PLATONIC INVESTIGATIONS

STUDIES IN PHILOSOPHY
AND THE HISTORY OF PHILOSOPHY
General editor: Jude P. Dougherty

Studies in Philosophy
and the History of Philosophy   Volume 13

Platonic Investigations

edited by Dominic J. O'Meara

THE CATHOLIC UNIVERSITY OF AMERICA PRESS
Washington, D.C.

Copyright © 1985 by The Catholic University of America

All rights reserved

Manufactured in the United States of America

LIBRARY OF CONGRESS CATALOGING IN PUBLICATION DATA
Main entry under title:
Platonic investigations.
 (Studies in philosophy and the history of philosophy; v. 13)
 Includes indexes.
 1. Plato—Addresses, essays, lectures.
 I. O'Meara, Dominic J. II. Series.
B21.S78 vol. 13 [B395] 100 s [184] 84-23906
ISBN 978-0-8132-9090-0

Table of Contents

Preface	vii
Abbreviations	ix
1. Plato's Metaphilosophy, Charles Griswold	1
2. Plato and the Story, Gerard Watson	35
3. The Body of the Speech: A New Hypothesis on the Compositional Structure of Timaeus' Monologue, Rémi Brague	53
4. Platonism and Socratic Ignorance, Leonardo Tarán	85
5. Self-knowledge in Early Plato, Julia Annas	111
6. Rational Prudence in Plato's *Gorgias*, Nicholas P. White	139
7. Platonic Provocations: Reflections on the Soul and the Good in the *Republic*, Mitchell Miller	163
8. Plato's Unnatural Teleology, James Lennox	195
9. The Primacy of ΟΥΣΙΑ: Aristotle's Debt to Plato, Daniel Devereux	219
10. Plotinus on How Soul Acts on Body, Dominic O'Meara	247
Index of Names	263
Index of Texts in Plato	267

Preface

This collection of new essays on Plato consists for the most part of papers delivered at The Catholic University of America in the fall of 1983 as part of the Matchette Lectures on "Plato and His Legacy." Papers having to do with the significance of particular formal and literary aspects of the Platonic dialogues—the dialogue form itself, the use of myth, literary composition—open the collection and are followed by discussions of certain philosophical issues in individual dialogues (here also hermeneutical issues are, of course, by no means absent). At the end are to be found two papers concerned with some aspects of Plato's legacy in Aristotle and Plotinus.

A standard set of abbreviations of the titles of works by Plato and Aristotle has been adopted. I owe much to Dean Dougherty and the members of the School of Philosophy of The Catholic University of America who together organized the lecture series, to Charles Griswold who provided some fruitful and opportune advice, and to Pat Corrigan who prepared the Indices.

D. J. O'M.

Abbreviations

The following abbreviations of the titles of Plato's and Aristotle's works have been used:

ARISTOTLE:

Anal. Prior.	:Analytica Priora (Prior Analytics)
Anal. Post.	:Analytica Posteriora (Posterior Analytics)
An.	:De Anima (On the Soul)
Cael.	:De Caelo (On the Heavens)
Cat.	:Categoriae (Categories)
Div. per Som.	:De Divinatione per Somnum (On Prophecy in Sleep)
EE	:Ethica Eudemia (Eudemian Ethics)
EN	:Ethica Nicomachea (Nicomachean Ethics)
Gen. An.	:De Generatione Animalium (Generation of Animals)
Gen. et Corr.	:De Generatione et Corruptione (On Coming-to-be and Passing-Away)
Met.	:Metaphysica (Metaphysics)
Part. An.	:De Partibus Animalium (On the Parts of Animals)
Phys.	:Physica (Physics)
Rhet.	:Rhetorica (Rhetoric)
Sens.	:De Sensu (On Sense)
Soph. El.	:De Sophisticis Elenchis (On Sophistical Refutations)
Top.	:Topica (Topics)

PLATO:

Alc.	:Alcibiades
Ap.	:Apology
Chrm.	:Charmides
Cra.	:Cratylus
Cri.	:Crito
Criti.	:Critias

Def. : *Definitions*
Ep. : *Epistles*
Epin. : *Epinomis*
Euthd. : *Euthydemus*
Euthphr. : *Euthyphro*
Grg. : *Gorgias*
Hp. Ma. : *Hippias Major*
Hp. Mi. : *Hippias Minor*
La. : *Laches*
Lg. : *Laws*
Ly. : *Lysis*
Men. : *Meno*
Phd. : *Phaedo*
Phdr. : *Phaedrus*
Phlb. : *Philebus*
Plt. : *Politicus*
Prm. : *Parmenides*
Prt. : *Protagoras*
R. : *Republic*
Symp. : *Symposium*
Sph. : *Sophist*
Tht. : *Theaetetus*
Ti. : *Timaeus*

1 PLATO'S METAPHILOSOPHY*
CHARLES GRISWOLD

Although the title of the present essay is somewhat jarring, it accurately expresses the issue I would like to discuss in this paper. Specifically, I would like to examine three questions: Does Plato have a "metaphilosophy"? If so, what is it? And finally, how does he go about defending it? My interest in these questions arises from a longstanding effort to assess the philosophical significance of Plato's use of the dialogue form. In particular, it stems from an effort to understand why the conversations depicted by Plato are so occasional and provisional in character; why the origination of philosophy is an omnipresent theme in the dialogues; why Plato seems obsessed with refuting the sophists, poets, popular rhetoricians, and other critics of philosophy; why Plato always maintains a distance from his dialogues in that he does not cast himself as one of the *dramatis personae*; and finally what the role of irony is in the dialogues. I will explain in a moment the connection between these issues and the question of metaphilosophy. It seems fairly clear that whatever Plato means by "philosophy," it is not quite the same as what contemporary textbooks mean by the term. Both Plato and Socrates are unique in their radical dedication to dialogue as a medium for philosophizing (written dialogue in the one case, spoken dialogue in the other). Moreover, few philosophy professors would dare advocate Socrates'[1] bizarre claims that the one thing he understands is erotic matters, that he possesses an "ἐρωτικὴ τέχνη" and that philosophy is divine erotic madness.

The whole issue of the role of "dialogue" or "dialectic" (for now I will not distinguish between them) in philosophy has recently come to

---

*This paper was presented on December 2, 1983, at the Catholic University of America as part of the Fall Matchette series on "Plato and his Legacy." The paper was also presented at the Iowa State University (March 28, 1984), and as part of the "Plato" panel at the annual meeting of the American Political Science Association (Sept. 2, 1984). I would like to thank Thérèse-Anne Druart and David Levy for their comments on earlier drafts.

1. In this paper I will be referring only to the Platonic "Socrates."

the fore once again thanks to the criticisms of nondialectical, systematic rationality put forward by (if I may vastly oversimplify the genealogy) descendants of both Nietzsche (such as Heidegger, Gadamer, Derrida, Foucault, and Rorty) and Hegel (such as Rescher and Habermas), as well as by philosophers of science such as Kuhn and Feyerabend. These critics themselves fall into at least two major camps, the one (to which Rorty and Derrida belong) hostile to philosophy as such, the other critical of nondialectical philosophy but partisan to dialectical philosophy (Hegel, Rescher). Thus, in spite of their common opposition to nondialectical philosophizing, these two camps have a debate of their own. This second debate is more radical than the debate between dialectical and nondialectical philosophers because it concerns the viability of philosophy *simpliciter*. I believe that an understanding of these two levels of debate can be of considerable assistance in clarifying the puzzling aspects of Plato's work mentioned above (the use of the dialogue form, and so forth).

I will begin by establishing a working definition of "metaphilosophy." Having then discussed the two metalevel debates, I shall try to show how sound metaphilosophical considerations make Plato's choice of the dialogue form and the associated phenomena mentioned above intelligible. This demonstration will require, however, a fairly detailed discussion of several other figures in the history of philosophy. The form of my argument looks like an example of "rational reconstruction." I do believe, however, that there is sufficient evidence in Plato's dialogues to indicate that the argument I will be presenting was, in general outline, understood and endorsed by Plato.

I

The term *metaphilosophy* is a recent invention. It seems to have been coined by, not surprisingly, a follower of the later Wittgenstein, in order to refer to the "investigation of the nature of philosophy, with the central aim of arriving at a satisfactory explanation of the absence of uncontested philosophical claims and arguments."[2] The preposition

---

2. The quotation is from Morris Lazerowitz' "A Note on 'Metaphilosophy'," *Metaphilosophy* 1 (1970): 91. It seems, according to this definition, that "metaphilosophy" is to analyze the causes of philosophical disagreement, with the aim of discrediting these causes and showing that the entire disagreement is a mistake. This strategy obviously has a precedent in Kant's treatment of the "dialectic" of reason. For this and other reasons I will propose that "metaphilosophy" should be understood, in its primary sense, in terms of the Kantian framework. This is the sense in which I will be using the term in the body of the paper. However, I have no objection to a looser, secondary, sense of the term, such that any reflection from any standpoint about the nature of philosophy can be called "metaphilosophy." In this secondary sense one might speak of "metaphilo-

meta had, of course, long since been put to work by philosophers intent on carving out a discipline that is one step above, or prior to, its object. The term *metacritique*, for example, was used by Herder in this sense.³ Even the term *metaphysics* is used by Kant in the distinctly non-Aristotelian and by now familiar sense of "the study of the conditions for the possibility of" a given science. Indeed, Kant repeatedly remarks that the *Kritik der reinen Vernunft (KRV)* is itself an example of the new "metaphysics" (e.g., B22–24, A841 = B869 ff.; see also Axix–xxi). Kant also characterizes the *Critique* as a "treatise on the method" (Bxxii) whose purpose is to determine the limits of reason in advance of particular attempts to reason. Since reason itself undertakes this task, Kant holds that in the *Critique* reason is "occupied only with itself" (A680). Since reason alone can judge of itself, all claims to knowledge are brought before it as before a "tribunal" (Axi, A751 = B779). Knowledge of "transcendental" rules or concepts will thus perform a veridical function (B26).

The second level, or transcendental, focus of "criticism" requires a concentration on *form*. The *KRV* studies our (formal) knowledge of objects, not objects themselves, a knowledge that is not itself an "object" in the same sense (A402). This metalevel project thus consists, as Kant repeatedly says with respect to reason's "critique" of itself, in *self- knowledge* (Axi, A735 = B763, A849 = B877). The project thus seems fully in keeping with the *goal* of philosophy as traditionally understood.

In the simplest terms, metaphilosophy is the effort to philosophize about *how* we reason about things and so to understand, "before" we reason about them, what we can and cannot know. Thus metaphilosophy in the primary sense of the term is naturally understood within the Kantian framework just adumbrated. This framework, anticipated by Descartes (and still more clearly by Locke), is definitive of a great deal of modern philosophy, according to modern philosophers themselves. The rise of the notion of subjectivity, the emphasis on certainty as a criterion of knowing, the description of knowledge in terms of formal rules and concepts, the thesis that knowledge is an instrument or τέχνη, as well as the concern for method, system, scientific procedure—all characterize the tradition derived from the Cartesian-Kantian "turn" to a metaphilosophical interpretation of the Delphic

---

sophical" objections to the Kantian framework. For a helpful discussion of the whole issue of metaphilosophy, see R. Pippin's "Critical Methodology and Comprehensiveness in Philosophy," *Metaphilosophy* 9 (1978): 197–211.

3. For the reference, see L. W. Beck's excellent "Toward a Meta-Critique of Pure Reason," in *Essays on Kant and Hume* (New Haven: Yale University Press, 1978), p. 25.

"know thyself." Though Kant in particular denies that this amounts to a metaphysics of the self in the classical sense (the *Paralogisms* is an attack on the possibility of such a project), he admits that the "transcendental conditions" of knowledge are, in some difficult to define sense, "in us."

The metalevel study of the conditions of our knowledge of objects cannot, as I have already suggested, list these same objects *as* conditions, unless it is to move in a circle. Hence the turn to metaphilosophy results in something like the substitution of "epistemology" for "ontology," or at least the view that the former is logically prior to the latter (*KRV* A247 = B303). This is why metaphilosophy has an endlessly "preparatory" or "anticipatory" nature (*KRV*, B26). Of course, even *this* tradition of modern philosophy is full of revolutions and counterrevolutions. But there is a family resemblance between them; the quarrel is an intramural one. Each new claim to legitimate rule rests on an intensification of the "critical" turn; new, more rigorously drawn limits (whether "transcendental," "logical," "categorial," or "linguistic") of reason are constantly touted, and the work of one's predecessors rejected as sloppy, speculative, unscientific, guilty of transgressing the bounds of what is knowable, and so forth.[4] Even the history of German Idealism, I think, should be read in this way.[5]

In my opinion, the logic behind this turn to "critical" philosophizing—that is, to metaphilosophy—is very persuasive. There really is a problem concerning *beginnings* in philosophy, and metaphilosophy concentrates on this problem directly. Moreover, there would simply

---

4. I do not want to claim that every modern philosophy fits this description. Heidegger, for example, would seem to represent an exception. But even the "fundamental ontology" of Heidegger's *Sein und Zeit* has a strongly Kantian bent, a fact that has been noted often enough.

5. Consider, for example, Kant's criticism of Aristotle for having discovered the forms of judgment in a wholly empirical way, whereas what is required is a "deduction" of these categories (*KRV* A81 = B107). Fichte turned around and made a similar criticism of Kant. See Fichte's "Second Introduction to the *Science of Knowledge*," in *Fichte: Science of Knowledge (Wissenschaftslehre), with First and Second Introductions*, trans. P. Heath and J. Lachs (New York: Appleton-Century-Crofts, 1970), p. 51. Hegel then accused both Kant and Fichte of having failed on the same score. *Science of Logic*, trans. W. H. Johnston and L. G. Struthers, 2 vols. (New York: Humanities Press, 1966), 1: 87–91; and the *Logic* in the *Encyclopaedia*, par. 41–42. See also the comments about Kant, and the general demand for an "unconditioned" starting point for philosophy, in Schelling's 1794 essay "On the Possibility of a Form for all Philosophy," trans. F. Marti, *Metaphilosophy* 6 (1975): 1–24. Certainly the first, "epistemological," part of Hegel's *Phenomenology* is an indirect criticism of nonreflexive pre-Hegelian epistemologies. For an interpretation of Hegel's "metaphilosophy" that is consistent with my remarks about Hegel, see Terry Pinkard's "The Logic of Hegel's *Logic*," *Journal of the History of Philosophy* 17 (1979): 417–435, and the articles by Pippin cited in notes 2 and 14 of the present essay.

seem to be a difference between knowledge claims that are *made*, and those that are *used* in the claims themselves; between claims made on the "object level," and evidence used to support the claims; or between what Hegel calls the "truth" and "knowledge" of claims. Still further, there would seem to be a difference between, on the one hand, the metalevel rules that allow one to define the problem or area one wishes to investigate, the rules for investigation, as well as the rules that determine when the investigation is complete, and on the other hand the investigation itself. Just as (to use one of Kant's own analogies) a language possesses a grammar containing its rules, so knowledge claims possess a metaphilosophy (a "transcendental grammar") containing the rules for making knowledge claims. This argument looks like a distant epigone of the Platonic demand for an "ascent" to the Forms.[6]

In sum, before we make a claim to know an object, we must know our knowledge of this object (*KRV* A11 = B25). Arguments *ad rem*, that is, prove little in philosophy; they do not answer the *quid iuris* question. Philosophers must first locate the "ἀρχή," and this ἀρχή seems necessarily to be a "concept" of knowledge, not of being. For, to repeat, every statement about "what is" is an implicit knowledge claim, which therefore reflects assumptions we are making in formulating the claim. Moreover, it does seem to be a distinguishing mark of philosophy to be self-reflexive; while other branches of knowledge cannot serve as the instruments for self-reflection (there is no biology of biology, only a philosophy of biology), philosophy alone possesses this capacity. So persuasive is this formulation of the self-knowledge issue that most modern interpreters of ancient philosophy assume without further ado that Plato too *must* have had an "epistemology," in however primitive a form. It is thus typical to find modern philosophers construing the history of philosophy as a continuous development towards the goal they believe themselves to have reached: namely that of specifying the "architectonic" (e.g., *KRV* A856 = B884 and context),

---

6. As Beck notes, Kant "compares his procedure to that of the grammarian 'who studies a language in order to detect the rules for the actual use of words and to collect elements for a grammar'." What Kant calls "transcendental grammar" is the doctrine of the elements of this grammar, elements thanks to which we can "spell" knowledge and experience. "Toward a Meta-Critique," p. 26. A letter/syllable metaphor is used in several of Plato's dialogues, but with the intent of illustrating the necessity of knowing the "forms" or "elements" in an ontological, not an epistemological sense. See *Plt.* 277e ff., *Phlb.* 17b, 18b–d and context; consider also *Sph.* 253a ff. and *Tht.* 201e ff. Whether or not knowledge of Plato's letterlike Forms yields a grammar (i.e., the rules) for the correct "spelling" of appearances is a matter of some controversy. Still, both Plato and Kant seem to demand some sort of ascent from the "book" of nature to its more intelligible and "prior" founding principles.

the "logic," "syntax," or the "grammar" of reason. Critical metaphilosophy, in short, seems to be an intensification (and inevitably also a correction) of philosophy as traditionally understood.[7]

Our metaphilosophically oriented philosophers also claim that there is no way of ending the proverbial disputes of the philosophers,[8] of distinguishing between defensible and undefensible philosophies,[9] or of answering scepticism convincingly,[10] unless some new, more self-conscious "method" is brought to light (*KRV* A751 = B779 ff.). The reasoning here is, again, persuasive.

II

I would like to bring this discussion to bear on Plato. We should admit from the start, I think, that judged by the standards of meta-

---

7. This "intensification" would also have to be interpreted as a *narrowing* of the notion of "philosophy" to "theory of knowledge," i.e., to a *foundation* specifying science. For a good account of this narrowing as well as of the rise of "histories of philosophy" which proceed along the lines just adumbrated (the ancients-as-primitive-epistemologists story), see Rorty's *Philosophy and the Mirror of Nature* (Princeton: Princeton University Press, 1979), p. 131 ff. As Rorty points out, the terms "theory of knowledge" and "epistemology" (*Erkenntnis Theorie, Erkenntnislehre*) were invented in the early nineteenth century, along with the whole notion of philosophy as a professional academic discipline.

8. Philosophical disputes (such as those portrayed in Plato's dialogues) do frequently seem to assume too *much*, and do seem fruitless because the disputants have not clearly seen their own, and each other's, assumptions and because they have not agreed on a decision procedure to settle their disputes. Earlier philosophers (so the charge goes) just did philosophy naively, without sufficient self-reflection; they philosophized dogmatically, and were therefore unable to locate the common "a priori" structure of reason that could serve as a "tribunal" (see *KRV* Axi). They disputed about topics whose solution transcends the power of reason, and thus "wrestle with their own shadows," as Kant puts it (*KRV* A756 = B784). Hume presents a similar argument in the Introduction to the *Treatise*.

9. That is, it seems that an object level knowledge claim cannot serve as a basis for ranking claims, since it itself has to be evaluated in the manner described above. The alternative to such evaluation would seem to just be dogmatism. For example, someone who claims that his conception of God is the only true one cannot dismiss other claims merely by asserting that his conception is the true one; for that just amounts to asserting that it is true because he says it is. Since the reasons he offers in favor of his conception are not accepted by his opponents, the dispute is undecidable unless we ascend to a higher plateau on which references to God are replaced by discussion of the possibility of referring meaningfully to the divine. This is precisely what Kant, for example, does in the *Transcendental Dialectic* of the *KRV*.

10. The epistemological formulation of the self-knowledge issue by some modern philosophers is thought to answer dogmatic scepticism (the view that nothing can be known) by clearly delineating what can, and cannot, be known. The answer, that is, is twofold: our metaphilosophers grant the sceptic that certain things cannot be demonstrated satisfactorily (in Kant's case, these would be the "transcendental Ideas," such as those of the existence of God, Freedom, Immortality); but they insist that within well-defined boundaries scientific knowledge does exist. So long as we are unclear about our metaphilosophy, they argue, a convincing response to the sceptic is impossible. The

philosophy, Plato seems hopelessly naive and clumsy. His dialogues contain no systematic doctrine of logic or of the a priori principles of knowledge. Plato does not even furnish us, as Aristotle does in book VIII of the *Topics*, with a systematic analysis of dialectical reasoning. Most of Plato's discussions about the nature of philosophy are framed against a moral or political canvas, and so avoid the purely theoretical discussions we would expect from a self-conscious thinker. The Platonic discussions of the matter tend also to be stated in a literary or poetic form (philosophy is "midwifery," and so forth), and so fail to measure up, as Hegel and countless others have said, to the demands of "scientific" thinking.[11] That is, there is a close connection between Plato's dialogue form of writing and his seeming inarticulateness in metaphilosophical matters. The one dialogue which would have dealt directly with metaphilosophical problems, namely the *Philosopher*, was never written, though it is promised in the *Sophist* and *Statesman*. And on the occasion when Plato brings the mature Socrates together with the one person competent to enter into a good metaphilosophical discussion with him, namely the Eleatic Stranger, Plato has Socrates sit in virtual silence. Yet this is the only time in the Platonic dialogues in which two mature philosophers are brought together.[12]

To be sure, there are indications in the dialogues that Plato understood, in principle, what a Kantian "critique" would be like. The discussion in the *Charmides* about an "*episteme* of *episteme*," and the various descriptions in the later dialogues about the "method of division and collection," constitute some evidence of that. But the *Charmides* ends in *aporia*, self-reflexive *episteme* is dismissed as an impossibility, and the method of division and collection never replaces for long the haphazard movement of dialogue. In the *Theaetetus* Plato seems to be groping for an epistemology, but of course that dialogue also ends in *aporia*. There are some statements in the dialogues which look like fragments of an epistemology, such as the occasional talk about "ἀνάμνησις," about the difference between knowledge and belief (δόξα), and so on. But such talk is often cast in the form of a myth (as in the *Phaedrus*) and is never presented systematically and in a manner that is unencumbered by digressions, rhetorical pronounce-

---

sceptic may question the very framework within which we adjudicate claims to know, and this a priori framework must first be established. For an excellent discussion of Kant's reply along these lines to Hume, see Beck's "Kant's Strategy," in *Essays*, pp. 3–19.

11. Hegel, *Lectures on the History of Philosophy*, trans. Haldane and Simson, 3 vols. (Atlantic Highlands: Humanities Press, 1974), 2: 9, 14, 17.

12. While Socrates' conversation with Protagoras looks like a conversation between mature philosophers, I do not count it as such since everyone in the dialogue, including Socrates and Protagoras, classifies the one as a philosopher and the other as a sophist.

ments, in short by the whole "dramatic" dimension. The incomplete epistemological doctrines even seem to change throughout Plato's career. None of this constitutes a reason for dismissing the epistemological (or metaphysical) passages in the dialogues as unimportant. But these passages are radically unsatisfactory from a metaphilosophical point of view.

Still more importantly, we repeatedly find that in his discussions about knowledge Plato just *assumes* or *asserts* that the Ideas exist, and *then* explains what "knowledge" is (e.g., *R.* 476a ff., 507a–b ff., 596a and context; *Phd.* 100b ff.). We do not seem to get an account of how we know these ontological assumptions to be true. Indeed, one is justified in wondering whether Plato has a "theory" of Ideas at all.[13] Thus in the *Phaedrus*, for example, *Episteme* is listed as one of the Ideas, the knowledge of which is the province of godly souls especially (247c–e and context). But in the *Phaedrus* little thought seems given to working out how we could claim to "know" even an Idea of Knowledge, or rather, to how we could know we know it. Similarly, the sun/Good analogy in the *Republic*, and the image of the divided line, do explain something about our knowledge, but without explaining how we know this very analogy to be true. In any case, the "ontological" principles of the *Phaedrus* and *Republic* seem to be beyond the grasp of merely mortal intellects. Correspondingly, the Platonic dialogues never supply us with a thorough discussion of the nature of "dialectic" (cf. *R.* 532e–533a; *Phdr.* 266b8–9 and context). To these points we must add that Plato's dialogues evidence a studious and frustrating avoidance of "technical" terminology. There is no Platonic analogue to book Delta of Aristotle's *Metaphysics*.

In sum, Plato's dialogues seem both fantastically naive—because of the absence of systematic reflection on the conditions for the possibility of knowing, as well as the ubiquity of unproven assumptions about the existence and nature of essences—and utterly inconclusive—because the assumptions always seem vitiated by the paucity, and poor logical structure, of arguments in favor of them as well as by the fact that they are presented in a rhetorical and dramatic context. The result would seem to be, depending which of these aspects one stresses, either dogmatism (supported, perhaps, by theories about Plato's "secret teaching") or scepticism (knowledge of ignorance, and nothing more). This is precisely the dilemma from which Kant seeks to extri-

---

13. For an extended argument for the view that Plato does not offer a "theory" of Ideas, see W. Wieland, *Platon und die Formen des Wissens* (Göttingen: Vandenhoeck und Ruprecht, 1982), pp. 125–150.

cate both himself and philosophy. The dilemma seems to arise from the fact that Plato has no "critical" metaphilosophy, even though he understood, in broad outlines, the notion itself. When everything is said and done, we seem drawn to the conclusion that Plato philosophizes unself-consciòusly.

Having said this, I would like to offer an alternative interpretation of the failure in Plato's dialogues to pursue systematic and metaphilosophically oriented self-knowledge. Plato's decision to write dialogues can and should be explained as part of a deliberate and plausible philosophical position. In order to present this interpretation, I would like to sketch out the two debates referred to at the start of this essay.

III

In the history of philosophy a movement critical of the very idea that philosophers should, or can, possess a metaphilosophy seems to dog every attempt to formulate one. The "constructive" efforts of the history of philosophy seem always shadowed by ever-present criticisms of "positive" or "systematic" philosophy. In recent years the criticisms have been developed, in a variety of ways and with a variety of intentions, by writers such as Nietzsche, Heidegger, Goodman, Gadamer, Derrida, and Rorty. One perfectly obvious, but very powerful criticism of metaphilosophy may be roughly stated as follows. Metaphilosophy either leads to an infinite regress or begs the question. If a metaphilosophy can itself be reasoned about, then we will require a meta-meta philosophy, and so on *ad infinitum*, there being no Archimedean point in philosophy. If we hold at the outset that the principles *about* which we wish to reason just are the only principles *for* reasoning, or if we simply stipulate or believe in our metaphilosophical principles, then we are assuming what we want to prove, namely that our claims to knowledge on the object level are reasonable. Metaphilosophy, after all, is a form of philosophy. That is, we are simply assuming, in advance of metaphilosophical analysis, the very principles that the analysis is supposed to uncover.

That the objection can be made with a variety of intentions is evident from the fact that Hegel—and not just some of the simply antiphilosophical thinkers mentioned above—also made this criticism of Kant. Since I regard Hegel's formulation of the criticism as unanswerable by the nondialectical advocates of metaphilosophy (such as Kant) who wish to avoid the criticism, and since the criticism will shed light on Plato's preference for dialectic, I would like to quote Hegel's own words:

A main line of argument in the Critical Philosophy bids us pause before proceeding to inquire into God or into the true being of things, and tells us first of all to examine the faculty of cognition and see whether it is equal to such an effort. We ought, says Kant, to become acquainted with the instrument, before we undertake the work for which it is to be employed; for if the instrument be insufficient, all our trouble will be spent in vain. The plausibility of this suggestion has won for it general assent and admiration; the result of which has been to withdraw cognition from an interest in its objects and absorption in the study of them, and to direct it back upon itself; and so turn it to a question of form. Unless we wish to be deceived by words, it is easy to see what this amounts to. In the case of other instruments, we can try to criticize them in other ways than by setting about the special work for which they are destined. But the examination of knowledge can only be carried out by an act of knowledge. To examine this so-called instrument is the same thing as to know it. But to seek to know before we know is as absurd as the wise resolution of Scholasticus, not to venture into the water until he had learned to swim.[14]

Hegel does not deny the need for metaphilosophy; on the contrary. But he insists that the project can only be completed dialectically, and correspondingly that the effort to set limits compels us to make increasingly comprehensive claims. Dialectic and the search for wholeness seem closely connected, at least for both Hegel and Plato (see below). Kant's effort to assign dialectical reason a noncognitive status is thus self-defeating. As is clear from Kant's own words, reason's (*Vernunft*) knowledge of the a priori conditions for the understanding (*Verstand*) cannot be obtained within those conditions. *Verstand* is mod-

14. Hegel, *The Logic*, pt. I of *The Encyclopaedia of the Philosophical Sciences*, trans. W. Wallace (Oxford: Clarendon Press, 1975), par. 10. The criticism is also accepted as definitive by Habermas, *Knowledge and Human Interests*, trans. J. J. Shapiro (Boston: Beacon Press, 1971), pp. 7–8. A similar criticism of Kant is accepted by Beck in "Toward a Meta-Critique." For example, Beck argues that Kant did not and could not demonstrate (given the *KRV*'s own doctrine of judgment) that all intuition is sensible (p. 24) or that time and space are the only two forms of intuition (p. 25), and still more fundamentally that Kant "has no explicit theory of how we come to know of the operations and faculties or abilities of the mind" (p. 33; italicized in the original). As Beck also remarks here: "It is regrettable that Kant did not say more about the peculiarities of self-knowledge"; in order to do so, Kant would have had to say more about "rational psychology." In order to construct a metacritique of Kant's philosophy it is necessary to use non-Kantian terms (p. 26). That self-knowledge cannot dispense with this "empirical" dimension is a very Platonic claim. For some criticism of Beck's suggestion that the "transcendental physiology" discussed in the "Architectonic of Pure Reason" chapter of the *KRV* might supply Kant with a viable "metacritique," see G. V. Agich, "L. W. Beck's Proposal of Meta-Critique and the *Critique of Judgment*," *Kant-Studien* 74 (1983): 261–270. Agich suggests that Kant's treatment of the metacritical problem is to be found in the notion of aesthetic judgment in the *Critique of Judgment*. For an excellent discussion of Hegel's dialectical efforts to avoid the self-reflexive problem he attributes to Kant, see R. Pippin's "Hegel's Phenomenological Criticism," *Man and World* 8 (1975): 296–314. Of course the problem of demonstrating "first principles" has a long history in philosophy. See Aristotle's discussion of the matter in the *Anal. Post.*, bk. I, ch. iii.

eled on τέχνη; but the knowledge of τέχνη cannot be an example of it. Τέχνη made reflexive negates itself. Hegel's criticism of Kant, and of nondialectical philosophy in general, has this *ad hominem* structure.

The Hegelian point is, in my opinion, shared by Plato. The least controversial evidence for this claim is the *Charmides'* criticism of an "*episteme* of *episteme*" (*episteme* is said to be analogous here to the τέχνη of mathematics). Socrates seems here to initially equate "*episteme* of itself, of all other *epistemai*, and of the lack of *episteme*" (166e) with self-knowledge and "knowing what you know and do not know," i.e., with his regular knowledge of ignorance (e.g., 167a–b). However, the two are not the same. Ironically, the very refutation of the "*episteme* of *episteme*" formulation *contributes* to the "knowledge of ignorance," and so to the self-knowledge, of those present.[15] As in Hegel's *Phenomenology*, a claim is allowed to "negate" itself and find its "truth" in a larger "whole." The negation is dialectical, and a moment in the larger dialogue. Our efforts to philosophize presuppose an ideal of "wisdom." Further evidence for the thesis that for Plato τέχνη, *episteme*, or method cannot "ground" itself without integrating itself into a broader conception of knowledge may be found in the *Phaedrus*,[16] as well as in the distinction in the *Republic* between "ascending" dialectic and "descending" τέχνη (511b–c and context). In sum: the criticism of nondialectical philosophy, which has been undertaken with such devastating effects by figures such as Hegel, seems conclusive. This brings us, then, to a more fundamental issue, namely that of the ability of dialectical philosophy to establish *its* own "metaphilosophy" without opening itself to the objections just directed towards the Kantian sort of metaphilosophy.

Hegel agrees that we must appeal to *some* standard in order to be able to say that we know even the conditions of knowledge; he holds, like Kant, that this standard is reason itself. Hegel argues that the efforts of Kant, Fichte, and others to "know" the limits of reason nondialectically, must terminate in a faith (or in some undefinable "intuition") which just stipulates that it "thinks" (perhaps with the putative guarantee of a benevolent God) the conditions of knowledge truly. Stated broadly, Hegel argues that Kant and Fichte share the Enlightenment's characteristic *faith in reason*. This result, Hegel thinks, can be avoided if we understand that the relationship between object- and

---

15. For a comprehensive interpretation of the *Chrm.* which supports my remarks about the dialogue, see D. Hyland, *The Virtue of Philosophy* (Athens: Ohio University Press, 1981).

16. See my "Self-knowledge and the 'idea' of the Soul in Plato's *Phaedrus*," *Revue de Métaphysique et de Morale* 86 (1981): 477–494.

metalevels of reasoning is itself dialectical. Dialectic is thus the solution to the seemingly impossible effort of philosophers to, as Rescher puts it, "pull ourselves up by our own bootstraps."[17]

As the discussion thus far suggests, the really fundamental dispute is not between Hegel and Kant, i.e., between proponents of dialectic and those of nondialectical epistemology, but between the dialecticians and the critics of philosophizing or "reason giving" as such. This latter debate is the second, and deeper, of the two debates I mentioned at the start of this essay. As a rule, these critics do not share in the philosopher's faith in reason. Nietzsche and his descendants, for example, fully agree with Hegel's criticisms of Kant and, more broadly, of nondialectical rationality. But they deny that the putative "circularity" or "completeness" of Hegel's system escapes a *petitio principii*. In a by now familiar move, they focus on the supposed *Aufhebung*, in the *Phenomenology of Spirit* and *Encyclopaedia*, of art and religion into "absolute knowledge." They assert that Hegel is simply showing that art and religion contain the "conceptual truth" that he has already read into them. In fact, so the objection runs, art and religion are not really assertions about "conceptual truth" at all. They are simply not continuous with philosophy. It is not the case, they claim, that (to take one example) poems secretly harbor philosophical questions. The questions exist only in the minds of philosophers, and all the grandiose claims made by philosophers on behalf of the supremacy of their questions are self-serving myths.

From this radical standpoint, Hegel's error is the same as that of all philosophers, indeed, of philosophy per se. The error derives from the philosophical effort to impose (and then to pretend to discover) a structure on all spiritual activity, a structure in terms of which philosophy inevitably emerges as dominant. A presupposition of the demand that one give a logos for one's opinions is that there is Truth, and correspondingly that there is a "whole" in terms of which opinions somehow reflect what really *is*. The effort to make the philosopher ruler of the life of the soul begins, so the objection continues, with Plato. Plato's harsh polemics against the poets, the sophists, and against those who just do not care about giving reasons for their views—in short, his effort to legitimize the philosopher's *quid iuris* question—simply sets the agenda for all philosophers.[18] The thesis that all signifi-

17. N. Rescher, *Dialectics—a Controversy-Oriented Approach to the Theory of Knowledge* (Albany: State University of New York Press, 1977), p. 56.
18. That is, although there are vast differences between the poets, sceptics, sophists, and others in terms of the radical disagreement at issue they can all be said to share a hostility or indifference to philosophy. Consider *Grg.* 502c–d (poetry as a kind of rhetoric which flatters the crowds); *R.* 596c–e and context (the sophists, painters, poets

cant forms of spiritual activity are incipient forms of philosophy is, we might say, Plato's legacy. Indeed, Nietzsche and Rorty *do* say just this. Socrates too, so Nietzsche argues, has a nondefensible, indeed absurd, faith in reason.[19] From the standpoint of the critics of reason, philosophical questions are pseudoquestions not worth asking, questions that carry no weight. Nietzsche argues that we should substitute the "aesthetic" justification of life for the philosophical effort to "justify" by appeals to "grounds" and "conditions."[20] The resolve to live well need not be supported by moralizing or metaphysical and theological considerations. At the very least, then, we seem left with an irreducible pluralism; philosophy is just one form of spiritual activity among others—one form of creativity, perhaps.

That is—to restate the main point of the previous paragraph—the really fundamental debate is the "ancient quarrel between philosophy

---

have the ability to produce imitations of all things); *Tht.* 160d and context (Homer, Heraclitus and Protagoras belong in the same camp); see too *Prt.* 316d–e (with which *Tht.* 180d should be compared), *Phdr.* 278c, *R.* 492b–e and context. The crucial diairesis of the human race seems to be, for Plato, that between the philosophers and everyone else. Similarly, the Platonic dialogues everywhere present us with a conflict between philosophy (Socrates) and the polis (Athens) as such. I do not mean to simply identify the modern critics of philosophy (such as Nietzsche and Rorty) with the ancient critics. I am not making the argument that the antiphilosophers in Plato's dialogues have Rorty's strategy in mind. But I am suggesting that the Platonic dialogue form makes sense if one supposes that Plato treated them as though they did have something like it in mind, and so treated them with an awareness of what is required to attack them successfully. Moreover, there *are* connections between modern and ancient critics of philosophy. E.g., on p. 157 of *Philosophy* Rorty says that if his recommendations are followed out, "We shall, in short, be where the Sophists were before Plato brought his principle to bear and invented 'philosophical thinking'." Throughout the book Rorty opposes himself explicitly to the "Platonic Principle." Thus on pp. 392 and 394 Rorty explicitly criticizes the philosopher's "quaestiones juris." Nietzsche's debt to Heraclitus, moreover, is well known. Much more can and should, of course, be said about these connections.

19. See "The Problem of Socrates," in *Twilight of the Idols*; also the *Birth of Tragedy*, trans. W. Kaufmann (New York: Random House, 1967), sections 14 and 15. On p. 106 of *Birth* Nietzsche writes: "In this contrast [between the theoretic and tragic world view] I understand by the spirit of science the faith that first came to light in the person of Socrates—the faith in the explicability of nature and in knowledge as a panacea." On p. 377 of *Philosophy*, Rorty declares that for the edifying philosophy "the Platonic notion of Truth itself is absurd."

20. *Birth of Tragedy*, pp. 22, 52, 141. Of course, I am quoting here from Nietzsche's first publication, one which he himself criticized subsequently. Though I cannot prove it here, the critical importance of art understood as an "aesthetic justification" is developed but not abandoned in Nietzsche's later thought. "Justification" does not, in any event, here mean what philosophers mean by it—else the phrase would express the very opposite of Nietzsche's thought on the matter (and does express with less ambiguity in later writings). Cf. *The Gay Science*, trans. W. Kaufmann, (N.Y.: Random House, 1974), bk. II, section 107: "As an aesthetic phenomenon existence is still *bearable* for us, and art furnishes us with eyes and hands and above all the good conscience to be *able* to turn ourselves into such a phenomenon."

and poetry," as Socrates puts it in the *Republic* (607b).[21] This remark in the *Republic* (along with its context), as well as many other passages, indicate that Plato understands that his *fundamental* argument is not with other philosophers, let alone with epistemologists, but with the hordes of antiphilosophers. This argument cannot be settled nondialectically (and for reasons I will examine in a moment, it is also very difficult to settle dialectically). I have tried to suggest thus far that the decision to consider the "quarrel" between poets and philosophers as the fundamental dispute makes sense in the light of the general problem of metaphilosophy. From this vantage point, two features of the Platonic dialogues are quite natural.

The first feature is simply the ubiquity of the effort to refute the poets, sophists, and popular rhetoricians in such a way as to justify the activity of philosophy. Both sophists and rhetoricians resemble the philosopher in their love of discourse and in their willingness to talk and dispute about all things (consider *Phlb.* 58a–59a, *R.* 596c–e, *Grg.* 452e–453a, *Sph.* 232c–233c). Characteristically, however, they care not about the truth but about persuasion. Hence, they are concerned not with giving reasons for insights with the aim of restoring to the soul forgotten knowledge and lost wholeness, but in controversy and refutation for the sake of "goods," such as reputation, wealth, power, and the like. The self-conscious critics of philosophy, to be sure, recognize that no one can escape making assumptions. They offer a variety of reflections on their own assumptions which seem to philosophers to lead to relativism, historicism, or nihilism. As Nelson Goodman puts it, philosophy is just one "way of world-making." Philosophy, we might say, has its own language game and its own history. The "ground" of a philosopher's assumptions then seems to consist in little more than the fact that he has faith in them, or believes in them, wills them, or finds them interesting and useful.

Thus, given that a basic and unavoidable "quarrel" concerns the viability of the philosophical enterprise, the constant (some have said wearisome) demonstration in Plato's dialogues that there are philosophical questions makes perfect sense. Plato's dialogues are full of characters who are, in one way or another, either hostile or indifferent to philosophy.[22] *The origination of philosophy itself out of the medium of*

21. For discussion of the *R.* passage, see my "The Ideas and the Criticism of Poetry in Plato's *Republic*, Book 10," *Journal of the History of Philosophy* 19 (1981): 135–150.

22. I do not wish to minimize the heterogeneity of the interlocutors in the Platonic dialogues. Some are outright antiphilosophers (Callicles), others are untried in philosophy but prominent in another field of intellectual activity (Theaetetus) or in political matters (Laches, Nicias). Still others are too young to have been tried in any field (Lysis). But the fact remains that none of those with whom the mature Socrates talks philosoph-

opinion is the most comprehensive theme in Plato's dialogues. This point is so preliminary that most philosophers have thought it absurd to make much of it. Most philosophers follow Hegel's lead here; his polemics against the critics of reason tend to be confined to the prefaces and introductions to his works—outside of his main argument, as it were. Yet it is precisely these polemics that are rejected by many proponents of popular rhetoric, sophistry, poetry, religion, and common sense.[23] I suggest that Plato understood this and was eager to *show* us the philosopher's response to his critics. The prefaces of other philosophers constitute the bulk of Plato's text. Perhaps this is an indication that Plato would agree with Hegel's critics that Hegelian dialectic begs the really fundamental question. However that may be, it is a fact that dialogue after dialogue raises, at one point or another, the question "why philosophize?" Does not this question go right to the root of the dispute between philosophers and nonphilosophers? Would not an answer to this question require a comprehensive justification of the whole project of "giving reasons," and so an account of a universe in which it makes sense to want to give reasons? With the madness attributed in the *Phaedrus* to philosophy itself, Plato's dialogues seem obsessed with the fundamental questions concerning the justification of philosophy.

Moreover, the experience of controversy, which is tirelessly depicted by Plato, shows (as does our own experience in the matter) that fundamental disagreements can be extremely difficult to resolve. Refutations of philosophical positions are rarely, if ever, conclusive. A clever interlocutor can always find an answer somewhere in the vast sea of discourse. Every proposition and argument seems to depend on and lead to myriad others. A discussion limits itself to this or that topic and leaves the rest undefined. But a clever arguer can always build a bridge to a related topic or to related aspects of the present topic under discussion.

And if it is the case, as I have been suggesting, that the defense of philosophy is a prime theme of Plato's dialogues, and that this defense is best accomplished in the medium of a dialogue with the critics of philosophy, then we have the basis for an explanation of another very

---

ically is a philosopher. I am far from denying that there is constructive philosophizing in the dialogues, or that the epistemological and metaphysical discussions (though fragmentary) are important and interesting. I shall in fact argue below (section VII) that when properly understood the dialogue form leads to, indeed requires, consideration of several metaphysical theses.

23. For an interesting discussion, with reference to Hegel, of the issue of prefaces, see J. Derrida, "Hors Livre," in *La Dissémination* (Paris: Seuil, 1972), pp. 9–67. The problem of the status of the Introductions to Hegel's works has, of course, been extensively discussed in the literature.

odd feature of the Platonic texts, namely that they do not contain a discussion between two mature philosophers. As I said above, the occasion for such a dialogue exists in the *Sophist* and *Statesman*; Socrates' silence there is dramatic. But a dialogue between him and the Eleatic Stranger would be a departure from Plato's overriding concern with the problem of the genesis of philosophy—a genesis that is no longer a live issue in a conversation between mature philosophers.[24]

However, understanding what kind of debate Plato wants to carry on does not fully explain why he wrote *dialogues*. I would like to turn next to this issue.

IV

I begin by noting that, as the debate between dialecticians and their critics suggests, it is not possible to successfully attack *or* defend philosophy *directly*, a fact that sheds light on the form of Plato's texts. I would like to discuss this point by reverting to the just mentioned debate.

The cleverest of those who reject the rationality of the love of wisdom understand that to argue *against* philosophy is to engage in it and so, it seems, to fall prey to the same dialectic of reason which they turned on those who argued *for* philosophy. The notion of a "limit" to reason, as Hegel insists, is a dialectical one. Consider the self-refutation of those who *argue* that, say, reason is (unlike faith) powerless to grasp "objective truth"; in arguing this they are claiming that something is objectively true. It is as though someone were to write a weighty book in which it is claimed that writing books is something a serious philosopher should never do. The inconsistency here is of the "pragmatic" sort, as it is called today; it turns on conflict between λόγος and ἔργον (on the *Phaedrus* and *Seventh Letter*, see below).

The self-refutation seems to point to Hegel's famous view that "the truth is the whole." However, our clever critics of dialectical philosophy have a way of showing that there is no "whole" in the sense required. They practice a form of elenchus and criticism called "deconstruction" (a term derived from Heidegger). The critique proceeds on purely *ad hominem* grounds; one shows one's opponent that within his

---

24. The best discussions of Socrates' near complete silence in the presence of the Eleatic Stranger are to be found in M. Miller's *The Philosopher in Plato's Statesman* (The Hague: Nijhoff, 1980), and S. Rosen's *Plato's Sophist: the Drama of Original and Image* (New Haven: Yale University Press, 1983). For some further discussion of the reasons for the absence in Plato's texts of a dialogue between mature philosophers, see my "Reflections on 'Dialectic' in Plato and Hegel," *International Philosophical Quarterly* 22 (1982): 126–129.

own framework the argument is either question-begging, incomplete, or leads to an infinite regress. The success of the critique depends on the critic not making any claims to knowledge not also made by his opponent (except, perhaps, a sly claim to "knowledge of ignorance"). Thus Rorty characterizes his approach as "reactive" and "parasitic."[25] Only the critic's *intention* should distinguish him from his opponent. The strategy of these critics necessarily involves an element of ruse, dissemblance, and irony.[26] This strategy is familiar to us, of course, from Plato's Socrates, as well as from the "classical sceptics."[27] Thus there is a significant resemblance between the procedure of the critics of reason and that of its Socratic defenders.

The critic will try to show, then, that the defense of dialectical reason is necessarily question-begging, and therefore that it too cannot be argued directly. He will then try to suggest that the defense of reason is also interminable (Kant's "tribunal" of reason to one side). Since

25. *Philosophy*, pp. 366, 369, 377. On p. 317 Rorty compares his position to that of "the informed dilettante, the polygramatic, Socratic intermediary between various discourses."

26. For an excellent discussion of Derrida and dissemblance, see V. Descombes, *Modern French Philosophy*, trans. Scott-Fox and Harding (Cambridge: Cambridge University Press, 1980), ch. 5. Similarly, N. Garver concludes his "Derrida on Rousseau on Writing" by remarking that "In the end, when we survey the ground that Derrida would have cleared by his call for us to recognize the full honor and priority of writing, we find no metaphysics, no logic, no linguistics, no semantics, and no grammatology left to carry on, but only the brilliant scholarly mischievousness." *Journal of Philosophy* 74 (1977): 673. Cf. the strikingly similar terms with which Feyerabend characterizes his own rhetoric: "Always remember that the demonstrations and the rhetorics used [in this book] do not express any 'deep convictions' of mine. They merely show how easy it is to lead people by the nose in a rational way. An anarchist [i.e., Feyerabend] is like an undercover agent who plays the game of Reason in order to undercut the authority of Reason (Truth, Honesty, Justice, and so on)." *Against Method: Outline of an Anarchistic Theory of Knowledge* (London: New Left Books, 1975), pp. 32–33. In the footnote to this passage, Feyerabend suggests a comparison between his strategy and Dadaism (see also p. 21, n. 12).

27. On the point in the context of the classical sceptics, see M. Frede's "The Sceptic's Two Kinds of Assent and the Question of the Possibility of Knowledge," a paper delivered to the Princeton colloquium on ancient Greek philosophy (Dec. 1982). Frede distinguishes between two kinds of sceptical assent, that of the "dogmatic sceptic" and that of the "classical sceptic." The former defends the view that nothing is or can be known, thereby making an implicit knowledge claim and contradicting himself. The latter (Arcesilaus and followers, Sextus Empiricus) does not make this claim, so avoiding the reflexive problem, and limits himself to showing on his opponent's ground that his opponent's claims fail. This is precisely the strategy of Rorty and Derrida. Frede also argues that the classical sceptics believed themselves to be following in Socrates' footsteps here. The "assent" given by the classical sceptic to the view that nothing is or can be known is not, according to Frede, a claim but an "impression," an "acquiescence." It is just this sort of feeling that Rorteans and Derrideans want to generate in dogmatic philosophers so as to turn them away from the search for "Truth." Rorteans and Derrideans want to do this in such a way as to escape the "having a view about not having views" paradox.

the *hope* of the closure of philosophical discourse animates philosophers, the critic of reason may thus succeed in *persuading* the philosopher that philosophy is a hopeless, Sisyphean task. This persuasion is not, in the final analysis, an argument. It is a rhetorical effort to shake the philosopher's faith in reason by raising ever more difficult metaphilosophical questions that the philosopher cannot yet answer and soon despairs of ever answering. Elenchic deconstruction is dialectic unaccompanied by the insight that there is a Whole; hence the great emphasis placed by the critics of reason on fragmentation, partiality, dissolution, difference, otherness, nonbeing. It is Socraticism without the Good.

In this way a philosopher is prepared to receive that insight which comes in the dead of night as the soul silently looks into itself, the insight which extinguishes the desire for reason-giving and kindles the poet's desire for "creativity," the intellectual's interest in cultured "conversation," the believer's resolve to trumpet his faith regardless of what is said or done, the sceptic's desire to free himself from the illusions of the love of wisdom, the orator's desire for power through the art of persuasion. In one way or another, the philosopher is prepared to imitate the self-negation of Wittgenstein's *Tractatus* and to leap into a more profitable, or at least satisfying, way of life. Neither the self-negation nor its result are supposed to constitute "a philosophy." In the final analysis, none of the sceptics or critics of reason has a "position." To even announce that he has a position, let alone that there are arguments in favor of it, is already to concede the game to the philosophers. As Rorty puts it, ". . . edifying philosophers [such as Rorty] have to decry the very notion of having a view, while avoiding having a view about having views. This is an awkward, but not impossible, position."[28] It may be replied that Rorty is advancing a "view" at least while he is engaging in debate with his opponents; but there is no reason for Rorty to deny it. Derrida too freely confesses that the terminology used in his own deconstructivist program must itself be deconstructed, put "sous rature."[29] An unending series of polemics that undermine

---

28. Rorty, *Philosophy*, p. 371. Rorty continues a few lines later: "Perhaps saying things is not always saying how things are. Perhaps saying *that* is itself not a case of saying how things are." The "perhaps" is the nub of the matter. Rorty wants to affirm these propositions, and Plato and Hegel to deny them.

29. Derrida, *De la Grammatologie* (Paris: Minuit, 1967), pp. 73, 102–103, passim. On p. 38 and context Derrida comments on the Heideggerean origins of the "sous rature" strategy. Even the translator of this book indicates that her comments too about Derrida deconstruct themselves. See the closing remarks of G. C. Spivak's "Translator's Preface" to *Of Grammatology* (Baltimore: Johns Hopkins Press, 1974). For Rorty's evaluation of Derrida (who is referred to only in passing in *Philosophy*) see his "Philosophy as a Kind of Writing: an Essay on Derrida," in *Consequences of Pragmatism* (Minneapolis: University

themselves even as they undermine others is the deconstructivist's way of avoiding being either reduced to silence or being forced to appeal *in propria persona* to a priori standards.

In sum, if reason cannot be either defended or attacked directly, then both the defense of and attack on reason must be dialectical. Not only are there (if one accepts the just mentioned proposition) no irrefragable systems or doctrines, and no unquestionable metaphilosophies, the defense of philosophy cannot be successfully generated in the absence of fundamental objections to philosophy. Like Hegel, Socrates reduces nonreflexive objections to absurdity by asking for *their* grounds (as in his critique of Protagoras in the *Theaetetus*). However, the debate between critics and defenders of reason more closely resembles Platonic dialogue than Hegelian dialectic, and it is here that a preliminary distinction between dialogue and dialectic should be drawn. The debate cannot fairly be seen as the dialectical self-explication of Reason. That is, it does seem that Hegel's decision to confine this dispute to prefaces and introductions, and to reconstitute it in terms of abstractly formulated "positions," is open to the criticism that he is begging the question. If one wishes to avoid this criticism, the dispute would have to be seen as taking place not between positions, but between the persons who hold them. In a dispute as radical as the one I have been discussing, the philosopher is compelled to question not just this or that doctrine, but also why anyone should be persuaded by the metaphilosophical view that philosophy as such is possible. In this sort of dispute, there are no "commensurating" principles (to borrow Rorty's terminology); hence a regression to the level of individual agreement is inevitable. As Socrates claims at the end of the *Phaedrus*, this dispute is best undertaken in the responsive medium of the "living" word. And, of course, this is precisely what all of Plato's "published" (if one may use the word) works depict.

Thus Platonic dialectic is crucially dependent on someone's asserting or denying something, agreeing to defend what he says, agreeing to say what he means, and acknowledging consequences of his position when they are pointed out to him (all of which is regularly insisted upon by Socrates).[30] The Platonic dialogue with the critics of

---

of Minnesota Press, 1982), pp. 90–109; and "Derrida on Language, Being, and Abnormal Philosophy," *Journal of Philosophy* 57 (1977): 673–681. Rorty clearly endorses Derrida's project, though in the former essay he sounds the alarm against the vaguely "luminous, constructive" aspects of *De la Grammatologie*. On p. 390 of *Philosophy* Rorty refers to his own book as an effort to "deconstruct the image of the Mirror of Nature" (cf. p. 192).

30. It is true that Socrates sometimes remarks that what counts is the logos, not who

philosophy is inescapably "empirical," unscientific, a posteriori, occasional, and rhetorical. Another reason that the debate between defenders and critics of philosophy must take the form of a dialogue (Plato) and not of a dialectic of positions (Hegel) is that, as noted above, the critics of philosophy deny that they have a "position" in the first place.

If the present line of reasoning is accepted, then we can see that, and why, Socrates cannot "justify" or "demonstrate" his own activity except by coming across or finding someone who is *not* already persuaded by its possibility and worth. Socrates cannot ever allow himself to claim that the critics of reason have been permanently refuted. He can claim to have refuted an antiphilosophical position only to the extent that he has refuted the person who holds it. And this limits him to a finite number of demonstrations, whose occurrence is contingent on a number of factors. Thus he must, as he explains in the *Phaedrus*, spend his time inside the walls of the city, rarely wandering out to peaceful nature; for the "open country and the trees do not wish to teach me anything, whereas men in the town do" (*Phdr.* 230d4–5). Unless Socrates can *persuade* his interlocutors to agree that there are philosophical questions, he cannot allow himself to persuade himself of it.

Correspondingly, philosophical rhetoric is unavoidably pedagogic. As Socrates puts it in the *Phaedrus*, rhetoric is "psychagogia," i.e., the leading of the soul. Socrates accomplishes this "leading" by getting his interlocutors to *desire* philosophy; hence the unendingly protreptic character of the Platonic dialogues. This is one reason why Socrates claims that the only thing he understands is erotic matters ("τὰ ἐρωτικά"; *Symp.* 177d7–8), and that he possesses an "ἐρωτικὴ τέχνη" (*Phdr.* 257a7–8). It is as though eros is the basis of Socrates' defense against scepticism. The philosopher is characterized by the fact that he cannot be satisfied with himself unless he knows why he is satisfied; that is, he remains unsatisfied until he can know himself discursively.[31] Obviously, Socrates' erotic art is meant to destroy the self-satisfaction of his interlocutors, a turn of events which is essential to Socrates' demonstration of the view that philosophy is not optional. The "post metaphysical conversation" advocated by Derrida and Rorty would

---

holds it, and that what is important is the truth regardless of whether anyone else cares about it. And the *Phlb.* presents us with a rather formalized looking debate in which "positions" confront each other (see the very start of the *Phlb.*). Nevertheless, Socrates always investigates a position dialogically.

31. For a fascinating discussion of this point, see A. Kojève's "Philosophie et Sagesse" (pt. I) in *Introduction à la lecture de Hegel* (Paris: Gallimard, 1947), pp. 271–282.

amount, from Socrates' perspective, to talk unanimated by the desire for truth. It would amount to unerotic rhetoric, in short. Socrates cannot refute his adversaries directly, or simply announce some metaphilosophical program of his own. He can refute them indirectly if he can change their intentions; hence the crucial role of rhetoric for Socrates, and specifically of dialogical rhetoric. Socrates' erotic art is the art of questioning and answering, and so of carrying on a conversation; it is the work of φρόνησις. These strange claims make sense if we understand Socrates to be concerned above all with the defense of philosophy in the sense that I have outlined.

To sum up: if reflection on the "beginnings" of philosophy is unavoidable, if the fundamental question of metaphilosophy concerns the "quarrel" between the proponents of philosophy and its various critics, if philosophy cannot be attacked or defended directly, and finally if the defense of philosophy requires a conversation with the critics of philosophy (and not just with abstract formulations of their "positions"), then it makes sense for a philosopher who agrees to all this to write *dialogues*.[32]

Nevertheless, one might object, my comments about Socrates' rhetoric and erotic art seem to reduce philosophy to the art of persuasion. The indirectness of the Socratic defense of philosophy seems to sabotage it. How will the dialogical defense of philosophy establish anything of a "positive" nature? I would like now to make some comments about this question.

V

In the *Meno*, Meno offers his famous "paradox," the conclusion of which is that learning is impossible. If we do not at all know what we are looking for, we cannot seek it. There are many things we do not know, and we would be unable to select one of them as that which is to be investigated. Even if we hit upon what we do not know, we would not know that it is the thing we were seeking (*Meno* 80d). Socrates immediately restates the puzzle in the form of a dilemma, and omits the last of these points.

It is striking that in the *Meno* Socrates twice inveighs against the laziness and intellectual cowardice to which Meno's paradox would lead (81d, 86b). "Trusting" (πιστεύων; 81e1) in the view that it is nec-

---

32. I am not arguing that I have specified the only reasons why Plato wrote *dialogues*. A fuller treatment of the matter would have to consider, among other things, Socrates' criticisms of writing at the end of the *Phdr.* For some discussion of these criticisms, see my "Style and Philosophy: the Case of Plato's Dialogues," *Monist* 63 (1980): 530–546.

essary to inquire, we are braver and less idle. Socrates here uses the language of war, thus trumpeting his courage; on behalf of the worth of inquiry "I am determined to do battle, so far as I am able, both in word and deed" (86c1–2; Lamb trans.). Similarly, at a difficult juncture in the *Laches* Socrates urges his interlocutors on with the remark that they must endure further conversation, lest courage laugh at them for their cowardice in the search for courage (194a1–5; cf. *Euthd.* 306d1, 307c3). Although Socrates is never, in the Platonic dialogues, explicitly referred to as courageous (with the ambiguous exception of *Symp.* 219d5), courage is the one virtue he attributes in his *Symposium* speech to eros (203d5). The erotic Socrates certainly exhibits the sort of courage in question. He also says in the *Symposium* that eros is a "philosopher through all of life, a clever sorcerer and enchanter and sophist" (203d7–8). Socrates concludes his encomium of eros by saying that now as before he worships "eros' power and courage" (212b7–8). The fainthearted misologist is, it seems, unerotic.

But the sceptic might argue that the emphasis on courage is a sign that Socrates' "knowledge of ignorance" is "justified" *only* by an individual's desire for it, and so only for that individual. The exhortations to have courage may be necessary precisely because there is no rational justification for the philosophical enterprise. Courage seems to be a substitute for the possession of wisdom. It is striking, in fact, that philosophers such as Nietzsche and Heidegger, who reject the Platonic ideal of wisdom, emphasize heavily the importance of courage, resoluteness (Heidegger's *Entschlossenheit*), and the will. In still another tradition of thought, Socratic courage would be replaced with faith. I am far from suggesting that Socratic courage and Heideggerean "Entschlossenheit" are the same. But on many occasions Socrates seems to argue that we ought to philosophize even though we cannot really prove that it makes sense to do so. A function of many of the myths in Plato's dialogues seems to be to reassure us that there are grounds for the hope that philosophy is a worthwhile enterprise; but myths are not proofs.

Without commenting on Meno's (nontrivial) puzzle in detail, I would like to point out Socrates' answer to the sort of objection just adumbrated. The refutation has two parts. The first is a short myth about the soul, and its affinity with the natural whole. The second is a demonstration (ἐπίδειξις) of somebody "learning," or rather, "recollecting," something. That is, Socrates does not provide a direct rebuttal of Meno's radically sceptical position. Instead he tries to *show* Meno a *deed* from which Meno is himself compelled to draw the conclusion that his own puzzle can be answered. This demonstration of an absolutely fundamental point (namely, that there is, loosely speaking, "learning") illustrates a crucial feature of Socrates' indirect refutation of the critics of philosophy, namely the reliance on the *deed* of learning which is itself generated through questions and answers. Meno is supposed to learn not the solution of the geometrical problem but the solution to a "meta" problem about learning. The slave boy is said to "recollect" the solution to the former; but in spite of Socrates' remark at 82a, it cannot be said that Meno "recollects" that the boy *is* recollecting. There is no metarecollection. Nevertheless, Socrates' indirect demonstration to Meno confirms his view that philosophical knowledge cannot be taught in the way that other kinds of knowledge can be.

Socrates concedes that he is not confident of every point in his demonstration in the *Meno*—indeed, how could he be certain of the myth that preceded it, or the thesis that learning is recollection of previously known truths?—but he affirms in the strongest possible terms that we should inquire into what we do not know. As I have already noted, he is willing to do battle, both in word and deed, for the proposition that we should seek the truth. As Socrates says, Meno's paradox reduces dialogue to eristics, i.e., to disputation devoid of the *desire* for the truth (a description that seems to fit Derridean and Rortean critics of reason). This is the bottom line of the battle with the critics of reason. It is not, as I have argued, a line that Socrates can draw nondialectically. Socrates' *ad hominem* argument against those who reject the possibility or worth of philosophical inquiry uses not just their words, but also the evidence of deeds, to persuade them otherwise. That is, a crucial refutation of the sceptics is simply the deed that *there is learning* (in a sense other than memorization). The refutation works only when the sceptic has either learned or acknowledges that someone has just done so; hence, once again, the necessarily occasional, empirical, and contingent character of Socratic dialogue about these fundamental issues. As Gadamer remarks, "There is no such thing as a method of learning to ask questions, of learning to see what needs to be questioned."[33] Philosophy certifies itself in the perfect tense. Differently put, Socrates' "erotic art" submits his interlocutor to the power of the question and the corresponding insight that the way one is leading one's life is not satisfactory. Our lives are not linguistic constructions, and Socrates' ability to arouse us to understand our lives better than

---

33. *Truth and Method*, trans. Sheed and Ward, Ltd. (New York: Seabury Press, 1975), p. 329. For a very strong statement of the view that for Plato philosophical knowledge cannot be stated in "propositional" form, see W. Wieland's *Platon und die Formen des Wissens*.

we think we already do *shows* us that the questions are real and worth pondering.

Until Socrates can yoke his critic into the activity of philosophizing, then, he lacks his most potent weapon against him; namely, the deed of philosophizing itself. The inference from this experience is the proposition that there are philosophical questions, an understanding of which brings one closer to what is. This inference from the deed, however, cannot itself be presented separately as a doctrine or teaching, at least not successfully. This is why the *Meno's* "slave boy passage" contains *two* conversations: one between Socrates and the boy and another between Socrates and Meno about the conversation between Socrates and the boy.

VI

If *showing* (rather than merely *saying* or *asserting*) the viability of philosophizing is a necessary component in the dialogical refutation of the critics of philosophy, then Plato's use of the dialogue form once again makes sense. In a way that is strikingly similar to Hegel's view that the demonstration of a philosophical standpoint is just the history of the experience of "consciousness" coming to know itself, Plato's dialogues contain no assertions by Plato, only depictions of people becoming and failing to become philosophers. Just as Hegel offers, not a treatise in which he "criticizes" various positions, but rather a "phenomenology" in which various nonreflexive positions show their defects and rewrite themselves in a more satisfactory way, so Plato presents us with dramatic *imitations* of the practice of philosophizing. Indeed, by withholding his own answers from his texts Plato seduces the reader into finding an answer for himself (just as Socrates did with respect to his interlocutors). The point of this maneuver is not simply a subjective or pedagogic one. On the contrary, given that the fundamental debate concerns the defense of philosophy, and given that this defense is necessarily dialectical, it is of the utmost importance that Plato draw the reader into philosophizing and only *then* allow him to reflect on the extraordinarily difficult problem of "justifying" this activity. Thus poetry and $\mu\iota\mu\eta\sigma\iota\varsigma$ are indispensable to Plato's presentation of the nature of philosophy.[34]

34. Indeed, thanks to its nontechnical nature, Plato's dialectical poetry may escape the charge frequently brought against Hegel's ostensibly "descriptive" phenomenology, namely that it is structured in such a way as to prejudice the process in favor of the author's position. Plato does not construct *doxa*, he "imitates" it; although, admittedly, this is not the same as just copying or mirroring it. For further discussion of the Hegel/

We now have, moreover, a further explanation of Plato's distance from his own texts. Simply put, the fact that Plato nowhere contributes to the discussions he portrays allows him to convey something about the nature of philosophy without asserting it in his own name to be so. If he did assert it, he would be open to the kind of criticism Hegel leveled against Kant, and which the critics of philosophy have frequently leveled against philosophers. An extradialogical postscript or preface by Plato would amount to a short treatise by him about philosophy; it is easy to see, from what I have said above, that this move would immediately fall prey to the difficulties already mentioned. Plato cannot stand outside his thought and set limits to it from some supradialectical standpoint. But, we now want to ask, is there any way for Plato to supply us *indirectly* with a commentary on what he is trying to accomplish without falling into self-contradiction?[35]

In order to see that the answer to this question is affirmative, it is necessary to compare something that is said in one of the dialogues with the deed of the dialogue itself. I am thinking of Socrates' criticisms of writing presented at the end of the *Phaedrus*. Plato wrote the criticisms, a fact which shows—to make a long interpretation short—that he both rejects the criticisms (since, unlike Socrates, he wrote) and that he accepts them (since he wrote dialogues). Plato accepts Socrates' arguments in favor of dialectical discourse, but he thinks that he has found a form of writing which blunts Socrates' criticisms of writing. On the essential points about the nature of philosophy, that is, Plato and the Platonic Socrates are in agreement. By recording all this Plato allows us to understand his philosophical reasons for writing *dialogues*.[36] He also allows us to see the limitations of writing, and the need for our engaging in spoken philosophical dialogue. This is Plato's silent postscript to his texts. Just as Socrates "answers" Meno's sceptical paradox with an exhibition of somebody learning, so Plato "answers" the critics of philosophy with a similar depiction. In each case, the onlooker is and must be left to draw his own conclusions. Plato's deed of writing dialogues supplies a basis for an indirect self-commentary.

Plato relationship, see R. Bubner, "Dialog und Dialektik oder Plato und Hegel," in *Zur Sache der Dialektik* (Ditzingen: Reclam, 1980), pp. 124–160.

35. I am putting aside here the complicated question of the *Epistles*. As Gadamer argues in his "Dialectic and Sophism in Plato's *Seventh Letter*," ch. 5 of *Dialogue and Dialectic: Eight Hermeneutical Studies on Plato*, trans. P. C. Smith (New Haven: Yale University Press, 1980), even the *Seventh Epistle* (which may well be genuine) presents certain hermeneutical problems to the interpreter.

36. For further discussion, see my "Style and Philosophy: the Case of Plato's Dialogues."

The relationship between Plato and Socrates in this matter of writing looks rather like one of Hegel's "determinate negations." Or, to put it in more Platonic terms, Plato's qualified acceptance of Socrates' conception of philosophy is indicated *ironically* by Plato. Irony is the medium in which Plato can express his "philosophy of philosophy" without compromising his own view on the matter. Hence there is a good philosophical rationale for Platonic irony.[37]

I note that to the extent to which the articulation of Plato's self-commentary depends on his "negation" of Socrates in the manner just referred to, Plato's defense of philosophy *must* be conveyed through the artifice of the written word. The written word is at one remove from the "ensouled" activity of dialectic (*Phdr.* 276a8 and context) which itself is at one remove from the Ideas. The written word affords Plato an indirect commentary about the nature of philosophy, but the dialogue form of writing releases him from the ensuing consequences which plague metaphilosophical self-reflection. Contrary to Socrates' remarks at the end of the *Phaedrus* about the inability of the written word (unlike the spoken) to defend itself, the present argument suggests that it is by virtue of being written that Platonic philosophizing can defend itself.

A final aspect of Plato's dialogues which makes some philosophical sense if we keep in mind the roots of dialectic as I have specified them is the lack of closure in the Platonic *corpus* as a whole. It seems that if Plato had written one more or one less dialogue, the unity of the *corpus* would suffer little, precisely because its unity derives from a common goal, not the systematization of the means. Moreover, it is difficult to see how any one dialogue could explicitly claim to "close" or "complete" Platonic philosophy without falling prey, once again, to the usual objections against "metaphilosophy" (in the primary sense of the term). Perhaps this is why the *Philosopher*—a dialogue that might have been the "definitive" statement of Platonic philosophy— was never written.

If one goes along with my general argument concerning Plato's use of the dialogue form, his choice of the positions he wants to argue with, his distance from his own texts, his irony, and the lack of closure in the *corpus*, then it would seem that Plato does not so much have "a philosophy" as a philosophy about the making of philosophical claims.

---

37. There's a good deal more to be said about Platonic irony, and its difference from Socratic irony, than I have said here. For some discussion of the issue, see W. Boder, *Die sokratische Ironie in den platonischen Frühdialogen* (Amsterdam: B. R. Grüner, 1973), and R. Schaerer, "Le mécanisme de l'ironie dans ses rapports avec la dialectique," *Revue de Métaphysique et de Morale* 48 (1941): 181–209.

But this cannot be said to amount to a "metaphilosophy" in the primary sense of the term. However, to restate an objection already discussed above, all this still doesn't seem to allay the old suspicion that Socratic and Platonic philosophizing is essentially "negative," elenchic, parasitic on the claims of others, and without any "positive" content of its own—as barren as the "midwife" Socrates claims to be. Are there, however, "ontological" consequences of Socratic and Platonic philosophizing (as I have adumbrated it) which mitigate the just mentioned criticism?

VII

The answer to this question is, I think, affirmative. In keeping with what I have said above, I suggest that we understand these consequences not so much as "theories" posited to round out an epistemology, but as reflections on the implications of the fact that there is philosophical learning and inquiry (in a sense other than memorization). As Gadamer puts this point: "The assumption that there are ideas remains for Plato an inescapable conclusion to be drawn from the nature of discussion and the process of reaching an understanding of something." And "the purpose of the Socratic art of conversing was to avoid being talked out of the fact that there is such a thing as the Just, the Beautiful, and the Good."[38] That is, inquiry, or philosophical questioning, or simply understanding something, have implications concerning the presence of intelligibility. In the *Republic*, Socrates explains this in terms of the sun-like Good. In the *Philebus*, he asserts that the Good shows itself as measure, symmetry, appropriateness, truth, and beauty (64e–65a, 66a–b). In the *Phaedrus*, Beauty is cited as the principle underlying the presence of intelligibility. In the myth of the *Meno* Socrates speaks of "all nature being akin" (81d). In the *Gorgias* he says that "heaven and earth, gods and men, are held together by the principles of sharing, by friendship and order, by self-control and justice; that, my friend, is the reason they call this Whole 'cosmos,' and not disorder or licentiousness."[39] There is a Whole ordered according to the principles of geometrical equality (*Grg.* 508a). This is an implication of the "aporetic" as much as the "nonaporetic" dialogues.

Plato would want to argue for all this indirectly and in an *ad homi-*

---

38. "Dialectic and Sophism," pp. 119, 117. A similar view is argued at length by Wieland, *Platon*, pp. 125–150. Consider also *Prm.* 135b5–c3.

39. The translation is W. C. Helmbold's, slightly amended. *Plato's Gorgias* (Indianapolis: Bobbs-Merrill, 1952), p. 83.

nem way. He might say (and does say in the criticism of Protagoras in the *Theaetetus*) that that to which we implicitly appeal in defending or attacking reason is the truth of our own thoughts and assertions—even if these be directed against the very notion of truth.[40] Even the antiphilosopher's inner dialogue with himself assumes, Plato wants to argue, the *presence* of the very intelligibility and wholeness that he thinks is the fabrication of the philosophers.

Deconstructivists who truly understand deconstruction do indeed truly understand something; they *see* their own point, as well as their opponent's point, and they do so in the light of intelligibility. The true "shapes" and "looks" (εἴδη, ἰδέαι) of things cannot be entirely inaccessible; for even the efforts to deny their accessibility or existence assume them. Or at least, this is the sort of deeply reflexive strategy Plato uses at this level of the argument. He then wants, of course, to introduce other notions to draw out his point. That of ἀνάμνησις, for example, expresses (among other things) the thought that the soul by nature knows something of what *is* (*Phdr.* 249e4–250a1). Plato's language in these matters necessarily becomes imprecise, metaphorical, or analogical; poetry is not dispensable for the Platonist. But there is also a good deal to be said about the "logic" of these εἴδη and about their instantiation in language, as well as about the nature of the soul. I am not arguing that the sorts of metaphilosophical issues considered in this paper somehow exhaust Platonic philosophy or the actual discussions Plato presents in his dialogues. In fact, my explanation of Plato's choice of the dialogue form of writing requires the philosopher to philosophize about the many issues that are in fact discussed in Plato's dialogues, as well as in the history of philosophy. For progress in these "object level" discussions is the evidence for the metalevel inferences concerning the εἴδη.

Now, there are responses to this Platonic *ad hominem* attack on the critic of philosophy which need to be considered. The critic can simply ignore it, reject it, or simultaneously both deny and affirm it. In each case dialogue seems to grind to a halt; and insofar as the success of the attack depends on the opponent's admission that he is wrong,

---

40. That is, however "subjective" or "relativist" a position may be, Socrates seeks to show that it ultimately must know itself as "true" in a sense that is not just subjective or relativist. For an excellent discussion of Socrates' criticism in the *Tht.* of Protagoras along these lines, see M. F. Burnyeat's "Protagoras and Self-Refutation in Plato's *Theaetetus*," *Philosophical Review* 85 (1976): 172–195. Burnyeat concludes that "No amount of maneuvering with his relativizing qualifiers will extricate Protagoras from the commitment to truth absolute which is bound up with the very act of assertion. To assert is to assert that *p*—as Passmore puts it, that something is the case—and if *p*, indeed if and only if *p*, then *p* is true (period). This principle, which relativism attempts to circumvent, must be acknowledged by any speaker" (p. 195).

the attack fails. The impossibility of dialogue with the Homericists/ Heracliteans (and implicitly the Protagoreans as well) is vividly described by Theodorus (*Tht.* 179e–180b). As a matter of fact, the antiphilosophers reject the very idea of a "dialogue" in the philosophical sense (along with the idea, discussed above with reference to the *Meno*, that there is "learning" in any philosophically suggestive sense), as Socrates explicitly notes in his attack on Protagoras.[41] Thus Socrates' dialogues with such persons are, one might argue, protodialogues, for they are not animated by a *mutual* search for truth (hence they border on the eristic). But in the face of a sufficiently tough or clever opponent, it would seem that even this protodialogue must falter and, as in the *Gorgias*, that the philosopher must end up conversing with himself. The antiphilosopher in question professes no care for the truth and therefore does not mind being labeled "irrational" in the philosopher's sense; all that is just an expression, for him, of the very framework that he has rejected. That is, having argued that, for Plato, dialogue with the critics of philosophy is necessary, we now begin to wonder whether it is possible even in the "indirect" senses I have discussed. Do we have, in effect, a necessity for an impossibility?[42] In the last section of this paper I would like to take a brief look at this issue.

41. *Tht.* 161e; if Protagoras' position is right, then Socrates' "maieutic art" is "laughable," as is "the whole business of dialectic (*dialegesthai*)."

42. It is fairly clear, for example, that Rortean "conversation" between an advocate of normal discourse (discourse governed by an agreed upon set of neutral commensurating principles which tell us how to settle a debate; examples of such discussion being systematic philosophy and epistemology) and an advocate of a certain species of abnormal discourse (the "edifying" philosopher who violates the metarule that all changes in normal discourse should be warranted by the discovery of a new set of commensurating rules) is impossible. Rorty initially sets up "hermeneutics" as "the study of an abnormal discourse from the point of view of some normal discourse" (*Philosophy*, p. 320) in the hope of generating a "conversation" between the two (p. 318). But hermeneutics soon collapses into edifying philosophy, the point of which is to keep the conversation going (p. 372, 77; cf. p. 366). The reason for this collapse is surely that Rorty understands hermeneutics from the start as generating a conversation that does *not* reach for Truth or Agreement in the sense assumed by the advocates of normal discourse (pp. 315, 318, 372). When he says that this conversation is "hermeneutics with polemical intent" (p. 365) he is simply conceding what he says throughout: there is no argument or genuine exchange possible between normal and edifying philosophers (pp. 181, 364–365; *Consequences* pp. xliii, 98). The two sides are not playing by the same rules or even the same metarule (the one that stipulates that we both want to learn the Truth). Since the conversation between normal philosophers is of no interest (for it would not be sufficiently radical) Rorty is presumably promising us conversation between edifying philosophers. But such a conversation seems impossible, since edifying philosophers are "reactive" and "parasitic," and so "having sense *only* as a protest against attempts to close off conversation by proposals for universal commensuration...." (p. 377; emphasis added). Edificationists can not react to each other. Indeed Rorty warns that to introduce "abnormal discourse *de novo*, without being able to recognize our own abnormality, is madness in the most literal and terrible sense" (p. 366). Moreover, the normal/

VIII

The idea that a very intelligent person (such as Protagoras or Derrida) could profess no interest in the love of wisdom is, we must admit, profoundly disturbing. It would be easy to dismiss their failure to give in to Plato's "deeply reflexive strategy" mentioned above as a sign of a stupidly obstinate streak, a character defect, or some such. That is, it would be easy to dismiss their disagreement as a sign of their deficiency, not as a sign that there is something wrong with the sort of *ad hominem* argument sketched above. Thus Aristotle terms a "vegetable" the man who resolutely rejects the principle of noncontradiction (*Met.* IV, 4, 1006a15, 1008b13).[43] Plato also sees, as Aristotle does, that the debate is *so* deep that *everything* is at stake, and that nothing of "philosophy" will survive if the other side wins (we cannot proceed with our metaphysics until we have settled this debate in our favor); and Plato certainly thinks that philosophy is the superior of the two. But Plato seems unwilling to let the insult be the last word, and this because he seems especially aware of just how difficult it is to "win" the quarrel between philosophy and its critics without begging the question. I have argued that the dialogue form, and everything associated with the genre as it is molded by Plato, can be understood as consequences of these observations.

But, to repeat, a true mediation between philosophy and its critics may well seem impossible. However, the rhetorical, dramatic, or mimetic dimension of Plato's dialogues may serve as a partial response to this point. This pervasive and sustaining dimension represents what might be called the world of ordinary experience, the "life-world," or to use a more Platonic expression, the "political." Even the debates with the anti- or nonphilosophers emerge, in Plato, from this context, and they never lose touch with it. These debates could have been structured by Plato "academically," without this elaborately crafted context, but they are not. That is, it seems that when faced with the ultimate challenge or "quarrel," Plato thinks he can draw on prephilosophical experience. At least two reasons for this suggest themselves.

---

abnormal dualism is permanent; though the future of philosophy cannot be predicted, this dualism will necessarily be present.

43. I do not mean to imply, of course, that Aristotle uses the insult without argumentation. It is worth noting that even Rorty wants to distinguish between the sane, on the one hand, and the "stupid," "psychotic," and "moronic," on the other. Conversation is worthwhile only with the sane. *Philosophy*, pp. 190, 349 (cf. the reference on p. 366 to "madness in the most literal and terrible sense"). Presumably Rorty does not think that the sane/insane distinction boils down to the normal/abnormal discourse distinction. But then how does he account for it?

First, the prephilosophical is not already a construction of the philosopher, and so provides a common starting point for philosophy as well as its critics, thus eliminating one basis for accusing the philosopher of begging the question. The framework that contains distinctions such as those between truth and judgments about the truth is not, on this account, a philosophical construction but a fact of life. In Plato's dialogues even the fundamental philosophical problems are depicted as arising out of the rich tapestry of ordinary experience and not (as is so often the case today) from an "academic" tradition. Moreover, if agreement is the "starting point" of philosophizing, then the starting point is unsystematic. This starting point is opinion, the multihued, receptaclelike medium in which the "Whole" is reflected. That opinion is the context of philosophizing in Plato has frequently been thought, particularly by metaphilosophically oriented philosophers, to constitute its weakness. But given the problems I have discussed concerning the beginnings of metaphilosophy itself, Plato's doxic starting point is a virtue, not a vice. Opinion is not an axiom or theoretical construction; it gives us an *already intelligible*, but nonmethodological, "beginning" for our philosophizing. Thus, for Plato, opinion is not a starting point that can ever be left behind. These points help to explain Plato's decision to write dialogues.

Moreover, the "political" does already contain and exhibit the threads of the great issues: those of life and death, self-interest and justice, freedom and slavery, war and peace, desire, power, and so on. It also exhibits, unavoidably, moral judgments and moral sense, along with their naive realism (see below). It seems to me that, in the final analysis, it is only by returning to this level—the level that defines what our concerns should be and defines the issues as real, the level in which our basic moral intuitions (such as "the courageous man is better than the coward") are grounded—that Socrates can draw his opponent into a context from which the origination of philosophy can command assent. Moral judgments in this sphere are not viewed by people in a relativistic or historicist way. Allegiances to family and country are deeply felt. The force of moral opinion is enormous. And the stakes in both war and peace are of universal import. In his debates with nonphilosophers Socrates appeals regularly to all this; for example, he frequently tries to shame his interlocutors into changing their outlook.[44] Correspondingly, Plato's phenomenology of human life is not value neutral, in the way that Heidegger's phenomenology of *Dasein* is. For Plato, philosophical rhetoric is always tied to the po-

---

44. On shame, see *Symp.* 216b, *Phdr.* 243c, *Grg.* 461b, 482d, and *Prt.* 248c.

litical (in the broadest sense of the term); this cannot be said of the comparatively apolitical thought of Wittgenstein, Heidegger, Rorty, and Derrida. Plato's wager is, I think, that the "political" dimension of human experience is more or less stable throughout history. Hence his portrayals of it can function as mirrors in which we can recognize, and be reminded of, our own moral intuitions—above all, the intuition that the great issues of life are great because they are somehow tied to the truth and the good in nonrelativistic senses of the terms.

Socrates is known for his criticisms of δόξα; but these do not amount to anything like a complete negation of it. His ability to drive home the power of the question brings him into conflict with the polis. But in his view that these "moral" issues are to be understood as "real" (and not just as social or linguistic conventions) he is at one with the polis, even though he wants to show that ordinary moral intuitions, when thought through, "really" depend on things like "recollection" and "Ideas." Rorty's postmetaphysical culture, by contrast, is considerably more alien to common sense than Socrates' analyses of true virtue. His deconstruction of philosophy seems to me to also entail a deconstruction of the political.[45] Rorty does, to be sure, talk about moral commitment; indeed, he does so in the last sentence of *Philosophy and the Mirror of Nature*. One wonders what he could possibly mean by such talk. Indeed, one wonders what it would mean to say, on Rortean grounds (if that is the right word), that one should have a moral commitment to keep a "conversation" going.[46]

---

45. Rorty says that there are human rights "worth dying for" (*Philosophy*, p. 177); but do people die while self-consciously holding that these rights "have been granted or denied, in the way in which social and intellectual historians understand this" (p. 178)? Not even intellectuals would die for rights so understood; even they revert to the naive realism of common sense, a realism with which Plato is much more sympathetic. That is, there is something terribly "theoretical" about the sort of position Rorty wants to advocate. Just as Rorty does not want to either affirm or deny the existence of God, and hopes to just set aside the "vocabulary of theology" since he does not see the point in using it (*Consequences*, p. xiv), so too he would presumably want to set aside the political rhetoric (which is usually contaminated by religious rhetoric) with which nations everywhere define themselves. But then Rorty is fairly clear in his view that the whole "mirror of nature" image, along with the notion that our ideas correspond to some reality out there, do not express a "pre-analytic intuition" (*Philosophy*, pp. 34, 158–159; yet see pp. 22, 286). I find this very doubtful. On "intuitive realism," see Rorty's response in the Introduction to *Consequences*.

46. Rorty's quasi-Sartrean talk about the "burden of choice" (*Philosophy* p. 376) imposed on us by the absence of commensurating discourse is presumably the basis for his criticisms of "totalitarianism" and the "secret police" (pp. 333, 351, 389), for the latter tend to extirpate conversation. To make sure that the conversation continues and the burden is not lifted is the "moral concern" of the philosopher (p. 383, 394). Presumably giving up the burden of choice is bad because it leads to "dehumanization" (p. 377),

But what if, to borrow the terminology of a recent reviewer of Rorty's *Philosophy*, our antiphilosopher is a "cheerful nihilist"?[47] What if he is simply insensitive to all the compelling moral issues embedded in political life or if he "deconstructs" political life? At this point (given that all our other strategies have been exhausted) the limits of dialogue really are reached, and such a person is dialogically irrefutable. Plato certainly does not mask this fact. But his depiction of it actually leaves the reader with more than this breakdown would suggest. Understanding the limits self-consciously and dialectically, with full awareness of all the pitfalls, and with the deeds and words of both philosopher and his opponent in front of us, we are justified in drawing the conclusion that the unexamined life is not worth living.

Howard University

"bad faith" (p. 383), "self-objectification" (pp. 378, 389; cf. 349). But why is all that so bad? What if dehumanization becomes, at some point, a self-description which people find "interesting" and "new" (pp. 321, 359)? And if their "present moral intuitions" (p. 306) were totalitarian? Rorty must say that there would be something wrong with this. But here Rorty reaches a point that cannot be relativized further without destroying the force he wants to attribute to his own words. Rorty must have some description of human nature, and of its debasement, which is not just true for his "linguistic conventions" or "social practices." As always in coherent statements of liberalism, there is a hidden metarule that all views must be tolerated except the view that tolerance cannot be tolerated. Otherwise we fall prey to what K. Popper calls the "paradox of tolerance," i.e., the fact that "Unlimited tolerance must lead to the disappearance of tolerance" (*The Open Society and its Enemies*, 5th ed., Princeton: Princeton University Press, 1966, 1: 265).

47. The remark is S. Rosen's, in his review in *Review of Metaphysics* 33 (1980): 801. Rosen also takes note of other important defects in Rorty's interpretation of Plato.

2 PLATO AND THE STORY

GERARD WATSON

In a curious passage in the *Symposium* Plato reflects on the nature of human identity. The passage seems to occur almost incidentally, a casual observation, as it were, on a commonplace phenomenon, meant merely to highlight the more important statement that the cause of love among animals and humans is the desire for immortality. Plato says that we talk of people remaining the same, and think of them as continuing one. Yet, when we consider it, this is a strange form of identity. In fact, there is neither unity nor continuity: there is continual renewal and replacement and this gives the illusion of unity. The lack of continuity is most obvious physically, in things like hair or flesh. More remarkable, however, is psychic discontinuity. We say we are the same, yet there is constant change of our opinions, fears, desires. Even what we dignify by the name of knowledge (*epistēmē*) is not fixed.[1] We forget some things we knew and we learn others, and any particular branch of knowledge is an image of the person who possesses it: it is constantly disappearing and being replaced, but because the process is not interrupted it seems as if the continuity is unbroken (207d–208b).

It is possible that the passage *is* quite casual, and that Plato is simply poking fun at his medical colleagues as he does elsewhere in the dialogue, making his contribution to their debate on the unity of man. We find an instance of this in the Hippocratean *Nature of Man*. The writer there begins with some disparaging remarks on other theorists before turning to the medical men. "When we come to the physicians," he says, "we find that some assert that man is composed of blood, others of bile and some of phlegm. But these, too, all make the same point, asserting that there is a basic unity of substance, although they each give it a different name and so change its appearance and

---

1. Plato is probably playing with a derivation of *epistēmē* from *ephistēmi* (cf. Aristotle, *Phys.* 247b11), but he is also drawing attention to the dignity and fixity expected from it.

properties under stress of heat and cold, becoming sweet or bitter, white or black, and so forth. Now I do not agree with these people either, although the majority will declare that this, or something very similar, is the case. I hold that if man were basically of one substance, he would never feel pain, since, being one, there would be nothing to hurt."[2] But if there is fun, it is, as is so often the case in Plato, fun mixed with very serious matter. If there is unity in man, can the constituents of the unity be merely physical?

Plato is asking an important question, and he is asking it even more clearly than he does in the *Theaetetus*. In the latter dialogue he is concerned with the problems of perception, knowledge, and change, preoccupations that are basic to his philosophy. Here Plato represents Protagoras beginning to reply to criticism of views alleged to be his and which have been put into his mouth. Protagoras will say: "Do you think anyone is going to concede to you that when one is no longer experiencing something, one can have present in one a memory of that thing which is itself an experience of the same sort as the original one? Far from it. Or again, do you think anyone is going to hesitate to admit that it's possible for the same person both to know and not to know the same thing? Or, supposing someone is afraid to say that, do you think anyone is ever going to grant that a person who is altering is the same person as he was before the altering began? Or rather, that one is a person at all, and not people, coming into being in unlimited numbers, too, as long as alteration goes on?" (*Tht.*166b).[3]

The *Theaetetus* passage is, I think, a clear indication that Plato is not simply poking fun in the *Symposium*. He is, in fact, referring to a central topic in his philosophy, what he refers to in the *Sophist* as the battle of the gods and giants. He is concerned to assert himself against those who "define reality as the same thing as body, and as soon as one of the opposite party asserts that anything without a body is real, they are utterly contemptuous and will not listen to another word" (*Sph.*246b).[4] Plato is asking whether, according to medical theory, it is seriously meant that we are merely blood, phlegm, or bile? Is there no higher center of consciousness whereby we both remember and de-

---

2. *The Nature of Man* 2, trans. by Chadwick and Mann, in *Hippocratic Writings* ed. G. E. R. Lloyd (Pelican, 1978). Lloyd (p. 11) attributes the work to Polybus, the son-in-law of Hippocrates, and says (p. 38) of the reference in the opening chapter of that work to current debates: "The implication is that the question of the ultimate constituents of the human body was, at this time, the subject of competitive public debates in which several speakers participated and the audience itself decided who was the winner." The point is of interest for the *Symposium*. Cf. ibid., *The Science of Medicine* 2 and *Tradition in Medicine* 20.
3. McDowell's trs.
4. Cornford's trs.

sire, and feel guilt or pride at what "I" have done or been? Are we just a series of incidents? Is there no connecting thread? If there is no fixity can there be any reliability? And if there is no unity, no continuity, can there be responsibility? Is there moral accountability? If there is, what is it that provides the unity or continuity in personality and so gives meaning to what is otherwise a psychic and physical hotch-potch?

In the context of the *Symposium* it seems almost perverse to hold that 207c–208b in particular precludes a belief in the immortality of the soul.[5] One could only adopt such a position by ignoring the context. Part of the context is an earlier passage in the *Symposium* where the emphasis is again on the broken nature of man. This is the story as told by Aristophanes of how human beings came to be the way they are (189c ff.). For the nature we had once was not what we have now but something quite different. We were whole and rounded. Human beings, indeed, were so strong, vigorous, and proud that they dared to attack the gods. And so Zeus split man in two, and as a result each of us is now merely a σύμβολον of a man, a broken token whose meaning is only clear when the other half is found. That is why we go around seeking for the other half. There is in us a longing that drives us on in an attempt to restore our ancient unity. The longing for unity is clear in physical love. But there is more than physical love in question. It is some mysterious restoration of unity that the soul is seeking in friendship. "It is clear that the soul of each has some longing, besides physical enjoyment, some longing which it cannot clearly state but can only surmise and obscurely hint at" (192d).

Man's salvation, then, for Aristophanes depends on some memory of wholeness, completeness. It is the persistence of *eros*, loving desire, which encourages him to hope that if we behave well we will be made happy by being restored to our original state. *Eros* is the mixture of memory and desire, it forms the link between the perfection at the beginning and the perfection we hope for at the end. It therefore is the mysterious force that provides the unity which gives meaning to man's life, in spite of physical and psychical discontinuity. Although knowledge is included in the vision of the original perfection, *eros* is more than knowledge. The drive persists even when the vision is no longer present. It is the desire for, and pursuit of, completeness. The longing may be obscure but it is unfailing.

It may be objected that we are not entitled to take Aristophanes' speech as containing serious views of Plato. In a very recent commentary, for instance, Dover says that "What precedes Socrates' interroga-

---

5. See the theories of Morrison and Hackforth referred to by Dover in "The Date of Plato's Symposium," *Phronesis* 10 (1965): 16.

tion of Agathon . . . is not philosophical," and he says with specific reference to Aristophanes' speech that "Plato later makes Diotima reject and condemn its central theme (205de, cf. 212c)."[6] If we turn to the first of these references we read "'There is indeed a theory,' Diotima continued, 'that lovers are people who are in search of the other half of themselves, but according to my view of the matter, my friend, love is not desire either of the half or the whole, unless that half or whole happens to be good. Men are quite willing to have their feet or their hands amputated if they believe those parts of themselves to be diseased.'"[7] To call this a rejection or condemnation of the central theme of Aristophanes' speech is, however, to adopt a very literal-minded approach to Plato, and such an approach can lead to a disastrous amount of wasted ink, if nothing worse. It would be ham-fisted to take literally Socrates' statement at the end of the *Charmides*: "Now I have been utterly defeated and have failed to discover" what *sōphrosunē* is (175b), or, in the *Laches* "Then, Nicias, we have not discovered what courage is" (199e). A literal acceptance of the *Phaedrus* (275cff.) would largely absolve us from the duty of reading Plato at all.

Aristophanes' speech is, of course, exuberant and to some tastes perhaps even excessive. But Plato's use of the speech is central to his method.[8] Aristophanes' speech is picked out for attack because Plato wishes to draw attention to it. But criticism does not imply total rejection. Throughout the dialogues suggestions that Plato would agree with are put forward only to be plucked at, made fun of, and, finally, apparently, thrown aside. *Aporia* is designed to provoke wonderment which will ensure enduring interest. One of the most elaborate examples of the technique is the criticism of the theory of Forms in the *Parmenides*. No one can, I think, seriously believe that Plato was simply, because of this criticism, rejecting the theory of Forms. It is always dangerous to ignore the context in Plato. In his recent book on the *Parmenides* Allen has done well to draw attention to Kitto's *Form and Meaning in Drama*, with a quotation from which he prefaces his discussion. In the *Symposium*, Aristophanes' story to explain eros takes up motifs from the earlier part of the dialogue, is in turn taken up by the discourse of Diotima, and is finally recalled in Alcibiades' comparison

---

6. *Plato Symposium* (Cambridge, 1980), pp. 5 and 113. Cf. Bury's commentary, p. lvii, where Aristophanes is ranked with the "men of *unphilosophic* mind" (his italics). Even the normally sympathetic Stewart says that the speech is "so barbarously grotesque that one has difficulty in recognising it as a Platonic myth," *The Myths of Plato* (London, 1960²), p. 378.

7. Penguin trs.

8. See, for instance, how Lysias is allowed to introduce the important love-as-madness theme in *Phaedrus* 231d.

of Socrates to the Silenus figures, the beings which can be unfolded to disclose two realities when we thought there was only one.[9] It is Aristophanes who has the honor to be the last man speaking to Socrates before the party ends with a discussion of the combination of tragedy and comedy, something that is central to Plato's whole presentation of Socrates.

The *Symposium* is among other things a discussion of what knowledge really is, what it would be like to be fully in possession of wisdom. We are told that man's normal condition is to be a seeker after wisdom, and that it is essential that he persevere in this quest. Nevertheless, his knowledge normally is partial, broken, questionable, vague, puzzling, a patch of obscurity more than a pool of light, something which, as Socrates says of his own *sophia*, is "like a dream" (175e).[10] In the *Symposium* Plato is using Aristophanes' speech to highlight the puzzle of man's nature, a puzzle that cannot be solved by merely physical explanations. The physical questions are interesting, and Plato was interested in the medical discussions. But his serious point is that to confine oneself to the physical in an attempt to understand man, his unity and meaning, would be as ridiculous as to accept Aristophanes' story of the physical separation as the *complete* explanation of why man has the mysterious longings we call love. But his story does contain the truth that each of us is something in search of a meaning. We, and the meaning, are incomplete, like a jigsaw puzzle with pieces missing. Yet there are enough pieces already fitted together to make us feel sure that the picture can be completed, and we will not be able to rest until we have the full picture. It is as if we had glimpsed the full picture once and memory stimulates us to aim for its completion.

But how are we to ensure perseverance in these uncertain conditions? There have to be encouragements and reminders. There is constant reference to such throughout the dialogues. In the *Phaedo* Cebes tells Socrates that "perhaps there is in each one of us a little child who's afraid of these sorts of things. Try to persuade him not to be afraid of death the way he's afraid of bogey-men." Socrates answers: "What you should do is to say a magic charm over him every

---

9. See *Symp.* 221d–222a.
10. This recalls Socrates' comment on the newly acquired conscious knowledge of slave boy in *Meno* 85c. Both passages (and there are many others in the corpus) point to Plato's awareness of the difficulty of acquiring real knowledge. Socrates is making an ironic contrast between his knowledge and Agathon's brilliance, and tells him "Wouldn't it be wonderful, Agathon, if wisdom were like water, and flowed by contact through a straw." (Bluck, in a revealing note on *Meno* 85c9, writes: "As Thompson observes, at *Symp.* 175e Agathon says that his own wisdom is slight and doubtful, like a dream" [Greek in original]. Irony is obviously a dangerous weapon).

day until you have charmed his fears away" (77e). The spell-like repetition is given a distinctive twist in the *Meno* (85c) where, after the geometry display, Socrates says about the slave boy: "At present these opinions, being newly aroused, have a dream-like quality. But if the same questions are put to him on many occasions and in different ways, you can see that in the end he will have a knowledge on the subject as accurate as anybody's." In the *Symposium* itself it is Socrates who is the enchanter.[11] Alcibiades talks of his ability to inspire others in some inexplicable way, and compares him with Marsyas whose music can "by reason of its divine origin throw men into a trance, and so mark off those who yearn to enter by initiation into union with the gods. But you, Socrates, are so far superior to Marsyas that you produce the same effect by mere words without any instrument" (215c). Finally we must mention a passage in the *Republic* which has become practically notorious, the passage on the necessity of contriving "some magnificent myth." Such a story would in itself carry conviction to the whole community, and such persuasion is vital for the state (414).

Stories themselves are the most important form of incantation, and Plato himself was obviously a born storyteller. This is clear even in the little observations from life, as in the *Protagoras*, for instance: "As I looked at the party I was delighted to notice what special care they took never to get in front or to be in Protagoras' way. When he and those with him turned round, the listeners divided this way and that in perfect order, and executing a circular movement took their places each time in the rear" (315b).[12] Or it can be seen in the picture in the *Gorgias* of the captain who has brought people from Egypt or Pontus for two drachmae, and disembarks at the Peiraeus, "and the man who possesses this skill and has accomplished all this lands and walks about on the shore beside his ship $\dot{\varepsilon}\nu$ $\mu\varepsilon\tau\rho\dot{\iota}\omega$ $\sigma\chi\dot{\eta}\mu\alpha\tau\iota$" (511e).[13] An entire character is presented in the three Greek words—competent, self-confident, proud of what he can do, and in no way tempted to try to exceed his capacities. In the *Gorgias* also there is a satisfying Hans Christian Andersen suddenness and decisiveness in Zeus' arrangements to ensure fair judgment: "They must be judged stripped" (523e).[14]

This last is, of course, taken from the myth towards the end of the

---

11. Cf. *Tht.* 149cff. on midwives and incantations, and Socrates, the midwife's son.
12. Penguin trs.
13. Penguin trs.
14. See Dodds' note ad loc. on the implication that the senses are a hindrance, not a help, to clear thinking.

Gorgias, one of the many eschatological myths in Plato which he evidently delighted in telling. We are inclined to say it came naturally to him. But this should not be taken to mean that Plato slipped into story-telling unconsciously. On the contrary, he was highly conscious of the importance of the story as such, a point we will return to when talking of the *Phaedrus*. Plato's moral concern sometimes had an unfortunate effect on his theory of art, and as a literary theorist he often compares unfavorably with Aristotle. In the *Poetics* Aristotle can be found to be at variance with Plato, and is at pains to correct him even when he does not mention his name. Aristotle is well aware of the importance of the story.[15] But in this instance at least he is simply following in the footsteps of Plato.

It is interesting to see how Plato will develop a prosaic statement of a philosophical point of view, such as that in *Phaedo* 82e–83a, into a story such as that of the Cave in the *Republic*, which grips the imagination and seems to say something more general about the whole human situation. The *Phaedo* says: "Every seeker after wisdom knows that up to the time when philosophy takes it over his soul is a helpless prisoner, chained hand and foot in the body. . . . And philosophy can see that the imprisonment is ingeniously effected by the prisoner's own active desire, which makes him first accessory to his own confinement. . . ." But in the *Republic* we can *see* the willing prisoners in the cave, their eyes glued to the wall, as if it were a television screen running a neverending series of *Dallas*, and no more willing to be moved than they would be by the announcement of a lecture on metaphysics in the next room, without slides. "They resemble ourselves." It is because Plato is so aware of the power of the story that he is so critical of the stories in which his own tradition was so rich.

Time and again in his work Plato turns deliberately and of set purpose to the story at a key point in the argument. The *Protagoras* is typical of his attitude (even if the story is not his own, although I believe it is). When it becomes necessary to show that virtue can be taught, Protagoras ponders: "Shall I make my demonstration to you . . . by telling you a story (*muthon*) or shall I attempt to set it out in argument (*logōi*)? . . . I think it might be nicer to tell you a story" (320c). In the *Gorgias* Socrates states: "To enter Hades with one's soul loaded with injustice is the supreme misfortune. I can tell you a story (*logon*) that proves this if you like." He grants that "You may consider it fiction," but that for his part "I am persuaded by these stories" (522eff.). He

---

15. See chs. 7–14 of the *Poetics* (1450b21ff.). Cf. *Met.* 982b18: "the lover of stories is in some sense a philosopher," and his own confession about himself fr. 668 Rose.

again offers to tell a fine story (*muthon legein kalon*) in the *Phaedo* (110b), and says after telling it (114d): "Of course, no reasonable man ought to insist that the facts are exactly as I have described them. But that either this or something very like it is a true account of our souls and their future habitations—since the soul would appear to be something immortal—this, I think, is both a reasonable contention and a belief worth risking."[16] In the *Statesman* he emphasizes the importance of using a great amount of myth in the attempt to obtain a portrait of the *politikos*, and urges: "So come now, pay attention to my story, as children would" (268d). Finally, we are told in the *Seventh Letter* (335a) that we are to keep faith "in the sacred stories (*logois*) which have come down to us from antiquity which tell us that the soul is immortal and that when it is separated from the body it must face judges and suffer the greatest punishments."

From these examples it is clear that we must not read too much into the distinction of *logos* and *muthos* in the *Protagoras*, and we must not presume that the distinction is always absolute. In the *Laws* Plato discusses the legal punishment for the murder of relatives (872c ff.). But in addition to the punishment laid down by the law he feels that reference should also be made to vengeance exacted by the gods and how "Justice stands on guard to exact vengeance for the spilling of the blood of relatives." This has been stated clearly for us by the priests of old, "this *mythos* or *logos* or whatever we ought to call it" (872d). And he refers back a couple of pages to the reference to divine vengeance for murder in general (870d) which is introduced with the words: "we must tell the story (*logon*) which is so strongly believed by so many people when they hear it from those who have made a serious study of such matters in their mystic ceremonies."[17] Again, in 927a he refers to stories (*logoi*) according to which the dead can interfere in the lives of the living, and once more he recalls an earlier passage (865d) where we are warned against looking down on old statements from the ancient stories (*muthoi*).

We should take particular note of what is said about *logoi* in the *Phaedrus*. There we have a number of speeches, from Lysias and Socrates, and included are discussions of the various kinds of madness, the myth of the chariot, and the story of human existence, or at least human philosophic existence, in the history of the cicadas. And so they turn finally to what good speaking must be. The first essential, recalling a point made in 237bc, is that the speaker must have knowledge of the truth about his subject (259e). Then we must avoid being misled

---

16. Penguin trs. modified.   17. Penguin trs.

by apparent likenesses. We are particularly liable to be misled by certain words. "Just," for instance, and "good" might mislead us in a way that "iron" or "silver" would not. It is because Lysias has failed to recognize or make clear what an ambiguous word "love" is that he has gone astray. He has got things back to front, he is like a man swimming on his back, in reverse. The true way is different. "I think you would agree that any speech (*logon*) ought to have its own organic shape, like a living being; it must not be without either head or feet; it must have a middle and extremities so composed as to fit one another and the work as a whole" (264c).[18]

This last statement made a deep impression on Aristotle.[19] Plato in fact does not expand it, and once again he certainly does not labor it. Nevertheless, it forms a climax in the discussion, coming as it does after the practical examples to give a memorable summary of what the *logos* in theory should be, and preceding the important new method of collection and division which it introduces. *Logos* is used in the widest sense of rational effective speech. Because of the attention paid to rhetoric in the dialogue, there is a temptation to confine the statement to forensic or epideictic oratory. Socrates, however, emphasizes twice that the term is not to be confined (258d, 261ab); his own speeches have been concerned with the highest realities, and Lysias' speech itself has been dealing in undisturbed ignorance with a highly important but highly ambiguous philosophical term.

Plato does not of course use the concept of symmetrical or asymmetrical relations in this context. When, however, he says here that the *logos* should be like a living being, it is hard not to believe that he was not also thinking that the human living organism should be like the *logos*, and in the human organism what for Plato was primary was not the body. The human life must have unity. If, therefore, he thinks of the life-*logos* relationship as symmetrical, the story (*logos* or *muthos*) takes on an even more important function than that which we have seen. We saw that from one point of view Plato's stories are spells, enchantments, or charms meant to keep away the darkness of uncertainty. "We should use such accounts to inspire ourselves with confidence; and that is why I have already drawn out my tale so long" (*Phd*.114d).[20] But now the *logos* or story is seen under a different aspect, both as the product of the mind and as the representation of it. The *logos* that emerges from man is by its very existence an affirma-

---

18. Penguin trs. See De Vries' comm. ad loc. for further parallels in Plato.
19. See especially *Poetics* 1450b25ff.
20. Penguin trs.

tion of his unity and a reassurance that his existence has direction and meaning. "Don't take it as a matter of course, but as a remarkable fact, that pictures and fictitious narratives give us pleasure, occupy our minds" (Wittgenstein, *Philosophical Investigations*, 524).

The stories, then, in Plato are complementary to the close argumentation (*logos* in the narrow sense) of which the dialogues are for the most part constituted. In the unity of his work the argumentation or attempted dialectical demonstration and the story (*logos* or *muthos*) are intimately intertwined. The combination has the effect of making Plato much more tentative about the possibility of establishing central philosophical positions than has often been assumed, and particularly than has been assumed in the last fifty years or so with the emphasis on Plato as the dogmatic philosophical theorist. That is not to suggest for an instant that Plato lacks conviction. His central conviction is that words as uttered by a good man like Socrates have meaning and consistency. If our words did not have meaning we could not make any sensible statement. If we could not do that we could not be conscious of ourselves as human beings. It is because words do have meaning that we can have true beliefs about right human action, and that consequently we feel the obligation to live by these beliefs. In the *Theaetetus* Plato is appalled that Protagoras could begin his book, actually called *Truth*, with the words "man is the measure of all things" (161cd). Just as well make the pig or the baboon or the tadpole the measure, if there is nothing more to humans than perception.[21] Plato takes it simply for granted in the first place that the human being has criteria for deciding right and wrong. They are based ultimately on the distinction in the human being between *epistēmē*, which here only humans have, and *aisthēsis*, which the animals share. But to *prove* that distinction requires long and complicated argumentation, such as is attempted in the *Theaetetus*. And the argumentation is so complicated and so open to question that at each stage, whether in regard to beginning, middle, or end, it may need to be substantiated by the story. The two must work together to confirm and perpetuate wisdom.

The beginning in Plato's account of man's story concerns recollection and preexistence, the middle concerns mortal existence and the values that give it meaning, and the end the question of immortality and the fate of the soul. Each stage is subject to uncertainties. This, of course, has long been recognized,[22] but it has become so fashionable

---

21. I have suggested elsewhere that the Stoics must have found the *Tht.* particularly stimulating for the development of their views on animal versus human knowledge. See my forthcoming *Phantasia in Classical Thought*.

22. See Stewart, op. cit., pp. 86f., 305f. on the views of Leibniz, Hegel, and Coleridge.

in the last fifty years to accuse Plato of dogmatism that it is necessary to turn back briefly to what Plato actually says. The review will be brief because a proper examination would fill some books and not just an article. Moreover, on topics like these views tend to be fixed, and a short exposition is as likely, or unlikely, to change opinions as a long one. We are not treading on virgin soil.

Let us turn first to the question of preexistence and, arising from that, recollection. The earliest reference to preexistence is in the *Meno* where he gives as his authorities for it "priests and priestesses," Pindar, "and many another of the poets": "see whether you think they are speaking the truth" (81ab). Plato next connects preexistence and immortality: "They say that the soul of man is immortal: at one time it comes to an end—that which is called death—and at another is born again, but is never finally exterminated." And from beginning and end flows an obligation for the middle: "On these grounds a man must live all his days as righteously as possible." Immortality and preexistence are then linked explicitly with recollection, and it is concluded that "seeking and learning are in fact nothing but recollection," a doctrine Plato recommends as producing "energetic seekers after knowledge" (81d; cf.86bc). Socrates then proceeds to demonstrate the doctrine in the geometry lesson with the slave. It is agreed by Meno at the conclusion that the slave's true opinions on the properties of the square were "somewhere in him," and Socrates adds that these opinions have "a dream-like quality," but that "if the same questions are put to him on many occasions and in different ways . . . in the end he will have a knowledge of the subject as accurate as anybody's" (85c). Finally, Socrates states that what has been said about the knowledge of geometry can be generalized and applied to all subjects.

This is commonly taken as the justification for a doctrine of preexistence and recollection in Plato. But in fact everything that has been said in the dialogue on the topic is qualified by the closing exchange between Meno and Socrates, before they return to the question "What is virtue?" When Meno says that he thinks Socrates is right, the latter replies: "I think I am. I shouldn't like to take my oath on the whole story, but one thing I am ready to fight for as long as I can, in word and act: that is, that we shall be better, braver and more active men if we believe it right to look for what we don't know than if we believe there is no point in looking because what we don't know we can never discover" (86bc).[23]

Plato seems to be saying that it is certain that we shall be better,

23. *Meno* trs. all Penguin.

more spirited, and active, less inclined to despair, *if* we have such a belief in preexistence and innate knowledge. He is clearly not saying that the belief itself is certain.[24] It is important to remember this point when the topic is recalled in the *Phaedo* (72e ff) and used to underpin the theory of Forms as there unfolded, as well as supplying a suasory argument for the immortality of the soul. The *Phaedrus* too is concerned with the vision that enables us to make sense of the universe. That we must, in a literal way, have had this vision in a state of preexistence is not at all so clear.

Closely connected with preexistence and recollection is what is important for the middle of man's story, the theory of Forms. Taken in its literal sense this seems to imply that we have actually seen at some stage the Equal Itself, the Beautiful, the Good, the Just, the Holy. It is useful to try to imagine what one would be looking at when contemplating the Equal Itself. It is interesting also that Plato chose this example as the introduction to the formal exposition of his theory in the *Phaedo*. Would not Beauty have been easier? It looks like a warning which states that we all know well in physical instances what it means to say that things are equal, but that we should also be aware that we cannot point to coercive physical justification of this knowledge. The knowledge of what equality is could never be gained from the senses. The ability which we have to state that things are equal derives from some mysterious power of the mind (since it cannot be the senses) by which we can estimate things which fall beneath our senses *as if* from a model which stands to hand. Plato makes it quite clear that the emphasis is on "as if." Later on in the *Phaedo* (100b) he discusses theories of causality and says: "I am assuming the existence of absolute Beauty and Goodness and Magnitude and all the rest of them." He then (100c) says that he takes it that "whatever else is beautiful apart from absolute Beauty is beautiful because it partakes of that absolute Beauty." But he is not going to get into an argument about what "partakes of" might mean. He says: "I cling simply and straightforwardly and no doubt foolishly to the explanation that the one thing that makes that object beautiful is the presence in it or association with it (in whatever way the relation comes about) of absolute Beauty" (100d).[25] He states quite clearly immediately that he is not being specific on the exact nature of the relation; he is sure only that it is because there exists some fixed reality that we can talk about the multiplicity of secondary phenomena which fall beneath our notice. A few pages later he puts it as fol-

---

24. Stewart, op. cit., p. 306 suggests that what Plato is really asking is: "How are we to save ourselves from scepticism and accidie?"

25. There is a difficulty in the reading, but it does not interfere with our argument.

lows: "It was agreed that the various Forms exist, and that the reason why other things are called after the Forms is that they participate (μεταλαμβάνοντα) in the Forms" (102b).

We human beings are enabled to talk to one another because there are Forms and because they are related in some way to the world we are in contact with through the senses. Plato is convinced that human conversation, as distinct from animal communication, has or can have meaning because of the Forms and their relation to the sensible world. But the nature of the Forms and the nature of this relation remains a mystery: one need only look at the *Parmenides* 130a–135d. I am absolved from doing so by the fact that it has been so excellently and recently by Allen. What is not to be doubted, however, is that, after all the objections, in the end there must be something to explain why human language has meaning. Parmenides concludes the section: "Nevertheless, if, in the light of all the present difficulties and others like them, one will not allow that there are characters of things that are, and refuses to distinguish as something a character of each single thing, he will not even have anything to which to turn his mind, since he will not allow that there is a characteristic, ever the same, of each of the things that are; and so he will utterly destroy the power and significance of thought and discourse" (135bc).[26] Plato may be tentative about Forms and the exact nature of their relation to the world; but he is certain that there is meaning in the world.

Finally we must turn to what is for Plato the end of man's story, the afterlife. This raises three obvious questions, the immortality of the soul, its reward or punishment after death, and the notion of the transmigration of souls. In regard to the first there seems to be little doubt: Plato appears to believe in the immortality of the soul. But does he think he can prove it? Some scholars have no hesitation in saying yes.[27] The *Phaedo* is the longest *ex professo* account of attempts to prove it, and there at the end of the proofs that have been offered for immortality Socrates says: "Then it is certain as anything can be, Cebes, that soul is immortal and imperishable, and that our souls will really exist in the next world." The replies to this are interesting and worth studying: "Well, Socrates," said Cebes, "for my part I have no criticisms, and no doubt about the truth of your argument. But if Simmias here or anyone else has any criticism to make, he had better not keep it to himself; because if anyone wants to say or hear any more about this subject, I don't see to what other occasion he is to defer it."

---

26. Allen's trs.
27. Hamilton, Penguin trs. p. 50, is just one recent example. They could be multiplied.

Even Cebes in his claim that he has no doubt about the truth of the argument seems to protest too much. He feels silenced rather than satisfied; and Socrates indicates his dissatisfaction (and Plato's own) by his appeal to Simmias to make his objections *if* he has any to make. Simmias states politely that as a matter of fact he now has no doubts; and adds immediately a qualification that is a striking echo of a famous statement by Protagoras: "All the same, the subject is so vast, and I have such a poor opinion of our weak human nature, that I can't help still feeling some misgivings." And Socrates does not then express shock or horror: he urges further examination in the hope of further refinement and the ultimate attainment of truth "in so far as it is possible for the human mind to attain it" (106e–107b).[28]

If this is the case in regard to the immortality of the soul there is not much need to labor the point in regard to its state after death and the possibility of reward and punishment. Plato tells stories about the state of the soul after death, and nowhere in his dialogues does he make it clearer that he is not claiming certainty and that he must not be tied to a literal interpretation.[29] It would seem, I think, to most moderns that Plato should be even more hesitant about theories of transmigration. Indeed, perhaps he is; but again, most modern critics do not seem disposed to raise the matter. This, of course, may well be due to total indifference to an idea that seems so remote to our way of thinking. On the other hand, it is such an extraordinary idea that it is worth our while to look at some contexts where Plato refers to it, just in case we are simply taking it for granted that he was really attached to the notion.

In the *Meno*, as we have seen, the notion of reincarnation is used to provide a context for the new theory of recollection, which in turn is being used as an explanation for some of our most deeply held convictions. The next detailed exposition of the notion occurs in the *Phaedo*, after an argument that it is natural for body to disintegrate rapidly, but for soul "to be quite or very nearly indissoluble" (80b). The pure will go to the pure. But only the soul that is absolutely pure when it leaves the body may attain to the divine nature (82bc). Others, through craving for the corporeal, are imprisoned once more in a body: some, in accordance with their conduct during life, into perverse or predatory animals, and others, the happiest, those who have cultivated self-control and integrity, but without philosophy, "will probably pass into some other kind of social and disciplined creature

---

28. Penguin trs.
29. See the introductions and endings to the eschatological myths.

like bees, wasps, and ants; or even back into the human race again, becoming decent citizens" (82b).[30] The *Phaedrus* contains a much more elaborate account, but again with different arrangements made for the philosophers, sinners, and the just. In the case of the latter, "both sorts alike must draw lots and make choice of their second life, each soul according to its own pleasure," an apparent reference to the myth of Er in the *Republic*. "At this moment a human soul may take upon itself the life of a beast, or a soul which was originally human may change from beast back to man" (249b).[31]

Are these accounts to be taken literally? Surely not. We have already seen in the *Phaedo* the general conclusion at the end of the "account of our souls and their future habitations": "no reasonable man ought to insist that the facts are exactly as I have described them" (114d). Immediately after the introduction of transmigration specifically, he says: "Do you feel that my account is inadequate? Of course it is still open to a number of doubts and objections, if you want to examine it in detail" (84c). The tone of the whole discussion here does not seem to indicate that Plato was entirely in earnest: the mention of the ghosts flitting around tombs (81cd), the specification of the animals, the birds, and the bees (81e–82b). (Indeed, Plato's general attitude to animals points in the same direction.) And in the *Phaedrus* we need not believe in a literal transmigration of souls any more than we believe in a literal chariot and horses.

What Plato does want us to believe about the end of our life-story is what he wants us to believe about the beginning and middle: that it is reason that must guide our lives, and that it is because we humans have reason that we are bound to live well and are individually responsible for what we do. As the key sentence in the story in the last book of the *Republic* puts it, "the responsibility lies with the soul that makes the choice." Living well, according to reason, means accepting the primacy of the unseen which is perceived only by the mind. Most of us are, however, like the prisoners in the cave, enslaved to the shadow world. We keep returning to it from the unseen world we should live in, like weak-minded people who cannot face reality and drift back recurrently to a world of dreams which they make their real world. Most of us feel more at home in the dream world, and that is why Socrates, who lives always in reality, looks to us *atopos*, out of place,[32] and his wisdom appears unreal, dreamlike, ὥσπερ ὄναρ οὖσα.

---

30. Penguin trs.
31. Penguin trs.
32. See *Symp.* 175a, 203d, 215a, 221d.

Alternatively, we are animals who do not possess the reason which would enable us to look up from the world of the seen. We behave, a great part of the time, like wolves, hawks, or kites, or, apparently (but only apparently) harmlessly, like pigs, baboons, or tadpoles, and, at best, like bees or ants.

The realization that this is our situation depends on the mind, however, and that, as Plato knows, is the nub of the difficulty. He did not use the *dunamis-energeia* distinction in the systematic way in which Aristotle did, but, as he showed as early as the *Euthydemus*, he was well aware of the distinction.[33] We have minds, but they are not always in act, because of things like sleep at night or, more insidiously, because of our normal way of life which Plato sees as day-dreaming. We have to be reasoned, lulled, or shocked into seeing the world as it is. Through mind we see the works of mind: if we had not mind we would not see them. We see order where without mind we could not see it, and we presume that if there is order, there is mind.[34] In reasoning of this sort the circle may appear to be blatantly vicious, and yet there is in reason no other way. Because the mind can perceive things that sense cannot see, it is higher than *aesthēsis*. Humans have it and animals do not. Mind, however, once given, imposes its own demands. It gives a superior vision, particularly of beauty which, because of its degrees, points beyond itself and so creates a desire that cannot be satisfied by the seen. The god of the unseen has laid everyone under his spell (*Cra.* 403d).

Nevertheless, we live in bodies too, and it is through the senses that we are in contact with the world that impinges most vividly upon us. Yet the knowledge we gain through the senses is unstable and unreliable, offering superficial certainties which even at the physical level are utterly misleading. At the moral level they may be ruinous yet irresistible because they are unchecked by any critical mind. In fact, sense-awareness may be so seductive that if the mind ever does become critical again, its criticism will not last for long. And if it should succeed in remaining critical for a while, sense-impressions may be so overwhelming that the certainties of the mind are shaken and even the thinker is cast back into his customary state of doubt—hence, the experience described in *Symp.* 207d ff., the constant change of opinions, fears, desires, the instability of even apparent pieces of knowledge; hence our wavering and indecision, and the disconnected nature of our lives.

---

33. See *Euthd.* 280cd for the *ktēsis-chrēsis* distinction.
34. See especially *Laws* 888e ff. on the supreme importance of believing that mind rules the world.

Yet we cannot endure the feeling of the lack of integrity, for the higher vision too is part of our human nature. "It is impossible for a soul that has never seen the truth to enter into our human shape; it takes a man to understand by the use of universals, and to collect out of the multiplicity of sense-impressions a unity arrived at by a process of reason" (*Phdr*.249b). "Beauty was once ours to see in all its brightness. . . . Whole were we who celebrated that festival" (250bc).[35] So memory revives our yearning for the past. Yet the doubts too will revive. And that is where ordinary reasoning must be assisted. Certainty about the unseen world must be secured, and the soul must be charmed or lulled into unconcern with anything else; assurance must be given that the certainty will last. The story suits these purposes. It arises from the same source as philosophy, and it aims at the same end. Its source is wonder, puzzlement, or amazement that things could be so. This was something that Plato was well aware of and which Aristotle repeated after him.[36] For Plato the whole world and all that was in it was a source of wonder. He wants to grasp it in its entirety, to be, again according to the *Republic*, a spectator of all time and all being. The philosopher seeks after the meaning of the universe just as someone hearing a mysterious story for the first time tries to grasp its meaning. Suddenly, in Plato's account, the meaning strikes him and the pieces fall into place. The revelation is like that which is talked about in the *Symposium* or the *Seventh Letter*: "the man who has been guided thus far in the mysteries of love . . . will suddenly have revealed to him a beauty whose nature is marvellous indeed, the final goal of all his previous efforts." "The truth flashes upon the soul, like a flame kindled by a leaping spark."[37] Everything that had been hinted at and merely foreshadowed beforehand is revealed in the end, suddenly as in a flash of light.

So the proper story in Plato is no longer a story just *about* the world: it is an image of the world and of man's place in the world. Our world is thereby seen to have a beginning, middle, and end, going from God to God, with the middle portion we call life the process of becoming like to God. The story of life often seems disjointed and unsatisfactory, rough and unfinished like Eros himself in the *Symposium* or as Socrates would have appeared to the casual observer. But in such cases only the surface is seen. In the life of a man like Socrates there is a hidden unity and completeness which changes of hair and flesh do

---

35. Penguin trs.
36. *Tht.* 155d is taken up by Aristotle, *Met.* 982b12ff. and associated with the love of the story.
37. *Symp.* 210e, *Ep.* vii, 341c. Penguin trs.

not affect, and which cannot be improved by a hundred reincarnations. The revelation of that hidden meaning provides the conviction no other experience can shake. His fate may look like a tragedy; in fact, his story has a happy ending with his descent into the cave to point his fellow citizens once more towards the light.

St. Patrick's College, Maynooth

THE BODY OF THE SPEECH
3 A New Hypothesis on the Compositional Structure of Timaeus' Monologue*

RÉMI BRAGUE

THE LITERARY WORK AS THE IMAGE OF AN "ANIMAL"

Even if one knows Plato only slightly, one can hardly ignore the passage from the *Phaedrus* in which Socrates contends that no author anxious to write in an artful way would compose any literary work without his marshalling its parts into a definite order. No written work should be a patchwork of disorganized elements. Socrates furnishes us with an image of what a properly composed work ought to look like:

> Any discourse ought to be constructed like a living creature (ζῷον), with its own body, as it were; it must not lack either head or feet; it must have a middle and extremities so composed (γεγραμμένα) as to suit each other and the whole work.[1]

This comparison owes a great deal of its richness to the double meaning of the words upon which it hinges. No translation can convey adequately the ambiguity of the Greek, and western literary theory had to break it into its two components.[2] On the one hand, the Greek noun ζῷον means (a) a living animal, a horse, or a dog, as well as (b) its pic-

---

*This paper belongs to a series of preliminary studies towards a work on the *Timaeus*. The hypothesis I develop was first presented during a course taught at Pennsylvania State University, department of Philosophy (Winter 1979–1980). I should like to thank all the friends and/or teachers who were so kind as to read a first draft, and especially Jacques Brunschwig (Paris-Nanterre) and Charles Griswold (Howard University, Washington, D.C.) whose comments proved very helpful and encouraging. The final version owes a great deal to the care of Dominic O'Meara (University of Fribourg).

1. *Phdr.* 264 c 2–6; I quote *Plato's Phaedrus*, translated with Introduction and Commentary by R. Hackforth (Cambridge, 1952), p. 128.

2. The first one is the well-known *ut pictura poesis*. The second one, that compares the literary work with an animal, is not as frequent. See for example Cervantes, *Don Quixote*, 1: 47.

torial representation. On the other hand, the verb γράφειν means (a) to write, as well as (b) to draw a picture. Playing on these words enables Plato to assume the equivalence of two sets of things:

1) Animal–picture. No unbridgeable gap is supposed to separate a living animal from a painted one. This has a bearing on what is at stake in Socrates' comparison, namely, the unity of a ζῷον. The unity of a living animal is meant to be on an equal footing with the unity of a picture. In particular, the picture of an animal is to be one in the same way as the animal itself is one. Thus, we discount the difference between an organism and a heap of parts, between the living and the lifeless, between what is ensouled and what is deprived of a soul. Whereas the animal possesses an inner unity, a picture as such (i.e., not as a colored canvas, but as a picture *of* something) has unity only for him who is looking at it as such. The latter kind of unity does not subsist outside of the observer's mind that compares it with the unity of the original. The picture is one as a representation. This leaves open the question of whether every picture is a representation of something.

2) Written work–painted work. We can find this assimilation in another passage of the same dialogue (275 d 4–9), a passage in which the word ζῷον is not, however, to be read. The composition of a literary work is analogous to the placing of colored spots on a painted surface. Therefore, a literary work is skillfully done when it reproduces the proportions of its model. This leaves open the question whether a literary work has a model, and, if so, what kind of model. Besides, this blurs the distinction Plato draws elsewhere between "eikastic" and "phantastic" imitation.

Be this as it may, we are confronted with two assimilations which we can schematize in the following way:

written text–painted image   (or)   picture–living animal
(γράφειν₁) (γράφειν₂)   (ζῷον₂) (ζῷον₁)

These assimilations are the basis of Socrates' thesis in the *Phaedrus*, according to which a written work is like an animal: like an harmoniously built body when it is artfully written, like a monster when this is not the case.

The dialogue in which such a rule can be read, the *Phaedrus*, should normally be expected to be its most perfect application. But it is far from being composed clearly. On the contrary, its plan deludes us, so that it is, at least in appearance, the most confused dialogue in the whole Platonic corpus. This paradox is typical of Platonic irony. It may be grounded in the teaching of the dialogue itself, a possibility we will not examine here.[3]

If we look for a Platonic text that can embody the rule that the *Phaedrus* formulates, the *Phaedrus* itself must be left aside. On the other hand, this text is more likely to be found in the *Timaeus* than in any other dialogue. The only other place in Plato where the comparison Socrates draws in the *Phaedrus* occurs is at the beginning of the *Timaeus*. The passage is a crucial one, because it explains the very fact that the dialogue takes place. Socrates confesses he is not wholly satisfied with the ideal regime (πολιτεία) he had just outlined for his guests the day before. He longs to see how a city with such a regime would behave when engaged in real warlike feats. He feels like "a man who has been looking at some beautiful animals (ζῷα), either wrought by painting, or even living in truth, but remaining still, and who wishes to watch them in motion." (*Ti.* 19 b 6–8) The important point here is that the painted animal, or picture (ζῷον$_2$), and the living animal (ζῷον$_1$), are left undistinguished. To be precise, the distinction is mentioned stealthily, and discarded as irrelevant in the same breath, once the decisive criterion is the presence or absence of motion. At any rate, the passage of the *Timaeus* formulates explicitly the assimilation of the painted animal to the living one, a point that was buried in the *Phaedrus*.

The later course of the *Timaeus* does fulfill the program Socrates had delineated, but it qualifies it. It does so by giving one more dimension to the comparison of a literary work with an animal: Socrates' speech, in his own eyes, was like a picture (ζῷον$_2$); now this picture represents an animal. This is not self-evident, for a literary work can be compared with a picture without this picture having to represent an animal. The word ζῷον means a picture of a living being in general, regardless of whether it represents an animal or, say, a man or a plant.[4] But in the *Timaeus* the treat Socrates is presented with, Timaeus' speech, deals with an animal. Furthermore, this animal is no longer the various animals (cities or citizens) Socrates mentioned (19 b 6), but it is *the* Animal *par excellence*, that is, the physical universe conceived as the only Living Being that really deserves this name—a theme Timaeus harps upon throughout his whole speech (30 b 8, d 4, 32 d 1, 33 b 3, 69 c 1, 92 c 7). The subject-matter of Timaeus' speech is an animal. As a literary work, it has to be composed like an animal. As dealing with the universe, it has to reproduce "the Animal" faithfully.

3. Cf. Charles Griswold, *Self-knowledge in Plato's Phaedrus* (forthcoming).
4. Cf. Herodotus, III, 88, 3, and I, 203, 2.

It has to be the picture of a living being, something like a ζῷον ζῴου. Therefore the structure of the speech will have to correspond to the structure of its object—the world as an animal.

THE WORLD AS AN ANIMAL

We cannot understand the structure of Timaeus' speech as long as we do not understand the structure of the world as an animal. In order to do that, we should quote and comment upon the whole dialogue. Fortunately, a passage from the first part furnishes us with rather general indications on the shape of the world as animal. I shall reproduce it in its entirety, and reflect on its implications:

> And for shape he gave it that which is fitting and akin to its nature. For the living creature (ζῷον) that was to embrace all living creatures within itself, the fitting shape would be the figure that comprehends in itself all the figures there are; accordingly, he turned its shape rounded and spherical, equidistant every way from centre to extremity—a figure the most perfect and uniform of all; for he judged uniformity to be immeasurably better than its opposite.
>
> And all round on the outside he made it perfectly smooth, for several reasons. It had no need of eyes, for nothing visible was left outside; nor of hearing, for there was nothing outside to be heard. There was no surrounding air to require breathing, nor yet was it in need of any organ by which to receive food into itself or to discharge it again when drained of its juices. For nothing went out or came into it from anywhere, since there was nothing: it was designed to feed itself on its own waste and to act and be acted upon entirely by itself and within itself; because its framer thought that it would be better self-sufficient, rather than dependent upon anything else.
>
> It had no need of hands to grasp with or to defend itself, nor yet of feet or anything that would serve to stand upon; so he saw no need to attach to it these limbs to no purpose. For he assigned to it the motion proper to its bodily form, namely that one of the seven which above all belongs to reason and intelligence; accordingly, he caused it to turn about uniformly in the same place and within its own limits and made it revolve round and round; he took (ἀφεῖλεν) from it all the other six motions and gave it no part in their wanderings. And since for this revolution it needed no feet, he made it without feet or legs. (33 b 1–34 a 8; Cornford, 54)[5]

Timaeus' method in the description of what the universe looks like as a whole is a negative one: he strips the universe of all that normally belongs to animals. It has been pointed out that the passage can be interpreted as an unspoken critique of the archaic world-view according to which the universe is a huge animal, each of whose limbs corresponds to a part of the world—some Greek equivalent of the Indian

---

5. I use *Plato's Cosmology*. The Timaeus of Plato translated with a running commentary (by) F. M. Cornford (London, 1937). (In abbreviation: Cornford.)

myth of Prajapati.[6] Timaeus' speech accordingly would have to be related to the Eleatic "demythologizing" tradition. Some fragments of Eleatic thinkers can indeed be read against the background of an analogous myth, for example fragment 24 Diels-Kranz of Xenophanes or fragments 29 and 134 Diels-Kranz of Empedocles.[7] As a first approach, this is perfectly legitimate. Nevertheless, if we scrutinize our passage from the *Timaeus* more carefully against the background of the fragments I have just mentioned, several original features appear. Since Xenophanes' fragment only asserts that something (probably the one God) sees, thinks (?), and hears as a whole—which implies it has no eyes, no ears, and no organ for thought (νοεῖν), I shall focus mainly on Empedocles.

Fragment 29 of Empedocles reads as follows: "No two branches spring from his back, no feet, no swift-moving knees, no parts of generation, but he was a Sphere every way equal to itself."[8] No particular stress is laid on the order in which the organs are enumerated, and discarded. Empedocles mentions the arms, the feet, the knees, the sexual parts. This to-and-fro movement in the description, by being disorderly, brings into relief the still balance of the Sphere. In the *Timaeus*, on the contrary, the organs disclaimed are mustered in a rigorous order. Timaeus goes from top to toe and he eliminates all that is under the cranial box. The organs that are successively eliminated are: the eyes, the ears, the nose (and with it, without its being mentioned, the whole respiratory system), the mouth (and again with it, we may surmise, the digestive system in its entirety, although only its other end is alluded to), the arms, the legs, and the feet. Sexual parts are not mentioned by name. Since, for Timaeus, they are scarcely more than an appendix to the digestive system (91 a 4–7), it is normal that they be tacitly excluded together with it.[9] In this way, the body is

---

6. For a study of some important Greek versions of this mythical world-view, see W. Kranz, "Kosmos und Mensch in der Vorstellung frühen Griechentums," in *Studien zur antiken Literatur und ihrem Fortwirken*, Kleine Schriften (Heidelberg, 1967), pp. 165–196 (The essay was first published in 1938).
7. See Cornford, pp. 55 f. and D. O'Brien, *Empedocles' Cosmic Cycle: A Reconstruction from the Fragments and Secondary Sources* (Cambridge, 1969), p. 144 f.
8. I quote Cornford's translation, p. 56. There is a more recent translation: *Empedocles: The Extant Fragments*, edited, with an introduction, commentary, and concordance by M. R. Wright (New Haven and London, 1981). But the editor conflates fragments 28 and 29 Diels-Kranz into one (her own n. 22, p. 188).
9. It may be the case that these parts are alluded to in 33 d 5 f. If we understand βάσις (34 a 1) as substantivizing the verb βαίνειν ("to mount," "to cover," see *Phdr.* 250 e 4), the sentence can be interpreted, not as a slight redundancy, but as a periphrase for male sexual parts—the epic word μήδεα Empedocles makes use of refers only to these. But this is rather unlikely.

methodically scanned from head to foot. The order chosen by Timaeus is the most rational one when a human is concerned, whereas another order would probably be more apposite if another animal were examined: for example, the same operation, on a dog, would have to begin with the nostrils and continue with the mouth, the eyes, the ears, etc. The body that gives the description of the world's shape its counterpart is a *human* body. What the world is said *not* to be is first and foremost a human.

Fragment 134 of Empedocles reads as follows: "For he is not equipped with human head on a body, [two branches do not spring from his back,] he has no feet, no swift knees, no shaggy genitals, but he is mind alone, holy and inexpressible, darting through the whole cosmos with swift thoughts."[10] The first part to be eliminated is the head, followed by the limbs. For the head, no more and no less than the other limbs, is something that stands out from the bulk of the body. The universe is, so to speak, truncated, reduced to a trunk that is mere thought—a thought lodged in the trunk, more precisely in the midriff (see the word φρήν at line 4). In the *Timaeus*, on the contrary, the head only is left. All that is not the skull is discarded more or less explicitly. The universe is like a skull deprived of the remnant parts of its body. If the universe resembles a skull, it is normal that the skull, in its turn, should look like the universe. This is exactly what Timaeus says farther on in the first section of his speech when describing human anatomy: "copying the round shape of the universe, they confined the two divine revolutions in a spherical body—the head, as we now call it—which is the divinest part of us and lord over all the rest. (*Ti* 44 d 3–5; Cornford p. 150) Let us notice that the skull that resembles the universe is not any skull whatsoever, but the human skull. For, in the other animals, the soul's motion has been impaired and has consequently lost its normal course, i.e., the circuit. It is accordingly lodged in lengthened skulls (91 e 8–92 a 2). The universe resembles a human head. Conversely, man resembles the universe because of his head. He could be compared best with the universe if he could shrink to his head.

THE PROBLEM

Thus far, I hope to have established something like premises for a syllogism that still requires a clear formulation.

The speech that has the world for its subject-matter must be iso-

---

10. Quoted from Wright (see n. 8), n. 97, p. 253.

morphic to the world itself. We may note that this theme is a familiar one in ancient thought, before and after Plato. For instance, in Democritus, whose influence on the *Timaeus* can scarcely be denied, we find the well-known analogy of elements with letters—an analogy the word στοιχεῖον contains in a nutshell, which implies that the world is made out of atoms in the same way as a poem is made of letters.[11] It is not a far cry from this assumption to the claim that a poem must imitate the world.[12] As far as Plato is concerned, we can deduce this isomorphism from some points made above: the structure of a properly composed literary work must be similar to the structure of an animal; the better composed a literary work, the more perfect the animal it imitates; consequently, the most perfect literary work will have to be similar to the most perfect animal, i.e. the world.[13] This should be the case first and foremost for the *Timaeus*, the subject-matter of which is precisely the world as the most perfect animal.

The structure of the world is isomorphic to the human structure. Again, this is in keeping with the old idea according to which man is a small world, a microcosm. This idea was probably first formulated by Democritus and is to be read in Aristotle.[14] But it emerges in some passages of Plato.[15] As for the *Timaeus* itself, although the idea never receives an explicit formulation, it is present in the background.[16] Moreover, I have just pointed out that the universe is conceived on the model of a human head.

We should be allowed to draw from these two premises I have just posited the conclusion that the *Timaeus* is likely to imitate the human structure. But how could this be possible? It looks like we are facing a blatant contradiction: I have shown that the universe is both like and

11. On Democritus' well-known analogy of writing, see the very suggestive remarks of K. von Fritz, *Philosophie und sprachlicher Ausdruck bei Demokrit, Plato und Aristoteles*, (Darmstadt, 1963 [= New York, 1938]), pp. 24–26.

12. See Macrobius, *Saturnalia*, V, 1, 19 (p. 243, ed. J. Willis, Leipzig (Teubner), 1963): Vergil's eloquence, by its variety, is equal to the overflowing variety of earth. For later developments of this theme, see S. K. Heninger, Jr., *Touches of Sweet Harmony. Pythagorean Cosmology and Renaissance Poetics* (San Marino, Calif., 1974), in particular "Poem as Literary Microcosm," pp. 364–397.

13. This conclusion is drawn by the *Anonymous Prolegomena to Platonic Philosophy*, Introduction, Text, Translation and Indices by L. G. Westerink (Amsterdam, 1962), p. 29 (15, 14 f.). For other references, see J. A. Coulter, *The Literary Microcosm: Theories of Interpretation of the Later Neoplatonists* (Leiden, 1976), in particular ch. 4, "Organism: the Microcosmic Analogue," pp. 95–126. Pp. 96 and 98 are especially relevant to my theme.

14. Cf. Democritus, frgt. 34 Diels-Kranz and Aristotle, *Physics* VIII, 2, 252 b 26.

15. See *Phlb.*, 29 a 6–30 d 8; *Menexenos*, 238 a 4 f.

16. See A. Olerud, *L'idée de macrocosmos et de microcosmos dans le* Timée *de Platon. Etude de mythologie comparée* (Uppsala, 1951), in particular ch. 1, "Les grands traits de l'idée de macrocosmos et de microcosmos dans le *Timée*," pp. 1–42.

unlike man. It is like man, in so far as it is conceived of as a *human head*; it is unlike man, in so far as it is conceived of as a human *head*— as a maimed man. It seems we shall have to choose either the universe or man. Now, the *Timaeus*, granted that its structure imitates something, should normally be expected to imitate the universe. For, on the face of things, the physical world, and not man, is its central topic, so that the whole dialogue, to quote the title of Cornford's commentary, constitutes "Plato's cosmology."

Since the universe is a perfect sphere, the *Timaeus* should imitate it by being composed like a well-rounded body. We can imagine several ways of meeting this requirement of a circular or cyclic structure.[17] In any case, such a work would fairly satisfy the ancient reader's taste in the matter of literary composition. Now, this is definitely *not* what Timaeus' speech does. In order to see this more clearly, let us examine briefly how the long monologue in which the *Timaeus* mainly consists is built. Its plan is clear to a certain extent. Plato not only indicates in which global program Timaeus' cosmological talk is scheduled to be given (27 a 2–b 6), but he sees to it as well that it teems with indications of order, that transitions are clearly marked, that points that have already been dealt with are recalled, while those still left are ushered in. Everything seems to have been composed in a rational and lucid way, so that the text might even seem somewhat didactic. Yet this very clarity may be dangerous; it may conceal the *principles* that underlie and govern the orderly succession of the various themes. These principles could possibly account for some details of the *Timaeus* that constitute its originality with respect to the literary genre it belongs to, i.e., the περὶ φύσεως poem (cf. 27 a 4),[18] such as the downplaying of some topics (meteorology—in the ancient meaning of the term) or, conversely, the introduction of some original feature, the most fascinating being certainly the passage on "place" with which the second section opens. Furthermore, it is a matter of common knowledge that Timaeus' monologue consists of *two* parts: the first one, from the beginning to 47 c 2, dealing with the works of "Reason" (νοῦς), the second one, from this point to the end, with the consequences of Necessity. This partition is all the more decisive in that it introduces a new principle of explanation by adding to the two mentioned first (paradigm and copy), that were apparently meant to be sufficient, a third

---

17. See B. A. van Groningen, *La composition littéraire archaïque grecque. Procédés et réalisations* (2d ed.: Amsterdam, 1960), p. 51 f. (with further references).

18. See the excellent article by P. Hadot, "Physique et poésie dans le *Timée* de Platon," in *Revue de Théologie et de Philosophie* 115 (1983): 113–133, in particular pp. 113 n. 1 and 119 n. 35 (with further references).

one whose nature is not immediately clear ("place"). I insist on this point, although it leaps to the eye, in order to discard the idea according to which Timaeus' monologue consists of *three* parts—a third one, beginning in 69 a 6, being devoted to the interplay of the two principles that had been first presented as independent from each other.[19] This is indeed the subject-matter of this subsection. But this does not allow us to discount the essential difference between the articulation in 69 a 6 and the earlier one in 47 e 2. For the former does nothing more than return to a starting point given previously (cf. 69 a 8), whereas the latter introduces something entirely new. Be this as it may, the very fact that Timaeus' speech consists of *two* parts introduces a decisive rift in the plan of the speech. The cut at 47 e is a fatal blow to the dream of a beautifully ordained circular or cyclic composition; at the same time, it is the most striking deviation from the literary genre of the περὶ φύσεως treatise (of the two sections of Parmenides' poem, only the second one is intended to deal with physical phenomena).

THE HYPOTHESIS

Now that I have stated the problem—"which is the model Timaeus' speech strives to imitate, man or the world?"—let me give my answer: Timaeus' speech imitates by its structure the structure of human body or, to be precise, of the whole made up by the head and the trunk. By their place and their relative lengths, the first section corresponds to the head, and the second one to the trunk. The secondary articulation that divides the second section into two approximately equal halves corresponds to the midriff. Some more parallels will have to be drawn later on, and justified to the best of my abilities.

For the time being, let me try to make this bold assertion more plausible. I contend that Plato purposely wrote the *Timaeus* so that the main character's monologue might have the same relative dimensions as the relevant parts of a human body. Now we learn from several sources that the ancient Greeks, particularly in Plato's time, were fascinated by the possibility of expressing the harmony of a beautiful object through mathematical ratios. This was the case for architectural works. But the most celebrated attempt at expressing beauty in numbers is undoubtedly Polyclitus' *Canon* ("the Standard"), a young man reclining on a spear—the statue was accordingly named the "Doryphoros"—whose handsome body was meant to represent the

---

19. *Pace* Cornford, p. 279.

ideal proportions of the human male.[20] Plato was familiar with Polyclitus' activity as a sculptor; he mentions him twice as such in the *Protagoras* (311 c 3, 328 c 6), a dialogue the title of which, by the way, mentions a sophist whose most famous saying (man as the measure of all things) might not be utterly foreign to the sculptor's undertaking. I am in no way suggesting that Plato intended in the *Timaeus* to write a text whose proportions are the same as the proportions of this or that statue. Among other reasons, let us not forget that we do not possess the original of the Doryphoros—this is the case for the overwhelming majority of the plastic works of the ancient world—so that we can only measure copies, the dimensions of which may vary. For this reason, I will make use, in the following, of the proportions of *every* human body.

Nevertheless, I should like to claim that the study of the proportions of the human body and the efforts at reducing them to ratios that the language of numbers can express can hardly have escaped Plato's attention. We may go even further than this merely negative assertion and notice that the philosopher betrays his interest in the mathematical harmony of the body. He does so in the very dialogue we are dealing with at present:

> Now the good is always beautiful, and the beautiful never disproportionate (ἄμετρον); accordingly a living creature (ζῷον) that is to possess these qualities must be well-proportioned (σύμμετρον). Proportions of a trivial kind we readily perceive and compute; but the most important and decisive escape our reckoning. For health or sickness, goodness or badness, the proportion (συμμετρία) or disproportion (ἀμετρία) between soul and body themselves is more important than any other; yet we pay no heed to this and do not observe that when a great and powerful soul has for its vehicle a frame (εἶδος) too small and feeble, or again when the two are ill-matched in the contrary way, the creature (ζῷον) as a whole is not beautiful, since it is deficient in the most important proportions; while the opposite condition is to him who can discern it the fairest and loveliest object of contemplation. Just as a body that is out of proportion because the legs or some other members are too big, is not only ugly, but in the working of one part with another brings countless troubles upon itself with much fatigue and frequent falls due to awkward convulsive movement, so is it, we must suppose, with the composite creature we call an animal (ζῷον). (*Ti.* 87 c 4–e 6; Cornford, p. 349 f.)

Let me point out some details. Timaeus draws a distinction between two kinds of proportions: some of them are perceived by the senses and consequently admit of a precise reckoning, whereas some, though more important, escape perception. In like manner he distinguishes

---

20. The most recent treatments are: H. von Steuben, *Der Kanon des Polyklet. Doryphoros und Amazone*, Tübingen, 1973, and R. Tobin, "The Canon of Polykleitos," *American Journal of Archaeology* 79 (1975): 307–321.

between the puny astronomical constants (the most conspicuous ones: day and night, months and years) to which we pay attention on the one hand, and, on the other hand, those we discount, namely the harmonious numerical ratios that govern the revolutions of the planets and the motions that, every time a Great Year is completed, bring the whole universe back to its initial state (39 c 6–d 2). The former impinge upon our senses so brutally that we cannot help taking notice of them: the light of the day replaces the murky night, the moon waxes and wanes, the heat increases and ebbs in the cycle of seasons. The latter ones, on the contrary, are not easy to notice, let alone to compute. This is still more difficult when the harmony Timaeus praises in our passage is concerned. How can we bring the visible harmony of the body and the soul's invisible one under the same reckoning? How can we compare the visible with the invisible? When Timaeus says that such an harmony is beautiful "to him who can discern (καθορᾶν) it" (87 d 8), far from adding a harmless clause, he hints at a momentous problem. The only means of perceiving the soul's hidden harmony consists in testing the speeches it produces.[21] By this token, in a well-built animal, the proportions of the body will have to correspond with the proportions of the speeches, since the latter can make visible the proportions of the soul. This will be all the truer if, as Timaeus teaches, the soul itself is lodged, part by part, in the various parts of the body.

Timaeus illustrates his assumption by borrowing a comparison from the safer domain of the body. He chooses the example of a man whose legs are too long. The choice of these particular limbs enables him to complement the theme of beauty with the consideration of utility—a theme other examples probably could not have allowed him to introduce so easily, because it is often the case that beauty and utility jar with one another.[22] The account of the drawbacks originating in too long legs is grossly exaggerated: it would better suit a man walking on stilts. Plato's intention is a comical one. We are reminded of a previous passage of the same dialogue (see below p. 67), a passage almost worthy of Aristophanes, or at least of the Aristophanes the *Symposium* sets on the stage (cf. 190 a 4–8), that, in an Aristophanic parody of an Empedoclean theme,[23] depicts the misfortunes of a head that no limb protects and that tumbles down holes to climb out of which it would be at greater pains than Thales in his well (44 d 9–e 2). The harmony

---

21. See *Charmides*, 154 e 4–6. The context of this dialogue is parallel with the passage examined now: curing the head implies curing the whole body, which in its turn implies curing the soul (see 156 e 2 f.).

22. See Xenophon, *Symposium*, 5: 5–7.

23. See Empedocles, fgt. 57 Diels-Kranz.

of the human body is halfway between total absence of everything but the head and excess of legs. The irony arises here from the fact that the human body, which is supposed to obtain health by imitating the shape (εἶδος) of the universe,[24] nevertheless receives for its model a world that is a mere head. We may thus wonder, in passing, whether human health is possible, in other words whether Timaeus' man is not essentially Hegel's "sick animal."

Be this as it may, the proportions of the human body are capable of beauty. Moreover, we are justified in believing that Plato conceived of the possibility of a precise and numeric determination of this beauty. We may elicit this assertion from a passage in the *Laws* in which the proportions of the body that define the animals reproduced by painting or sculpture are called "numbers" (ἀριθμοί):

> Now, imagine someone who didn't know the character of each of the objects that are imitated and represented. Would he ever be able to estimate the correctness of the finished article? This is the sort of point I have in mind: does it preserve the overall proportions (ἀριθμοί) of the body and the position of each of its various parts? Does it hit off the proportions exactly and keep the parts in their proper positions relative to one another? And what of their colours and contours? Have all these features been reproduced higgedly-piggedly? Do you think that if a man did not know the character of the creature (ζῷον) represented he would ever be able to assess these points?[25]

What is to be read in the *Laws* is still more likely to be present in the *Timaeus*: if the soul, and first of all the world-soul, is constructed out of some numerical ratios, the same must be true for the body that houses the soul. Furthermore, if Polyclitus was influenced by Pythagorean arithmetical mysticism,[26] such an influence is obvious in Timaeus, who comes from Locri, a stronghold of Pythagoreanism. At any rate I am not the first to compare the philosopher's dialogue with the sculptor's statue. One scholar has written, precisely concerning the Doryphoros:

> Ce qu'a pu faire l'esprit classique après la première moitié du Ve siècle, c'est développer tout d'abord,—parallèlement à l'étude de la nature—, une connaissance foncièrement *critique* des formes du corps humain. Nous sommes renseignés sur ce travail, et sur les conséquences qu'il eut à la période suivante, par certains passages du *Timée* (44 d), où Platon, pour le début du IVe siècle, a consigné encore des idées antérieures, utiles à l'explication du *Canon*

---

24. See *Ti.* 88 d 1 and 87 d 5—to be compared with the word σχῆμα that the first section made use of, in the same context (cf. 44 d 4).

25. *Lg.* II, 668 d 9–e 6. I quote Plato, *The Laws*, translated with an introduction by T. J. Saunders (New York, Penguin Books, 1970), p. 109.

26. See the note by J. E. Raven, "Polyclitus and Pythagoreanism," *Classical Quarterly* 45 (1951): pp. 147–152.

polyclétéen. On n'insistera jamais trop, par exemple, sur l'étonnante conception d'alors, qui comparait la tête humaine, siège du νοῦς, à la sphère céleste, et qui la disait même créée plus ou moins à l'imitation de cette sphère. N'y a-t-il pas eu là, notons-le, trace persistante du temps où la frontalité obligeait les statuaires à présenter le corps humain, de préférence, selon la *face antérieure*, dite principale?[27]

What is thus commonly admitted concerns only the obvious proximity of a small detail in the dialogue's *content* to the anthropomorphical method in Greek sculpture. Yet, I think it possible to expand this parallelism to the very form of Timaeus' speech. Its form contains, in my opinion, a teaching that can be related to the teaching conveyed by the content in order to complement it, even to qualify it.

I have endeavored to show that speculations on the numerical dimensions of the various bodily parts existed in Plato's time and even in Plato's works. Now I contend that the proportions of Timaeus' monologue reproduce some of the main proportions of a human body. Again, how is this possible? This supposes first that a literary work can be composed on the pattern of a visible object. Now we do possess several examples of such works. Guillaume Apollinaire's *Calligrammes* do not lack an ancestor, and their pedigree reaches back to Antiquity. The fifteenth book of the *Anthologia Graeca* contains half a dozen short pieces of poetry that reproduce the shape of a Pan's flute (n. 21, by Theocritus), of an axe, of Eros' wings, of a swallow's egg (nn. 22, 24, 27, by Simias the Rhodian), or of an altar (nn. 25 and 26, by Vestinus and Dosiades).[28] These poems were written during the postclassic period and I must honestly confess that, to the best of my knowledge, no earlier example is extant. On the other hand, such devices are easier to apply when short works are concerned. Yet, it has been suggested that the plan of a lengthy work such as the biblical *Book of the Proverbs* might be organized so as to imitate the "seven pillars" of wisdom's house that the text mentions in 9:1.[29] Generally speaking we know of the important part played by numbers in ancient poetry.[30] But counting lines is far easier than measuring prose works. Nevertheless, I should like to point out that the device my hypothesis supposes was made easier by the nature of an ancient book. In Plato's

---

27. Ch. Picard, *Manuel d'archéologie grecque*, La sculpture, II, Période classique, Ve siècle (Paris, 1939), p. 261.
28. Cf. U. von Wilamowitz-Moellendorff, "Die griechischen Technopaegnia," *Jahrbuch des kaiserlich deutschen Archäologischen Instituts* 14 (1899): 51–59.
29. Cf. P. W. Skehan, "Wisdom's House," *Studies in Honor of Louis F. Hartmann.* = *The Catholic Biblical Quarterly*, 29, n. 3 (1967): 162–180 (= 468–486).
30. Many examples are collected in E. R. Curtius, *Europäische Literatur und lateinisches Mittelalter* (8th ed.: Bern, 1973), 15th excursus on "Zahlenkomposition," pp. 491–498.

time literary texts were written on papyrus rolls and disposed in columns with the same number of lines, each of these lines containing roughly the same amount of letters.[31] The reader could count the columns at least as easily as we do with the pages of our modern books (which are *codices*). In this way the proportions of the *Timaeus* could be ascertained with a high rate of precision, regardless whether it was published on a very long single roll or, more likely, on two shorter ones.[32]

The facts I have just mentioned are hardly more than hints. They can help us over some preliminary difficulties. But, for a more complete justification, I can do little more than develop the details of my hypothesis.

THE MAIN ARTICULATION

The main articulation of Timaeus' speech is that between the first and the second section. If my hypothesis is right, it should correspond to the main articulation of the human body (apart from the limbs), i.e., the articulation of the head and the trunk.[33] To what extent does the first section correspond with the head? It is clear that this first section is intended to give an account of the world as it is governed by Reason (νοῦς). Now in the human body as it is conceived of by Timaeus, the seat of Reason is none other than the head (cf. 44 d 3–5). The head is spherical because it imitates the shape of the universe, which imitates in turn circular movement, a privilege granted to Reason alone (cf. 34 a 2 f.). Thus it is to be expected that the section that describes the universe as the work of Reason alone should correspond to the head, its seat in the human body.

Besides, it is as if the first section of Timaeus' speech looks at the human body from the point of view of the head and from this point of view alone. The only senses that are studied here (although they are dealt with from one side only) are those that are housed in the head and lack any connection with the trunk and its contents. This is the case for sight (45 b 2–47 c 4) and hearing (47 c 5–e 2). The other

---

31. Cf. H. Hunger, "Antikes und mittelalterliches Buch- und Schriftwesen," in *Die Textüberlieferung der antiken Literatur und der Bibel* (Munich, 1975), p. 43.

32. Cf. F. G. Kenyon, *Books and Readers in Ancient Greece and Rome* (2d ed.: Oxford, 1951), pp. 54 and 64.

33. Note that the first section adds up to 631 lines in Burnet's edition and the second one to 1640 (665 to 1710 in Rivaud's edition in the "collection Budé"). The ratio is 7 to 18, i.e., the ratio of the head to the trunk in Polyclitus' *Doryphoros*. I have measured the lengths on a photograph of the statue in the Naples museum that is acknowledged to be the best copy of the lost original.

senses are not mentioned, inasmuch as the sense of touch belongs to the whole body (cf. 65 b 5) while taste implies digestion and the digestive system, for which reason the tiny veins that receive tasted substances extend to the heart (cf. 65 c 7–d 1); as for the sense of smelling, it implies respiration and consequently the respiratory system, and odorant substances affect the whole cavity of our body, from the crown of the head to the navel (cf. 67 a 5 f.). The first section deals exclusively with what is to be found in the head, even if it does not examine *all* that is in it.

As for the other parts of the human body, they are mentioned in the first section. But they are mentioned only from the point of view of the head. This can be seen clearly enough from the following text:

> Copying the round shape of the universe, they confined the two divine revolutions in a spherical body—the head, as we now call it—which is the divinest part of us and lord over all the rest. To this the gods gave the whole body, when they had assembled it, for its service, perceiving that it possessed all the motions that were to be. Accordingly, that the head might not roll upon the ground with its heights and hollows of all sorts, and have no means to surmount the one or to climb out of the other, they gave it the body as a vehicle for ease of travel; that is why the body is elongated ($\mu\hat{\eta}\kappa o\varsigma$) and grew ($\check{\epsilon}\phi\upsilon\sigma\epsilon\nu$) four limbs that can be stretched out or bent, the god contriving thus for its travelling. Clinging and supporting itself with these limbs, it is able to make its way through every region, carrying at the top of us the habitation of the most divine and sacred part. Thus and for these reasons legs and arms grow ($\pi\rho o\sigma\acute{\epsilon}\phi\upsilon$) upon us all. (*Ti.* 44 d 3–45 a 2; Cornford, p. 150 f.)

Several traits strike us in this image of the human body: first, the upper and lower limbs are in no way distinguished from one another, as if man walked on all fours, like the child in the well-known riddle which the Sphynx put to Oedipus. Second, the limbs seem to be depicted as mere appendices of the head, as if they were more or less adventitious concretions simply grafted to its bulk. This is suggested by the verb $\pi\rho o\sigma\phi\acute{\upsilon}\epsilon\iota\nu$ in 45 a 2.[34] Finally, we feel as if the limbs were fastened to the head without the ghost of an intermediary, like shoots sprouting forth from a tuber.

Something is missing in this body: the trunk. How can we characterize this image of the body? Timaeus has just delivered us a small treatise in infant psychology (43 a 6–44 b 2). Now the secondary gods to whom the Demiurge has delegated the task of framing man are precisely children-demiurges, even if they escape the troubles that befall the newly incarnated soul in the case of man (cf. $\pi\alpha\hat{\iota}\delta\epsilon\varsigma$ in 42 e 6).

---

34. Cf. the use of $\pi\rho o\sigma\phi\acute{\upsilon}\epsilon\iota\nu$ in the myth of Glaukos, *R.*, X, 611 d 4 and its meaning in Aristotle (cf. Bonitz's index, p. 649 a 50–53).

It is as if Timaeus described the man they have just designed by drawing the image children have of their own body. Man, as the first section of Timaeus' speech describes it, is a perfect instance of what infant psychologists call a "tadpole-man", i.e. the first representation children give of their own body: a large, round head with eyes, but without any nose or mouth, and endowed with four thread-like limbs directly fastened to the head. No trunk, but "l'allongement du corps, sans qu'on puisse reconnaître s'il s'agit du tronc ou des jambes."[35] Such a body is seen from the point of view of the head. What we are shown looks like the image we get whenever we bend and look—with our eyes, from our head—at the rest of our body.

THE TRUNK

If the first section deals with "the works wrought by the craftmanship of Reason," and corresponds accordingly to the head, the second one, which gives an account of "things that come about of Necessity" (47 e 5; Cornford, p. 160), should be expected to correspond to the trunk. No wonder then that, whereas this part of the body was not mentioned in the first section, the second section expatiates on its fabrication by the demiurges and gives a detailed account of its contents (69 e 5–73 a 8).

Furthermore, even that which had already been studied in the first section is taken up afresh in the second one. But this takes place, if I may so put it, from the point of view of the trunk—that is, from the point of view of Necessity. The senses, now covered, are dealt with again from the point of view of their *objects*—a crucial point we may here merely note. The study of sight, for example, is made complete by a study of color and such. In the second section sensible qualities are dealt with in a reverse order with respect to the first one. In the latter the senses were mentioned twice: first, in the passage I quoted above on the structure of the world, in which the eyes, the ears, the nose, the mouth, and the hands were successively discarded and, second, in the theory of sensory perception sketched by Timaeus, who deals with the eyes before the ears. Now, on the contrary, he begins with what can be grasped by the sense of touch (61 d 6–65 b 4), which concerns the whole body, including the legs. He then studies taste (65 c 1–66 c 7), which involves all that is comprised between abdomen and the mouth. Then come odors (66 d 1–67 d 7), which affect the

---

35. H. Wallon and L. Lurçat, "Le dessin du personnage chez l'enfant," *Enfance* (1958), p. 179. Compare μῆκος in 44 e 3.

whole body from the navel to the crown of the head, sounds (67 a 7–c 3), and finally colors (67 c 4–68 d 8). The first section dealt with sight and hearing only. It gave no account of what there is in the bucco-nasal cavity, and with it, discounted taste and smelling.

The point of view of the trunk is the point of view of Necessity. The trunk is related to Necessity because it is the receptacle of what is for us necessary, in the most prosaic meaning of the term: exchange with the surrounding world, what will later be called metabolism, respiration and nutrition. This meaning, the commonest one, is the first Aristotle registers in his philosophical dictionary: "Necessary is said of the accessory causes without which it is impossible to live; for instance, respiration and food are necessary for the animal, since it is impossible that he should be without them."[36] Timaeus emphasizes the link between the trunk and this kind of Necessity with the utmost clarity. I content myself with quoting what he expressly says, a passage many commentators have already pointed out:[37] "all that comes in to give sustenance to the body is necessary." (*Ti.* 75 e 2 f.; Cornford, p. 299) Moreover, the framing of human body by the demiurges is explicitly said to be governed by Necessity:

> For a vehicle they gave it (soul) the body as a whole, and therein they built on another form of soul, the mortal, having in itself dread and necessary (ἀναγκαῖα) affections: first pleasure, the strongest lure of evil; next, pains that take flight from good; temerity moreover and fear, a pair of unwise counsellors; passion hard to entreat, and hope too easily led astray. These they combined with irrational sense and desire that shrinks from no venture, and so of necessity (ἀναγκαίως) compounded the mortal element. (*Ti.* 69 c 6–d 6; Cornford, p. 281)

Thus, the second section of Timaeus' speech, which deals with Necessity, corresponds as a whole to the trunk.

THE TRUNK'S INNER ARTICULATION: THE MIDRIFF

Thus far, the parallelism I am trying to establish holds only between the compositional joint of Timaeus' speech, which he distinguishes with great clarity, and the most visible articulation of human body. At present I must try to make this parallelism closer by showing that it helps to understand other details in this speech. In order to do that, let me examine how Timaeus conceives of the structure of the human body by quoting the passage that immediately follows the one I have

36. *Met.*, Δ, 5, 1015 a 20–22.
37. See for instance Cornford, p. 281 n. 3.

just quoted. The structure of human body is moulded on the repartition in it of the various parts of human soul:

> Now fearing, no doubt, to pollute the divine part on their account, save in so far as was altogether necessary, they housed the mortal apart from it in a different dwelling-place in the body, building between head and breast, as an isthmus and boundary, the neck, which they placed between to keep the two apart. In the breast, then, and the trunk (as it is called) they confined the mortal kind of soul. And since part of it has a nobler nature, part a baser, they built another partition across the hollow of the trunk, as if marking off the men's apartment from the women's, and set the midriff as a fence between them. That part of the soul, then, which is of a manly spirit (ἀνδρεία, θυμός) and ambitious of victory (φιλόνικον) they housed nearer to the head, between the midriff and the neck. (*Ti.* 69 d 6–70 a 5; Cornford, p. 282 f.)

Timaeus is describing what we call the trunk. He calls it by two names, one more popular (στήθη), one more technical (θώραξ)—a term that comprehends what *we* call "thorax," the chest, as well as what we call "abdomen," the belly. By so doing, he draws our attention to that usage. The word θώραξ had not yet any firmly technical meaning. This meaning only came to the fore in Plato's time.[38] It refers first to the breast-plate in a suit of armor, which enables Aristophanes to pun on it.[39] By adding the technical term to the more popular one Timaeus stresses an important fact: man as the demiurge framed him is originally a male capable of bearing arms, for woman will not emanate from primitive man before the second generation (cf. 90 e 6–91 a 1). The military metaphor is developed when the cavity (κύτος) of the breast-plate is mentioned (69 e 6).[40] The trunk is divided into two rooms by a fence constituted by the midriff. These two rooms are compared with the men's apartment and the women's one in the typical Greek house. Even if we may not speak of a male and a female soul, we must parallel maleness (70 a 1) with manliness (ἀνδρεία, 70 a 3).[41]

Thus the midriff plays an important part in the economy of the human body, and consequently in the mortal part of the human soul. For it separates what relates to reason (λόγος), that is, both mind (νοῦς) which possesses it and sends it down from the head where it has its throne, and spiritedness (θυμός) which at least can hear the discourse

---

38. Cf. A. E. Taylor, *A Commentary on Plato's* Timaeus (Oxford, 1928), p. 500 f.
39. Cf. *Wasps*, l. 1194 f.
40. Cf. Aristophanes, *Peace*, l. 1224—a scene in which Trygaeus uses the breast-plate as an ὄχημα. Cf. *Statesman*, 288 a 10 with J. B. Skemp ad loc. (*Plato's Statesman: A Translation of the Politicus of Plato with introductory essays and footnotes*, by J. B. S. (2d ed.: London, 1962), p. 180).
41. Cf. T. H. Martin, *Etudes sur le* Timée *de Platon* (. . .), Paris, 1981 (= 1841), t. 2, pp. 295 f. and 298 ff., as well as *The Timaeus of Plato*, edited with Introduction and Notes by R. D. Archer-Hind (New York, 1973 [= London, 1888]), p. 257 b.

of reason (70 a 5), on the one hand, from what is definitely unable to understand any discourse of reason whatsoever, on the other hand (71 a 3 f.; 77 b 5 f.). This deaf power is housed in the abdomen:

> That part of the soul whose appetite (ἐπιθυμητικόν) is set on meat and drink and all that it has need (ἔνδεια) of for the sake of the body's nature, they housed between the midriff and the boundary towards the navel, constructing in all this region as it were a manger for the body's nourishment. There they tethered it like a beast untamed but necessary (ἀναγκαῖον) to be maintained along with the rest if a mortal race were ever to exist. Accordingly, they stationed it here with the intent that, always feeding at its stall and dwelling as far as possible from the seat of counsel, it might cause the least possible tumult and clamour and allow the highest part to take thought in peace for the common profit of each and all. (*Ti.* 70 d 7–71 a 3; Cornford, p. 286)

This separation, important as it is, is not Timaeus' last word. On the contrary, he explains that there is a mediator that can bridge what first seemed incompatible: the liver, which is lodged just above the intestines so that it can transmit to the appetitive part that is irrational in its very essence some images proceeding from reason (71 a 6 f.; b 3). By the medium of dreams and of divination Reason, by alternately striking terror and soothing, can keep somewhat in awe the desires lodged in the bowels. The midriff is not only the fence that might suggest the name Plato first gives it (διάφραγμα, from δια-φράττειν). It has a mediating function as well. In keeping with etymology Plato sees in the φρένες (70 a 2) the bodily part that ties together what partakes in practical reason (φρόνησις) and what does not (71 d 5, e 4). The midriff and its place in the human body reconcile to some extent Reason and Necessity.

Now if we compare the place occupied by the midriff in the human organism on the one hand, with the composition of Timaeus' speech on the other, we observe that it corresponds with the articulation in 68 e 1 which I dealt with above. This articulation divides the second section towards its middle and introduces a subdivision intended to display the collaboration of Reason with Necessity. Timaeus nowhere says that the midriff divides the trunk into two strictly equal parts. But we know that the upper limit of the midriff, the solar plexus, is roughly halfway between the chin and the pubes. This is the case, at any rate, in the Doryphoros. If we look for the center of the second section, we will find it at 70 c or 69 c, depending on whether or not we take into account what follows 90 e 1 (more on this below, p. 72). Thus, it falls on this part of the body to enact in practice what the last section of Timaeus' account is meant to explain in theory, i.e., how Reason holds sway over Necessity. The influence of Reason is brought to bear by means of persuasion: Reason overrules Necessity by persuading it (cf. 48 a 4, 56 c 6). The λόγος becomes rhetorical in order to cope with what could possibly thwart it or, at least, with what is not spontaneously in tune with it.[42] In like manner, the liver influences irrational desires by ways analogous with the devices of rhetoric: the images it produces allure them (ψυχαγωγεῖν) (71 a 7) just in the same way as a skillful rhetorician allures his audience.[43] What is the case in the human body corresponds to what happens both in the universe and in the dialogue that is meant to describe it: the Demiurge takes over what necessarily arises from the nature of things, and orders this chaos so that the most beautiful world might arise. The section that deals with this cooperation opens at the very place that, in the human body, is occupied by the midriff, an organ that plays the same part in man.

SEXUAL PARTS

Thus the second part of Timaeus' speech is analogous, by its dimensions and main articulations, to the human trunk or, more precisely, to the account of the human trunk this very speech gives us. This is true for the beginning (the "neck") and for the middle (the "midriff"). Now I think the parallelism holds true for the end of both structures as well.

Both of them end with something like an appendix. As for the speech, Timaeus explains that he has almost fulfilled the task he had been set, namely expounding the coming into being of the universe as far as the generation of man (90 e 1–3, and cf. 27 a 5–7). What follows, then, is not strictly necessary but is added, so to speak, into the bargain. In this last passage Timaeus deals with sexuality and reproduction. His short treatise corresponds, by its place and proportions, to its subject-matter, the sexual parts. Now, as for human body, the status of these parts is exactly as ambiguous as the status of the corresponding passage. They too are not strictly necessary. For, although primitive man is said, in passing, to be a male (cf. ἀνήρ in 75 c 7), it remains unclear whether he has sexual parts and, supposing he has not, what his maleness consists in. On the one hand sexual parts seem fairly useless before woman is born. On the other hand, a passage like 76 e 1, that declares that the divine workmen *foresaw* the birth of

---

42. This rhetorical function of reason, far from being a derogation, may be indispensable to the self-knowledge of λόγος. For the importance of rhetoric for the soul's self-knowledge, see C. Griswold (cf. n. 3).

43. Cf. the uses of ψυχαγωγία in *Phdr.* 261 a 9 and 271 c 10.

women from the primitive male and sexual reproduction as its consequence, may suggest they were present. As the human trunk ends with sexual parts, so Timaeus brings the second section of his speech and with it the whole dialogue to a close by studying their formation, their functioning, and their results.

The passage devoted to these topics occupies a space that is approximately analogous to the one occupied in the real body of a human being (of a male human being, in this case) by the organs of generation. After a short introduction of the theme (90 e 1–91 a 4), the passage consists of two parts of almost equal length (some 30 lines): the first one begins with describing the sexual organs, and first of all the male one, and explains the operation of reproduction (91 a 4–d 5). The second one draws the pedigree of all animal kinds (plants are dealt with in 77 a 4–c 4) that come into being by degeneration from primitive man (91 d 6–92 c 4). Animals are the seed of man. By this token, the first paragraph corresponds to the penis, and the second one to the testicles. For it is a matter of common knowledge in Greek physiological theory that the testicles are the receptacle of semen, regardless where it originates.[44]

THE ABDOMEN

My hypothesis is grounded on human anatomy, expounded by Timaeus himself.[45] It may not be amiss to think that the organs whose place in the human body receives due treatment in Timaeus' speech correspond to the place of some contents of this same speech. Thus, as for the abdomen, the intestines are said to be located "between the midriff and the boundary towards the navel." (70 e 1 f.; Cornford, p. 286)

The expression ὅ πρὸς τὸν ὀμφαλὸν ὅρος, which Cornford renders very accurately, clearly says that some limit is present. But it is strangely vague and cramped, although its meaning is ascertained by the parallel passage in 77 b 4 f. We may wonder whether this lack in clarity

---

44. Plato mentions the testicles neither in the *Ti.* nor elsewhere in his works. The semen, according to Greek medicine, is produced either in the brain (Alcmaeon) or collects itself from the whole body (Democritus). It is led to the testicles through the spinal marrow (cf. Diogenes of Apollonia, fgt. 6 Diels-Kranz, t. 2, p. 65, 4f. with *Ti.* 91 b 1 f.). See Taylor (cf. n. 38) ad loc., p. 637 f., and E. Lesky, *Die Zeugungs- und Vererbungslehren der Antike und ihr Nachwirken*, Akademie der Wissenschaften und der Literatur, Abhandlungen der Geistes- und sozialwissenschaftlichen Klasse, 1950, n. 19, Wiesbaden, pp. 13 and 18–20.

45. Let me point out that Timaeus nowhere claims that the account he gives of human anatomy is an exhaustive one. For instance the kidneys are mentioned in 91 a 5, but we don't know their function—as if man were seen only from the front side.

could not possibly arise from the fact that primitive man, who was moulded by the gods and not born from a woman, cannot reasonably have a navel.[46] Or, if we suppose he has one, its presence cannot possibly have the same meaning for him and for us. As for us, the navel was useful during our life in our mother's womb, but now it is nothing more than a useless trace of the past. For the primitive human being, it must be the sign of a future. This man is made by the created gods in a way that reminds us of his creation by Apollo according to the myth Aristophanes tells in the *Symposium*. For in both cases we witness the creation of sexual reproduction out of a primitive nonsexual stage. In the *Symposium* the navel is for man (or for the half circle-man) what remains after a past operation (191 a 4 f.), and it permanently reminds men of their finitude. In the *Timaeus* it cannot serve as a remainder from birth for men of the first generation who precisely were *not* born. But it functions as a reminder of the menace of death. Now if we look for the place that the equivalent of the navel should occupy in Timaeus' speech, this place must be located halfway between the articulation that cuts the second section into two parts (the "midriff") and the end. Timaeus does not say clearly where the boundary he hints at is placed. But the navel, in concrete human bodies, is situated halfway between the midriff and the pubes. If we look for the corresponding point in the text, we find 81 c, the very middle of the short passage on aging and death (81 b 4–e 6).

As for the space that should be expected to correspond in Timaeus' speech with the part of human body situated between the navel and the sexual parts, the lower belly, it is devoted mainly to the study of diseases (81 e 7–87 b 9) and to a briefer account of the means of keeping them in check through proper care (87 c 1–90 d 7). Timaeus' compendium on pathology does nothing more than expand a part of the sentence that concluded the section on aging and death: whereas natural death is pleasant rather than not, it is "painful and contrary to nature when it results from disease and wounds" (81 e 2 f.; Cornford, p. 330). This assertion calls for an account of the reasons why disease is contrary to nature and painful, an account delivered in the section I am dealing with at present. Now I may be permitted to offer a tentative explanation of the place this section occupies: the lower belly is the place where a wound causes the greatest pain. This was at least a common opinion in Greece from Homer on, since we read in the *Iliad*: "midway between the privy parts and the navel, where most of

---

46. See Taylor (cf. n. 38), p. 502, on 70 b 1. The navel is mentioned in 67 a 6, however. But it is referred to as *ours* (ἡμῶν, 67 a 5), i.e., as belonging to men of a later generation.

The Body of the Speech 75

all Ares is cruel to wretched mortals."[47] So it *may* be the case that Plato chose to locate a theory of diseases in the place corresponding with the most sensitive part of the human body.

THE THORAX

We have just seen the parallels I suggest for the abdomen. Can we find analogous ones for the thorax? If my schema should prove true, the chest should correspond with the beginning of the second section. Can we find, in the relevant part of Timaeus' speech, a structure analogous to the structure he supposes to be that of the human chest?

The passage where the thorax is described reads as follows:

That part of the soul, then, which is of a manly spirit, and ambitious of victory (φιλόνικον) they housed near to the head, between the midriff and the neck, that it might be within hearing of the discourse of reason and join with it in restraining by force the desires, whenever these should not willingly consent to obey the word of command from the citadel. The heart, then, the knot of the veins and the fountain of the blood which moves impetuously round throughout all the members, they established in the guardroom. (*Ti.* 70 a 2– b 3; Cornford, p. 282 f.)

The comparison with a city, and above all with the city planned in the *Republic*, with its three classes, is obvious, and I shall do no more than mention it: the heart corresponds to the intermediary class of warriors, who receive orders from the headquarters and control the lower parts. The image is vivid, but has a drawback, insofar as it obfuscates the precision required by an anatomical description. We wish we could locate the heart with some precision. But where will we situate the "guardroom"—word for word, the house of the doryphors[48]—that Timaeus alludes to? If we admit again that the heart is located halfway between the neck and the midriff, we will have to look for its counterpart in Timaeus' speech about the middle of the first subsection of the second section, the part that extends from 47 c to 70 c (or 68 d 8). The middle point is 59 a if we choose 70 c for a limit, 58 b if we prefer 68 d 8. Nothing corresponds there very clearly with the heart's function in the human body, so that I may not draw any clearcut parallelism.

Yet I should like to propose a tentative solution: the content of the

47. Homer, *Iliad*, 13, 568 f., quoted from Homer, *The Iliad*, with an English Translation by A. T. Murray (Cambridge and London, 1925), p. 45. See *Scholia Graeca in Homeri Iliadem* (scholia vetera), recensuit H. Erbse, vol. 3um (. . .) (Berlin, 1974), p. 508, for further references. According to "Hippocrates," wounds of the bladder and of the intestines are lethal for the most part (see *Aphorisms*, VI, 18, t. 4, 566 f. Littré; *Coacan Prognostics*, 29,.§ 499, t. 5, p. 698 L.; *Diseases*, I, t. 6, p. 144 L.).

48. Cf. *Cri.*, 117 c 7.

passages that may be considered as the middle of the section we are dealing with consists of a group of passages that explain the mutual transformation of the primary bodies (Empedocles' four "roots," minus the earth): 56 c 8–57 c 6 describes what we might call "chemical warfare." The vocabulary is warlike in nature: the elements fight battles (μάχεσθαι in 56 e 5, 57 a 7, b 4), break through (κρατεῖν in 56 e 6, 57 b 2.7), gain victories and suffer defeats (νικᾶν in 56 e 5, 57 b 6), beat a retreat (ἐκφεύγειν in 57 b 6), and even voluntarily capitulate or change parties (cf. 57 b 1); 57 d 7–58 c 4 explains why elementary bodies must undergo a permanent change: the circular motion of the universe (περίοδος, 58 a 5) keeps movement going on forever; 58 c 5–59 a 9 enumerates several kinds of fire and deals with their action on fusible substances, that, molten by fire, solidify again when cooling. Now we could tentatively look for counterparts to these passages in the description Timaeus gives of the θυμός and of the heart that is its seat. The first passage could be compared with the warlike nature of θυμός, which clearly corresponds to the warriors in ideal city, and whose thirst for victory is stressed (cf. φιλόνικον in 70 a 3); the second passage would correspond to the circulation of blood (cf. περιφέρεσθαι in 70 b 2); the third one would remind one of the heart's innate heat (cf. μένος in 70 b 4; πῦρ in 70 c 3).

I am clear that the parallelism is far from being as likely as some of those I have pointed out thus far are, at least, hoped to be. It may be the case that the hypothesis I am proposing simply does not hold for the thorax, perhaps because of its interfering with other compositional needs. Or, as an alternative solution, I might ask whether the very fact that nothing in Timaeus' speech clearly corresponds to the θυμός may not convey some teaching.

THE HEAD

I have endeavoured to draw a parallel between the compositional structure of the second section of Timaeus' speech and the structure of the human trunk. Can I procede in the same way for the first section of this speech, that should be expected to correspond to the human head? The task in that respect is made more difficult by the fact that Timaeus does not furnish us with any hint on the head's internal structure, whereas he dwells at some length on the divine purpose that explains why it is not fenced round with thicker bones and flesh, why it rests on a sinewy neck, and why it is covered with skin and hair (75 b 2–76 d 3). For lack of such information as I could use with Timaeus' description of the trunk's inner structure, I shall have to rely on our knowledge of how a human head is built, without my being able to support my views with any Platonic text.

We easily see that the human head can be divided into two main parts in the same way as the trunk is divided into two approximately equal parts by the midriff (cf. 69 e 6–70 a 2, quoted above p. 70). If we look at a human head from the outside we will get two halves, the eyes functioning as a dividing line. This will prove all the truer if we choose the head of a better proportioned man. On the other hand the human head, considered from the inside, is divided into two unequal parts by the palate, that is the lower limit of the cranial cavity.

Can we discover some equivalent of this or these partitions in the "head" of Timaeus' speech? If we divide the first section of his account into two equal parts, we will get 37 c as the middle point. In Timaeus' monologue this is the point where the account of the making of the world-soul and of its motion makes way for the beginning of the well-known passage on time. Now this passage follows immediately the short section in which the Demiurge is said to "line" the world-soul, that is the invisible, with corporal, hence visible, reality (36 d 8–37 c 5; see especially 36 d 9 and e 6, with the pun σῶμα ὁρατὸν οὐρανοῦ). Thus far we moved in the realm of the Invisible. Now we enter the field of the Visible. This momentous shift from invisibility to visibility is followed by the lengthy section on time (37 c 6–39 e 2), a passage whose central theme, on closer inspection, is not so much time and its definition as the visible reality *par excellence*, i.e., heaven, the celestial vault and the stars that revolve on its backdrop,[49] in a (Greek) word: οὐρανός.

Now it so happens that the word οὐρανός is at the same time the only word that can designate in good Greek, at least in Plato's time (later on another word, οὐρανίσκος, "the small heaven," was introduced), the upper part of the buccal cavity, what we call the palate. This double meaning of the word for "sky" exists in Latin and in other languages.[50] In Greek its ambiguity afforded a golden opportunity for puns.[51] It might be that the passage of Timaeus' speech which he devotes to the heavens should correspond to the place the palate oc-

---

49. See my essay on the alleged definition of time in the *Ti.*, in *Du temps chez Platon et Aristote*, Quatre études (Paris, 1982), p. 11–71, especially p. 47 f.

50. Cf. Augustine, *The City of God*, VII, 8; PL 41, 200 f. and *M. Tulli Ciceronis De Natura Deorum*, libri secundus et tertius edited by A. S. Pease (Cambridge, Mass., 1958), p. 654 f. (ad II, 18 [49]) for all the references.

51. Cf. Athenaeus, VIII, 344 b; *Anthologia Graeca*, V, 105; Clement of Alexandria, *The Paedagogos*, II, 1, 4, 2.

cupies in the human head. Now this parallelism is not merely verbal; it has a deeper meaning. The vault of our palate is the boundary between the brain and the mouth, in other words, between silent thought and its verbal expression. In the same way the vault of heaven separates the "hyperuranian" realm of pure thought from its expression in the heavenly bodies whose ordered motion is the language that conveys to us the thoughts of the world-soul.[52]

As an alternative, or perhaps complementary, hypothesis, we could suppose the passage on heaven to be equivalent to the eyes. Their place in the human body corresponds better to the middle point of the first section—the "head" of Timaeus' speech. The sense of sight is dealt with only later, towards the end of the first section (45 b 2– 47 c 4), for reasons we probably could endeavor to guess—and cannot do here. Nevertheless the heaven would be a fitting counterpart of the eyes. First, because they often are compared to the celestial bodies. This is the case mainly with the sun, for the eyes are sunny in nature.[53] But other stars are not excluded. Plato himself indulged in this kind of poetic likeness: in an epigram he wishes he were like the sky, studded with stars, in order to be able to look at the beloved one with a thousand eyes.[54] To come back to the *Timaeus*, we may notice that heaven is the privileged object of sight: we have sight so that we might be able to contemplate the sky (cf. 47 a 1–5). The sight of the sky is privileged because it allows, even entices men who are potential philosophers to ascend from sensory perception to thought. For if we had no eyes to see the order of celestial phenomena we would be devoid of physics and philosophy (47 a 8–c 4; 91 e 3). Sight enables man to go beyond the palate of the universe up to its hyper-uranian brain and to decipher the secret thoughts of the cosmic mind (47 b 7).

The mouth is not dealt with in the first section, which discounts the sense of taste as well. We can, however, find its equivalent in the compositional structure of this section. Our task is made easier by the fact that Timaeus dedicates some sentences to this organ in the second section. In a very interesting way mouth is characterized as bearing the seal of two points of view—the Good and the Necessary:

The mouth was equipped by our makers for its office with teeth, tongue, and lips arranged as now, for the sake at once of what is necessary and what is best.

---

52. The theme, Babylonian in origin, of the stars as a divine language (cf. *Psalm* 19, 4), does not occur in Greek thought earlier than Plotinus (III, 1, 6, 20–23). Cf. F. Dornseiff, *Das Alphabet in Mystik und Magie* (Leipzig, 1922), p. 89 f.
53. Cf. Aristophanes' parody of Euripides in *Thesmophoriazusae*, 17, and Plato, *R.*, VI, 508 b 3.
54. The epigram is quoted in Diogenes Laertius, III, 29.

They devised it as the passage whereby necessary things might enter and the best things pass out; for all that comes in to give sustenance to the body is necessary; but the outflowing stream of discourse, ministering to intelligence, is of all streams the best and noblest. (*Ti.*, 75 d 6–e 5; Cornford, p. 299)

Among the organs, mouth is granted the privilege of being located at the meeting point of the two outlooks from which the *Timaeus* considers the universe. They are stated respectively in the first and in the second section of the account of the universe that is given there. The mouth depends on the Good for speech, on the Necessary for eating.[55] It paradoxically unites the noble and the base, in the same way as the sexual parts do.[56] Since the only difference Timaeus mentions is the direction (the way in or the way out), it is of the utmost importance that we should tell the one from the other, in order to be able to distinguish what comes in (the Necessary) and what goes out (the Good).[57] Now this distinction is precisely what remained blurred in the passage I examined at the beginning. For to speak of an "organ by which to receive food into itself or to discharge it again when drained of its juices" (33 c 4–6; Cornford, p. 55) amounts to discounting the fact that ingestion and excretion do not take place at the same point. It is as if human body were thought of as feeding itself in the same way as the universe does, i.e., on itself (cf. 33 c 8). We have to wait for the second section to find an explicit distinction between these two points. In the first section the distinction cannot be clear, for the point of view of the Necessary is not yet sharply distinguished from the point of view of the Good. In spite of this, it seems to me that the first section distinguishes those two points of view *implicitly*. For in my opinion we can find, hidden in its composition, an equivalent of the mouth. The mouth is represented by two passages that occupy the place the mouth occupies in human head. These two passages, which follow closely one another and are approximately of the same length (some twenty lines), are the only two speeches the Demiurge delivers. The place of the mouth is occupied by the works of the mouth.

The first speech addresses the newly created gods who are in charge of producing the living beings that still await creation (41 a 7– d 3). The second one addresses the souls that have just been mixed up from the remnants of the world-soul (41 e 3–42 d 2). The first one is in direct style: we hear the Demiurge speaking with Timaeus' voice.

---

55. Cf. Aristotle, *On the soul*, II, 8, 420 b 18–20.
56. Cf. Hegel, *Phänomenologie des Geistes*, WW 2, p. 271 Glockner; Baudelaire, *Mon coeur mis à nu*, 18.
57. Cf. *Matthew*, 15, 11.

The second one is in the indirect style: the Demiurge's words are related by Timaeus' words. The content of the first speech has the Good for its principle: if the gods are not such as the Demiurge could not undo them *de potentia absoluta*, yet only an evil being would wish to dissolve what has been made in agreement with the beautiful and the good (καλῶς, εὖ, 41 b 1 f.). Now the God is a good one (29 e 1). What presides over the making of the universe is care for the maximal perfection it is capable of (41 b 9 f.). Man's end is following what is divine in him (41 c 7 f.). As for the second speech, it expresses the rule of Necessity: souls must be implanted in bodies because it is necessary that it should be so (ἐξ ἀνάγκης, 42 a 3). Once they are incarnated, they will go through all the effects of incarnation, all that necessarily follows from it (ἀναγκαῖον, 42 a 5 and cf. above p. 69). The second discourse unveils what the first one concealed under the appearance of beauty: man will give birth to woman and to the other animal kinds, depending on whether man will have proved more or less equal to the part he has to play, a part Timaeus implicitly sums up in the idea of courage (cf. δειλοί in 90 e 7). The second speech allows the careful reader to make out what it does not explicitly say: the universe is perfect, i.e., it contains all the living beings (41 b 7–c 1) only because man, who is pregnant with all other animal kinds, by means of his very imperfection triggered the process that let them emanate from him. The price to be paid for the universe being perfect is man being imperfect, and his having to yield to temptation. It looks like man's fall is necessary, since the Demiurge can foresee it from the outset (cf. 72 e 4 and 76 e 1). By this token the second speech is instrumental to the first one, insofar as Necessity leads to the Good, just as this is the case in the structure of the universe at large. The two speeches, by their style and by their content as well, correspond to the mouth's two functions as they are distinguished by Timaeus. Mouth is the organ in which the persuasion of Necessity by Reason takes place; but it is itself the best example of what this persuasion is directed towards: the organ that embodies the utmost Necessity, namely the need for food, is at the same time the organ that Reason succeeds most perfectly in reshaping in order to put it at its disposal.

I have pointed out already that the first section, in its account of the senses whose organs are lodged in the skull, did not go farther than the sense of hearing. Timaeus' anatomical research does not go lower than bucco-nasal cavity. He does not explain the nature of the nose in the first section, which alludes to respiration only in order to exclude it together with its organ from the world-body (33 c 3 f.). But this would not suffice to prevent the equivalent of the nose, even if it does not receive an explicit treatment in the first section, from appearing in the composition of this same section, as I have just tried to show with respect to the mouth. Now this is not the case. Apparently nothing in the composition of the first part can be said to correspond to the nose. Nevertheless I may suggest an hypothesis. In the human face the nose is intermediary between the eyes and the theoretical faculty, on the one hand, the mouth and need, on the other hand.[58] The part it plays in the head is analogous with the part played in the system of the parts of the soul by the θυμός, the outlet of which is precisely the nose.[59] If, for some reason, the θυμός is lacking, the nose must be lacking as well.

SYNOPSIS

I have thus far been drawing a comparison between some elements in the compositional structure of Timaeus' speech and some parts, divisions or organs of the human body. I now recapitulate this parallelism in a synoptic table:

I put on this table all the parallels I have ventured to draw, regardless of their degree of probability, a degree that in my own opinion is not constant. This degree seems to me higher as more general features of Timaeus' speech (its general economy, its end, and such) are considered, and it sinks as we stoop to its minute details. Be that as it may, it seems to me that the parallelism I have drawn is obvious enough so as to be one of the keys to the compositional structure of Timaeus' monologue. I purposely said "*one* of the keys," for I am clear that some other "logographic necessities" must interfere with the imitation of human body. Consequently the key I am suggesting cannot be claimed to open all the closed gates of the dialogue—and there are a good deal of them. The other necessities I have just been hinting at can be of various kinds. The literary genre Plato intended to imitate (perhaps in order to parody it), the περὶ φύσεως treatise or poem, compelled him to make use of some literary devices and to mention some topics. We can spot as well some compositional choices that could possibly be explained by the teaching Plato wanted his dialogue to convey. For instance, the fact that the account of vision is located at the end of the first part, i.e., not at the place that corresponds with the place the eyes occupy in a normal human body, may be linked

---

58. Cf. Hegel, *Aesthetik*, WW 13, p. 389 f. Glockner.
59. Cf. Homer, *Odyssey*, 24, 318 f.

	HUMAN BODY	TIMAEUS' SPEECH	
head	⎧ brain ⎪ ⎨ eyes ⎪ palate ⎪ ⎪ mouth ⎩ (neck)	27c1 27c1–36d7 reasonings of Timaeus and of the Demiurge; the World-Soul 36d8–39e2 creation of the visible world: the heaven 41a7–d3 speeches of the 41e3–42d2 Demiurge 47e3	⎫ ⎬ Reason ⎭
trunk	⎧ ⎪ heart ⎪ ⎪ ⎨ midriff ⎪ liver ⎪ ⎪ navel ⎪ lower belly ⎪ ⎩ penis testicles	56c8–57c6 chemical warfare 57d7–58c4 circulation 58c5–59a8 fire 68e1ff. cooperation Reason/Necessity 71a3–72d3 liver 81c6–e5 aging and death 81e7–89d1 diseases & medicine 90e1–91d5 sexuality 91d6–92c3 generation of the other animals species	⎫ ⎬ Necessity ⎭

with one of the ways one could account for what is lacking in the first section, and consequently explain why a second explanatory method is required—why Necessity is necessary. At all events, a crucial question remains unasked, let alone unanswered: granted my hypothesis, why did Plato choose to give his "cosmology" a human shape? In order to give this question a full answer I should have to interpret the teaching of the *Timaeus* as a whole, which of course is another story.

Centre National de la Recherche Scientifique, Paris

4 PLATONISM AND SOCRATIC IGNORANCE
(with special reference to *Republic* I.)
LEONARDO TARÁN

Both "Platonism" and "Socratic Ignorance" have several different meanings, and since I am interested in pointing out the relationship between the two, I should first like to explain what I mean by each word. I trust, however, that in doing so I shall at the same time be making some progress in the development of my topic.*

By Platonism I mean Plato's philosophic thought as it is expressed in his dialogues, including not only his doctrine of absolute ethical standards, his conception of the soul, the theory of ideas, and so forth, but also his method. For in Plato's case it is impossible, if one wishes to do justice to the evidence, to separate the doctrine from the method and vice versa. His method includes the *elenchus*, the procedures of hypothesis and of collection and division, and the very way in which he chose to present his thought: the dialogue. Any or all of these may sometimes be subsumed under the name "dialectic," and more will be said about this in what follows. On the other hand, by Socratic Ignorance I mean in general Socrates' profession of ignorance, his often repeated assertion that he only knows that he does not know. But the Socrates and the Socratism with which I am here concerned are those to be seen in the Platonic dialogues. In other words, I am concerned with the Platonic Socrates, not with the historical Socrates, nor yet with the Socrates of Aristophanes, or Xenophon, or others.

---

*With some changes in its contents and with the addition of the footnotes (references have been kept to a bare minimum) this paper contains the text of a lecture delivered at The Catholic University of America on September 30, 1983. As printed here it is a résumé of part of a longer study on the subject of Platonism which is in preparation. I should like to thank Dean Jude P. Dougherty for his kind invitation and hospitality and Professor Dominic J. O'Meara for inviting me to submit my paper for publication in the present volume.

Plato's works—all of which are extant[1]—are generally divided into three groups. One group of dialogues is called aporetic because in them no positive conclusions are reached. These are believed to be the earliest works. We have then a series of dialogues, including at least the *Phaedo*, the *Phaedrus*, the *Symposium*, and the *Republic*; that is, the works of his artistic maturity, where the central doctrines of Platonism are fully developed. Finally, in yet another group of works the dramatic presentation is less lively whereas the philosophic issues and the treatment of them become more technical. These dialogues are considered to be the latest. They are the *Parmenides*, the *Theaetetus*, the *Sophist*, the *Politicus*, the *Philebus*, the *Timaeus*, the unfinished *Critias*, and the *Laws*.[2]

There is a widespread opinion among Platonic scholars (though perhaps not all of them would subscribe to the totality of the following propositions) that the aporetic dialogues—where Socrates examines and refutes certain definitions of the virtues and where no positive conclusions concerning the main issues are reached—represent the purely Socratic aspect of Plato's thought. Moreover, they contend that Plato himself, at the time he composed these works, had not yet developed the main tenets of his mature philosophy as they appear in the dialogues of his middle period, especially in the *Republic*. In short, the passage from the aporetic dialogues to those of the middle group (and *a fortiori* also to the later works) truly represents the evolution of Plato's own thought, his intellectual autobiography. For—so it is explicitly argued or implicitly assumed—if Plato had already developed his mature doctrine at the time he wrote the aporetic dialogues, there would not be any good reason why he should have composed a whole series of works where we find only refutations of mistaken views. Moreover, scholars have objected to Socrates' way of examining and refuting definitions in the aporetic dialogues. The very notion of So-

---

1. Cf. E. Zeller, *Die Philosophie der Griechen*, 2, i[5] (Leipzig, 1922): 436–437 and 437, n. 1.
2. On Plato's latest works cf. H. Cherniss, *AJP* 78 (1957): 225–266 = *Selected Papers* (Leiden, 1977), pp. 298–339; L. Tarán, *Academica: Plato, Philip of Opus, and the Pseudo-Platonic Epinomis* (Philadelphia, 1975), p. 17 and n. 60 and pp. 130–132 with references. In the "middle group" I have included those works which are less controversially assigned to it. As for the large number of works generally included among the aporetic and/or early dialogues, I am well aware that not all of them are aporetic (cf., e.g., the *Cri.*) and that not all of them are aporetic in the same way (contrast, e.g., the *Euthphr.* and the *Men.*); but for my purpose here it has sufficed to accept the category aporetic as a single whole and to make use of those works which have an aporetic end, even when in the case of the *Men.* the dramatic purpose of the dialogue requires that the aporetic result should not be openly stated. Cf. *Men.* 100 B 2–6 with Cherniss, *AJP* 58 (1937): 499–500 = *Selected Papers*, pp. 263–264. For the aporetic character of the *Protagoras* cf. 360 E–361 D.

cratic Ignorance is often seen as purely negative and sometimes buttressed with arguments that are fallacious and/or unfair to the other disputants. It is appropriate to notice, however, that most of the strictures modern scholars formulate against Socrates and his method of argument are already stated in Plato's own aporetic dialogues.[3]

Furthermore, Socrates' very method in the aporetic dialogues, the *elenchus*, that is, the testing and refutation of definitions by means of short questions and answers, is strongly objected to.[4] Thus, one of the most acute of its recent critics, Richard Robinson, in his *Plato's Earlier Dialectic*, contends that the *elenchus* involves hypocrisy and that it shows a negative and destructive spirit; that it tells one *that* one is wrong but not *why* one is wrong; and that in any case it would be more effective without the Socratic irony. He argues that in the middle and later dialogues the *elenchus* loses its irony, which shows that the irony is unnecessary. In his opinion the Socratic *elenchus* is always indirect, never uses an independent premise, and reduces the thesis to contradiction. Robinson objects also to the Socratic quest for definition, and does so mainly on two grounds: First, that in the early dialogues no justification is given for the absolute priority of what he calls "The What-is-X question," and that even the justification in the *Phaedrus* is insufficient, since we can and do make useful statements about X without being able to say what X is. Second, that the "What-is-X" question is the vaguest of all questions.[5]

Several of these criticisms of Socrates' procedure in the aporetic dialogues have been answered long ago. About them and others as well I shall have something to say in what follows.[6] What I propose to do here is, first, to comment on Socratic Ignorance and on its relation

---

3. Cf. esp. *Euthphr.* 11 B–C, *Ion* 533 C, *Men.* 79 E–80 B, *Gorg.* 482 C–484 C, 489 B–C, 497 B 6–7, *R.* 336 B–D, 337 A–338 B, P. Shorey, *What Plato Said* (Chicago, 1933), p. 513.

4. The *elenchus* as such need not result in the rejection of a proposition. In this paper, however, unless otherwise indicated, I refer always to the negative function of the *elenchus* which is connected with Socrates' profession of ignorance.

5. Cf. R. Robinson, *Plato's Earlier Dialectic*² (hereafter = Robinson; Oxford, 1953), esp. pp. 7–60. I have concerned myself chiefly with this work because it contains the most radical attack on what I have called Socratic Ignorance. I need hardly say that my discussion of the *elenchus* here is not at all complete and that it is limited to its relevance to my topic as described above. The following publications reached me after this paper had been written and could not therefore be taken into account: G. Vlastos, "The Socratic Elenchus" and "Afterthoughts on the Socratic Elenchus," *Oxford Studies in Ancient Philosophy* 1 (1983): 27–58 and 71–74, and R. Kraut, "Comments on Gregory Vlastos, 'The Socratic Elenchus'" ibid., pp. 59–70.

6. The two most important reviews of the first ed. of Robinson's book (Ithaca, 1941) are: P. Friedländer, *CP* 40 (1945): 253–259 = *Studien zur Antiken Literatur und Kunst* (Berlin, 1969), pp. 193–202, and H. Cherniss, *AJP* 68 (1947): 133–146 = *Selected Papers*, pp. 162–175.

to the *elenchus* throughout the Platonic corpus. Then I should like to test the interpretations and objections outlined above in a concrete case, that of the first book of the *Republic*. This will be done by offering a short analysis of it and by indicating its relation to the rest of the work.

I

Socratic Ignorance is not entirely negative. Socrates is not a sceptic. He believes that there is an essential difference between opinion, even correct opinion, and knowledge.[7] He thinks the truth can be discovered, and he urges his interlocutors to continue the search. Rather, Socratic Ignorance is to know that we do not know, and in Plato, including the aporetic dialogues, it is sharply distinguished from, and contrasted to, real ignorance, which is the false conceit of knowledge. Real ignorance or $\dot{\alpha}\mu\alpha\theta\iota\alpha$ is to believe that a false proposition or set of propositions is true. And it is one of the main functions of the *elenchus* to eliminate this false conceit of knowledge, to reduce the interlocutor to *aporia*, that is to bring him to the realization that he does not yet know and that what he thought he knew was merely an opinion, in most cases a mistaken one.[8] This cathartic function of the *elenchus* is the first necessary step towards further investigation, since as long as we believe that we already know we will not go on searching. I hope to show later on that these interrelated points were always central to Plato's thought. But we do not do quite full justice to this function of the *elenchus* by stating merely that it makes us "curious."[9] To do so disregards, for one thing, the paramount importance of ethical concern in Plato's thought from his earliest to his latest works. Moreover, I believe that it is illegitimate to dissociate Socrates' *elenchus* from the dramatic situation and from the subject-matter of the aporetic dialogues. For Plato did not write treatises but chose to present his thought in the form of dialogues and through dramatic conversations, which certainly are not records of conversations that Socrates actually held. We cannot therefore evaluate the arguments and Socrates' procedure without due regard to the dramatic situation, to the identity and the characterization of Socrates' interlocutors, and to the

---

7. The very *raison d'être* of the Socratic quest presupposes the distinction between opinion and knowledge, cf., e.g., *Ap.* 21 B–23 B; 29 D–E. Moreover, compare *Ap.* 22 B 8–C 3 with *Men.* 99 B 11–C 5, and note *Men.* 98 B 2–5, where Socrates claims to know that correct opinion is different from knowledge.

8. Cf., e.g., *Ap.* 21 B–D, 23 C, 29 B–C, D–E, *Ly.* 218 A–B, *Men.* 79 E–80 D with 84 A–C.

9. Cf., e.g., Robinson, p. 12.

kind of beliefs they are portrayed as holding.[10] In the aporetic dialogues Socrates is not represented as being interested in the "What-is-X" question in general but in examining definitions of moral concepts which his interlocutors advance. But the definitions he examines (which often become definitions by the effect of his questioning, since his interlocutors are usually not accustomed to abstract formulations at all[11]) are not put forward either in the course of a purely theoretical investigation or independently of the dramatic situation and of who the interlocutors are.[12] In fact Socrates examines and refutes definitions and ethical conceptions that were current in the Athens and in the Greece of his day, and some of which are to this day accepted in many quarters. Suffice it to mention the definition of Justice as the interest or advantage of the stronger, with its corollary that might is right.[13] Yet it is such definitions that propel history, for it is on the basis of them that human beings often attempt to justify their conduct, even when they care to justify it at all. The purpose of the aporetic dialogues described in what precedes may fittingly be called protreptic; protreptic for Socrates' interlocutors and also for us, Plato's readers. For though the literary conventions of the dialogue-form prevented Plato from making a direct appeal or reference to his readers, he nevertheless must have intended to present his dramas of ideas to presumptive readers. This protreptic aspect of the aporetic dialogues, though not the only one, is one of the main purposes of these works.

Socratic Ignorance and the *elenchus* are intimately related not only to the elimination of true ignorance, or $\dot{\alpha}\mu\alpha\theta\iota\alpha$, but to other notions as well. For, if we believe that we know what justice is when in fact we do not know, we will often act on the basis of our false conceit of knowledge. Hence the Socratic and Platonic doctrine that all wrongdoing is involuntary, since evil is ignorance but virtue is knowledge.[14] Moreover, the *elenchus* is connected with the Socratic procedure that

---

10. In connection with the last two points, cf., for example, the different characterizations of, and discussions with, Gorgias, Polus, and Callicles in the *Grg.*
11. Thus several of Socrates' interlocutors fail to understand the requirement of universality in a definition and point to what is at best a particular case of the virtue in question, cf., e.g., *Euthyphr.* 5 D ff., *La.* 190 E–191 E, *Men.* 71 E ff.
12. Note for example the connection of Euthyphro with piety, of Nicias and Laches with courage, and so forth.
13. Cf. the discussions with Polus and Callicles in the *Grg.* and with Thrasymachus in the *R.* and note 87 *infra*.
14. The connection of the Socratic *elenchus* and of Socratic Ignorance with the doctrine that all wrongdoing is involuntary since virtue is knowledge, is admitted by Robinson, p. 14. Cf. *Ap.* 26 A, *Prt.* 345 D ff. (cf. Cherniss, *AJP* 71 [1950]: 87 = *Selected Papers*, p. 269), 358 C–D, *Men.* 77 B–78 B, *Grg.* 466 D ff., etc.

consists in short questions and answers, which is sometimes in Plato called διαλέγεσθαι (to converse) and dialectic or διάλογος (dialogue). What is often disregarded is that, though sometimes in Plato the words mean "to converse" and "conversation" in the ordinary sense, they also have a related but more specific meaning. This meaning, which is emphasized when the Socratic procedure is contrasted with rhetoric, or with eristic, or with both, is "to argue" and "argument."[15] In such cases, the procedure of conversing by means of short questions and answers is merely the externalization of the process of rational discourse and thought. The Platonic Socrates is not opposed to long speeches as such, but to long speeches in which there is no argument or there is only the mere appearance of argument.[16] Hence, it is illegitimate to contend—as many critics, including Robinson, do—that in Plato's later works the dialogue-form, which is essential to the Socratic procedure, misfits the contents of such works. One may concede that in these later dialogues the conversation between the characters is less lively and less dramatic; but they still preserve the essence of the Platonic Socrates' method: the development of an argument by the examination of the different propositions and the links connecting them. In fact, in lengthy parts of the *Laws* (Plato's latest work) though the external dialogue is abandoned, the procedure is still dialogical or dialectical in the sense just described. The same is true of those parts of the *Timaeus* which are not purely "mythical."[17] And it is in two late works, the *Theaetetus* and the *Sophist*, that the very process of thought is identified with the internal dialogue of the soul with itself.[18] A conception, one may add, already anticipated in the *Apology*.[19]

Socrates' *elenchus* in the aporetic dialogues does not consist, *pace* Robinson, in indirectly reducing the thesis to contradiction without an independent premise. Rather, its function is to show that the definitions proposed by Socrates' interlocutors are incompatible with other beliefs they hold. And it is noteworthy that the only description of the

15. Cf. *Men.* 75 C–D, *Chrm.* 155 A with 162 D–E, *Ly.* 211 B ff., *Euthd.* 290 B–C, and *R.* 354 B 9–C 1 ὥστε μοι νυνὶ γέγονεν ἐκ τοῦ διαλόγου μηδὲν εἰδέναι, where, as the context indicates, διάλογος means "inquiry," "discussion," not "conversation," cf. R. Hirzel, *Der Dialog*, 1 (Leipzig, 1895): 4, n. 1, and P. Shorey, *Plato, The Republic*, 1 (Cambridge, Mass., and London, 1930): 107 and n. *c*.

16. Cf. *Grg.* 461 E–462 A, 471 E ff., *Prt.* 328 D–329 B, 334 A–335 C, 338 B–E, *R.*337 E–338 A, 343 B–344 C with 344 D 6–E 3 and 348 A–B, Cherniss, *Selected Papers*, pp. 24–31.

17. Cf., e.g., *Ti.* 27 E–29 D, 51 D–52 D, *Lg.* Book V, passim, R. Schaerer, *La question platonicienne*² (Neuchâtel, 1969), pp. 152–156.

18. Cf. *Tht.* 189 E–190 A, *Sph.* 263 E. Cf. also *Phlb.* 38 C–E, *Ti.* 37 B 3–C 5 (cf. A. E. Taylor, *A Commentary on Plato's Timaeus* [Oxford, 1928], p. 178 f.).

19. Cf. *Ap.* 28 E 5–6 φιλοσοφοῦντά με δεῖν ζῆν καὶ ἐξετάζοντα ἐμαυτὸν καὶ τοὺς ἄλλους.

method given in the Platonic corpus, that in the late *Sophist*, explicitly says as much.[20] Therefore, it ought to be intelligible for what reason the *elenchus* tells one *that* one is wrong but not *why* one is wrong.[21] Moreover, there is, I think, an additional reason. Plato believes that all teaching is indirect, for he denies that knowledge can be directly transmitted; that it can, as it were, be imposed from outside the knower. "No compulsive knowledge stays in the soul" says Socrates in the *Republic*,[22] and in the *Symposium* he explicitly denies that wisdom can simply pass from one individual to another.[23] But this conception of the acquisition of knowledge appears also in the *Meno*,[24] since the doctrine that knowledge is nothing but recollection implies it: it is the individual who must recollect the prenatal vision of the truth, a doctrine found also in Plato's later works.[25] The *elenchus* of the aporetic dialogues cannot tell one *why* one is wrong because to understand this requires positive knowledge, whereas the main function of the cathartic *elenchus* is to reduce the interlocutor to *aporia*. It is only after one has gone through this experience that the search for the truth can really begin. For it is only after such an experience, as Robinson himself recognizes,[26] that the soul has for the first time come to realize the essential difference between opinion and knowledge. But the procedure to be followed in the positive investigation of ethical universals, such as Socrates follows in the *Republic* from Book II onwards, is different from that of the aporetic dialogues. Here, too, the *elenchus* is necessary; but its function is more general than the purely cathartic one of the aporetic dialogues, which is intimately connected with So-

20. Cf. *Sph.* 230 B 4–8 and note 53 *infra*.
21. Robinson, pp. 17–18, himself takes the realization of *why* one is wrong in the strong sense of requiring knowledge. However, he is inconsistent in citing the explanation in the *Grg.* of "why" Pericles was mistakenly thought to be a good statesman as an exception to the general absence of the former *why* in the aporetic dialogues. For the discussion in the *Grg.* (503 B–D; 515 B–522 E) is based on the inconsistency of Callicles' own admission that Pericles was truly a good statesman with the Athenians' condemnation of him towards the end of his life. Hence it is inferred that Pericles' being considered a good statesman was due to the fact that he flattered the Athenians. In short, this is the typical procedure of the Socratic *elenchus* as practiced in the aporetic dialogues and as described in the *Sph*. Cf. notes 52–53 *infra*. Otherwise, one ought to say that the aporetic dialogues in many cases offer explanations of "why" someone went wrong.
22. *R.* 536 E 3–4.
23. Cf. *Symp.* 175 D–E.
24. Cf. *Men.* 81 A–E with 85 D–86 B.
25. Cf. *Phd.* 72 E–76 E, 91 E, *Phdr.* 249 B–C, *Ti.* 41 E–42 D with F. M. Cornford, *Plato's Cosmology* (London, 1937), pp. 144–146, *Plt.* 277 D 2–4 and 278 C–D with P. Shorey, *The Unity of Plato's Thought* (Chicago, 1903), pp. 43–44. Cf. further H. Cherniss, *Aristotle's Criticism of Plato and the Academy*, 1 (Baltimore, 1944): 47, n. 36.
26. Cf. Robinson, pp. 17 f.

cratic Ignorance. And even so the *elenchus* is not by itself sufficient to attain knowledge. For that we must also make use of the methods of hypothesis, as described in the *Phaedo* and applied in the *Republic*,[27] and of collection and division.[28] Thus, two additional interrelated purposes of the aporetic dialogues are to show us that some definitions of the virtues cannot be right and to induce us to inquire why they cannot be right.

Plato is from first to last opposed to relativism, and especially to ethical relativism, and the Platonic Socrates is always searching for absolute moral standards. Hence the definitions of the virtues must have as their objects ethical universals. And here at once we discover one of the main reasons for the failure of the definitions Socrates' interlocutors advance in the aporetic dialogues: they fail to point to the universal concept in each case. Thus, for example, all the definitions of piety that Euthyphro advances in the homonymous dialogue are shown to be mere instances of acts which may or may not be pious.[29] But it is precisely Plato's point that no act *per se* is absolutely good or evil,[30] and that to decide this in each case we must refer to an absolute ethical standard or pattern.[31] It is because they fail to meet this requirement that Euthyphro's definitions cannot abide in one place but are constantly running away.[32] Now in the aporetic dialogues Socrates' refutations do contain arguments that sometimes look and a few times are really fallacious; and in some cases these refutations are not absolutely decisive. But this is to be explained, among other reasons, by the fact that Socrates considers it sufficient in such cases to argue from the point of view of received and conventional opinions. This suffices for the purpose at hand precisely because those who advanced the definitions themselves accept the unexamined opinions and conceptions of conventional morality which their definitions and other beliefs reflect.[33] The main point is that Plato himself is not confused by such arguments and by such fallacies when they are present. It is well

---

27. Cf. *Phd.* 99 D–102 A with 107 B and *R.* 510 B–511 E with 533 B–D. Cf. P. Shorey, *University of Chicago Studies in Classical Philology* 1 (1895): 230–234 = *Selected Papers*, 2 (New York and London, 1980): 70–74; Cherniss, *AJP* 68 (1947): 141–144 = *Selected Papers*, pp. 170–173.

28. Cf. Shorey, *The Unity of Plato's Thought*, pp. 50–53, esp. p. 51, n. 377; and for *diaeresis* in the *R.* cf. Cherniss, *AJP* 68 (1947): 143 and n. 42 = *Selected Papers*, p. 172.

29. Cf. *Euthphr.* 6 D–E, 10 E–11 B, 15 B–C.

30. Cf., e.g., *Euthphr.* 11 A 6–B 1, *Euthd.* 280 D ff., *Men.* 87 E–89 A, *R.* 331 C, and the implications of the passages cited in n. 31 *infra*.

31. Cf. *Euthphr.* 5 C–D with 6 D–E, *Men.* 71 A–B with 72 C–D, 79 A–C, etc.

32. Cf. *Euthphr.* 11 B–E, 15 B–C, *Men.* 97 D–98 A.

33. In the aporetic dialogues Socrates' arguments always proceed on the assumptions accepted by his interlocutors. Cf. also the implications of κατὰ τὰ νομιζόμενα in *R.* 348 E and the second part of this paper.

to emphasize that Socrates in the aporetic dialogues does not claim to have established any positive doctrine; it seems futile to try, as some scholars do, to reconstruct the Platonic definition of a given virtue by means of what is considered to be the positive part of Socrates' argument.[34] It is after all Socrates himself who in the aporetic dialogues points out that we are still in *aporia*, that we still do not know what piety, courage, and such are, and that we must start again from the beginning.

Sometimes Plato goes further than this, as when Socrates in the *Laches* refutes Nicias' definition of courage though it contains what seems to be a valid Socratic and Platonic tenet, that courage is some kind of knowledge.[35] The point of doing this is to show that knowledge of "courage" is much more than merely expressing the conception in such words as may in a different context be acceptable as a valid definition of courage. In other words, he is not satisfied with an opinion, even if it be a correct opinion. Similarly, in the *Republic* Socrates argues against Simonides' and Polemarchus' definition that justice is to give to each what is due to him. This does not prevent him from later using this very notion as a "lower" conception of justice. But we must note that in its context in Book IV, after the preceding argument, based as it is on the principle of the division of labor, there is no essential connection between Socrates' definition and Polemarchus' in Book I.[36]

Another standard procedure to refute definitions is to obtain the interlocutor's agreement that the virtue in question, as defined, must be absolutely useful and, hence, good; that it must always contribute to our goodness and happiness. And this the definitions in the aporetic dialogues often fail to do. Here is then yet another aspect of the protreptic purpose of these works, for it points to the need of an absolute standard of goodness, to the idea of the good in the language of the *Republic*. In short, no definition is satisfactory if its author cannot refer it to an absolute standard of goodness and thereby be able to answer the objections brought against it.[37]

---

34. Cf., e.g., the many attempts to reconstruct from the *Euthphr.* Plato's definition of piety.

35. Cf. *La.* 194 C ff.

36. Note that Simonides' "to give to each his due" (331 E 3) is transformed into "to benefit friends and to harm enemies" (332 D 7), and that it is the original definition *as so interpreted* that Socrates considers to have refuted, as 335 E 1–5 shows. Contrast with 433 D–E and 442 E.

37. Cf. note 31 *supra*. Moreover, if, as I argue in part II, the first book of the *R.* was written by Plato as a proem to the whole work, then such passages as 531 E, 533 A–C with the application to the good in 534 B–C, show that the ability of δοῦναί τε καὶ ἀποδέξασθαι λόγον τοῦ ἀγαθοῦ is what will solve the puzzles of Book I and of the aporetic

The quest for definition in the aporetic dialogues being about ethical concepts and universals, it ought to be clear that Socrates is not concerned with the "What-is-X" question in general. One may at once add that none of the definitions advanced in the aporetic dialogues is an atomic proposition, as Robinson assumes in his criticism of the logic of the Socratic *elenchus*.[38] In fact, most often the definitions advanced by Socrates' interlocutors are so vague that he must obtain their agreement to additional propositions in order to clarify the meaning of the original definition. And then it is frequently the case that there is inconsistency between the latter and one or more of the additional propositions.[39] Robinson himself softens his criticism of the Socratic "What-is-X" question when he admits that Plato provides a context for such a question, which shows it to be a quest for essence. But it is necessary to add that it is a quest for the essence of ethical universals. Hence it is not an appropriate criticism of the absolute priority Plato assigns to the quest for definition to say that we can and do make useful statements about X without knowing what X is in the sense Socrates requires. For, strictly speaking, how can we evaluate and decide the claim of a Thrasymachus that injustice is the height of virtue and wisdom or that justice is the advantage of the stronger, if we do not first determine what justice is? And if not this, should we not at least demand from Thrasymachus a definition of justice and proceed to investigate it to determine whether or not it is consistent with his other related beliefs and/or in agreement with the facts? Such is precisely the implication of the point made in the *Phaedrus*:[40] If we had never seen a horse and wished to buy one, we might be easily persuaded to buy a donkey and think that it is a horse. However, in the case of things like horses, we do have some notion as to what they are once we have seen them. But the case of justice is different: without at least a preliminary definition we would not know what we are talking

---

dialogues. For these dialogues try to create puzzles and riddles that point to the solution given to them in the *R*. Cf. Shorey's paper "The Idea of Good in Plato's *Republic*," *Univ. of Chicago Studies in Class. Philol.* 1 (1895): 188–239 = *Selected Papers*, 2:28–79.

38. Against Robinson's misinterpretation of *R*. 380 C, *Grg.* 487 B, *Tht.* 155 B cf. Cherniss, *AJP* 68 (1947): 136 with n. 34 = *Selected Papers*, p. 165. On *R*. 341 C–343 A cf. note 101 *infra*. One may add that Plato's "middle and late" doctrine of the intercommunion of ideas (cf. *Phd.* 102 B–E, *R*. 476 A, *Sph.* 249 D–264 B, Cherniss, *Dialogue* 22 [1983]: 157 and n. 42) is incompatible with atomic propositions of any kind and that there is no evidence and no reason to suppose that the "early" Plato thought differently.

39. Cf., e.g., the summary of the arguments with Polemarchus and Thrasymachus in the second part of this paper.

40. Cf. *Phdr.* 259 E–261 A. For our purposes here *Men.* 71 A–B gives, *pace* Robinson, p. 51, the same justification of the absolute priority of the quest for definition as the *Phdr*.

about.⁴¹ Justice and all other ethical concepts are the most difficult for man to apprehend; and yet it is about such concepts that in Plato's opinion all human conflicts and disagreements revolve.⁴² In two later dialogues, the *Phaedrus* and the *Politicus*, Plato explains the reason for this from his own point of view. While most of the real entities have sensible likenesses, of the greatest and most precious, identified as justice, wisdom, temperance, and so on, no image has been made perceptible to man.⁴³ Even apart from the theory of ideas, however, moral concepts are abstractions, abstractions that are not easily apprehended because they do not have—as, for example, beauty does—images or instances directly perceptible to human beings. This to my mind is precisely one of the points to be learned from the aporetic dialogues: they show that those who readily advance definitions of ethical concepts and who act or are ready to act in accordance with them are really unable to fix their minds' eye on the concept in question.⁴⁴ Plato believes this to be extremely difficult and to require a long training and a long search by those so trained: after all it takes up most of the *Republic* for him to tell us what his conception of justice is. That his interlocutors in the aporetic dialogues are almost always unable to point to ethical universals and that Socrates is not in fact absolutely requiring that they give a definition by genus and specific difference is shown by some of the sample definitions he himself gives. Thus, in the *Meno*, Meno is unable to provide a satisfactory definition of virtue and Socrates tells him that he would be satisfied if Meno could point to a distinguishing mark of virtue and gives an example of what he means by this.⁴⁵ But Meno, who readily began by advancing a definition,⁴⁶ is shown to be incapable of giving such a distinguishing mark of virtue. In fact, he is irritated and even uninterested in the question.⁴⁷

To come back to the relation of Platonism to Socratic Ignorance, it seems to me illegitimate to try to determine, as many scholars con-

---

41. Cf. *Phdr.* 250 B, 263 A. Justice, like all other ethical concepts, is an abstract, not a concrete object apprehended by the senses. That much the "middle" Plato explicitly says (cf. also *Phd.* 65 D), and that much I trust will be granted to the early Plato, especially in view of the fact that the question about the existence of the virtues receives a similar formulation in the aporetic dialogues. Cf., e.g., *Euthphr.* 5 C–D, 6 D–E, *Men.* 72 C–D, *Prt.* 330 C–D, etc.
42. Cf., e.g., *Euthphr.* 7 B–D, 8 B–E, *Phdr.* 250 B with 263 A–B, *Plt.* 285 E–286 A.
43. Cf. *Phdr.* 247 D–E and 249 B–C with 249 D–250 D, 259 E–261 A and 263 A–B; *Plt.* 285 D–286 A.
44. Cf., e.g., notes 29–32 *supra* on *Euthphr.*
45. Cf. *Men.* 74 B ff., esp. 75 B–76 A with 76 C–E.
46. Cf. esp. 71 E–72 A.
47. 77 B ff., 79 E ff., 86 C ff.

fidently do, where in Plato's dialogues Socratism ends and Platonism begins. I do not mean by this to deny the validity of Aristotle's testimony to the effect that Socrates was engaged in the quest for ethical universals, whereas Plato was the first to separate the universal and to believe that the ideas exist apart from the particulars.[48] What I maintain is this: whatever may have been the philosophical doctrine of the historical Socrates, there is no point, in those of Plato's dialogues in which Socrates is the leading speaker, where one can note the passage from what is purely Socratic to what belongs to Plato alone. The same may be said about such a change taking place from one dialogue to another. It is noteworthy that when Plato felt, and meant to indicate to his readers, that the interests of his teacher were too remote from the doctrines he presents in the *Sophist*, the *Politicus*, the *Timaeus*, and the *Critias*, Socrates, though a *dramatis persona*, is not the main speaker. And in the *Laws* he is no character at all.[49] If, with the exceptions just noted, Plato decided to present the great majority of his views and doctrines as those of Socrates—as he does for example in the *Phaedo* with the very "discovery" of the theory of ideas—then we must infer that he wanted to convey to us the notion that his own philosophy is the natural result of Socrates' quest and teaching. Thus, if one wishes to argue that Plato eventually modified or entirely rejected the Socratism of his own earlier dialogues, one has to adduce evidence from Plato's own works that this is so. In my opinion there is none, and Socratism is from first to last a central tenet of Plato's thought. The fact that Plato later wrote dialogues containing his positive and constructive doctrine, is not by itself evidence that he had abandoned the Socratism of his earlier works. Nor is it a reason, either, for thinking

48. Cf. Aristotle, *Met.* 987 A 20–B 10, 1078 B 9–32, 1086 A 37–B 11 and compare with Socrates' intellectual autobiography in *Phd.* 96 A–102 A. It is noteworthy that *Met.* 987 B 31–33 καὶ ἡ τῶν εἰδῶν εἰσαγωγὴ διὰ τὴν ἐν τοῖς λόγοις ἐγένετο σκέψιν (οἱ γὰρ πρότεροι διαλεκτικῆς οὐ μετεῖχον) is a reminiscence of *Phd.* 99 E 4 ff. so that Aristotle is ascribing to Plato what the latter puts into Socrates' mouth in the *Phd.* Cf. W. D. Ross, *Aristotle's Metaphysics* 1 (corr. ed. Oxford, 1953): 172 and Cherniss, *Selected Papers*, pp. 48–49 with n. 50.

49. In the late dialogues Socrates is the leading speaker in the *Tht.* and in the *Phlb.* only, two works in which the subject matter and the procedure of discussion are clearly in Socrates' manner. In the *Prm.* Socrates is Parmenides' interlocutor in the first part only and is unable to meet the latter's objections to the theory of ideas. In the *Sph.* and in the *Plt.* Socrates takes almost no part in the conversation at all. The same is the case in the *Ti.* and in the *Criti.* The probability is that with the *Prm.*, *Sph.*, and *Plt.* Plato wished to indicate his indebtedness to Eleaticism and to related technical, logical and metaphysical problems not ostensibly connected with Socrates' quest for moral ideas. Similarly, the *Ti.* is a Περὶ φύσεως related more to Presocratic than to Socratic interests. And the detailed legislation of the *Lg.* is also foreign to the portrayal of Socrates in the early and middle dialogues, quite apart from the fact that too many things in the work would be anachronistically incompatible with Socrates.

that Plato's thought has been essentially modified in the passage from the aporetic to the later dialogues. For, as I have argued, there are good reasons to think that he wrote the aporetic dialogues for protreptic and other purposes which are not invalidated by his later works.

Be that as it may, several passages in his later dialogues show that Plato himself considered the position I have called Socratic Ignorance as of fundamental importance. Apart from the practice of the *elenchus* throughout the aporetic dialogues, it is in two works of this period that Plato describes and justifies its purifying or negative function: they are the *Apology* and the *Meno*.[50] In these works we find the distinction between true ignorance, which is the false conceit of knowledge, and Socratic ignorance, to know that one does not know. And though the two passages occur in different contexts they both stress the importance of the elimination of the false conceit of knowledge for the moral life and for the search for truth.[51] Now it is remarkable that this conception of the *elenchus* and of its function recurs in a passage of the *Sophist*,[52] a late dialogue, certainly later than the *Republic*, and that it is put into the mouth of the main speaker, the Eleatic Stranger, though Socrates himself is present at the conversation. And that is not all: the passage in addition contains a description of the very procedure followed by Socrates in the aporetic dialogues.[53] Moreover, another late dialogue, the *Theaetetus*, is itself a long *elenchus*, where three definitions of knowledge are examined and rejected by Socrates and where no positive conclusion is reached. Finally, in the *Philebus* and especially in the *Laws*, Plato's latest work, though

---

50. Cf. *Ap.* 23 A ff., 28 D ff., 39 C, *Men.* 80 A–D with 84 A–C and 85 C ff.

51. I cannot follow Robinson, p. 14, in his contention that the *Men.* and the *Sph.* show little trace of the strongly moral and religious setting in which the *Ap.* places the procedure of the *elenchus*. In the *Men.* the discussion with the slave-boy and his reduction to *aporia* is related to Meno's own *aporia* in 80 A–D and to the whole theme of the work which is the question of virtue. Cf. esp. *Men.* 99 E–100 B. On the *Sph.* cf. notes 52–53 *infra*.

52. Cf. *Sph.* 229 E–230 E.

53. After saying that ignorance is involuntary and that no one will ever learn anything about that of which he has a false conceit of knowledge (*Sph.* 230 A 5–8), the Eleatic Stranger describes the removal of the false opinion in these words: διερωτῶσιν (sc. τινές) ὧν ἂν οἴηταί τίς τι πέρι λέγειν λέγων μηδέν· εἶθ' ἅτε πλανωμένων τὰς δόξας ῥᾳδίως ἐξετάζουσι, καὶ συνάγοντες δὴ τοῖς λόγοις εἰς ταὐτὸν τιθέασι παρ' ἀλλήλας, τιθέντες δὲ ἐπιδεικνύουσιν αὐτὰς αὑταῖς ἅμα περὶ τῶν αὐτῶν πρὸς τὰ αὐτὰ κατὰ ταὐτὰ ἐναντίας. Two things should be säid against Robinson's interpretation: (i) the ethical purpose of the *elenchus* in this passage is to be seen in its being considered as a method of education (cf. also the moral tone of 230 D 6–E 3, translated in the second part of this paper); (ii) it is for this very reason that the irony which most often accompanies the *elenchus* in the aporetic dialogues is absent from this passage (n.b., however, that the man who is refuted is brought to shame and thus purified of his false opinions, 230 C 7–D 4).

there is no occasion to mention the *elenchus*, the greatest and worst ignorance is still identified with the false conceit of knowledge.[54] This notion, since Plato still considers that ignorance and wrongdoing are involuntary,[55] implies that for him the elimination of the false conceit of knowledge is the necessary first step towards the discovery of truth.[56]

II

One might argue, however, as in fact it has been done, that, though Plato never abandoned Socratism, nevertheless he later came to feel dissatisfied with it because its results are always negative.[57] One would think that the test case to discover what Plato himself thought about the function of Socratic Ignorance in his mature philosophy is the relation of the first book of the *Republic* to the rest of the work. Has not Plato himself prefaced the positive and constructive philosophy of the *Republic* with an aporetic dialogue? But here—as so many times in the course of Platonic scholarship—an attempt to give a more or less mechanical explanation of the evidence has stood in the way of a fruitful philosophical and literary approach. For since the second quarter of

---

54. Cf. *Phlb.* 48 C ff., esp. 48 E–49 E; *Lg.* 688 B–C, 689 A–C, 732 A, 863 C.
55. Cf. *Phlb.* 22 B, *Lg.* 731 C, 734 B, 860 D–E.
56. The elimination of the false conceit of knowledge is explicitly represented to be the function of the cathartic *elenchus* from the *Ap.* and the *Men.* to the *Sph.* (cf. notes 50–53 *supra*), and there is no reason to think that Plato thought differently when he wrote the *Lg.* In fact, the *elenchus* is practiced throughout the *Phlb.* and the *Lg.*, and in the latter work the first step in the argument is an *elenchus* by the Athenian Stranger directed against his interlocutors' notion that the aim of legislation in a well-ordered city is war (cf. 626 B–632 D). The reasons given in the text and in this note seem to be decisively in favor of thinking that even in the *Lg.* the cathartic *elenchus* and Socratic Ignorance are still of paramount importance in Plato's thought. I am not persuaded, however, by Hackforth, *CR* 59 (1945): 4, who sees the implied presence of the cathartic *elenchus* in *Lg.* 653 B.
   E. R. Dodds, *JHS* 65 (1945): 18, n. 14 = *The Greeks and the Irrational* (Berkeley and Los Angeles, 1951), p. 226, n. 19, maintains that in the *R.* and in the *Lg.* Plato in reality no longer accepts the Socratic *elenchus*. Concerning the *R.* see the second part of this paper and cf. also the future guardians' practice of the true art of disputation in contrast to ἀντιλογία (537 D–539 E). In the case of the *Lg.*, in addition to what has been said above, one must note that the higher education of the members of the Nocturnal Council is not given, for sufficient dramatic and philosophic purposes; but all the evidence suggests that for Plato the course of study was still the same as that of the *R.* (cf. Tarán, *Academica*, pp. 19–30). One of the main difficulties for Dodds is that he is bound to give the same interpretation to the *R.* as he gives to the *Lg.*; and this then forces him to take the eloquent passage *Sph.* 229 E–230 E as Plato's way of paying lip service to the Socratic *elenchus*.
   57. From different viewpoints such is the position of Robinson and also that of Giannantoni (cf. note 61 *infra*).

the nineteenth century many erudite scholars have contended that the first book of the *Republic* is shown in form, content, and style to be an aporetic dialogue which must therefore have been written early in Plato's life, particularly earlier than the *Gorgias*, and later attached to the rest of the *Republic* either exactly as it was written or with appropriate modifications.[58] Even if this interpretation were established, one would still have to discover why Plato attached this aporetic dialogue to the rest of the work. Why did Plato, at the height of his artistic and philosophic maturity, consider it appropriate to do so? In fact, however, there is no evidence, and it is highly improbable, that the first book of the *Republic* was conceived as a separate work. It is not the facts on which such a hypothesis rests that are wrong; it is the interpretation of them that must be rejected. For both in form and content Book I is an aporetic dialogue, and it is also true that its style is different from that of the rest of the *Republic*. What has struck scholars most is precisely the difference in style, and they believe that this is their most objective argument. In adopting this view, however, they explicitly or implicitly make an assumption that will not stand the test: namely, that Plato's style in certain matters—such as the way the interlocutors express agreement or disagreement—was unconscious. Yet it has been shown more than once that this is not so. The particles and other words used by Socrates' interlocutors depend on who they are and on what kind of discussion is going on, in other words, the style here, as almost always in Plato, has to do with the dramatic context and purpose at hand, and therefore style as such is not a valid criterion to determine the chronology of Plato's writings.[59] Since in form and content Book I, if taken in isolation, is an aporetic dialogue, it exhibits the style of such a work. So many things in it seem to point to developments in the later books of the *Republic* that most of the recent scholars who believe in the separate composition of Book I have asserted that such passages are later elaborations and interpolations by Plato himself. However, if one eliminated all such passages from the allegedly early part of the work, what would be left would constitute nothing but a farrago.[60] Therefore, this modification of the original

58. For a good bibliography on the controversy since the days of K. F. Hermann to about 1957 cf. Giannantoni's paper cited in note 61 *infra*.

59. Cf. esp. K. Vretska, *Wiener Studien* 71 (1958); 30–36 with references. Cf. also note 61 *infra*.

60. The scholar who has carried this separatist approach to the extreme is R. Preiswerk, *Neue philologische Untersuchungen zum 1. Buch des platonischen Staates* (Freiburg [Schweiz], 1939). For a thorough refutation cf. A. R. Henderickx, *Rev. Belge de philol. et d'histoire* 24 (1945): 5–46.

interpretation is nothing but an attempt to change the data in order to save the original hypothesis. On the other hand the Italian scholar Giannantoni, in an important paper,[61] rightly rejects the hypothesis that Book I is an early work and maintains that it was purposely written as a preface to the rest of the *Republic*. However, he believes that Plato did write it in order to show the insufficiency of Socrates' method in the aporetic dialogues, and that this is to be seen in the implicit and ironic criticism of Socrates at the beginning of Book II. It is necessary, then, to take a closer look at the content of Book I and at its relation to the rest of the *Republic*.[62]

Book I falls into three parts: (i) the dramatic introduction; (ii) the argument with Polemarchus; (iii) the argument with Thrasymachus.[63] Most of the first part consists of a conversation between Socrates and Cephalus. From several of the latter's statements Socrates collects a definition of justice: it is, without qualification, to tell the truth and to pay back one's debts. Yet as in some circumstances these very actions may be unjust, Socrates infers, and Cephalus agrees, that this is not the definition of justice. But it is, interposes Polemarchus, if one is to put any faith in the poet Simonides.

The purpose of the first part of the discussion with Polemarchus is to clarify what Simonides meant by saying "it is just to render to each his due." As it stands the definition is too vague. In answer to Socrates' objection to Cephalus, Polemarchus introduces a new proposition which he once more ascribes to Simonides: friends owe it to friends to do them some good and no evil. And he then admits that to enemies also one must render what is their due. However, he believes that what is *due* to an enemy from an enemy is what is *proper* (or fitting) for him, namely some evil. Thus the original definition is transformed and interpreted to mean, "justice is to benefit friends and to harm enemies."[64]

In the next section Socrates asks Polemarchus to point out the specific function of justice as so defined. The latter is unable to do this and is gradually reduced to the admission that he no longer knows

---

61. "Il primo libro della *Republica* di Platone," *Rivista critica di storia della filosofia* 12 (1957): 123–145.

62. In the summary and analysis of Book I that follows I have concentrated upon those aspects of it which are relevant to my purpose here. Because of what seems to me to be Robinson's misinterpretation of the Socratic *elenchus* and because he himself says that the first book of the *R*. may be regarded as an early dialogue (cf. Robinson, p. 7), I have also emphasized Socrates' method of discussion in Book I, which is an example of the procedure of the cathartic *elenchus* in *Sph.* 229 E–230 E. Cf. notes 52–53 *supra*.

63. Cf. *R*. 327 A–331 D = (i); 331 E–336 A = (ii); 336 B–354 C = (iii).

64. Cf. *R*. 331 E 1–332 D 9.

what he meant. But he still believes this: that justice benefits friends and harms enemies.[65] Consequently, Socrates proceeds to refute the definition outright.

This refutation takes up the rest of the discussion with Polemarchus.[66] By friends one may mean those who seem good friends or those who are really so though they do not seem; and similarly with enemies. Polemarchus first chooses the former alternative and is refuted by Socrates on the grounds that either (a) it will be just to harm those who do no wrong[67] or (b) it will be just to harm our friends and to benefit our enemies.[68] Consequently, Polemarchus chooses the alternative notion of friend, that is he who both seems and really is a good friend; and similarly with enemies. In that case the good man will be a friend and the bad man an enemy, and these are to be benefited and harmed respectively. But does it belong to the just man to harm anyone? From the analogy of the arts it is concluded that to harm men in respect to human excellence or virtue is to make them worse; and justice is a specific human virtue. Hence those who are so harmed become worse men and more unjust. The function of justice, however, is not to harm anyone; to harm is the function of injustice. Therefore, Simonides' definition *as so interpreted* cannot be right.[69]

At this point we have a violent interruption by Thrasymachus who, after criticizing Socrates' method,[70] offers the following definition: justice is nothing other than the advantage of the stronger.[71] Since Socrates agrees with Thrasymachus that justice is something useful, the meaning of "the stronger" must be investigated. Thrasymachus states that in all cases the ruling class legislates in its own interest and determines what is just. And he admits that also the inferiors' obedience to the rulers is just.[72] But as rulers are not infallible, when they err, they enact legislation which is not advantageous to themselves. Yet, according to the definition, whatever the rulers enact, it is just for their subjects to perform; hence according to Thrasymachus' own argument it is just not only to do what is of advantage to the stronger but also the opposite.[73] After a dramatic interlude,[74] Thrasymachus states that by

65. Cf. *R.* 332 D 10–334 B 9.
66. Cf. *R.* 334 C 1–336 A 10.
67. Cf. *R.* 334 C 1–D 8.
68. Cf. *R.* 334 D 9–E 5.
69. Cf. *R.* 334 E 5–336 A 10. Cf. note 36 *supra*.
70. Cf. *R.* 336 B 1–338 B 9.
71. *R.* 338 C 1–2.
72. *R.* 338 C 4–339 B 9.
73. *R.* 339 C 1–E 8.
74. *R.* 340 A 1–C 7.

the advantage of the stronger he meant what is really so, for the ruler as ruler cannot be mistaken, just as the physician and other craftsmen cannot be mistaken when they act according to their arts or crafts. The ruler as ruler (i.e., the perfect ruler) does not err, and so enacts what is best for himself, and this the subjects must do. Thrasymachus now claims that this is what he meant from the very beginning, so that what is just is to do what is for the advantage of the stronger.[75]

Socrates' objection is now based on the very analogy of the arts, introduced by Thrasymachus himself. Every art considers the advantage of, and is stronger than, that of which it is the art. Therefore no art considers the advantage of the stronger but of the weaker, which it itself rules. Thrasymachus, though reluctantly, expresses agreement.[76]

But he now delivers a speech in defense of his definition, accusing Socrates of not knowing the difference between the shepherd and the sheep. Shepherds fatten the cattle for their own advantage, not for that of the cattle. And similarly with rulers in our cities.[77] Two things are noteworthy in this passage. First, Thrasymachus has substituted the actual rulers in our cities for the ideal perfect rulers of his previous argument. Second, there is a remarkable shift in regard to justice. Hitherto, Thrasymachus had maintained that the just man is also the stronger, who rules for his own advantage; but he now calls this injustice, while the just man is he who is worsted. He now contends that injustice is more profitable than justice, that the highest form of injustice is tyranny, and the tyrant the happiest man. In short, Thrasymachus now openly espouses the cause of the immoralist.

The subsequent discussion has two parts. First Socrates argues that Thrasymachus in giving his description of the shepherd did not maintain his own analogy with the true physician. For according to the analogy of the arts the true shepherd would care only with providing the best for that which he rules, similarly with rulers in cities. Hence, Socrates does not at all concede that justice is the advantage of the stronger.[78]

However, a much more important matter seems to be Thrasymachus' contention that the life of the unjust man is better than that of the just man. Thrasymachus now clarifies his position: injustice is a virtue and justice, while not a vice, is simplicity or goodness of heart.

---

75. *R.* 340 C 8–341 C 4.
76. *R.* 341 C 4–342 E 11.
77. *R.* 343 A 1–344 C 8.
78. *R.* 344 D 1–347 E 2.

Injustice is goodness of judgment (εὐβουλία); the unjust are intelligent (φρόνιμοι) and good (ἀγαθοί), provided that they are capable of complete or perfect injustice (οἵ γε τελέως, . . . , οἷοί τε ἀδικεῖν).[79]

Socrates undertakes to refute this by establishing the following points: The unjust man, who according to Thrasymachus himself tries to have more (πλέον ἔχων) than anyone else,[80] will try to overreach (πλεονεκτεῖν) both his like and his unlike. On the analogy of the arts, however, which Thrasymachus himself introduced, it is shown that the expert will try to overreach his unlike but not his like. Therefore the unjust man is not wise but bad and ignorant. It is justice that is virtue and wisdom and, if so, is stronger than injustice. Hence, the just have a better life than the unjust and are happier, as justice is the virtue or excellence of the soul. And so injustice can never be stronger or more profitable than justice.[81]

Yet at the end of Book I Socrates himself says that something went wrong in the previous discussion, and that through his own fault.[82] I shall presently come back to this statement of Socrates.

Noteworthy in Book I is the eagerness of Polemarchus and Thrasymachus to introduce their definitions; and even Cephalus himself first mentions the question of the just and pious life.[83] A point of more fundamental importance, though usually neglected, is the dialectical development from Cephalus' definition of justice to Polemarchus' and from the latter to Thrasymachus' definition. Polemarchus begins by attempting to defend the definition Socrates collected from Cephalus' statements, and does so by appealing to the authority of Simonides. He then accepts two additional propositions, and thus the original definition, "justice is to render to each his due," is transformed into "justice is to benefit friends and to harm enemies." But Socrates, after showing that the function of justice cannot be to harm anyone, maintains that such a definition belongs, not to Simonides or other wise men but to tyrants and rich men who think they have great power to do whatever they wish.[84] There is then an obvious connection between the definition of Cephalus-Simonides as transformed by Polemarchus and Thrasymachus' conception of justice as the interest of the stronger and of the tyrant as the perfectly happy man; for it is precisely such a man who will benefit his friends and harm his ene-

---

79. *R.* 347 E 2–348 D 9.
80. Cf. *R.* 343 C 3 ff. N. b. D 5–6 πλέον ἔχοντα, and contrast with D 7–8; 344 A 1 τὸν μεγάλα δυνάμενον πλεονεκτεῖν, etc.
81. *R.* 348 E 1–354 A 13.
82. *R.* 354 A 13–C 3.
83. Cf. *R.* 330 D 4 ff., esp. 331 A 4–5 ὅς ἂν δικαίως καὶ ὁσίως τὸν βίον διαγάγῃ.
84. Cf. *R.* 335 E 1–336 A 7.

mies. Finally, it ought to be clear that there is an intimate connection between Thrasymachus' first position, namely that justice is the advantage of the stronger, and his later contention that the advantage of the stronger is injustice and that injustice is preferable to justice. Not only does Thrasymachus himself say as much, but it is clear that his conception of "the advantage of the stronger" has not changed[85] but that, as we shall see, it is considered from two different viewpoints. We may infer, then, that Plato has shown the danger lurking even in the conception of justice of a pious man like Cephalus,[86] and that he has skillfully indicated the connection between the popular notion that it is just to benefit our friends and to harm our enemies and the well-known position of the extreme immoralist held by Thrasymachus and others.[87]

The discussion with Polemarchus proceeds on two assumptions: that justice is useful and that it is good, and these assumptions Thrasymachus himself adopts at first.[88] However, his definition is so vague that he, like Callicles in the *Gorgias*, must specify what he means by "the stronger." Thus he advances the new proposition that in all cases the ruling class legislates in its own interest and determines what is just. Having said so much, he has to admit that obedience to the rulers is also just.[89] It is this last admission that proves to be fatal to Thrasymachus' definition of justice, for Socrates' objections are based on the relation between the rulers and their subjects. One may ask, then, why does Thrasymachus agree that obedience to the rulers is just? It is be-

85. Cf. *R.* 343 B 1–344 C 8, esp. 344 C 4–8.
86. Cf. 329 A–D, 330 A, 330 D–331 B. But for Plato Cephalus is one of those who ἔθει ἄνευ φιλοσοφίας ἀρετῆς μετειληφότα (*R.* 619 C 7–D1; cf. also *Phd.* 82 B 2–3), and hence lacks knowledge.
87. For the popular Greek feeling that it is right to benefit our friends and to harm our enemies, to requite wrong with wrong, and so forth, cf. Archilochus, frg. 126 (West); Solon, frg. 13, 5–6 (West); Theognis 869–872; Pindar, *Pyth.* II, 83–84; Aeschylus, *Sept.* 1049, *Agam.* 608, *Choeph.* 123; Sophocles, *Antig.* 643–644; Euripides, *Med.* 809, *Ion* 1046, frgs. 1091–1092 (Nauck); Xenophon, *Mem.* II, 3, 14, II, 6, 35, *Cyrop.* I, 4, 25; [Isocrates], *Ad Demon.* 26; Plato, *R.* 332 D, 335 E, etc. Cf. *contra* Plato, *Cri.* 49 B, *Grg.* and *R.*, passim. For "the advantage or the right of the stronger," "the power or licence to do whatever one wishes," and so forth as the popularly accepted canon of conduct in public and private life, cf. the debates in Thucydides III, 36–49 and V, 84–113; also III, 82–84 and IV, 61, 5; Plato, *Grg.* 466 A ff., 482 C–484 C, 491 A–492 C, 510 A–511 B, *R.* 336 A, 358 C ff., 367 C, *Lg.* 714 A–C. N.b. Glaucon's remark in *R.* 358 C 7–8 ἀπορῶ μέντοι διατεθρυλημένος τὰ ὦτα ἀκούων Θρασυμάχου καὶ μυρίων ἄλλων.
88. In the discussion with Polemarchus, note the question whether the just man is χρήσιμος or ἄχρηστος (332 E 5 ff.), the comparison of the just man to the ἀγαθὸς φύλαξ (333 E 3 ff.), and the assumption that justice is a human virtue (335 C 4 ff.). As for Thrasymachus, he himself defines justice as τὸ τοῦ κρείττονος συμφέρον (338 C 2), but when he later calls this injustice he maintains that injustice, not justice, is a virtue (348 C 2 ff., esp. D 3–5; 348 E 9–349 A 3).
89. Cf. *R.* 338 E–339 B.

cause, had he rejected that proposition, it would at once have been clear that he was adopting the position of the extreme immoralist; instead, he began by offering "the interest of the stronger" as a definition of justice along conventional lines, that is on the assumption that justice is useful and is a virtue.[90]

An additional point that needs to be emphasized is the importance of, and the prominence given to, the relation of justice to knowledge and wisdom. This is to be seen even in the discussion with Polemarchus. For one thing, his failure to point out the specific function of justice as he had defined it implies lack of knowledge. Yet even more significant is the procedure followed by Socrates in his outright refutation. The very introduction of the distinction between seeming and real friends and enemies already points to the distinction between opinion and knowledge. And one may ask: since Socrates refutes Polemarchus' conception of justice by showing that the function of justice cannot be to harm anyone, why does he not do so at once? Why does he first refute the two alternatives in the case of seeming friends and enemies? I submit that the probable reason of having him do so is Plato's desire to call attention to the necessity of facing the question of knowledge in connection with any conception of justice whatever.[91] In the case of Thrasymachus it is clear that the question of knowledge and wisdom is of fundamental importance throughout the argument. Yet it is precisely Thrasymachus' notion—based on the analogy of the arts, which he himself introduced—that the ruler, as ruler, must be perfectly wise that proves to be fatal both to his definition of justice and to his later open espousal of the immoralist's cause. It is therefore the more remarkable that, even though he blushes because Socrates has refuted him,[92] he does not withdraw his assent to the proposition that the unjust man must be wise; and this although he was given the choice of doing so early in the argument.[93] However, had he chosen the alternative "what appears to the stronger to be for his advantage," as Cleitophon proposed, it would have been clearly impossible for Thrasymachus from the start to identify justice with the interest or advantage of the stronger, since rulers sometimes err.

90. Cf. note 88 *supra*.
91. In the first part of the argument with Polemarchus (331 D–334 B) both the transformation of the original definition into "to benefit friends and to harm enemies" (332 C 5–D 9) and Polemarchus' inability to point out the specific function of justice as so defined (332 D 10–334 B 6) are based on the analogy of the arts. And at the end of this section Polemarchus says οὐκέτι οἶδα ἔγωγε ὅτι ἔλεγον (334 B 7).
92. Cf. *R*. 350 D 2–3.
93. It is clear that this is the main purpose of the interlude with Polemarchus and Cleitophon (340 A 1–C 7).

In the end he is unable to maintain both his definition of justice and his conception of a perfectly wise ruler. It is at this point that Thrasymachus shifts his ground by introducing the parallel between the ruler and the shepherd who fattens cattle for his own, not the cattle's, advantage. It now becomes clear that Thrasymachus has decided to disregard the question of those who are ruled. What is more, he states that it is only those who are worsted that will call their treatment injustice and will revile injustice.[94] One must note that at this point Thrasymachus' rulers are actual rulers, not any longer the ideal rulers of his previous argument.[95] Yet he still clings to his notion of the perfectly wise ruler, inconsistent as it is with his new notion of ruler, because his rulers must be capable of complete and perfect injustice, which requires knowledge.[96]

There is an even more significant shift in this second part of the argument with Thrasymachus. It is that now "the advantage of the stronger" is considered to be, not justice but injustice, and that injustice is pronounced to be not only useful but a virtue and wisdom.[97] This is the main difference (though there are others) between the immoralist's position of Thrasymachus and those of Polus and Callicles in the *Gorgias*: for it is only in the *Republic* that Plato presents us with the extreme immoralist who asserts that injustice is a good thing and the height of wisdom, provided that it is perfect and complete injustice.

As Socrates himself admits, the extreme immoralist cannot be refuted with arguments based on conventional principles;[98] for he rejects all such principles.[99] That in spite of this admission Socrates proceeds to confute Thrasymachus with arguments of this kind, is explained, I believe, by the following considerations: First, because here as elsewhere Plato desires to show that no contemporary sophist or rhetorician was a match for Socrates in argument. And he wished to do this particularly in a case where, as here, his interlocutor has abused Socrates and his cathartic method.[100] Secondly, because it is important to show that Thrasymachus' immoralism is not consistent[101]

---

94. Cf. *R.* 343 E 7 ff., esp. 344 C 3–4.
95. Cf. *R.* 343 B 1–C 1, n. b. B 4–5 τοὺς ἐν ταῖς πόλεσιν ἄρχοντας, οἳ ὡς ἀληθῶς ἄρχουσιν, κτλ. But these cannot be identical with the perfect rulers who, in so far as they have knowledge, are never mistaken (340 C–341 A).
96. Cf. 344 A–C. Cf. also note 79 *supra*.
97. Cf. note 79 *supra*.
98. Cf. *R.* 348 E 5–9, n. b. εἴχομεν ἄν τι λέγειν κατὰ τὰ νομιζόμενα λέγοντες.
99. Cf. *R.* 348 E 9–349 A 3.
100. Cf. *R.* 336 B–338 B.
101. It ought to be clear that Thrasymachus' conception of injustice as the advantage of the stronger and as a virtue is incompatible with his own conception, based on the

and that the extreme immoralist *à la* Thrasymachus can at least be neutralized along conventional lines of argumentation. Thus it is only at the beginning of Book II of the *Republic* that the cause of the extreme immoralist is put forward much more strongly and consistently by Glaucon and Adeimantus, who, unlike Thrasymachus, do not believe in it. Only then does Socrates undertake to show what justice is and why it is preferable to injustice.

The preceding analysis has emphasized the unity of the first book of the *Republic* by stressing the dialectical development of, and the connection between, Cephalus', Polemarchus', and Thrasymachus' definitions of justice and by calling attention to the paramount importance attached to the relation of justice to knowledge and wisdom. It is therefore reasonable to infer that Plato conceived Book I as an organic whole in which the discussion is so structured as to lead to the position of the extreme immoralist. Moreover, at the end of Book I Socrates himself implies that his refutation of the extreme immoralist has not been decisive, and at the beginning of Book II the latter's case is more consistently reformulated by Glaucon and Adeimantus. Therefore, we must conclude that Book I was purposely written as a proem (as Socrates calls it [102]) to the rest of the *Republic* and that it was probably composed after and not, as some think, before the *Gorgias*.[103]

---

analogy of the arts (340 C–341 C), that the ruler as ruler is perfectly wise, a proposition that he never withdraws. One should add that when Thrasymachus pronounces the advantage of the stronger to be justice, he is inconsistent; for on the analogy of the arts one would have to infer that justice is the advantage of the weaker. This point seems to have escaped Friedländer in his review of the first edition of Robinson's book (op. cit. [note 6 *supra*], p. 253 = p. 194); he says that 343 A 2 (ὁ τοῦ δικαίου λόγος εἰς τοὐναντίον περιειστήκει) implies that "Justice is the advantage of the weaker" is nothing but a more emphatic contrast to "Justice is the advantage of the stronger" than "Justice is not the avantage of the stronger." However, as the point made in 343 A 2 depends on the previous discussion, it is clear that "Justice is the advantage of the weaker" is an inference from the analogy of the arts, which Thrasymachus himself had introduced. Of course, this does not mean that Plato himself accepted "the advantage of the weaker" as a definition of justice.

102. Cf. *R.* 2:357 A 2.

103. The necessary connection of justice with knowledge in the rest of the *R.* is prefigured in the position of the extreme immoralist, who, as I have argued, makes knowledge and wisdom a necessary condition of the perfect injustice that will render him happy. We must note two things: (i) that in the interlude with Polemarchus and Cleitophon (cf. note 93 *supra* with the corresponding remarks in the text) Thrasymachus is given the opportunity to accept "what *appears* to the stronger to be for his advantage," but chooses instead the notion that the ruler *qua* ruler can never be mistaken (i.e., that the ruler as such must be wise); (ii) that in 348 E 6–9 Socrates says that if Thrasymachus had posited that injustice is beneficial, but had admitted that it is a shameful thing, "as some others do" (a position taken by Polus in the *Grg.*), it would have been possible to argue against him on the basis of conventional principles. I therefore infer that the *Grg.* must have been composed before *R.* 1; otherwise Plato would also have discussed the

Thus, the popular morality of the Greek world, its insufficiency and its connection with the extreme immoralist's denial of the moral life, are made by Plato to stand as a prelude to, and in contrast with, the ethical and political philosophy of his ideal state.

It is not the case, however, as Giannantoni thinks it is, that Book II implies criticism of the Socratism of the aporetic dialogues and of Socrates' procedure in Book I. For one thing, Socrates himself at the beginning of Book II says that he is in *aporia*,[104] even after he has been told by Adeimantus that he is the man to investigate the question of justice since he has passed his entire life in the consideration of this very matter.[105] Moreover, there are several reasons why Plato could hardly have meant to indicate at the beginning of Book II dissatisfaction with the Socratism of the aporetic dialogues. At the end of Book I it is Socrates himself who says that his previous discussion is unsatisfactory, and that through his own fault: for before determining what justice is he undertook to discuss whether justice is ignorance and evil or their opposites and whether or not it is preferable to injustice.[106] Now this statement of Socrates refers especially to his discussion with Thrasymachus.[107] What is more, Socrates' criticism of his own procedure here is the very criticism he directs against others in the aporetic dialogues: there it is he who insists that before investigating a predicate or quality of a virtue one must determine what the virtue in question *is*.[108] In addition, we must recall that even earlier in Book I Socrates had tacitly admitted that it is impossible to refute Thrasymachus' extreme immoralism along conventional lines.[109] A real answer to the immoralist requires a different type of argument and one that cannot be undertaken with Thrasymachus. In any case, Socrates'

---

alternative Cleitophon suggested. This interpretation is the exact opposite of that of the partisans of the separate composition of Book I. They argue that, as the *Grg.* is a more complex and elaborate dialogue than *R.* I, it must have been composed after it but before *R.* II-X. This argument of the separatists A. Diès (cf. his introduction to the "Budé" *R.* [in vol. VI of *Platon, Oeuvres complètes*, Paris, 1932], pp. xviii–xx) and others have countered with the remark that it begs the question, since we cannot know that *R.* I was ever an independent dialogue. To my mind, however, the arguments given above and the overwhelming reasons for thinking that *R.* I was purposely written as a prelude to the rest of the work suggest that the *Grg.* is earlier than the whole of the *R.*
104. 368 B–C.
105. Cf. *R.* 367 D–E.
106. Cf. *R.* 354 A–C, n. b. B 4–6.
107. For the two points mentioned as having been discussed "about Justice," (i) "whether it is evil and ignorance or wisdom and virtue" and (ii) "whether injustice is more profitable than justice," explicitly came up in the discussion with Thrasymachus.
108. Cf., e.g., *Euthphr.* 11 A 6–B 1; *Men.* 71 A–B and 86 C–E with 100 B 4–6; *Prt.* 360 E–361 D; *Grg.* 448 E.
109. Cf. *R.* 348 E–349 A.

self-criticism in Book I does not imply a rejection of all that went on in that book: the refutations of Polemarchus' and of Thrasymachus' definitions are not rejected. And even the argument against Thrasymachus to show that the unjust man is not wise is valid *ad hominem*, since it proceeds on Thrasymachus' own analogy of the ruler with the perfect practitioners of the arts. Hence, Socrates' statement that he knows nothing at the end of Book I is his usual assertion of Socratic Ignorance.[110]

Dramatically and philosophically it is the extreme immoralist's claim that injustice is virtue and wisdom that necessitates the type of discussion we find in Books II–IX. If this is so, and if Plato conceived Book I as a proem to the rest of the work, it follows that at the time he composed the *Republic* he still considered Socratic Ignorance as the first essential step towards his positive philosophical doctrine.

Socratic Ignorance and the purifying function of the *elenchus* bring about the mind's first realization of the difference between opinion and knowledge. Human beings are not born wise, particularly not morally wise. And he who has never experienced the discovery of his own false conceit of knowledge has hardly learned anything worth learning. As Plato says in the *Sophist*: "For all these reasons, then, we must say that the *elenchus* is the greatest and most important of purifications: and we must consider that the man who has not experienced it, even if he happen to be the Great King himself, is unpurified in respect to the most important matters, being uneducated and ugly in things in which it is proper for him to be most pure and fairest, if he is to be truly happy."[111] Plato's aporetic dialogues, then, are not testimony to a philosophy that he later abandoned or essentially modified, but are central to his thought from first to last. They portray the essence of man's moral quest and the very process of rational thought.

Columbia University

110. Cf. *R*. 354 B 9–C 3.
111. *Sph*. 230 D 6–E 3.

5 SELF-KNOWLEDGE IN EARLY PLATO

JULIA ANNAS

"Self-knowledge in Early Plato" may suggest a rather limited topic. For within what we accept as the Platonic corpus, Plato deals with self-knowledge only once, in the *Charmides*; and that discussion is itself baffling, appears marginal to Plato's main concerns, and seems to spring philosophically out of nowhere.

In this paper I am going to make, and to some extent follow through, the suggestion that the apparent isolation and oddity of the *Charmides*' discussion disappear if we regain the picture of Plato which the ancients had, and do so by regaining a wider view of the Platonic corpus. I am going to take up, and to treat as Platonic, two dialogues which nowadays are not generally held to be Plato's: the *Lovers* (*Erastae*; or *Rivals* (*Anterastae*)), and the *First* (or *Greater*) *Alcibiades*. (There is another, definitely un-Platonic dialogue called the *Second* (or *Lesser*) *Alcibiades*; since I have nothing to say about that, I shall refer to the longer work simply as the *Alcibiades*.) If we treat these dialogues as genuine, I shall argue, we may deepen our philosophical interpretation both of them and of some of Plato's other works; and we may also gain insight into some aspects of the puzzling concept of self-knowledge.

I shall not be arguing directly that these two dialogues are genuinely by Plato, partly because it would be dreary but mainly because it would be misguided. To do so would go along with the common assumption that the balance of proof is against these dialogues, so that the burden of proof lies with the person who wants to treat them as authentic. But even a cursory look at the history of scholarship on these dialogues shows that this assumption is not a reasonable one to make.

*This paper was first read as a Matchette Lecture at The Catholic University of America. It was greatly improved by discussion there and subsequently at the University of Oklahoma and the University of Texas at Austin. I am particularly grateful to Alex Mourelatos and Dominic O'Meara.

The *Lovers* is a short, slight work, containing no decisive indications either for or against authenticity. In antiquity one of Plato's editors had doubts about it, but we don't know his grounds for this.[1] There are many short dialogues which have come down under Plato's name; some—like the *Axiochus*, which contains Epicurean argument—cannot possibly be by Plato[2]; others, like the *Euthyphro*, have never seriously been doubted; others, like the *Lovers* and the *Hipparchus*, occupy a grey area (though it is worth noting that philosophers are much more skeptical about them than, for example, ancient historians are[3]). The argument of this paper will, I hope, make it plausible that the *Lovers* is an early work by Plato, but I do not claim any stronger case than this, nor do I see how one could be made.[4]

The *Alcibiades* is a different and a more surprising case. Throughout antiquity it was a famous work, often referred to[5] and echoed in a variety of literary works.[6] Cicero, among others, recalls its two most striking passages.[7] As we would expect, it was particularly well known

---

1. Diogenes Laertius IX, 37: Thrasyllus suggested that "if the *Lovers* is Plato's" Democritus may appear anonymously in it. We are given no reasons for the hesitation, and the suggestion is strikingly silly.

2. The *Axiochus* contains the extraordinary incoherence of materialist Epicurean arguments to show that nothing survives death, and dualist Platonic arguments to show that the immortal soul does so.

3. For example, apart from Friedländer ([4], 119–128 and 339–322) hardly any ancient philosophers think the *Hipparchus* to be Plato's—often on the grounds of the absurdity of the historical section; but historians do not share these doubts: see the forthcoming *Cambridge Ancient History*, vol. IV,[4] ch. 5.

4. On the *Lovers* see Souilhé, Carlini (1) and (2) and Isnardi. Apart from Thrasyllus' undefended doubts, the only grounds given for doubt are (1) dislike of the dialogue. Cf. Isnardi, "Nessuno vorebbe oggi sostenere la tesi dell'attribuzione a Platone di un'opera non solo di nessun valore teorico e di notevole trascuratezza e superficialità, ma che presenta chiaramente . . . il carattere di un centone di motivi desunti dai più vari dialoghi platonici." (2) distrust of the final passage in particular, see n. 37 below (3) the claim that the ideas we find in the *Lovers* must be late because they fit into a later context. This is inconclusive at best, and the unsatisfactory nature of the criteria used emerge clearly from the fact that while Souilhé and Isnardi favour Polemon's Old Academy, Carlini places it in the utterly dissimilar New Academy of Arcesilaus.

5. Aristotle does not refer to it by name, but may well show knowledge of it (see n. 23 below). Diogenes Laertius, or rather his source(s), accept it (III, 51). Alexander of Aphrodisias recalls a famous passage in the Preface to his *De Anima*; Epictetus III, 1.42 clearly refers to 131d; the Emperor Julian accepts the work as Plato's (*Oration* IX, 9). It clearly was well known in all philosophical schools.

6. Friedländer ([3] and [4]) sees echoes in Polybius' portrait of Scipio, and close reference in Persius' *Satire* IV. I am inclined to give less weight to these passages than Friedländer, since what they echo is not so much specific details of Plato's dialogue as the theme of an encounter between Socrates and the young Alcibiades, a theme treated by others. See, e.g., the fragments of Aeschines' dialogue *Alcibiades*, ed. Krauss (Leipzig, 1911). (Friedländer is otherwise very perceptive about this dialogue [(2) 41–6].) Persius, for example, is engaged in developing a sustained sexual joke for which he owes nothing to Plato.

7. *Tusculan Disputations* I, 52 (the real self is the soul, not the body) and V, 70 (the real

to philosophers in the Platonist tradition.[8] The Middle Platonists emphasized it, and some, including Albinus, made it the opening dialogue in a course on Plato's philosophy[9]—thus giving it the position that we today, with our rather different view of Plato, usually give to the *Euthyphro*. The Neoplatonists followed the Middle Platonists in this, especially since Plotinus echoes the work.[10] Several later Neoplatonists wrote commentaries on the *Alcibiades*, of which we possess those of Olympiodorus and, in part, of Proclus. Iamblichus followed the tradition of making the *Alcibiades* first in the reading order of Plato's ten major dialogues; the developments in these, he said, were all to be found in that work "as if in a seed."[11] Olympiodorus also thought it the best introduction to Plato's philosophy; he compared it to the *propylaeon* or entrance to a shrine (of which the *adyton* or holy of holies, incidentally, was the *Parmenides*.)[12] Nobody thought the *Alcibiades* to be a dubious work until Schleiermacher in the nineteenth century decided that it was too "insignificant and poor" to be Plato's.[13]

---

meaning of "know yourself" is "Know God"). See also *Somnium Scipionis* 26. For discussion of related passages, and the difficult question of Cicero's sources, see Courcelle, Boyancé, and Pépin. Pépin seems clearly right in finding in these passages both a commitment to a drastically dualist view of the soul-body relation, and a less drastic view which plausibly derives from Antiochus. But his hypothesis of an intermediary Stoic source for the drastic view seems unnecessarily speculative. The confusion is entirely typical of Cicero, who could quite well have read the *Alcibiades* for himself.

8. Pépin (2) gives an excellent account of the philosophical afterlife of the *Alcibiades* in the Platonist and Christian traditions. His chs. 4 and 5, in which he tries to make out a direct influence on Stoicism, are more conjectural and speculative, and also, I believe, depend on a questionable view of the soul-body relation in Stoicism.

9 . Diogenes Laertius (IV 62) knows of one teaching order of the dialogues beginning with the *Alcibiades*. Albinus in his *Introduction* says that the *Alcibiades* should be the first read of the dialogues, though interestingly not for the reasons the Neoplatonists were to give: the primary importance of self-knowledge. Albinus stresses rather the appropriateness of Alcibiades as the type of the eager and gifted young person ready to be turned towards philosophy (suggesting that the historical irony was lost on him). Of other middle Platonists, Harpocration wrote a commentary on it (see Dillon). Plutarch does not discuss it in the extant philosophical works, but cites it as Plato's for the fact that Zopyrus was Alcibiades' tutor (*Life of Alcibiades* 2).

10. See Pépin (2), 95–101. *Enneads* I 1,3,3; IV 4, 43, 20–1; VI 7, 5, 24 echo the *Alcibiades*.

11. Fr. 1 of the *Alcibiades* commentary (pp. 72–73 in Dillon's edition). The ten dialogues were: *Alcibiades, Gorgias, Phaedo, Cratylus, Theaetetus, Sophist, Statesman, Phaedrus, Symposium, Philebus*. (*Anon. Prolegomena to Platonic Philosophy* ed. Westerink, ch. 26.) See Pépin (2) ch. 3 for discussion of other Neoplatonist treatments of themes in the *Alcibiades*.

12. Olympiodorus, ed. Westerink, 10–11. The *Parmenides* is not in the list quoted in n. 11; the *Alcibiades* was established as "the introduction" to different conceptions of Plato's philosophy.

13. See Schleiermacher, 328–336 (and 325–328 for the *Lovers*). The influence of Schleiermacher's judgment is surprising, considering the total absence of grounds given other than taste. It is noteworthy that Schleiermacher is in fact ambivalent about both

To show that a work with such credentials is not really by Plato at all, one would expect indications of authenticity to be offered which are clear, unmistakable, and independent of any desire on the scholar's part for the work to be authentic or not. But when we look at the arguments brought against the *Alcibiades*, we find that specific objections—against language,[14] supposed anachronisms, and such[15]—are very few, weak, and usually not even presented as being conclusive.[16] The real objections have been two. One is aesthetic: scholars have found the style flat and the characterization weak. However, even if we grant this, it scarcely shows that the dialogue can't be by Plato, unless we think it a priori true that Plato's style is never flat, in which case we should in consistency feel doubts about large tracts of the *Philebus* and *Statesman*, not to mention the entire *Laws*. The other objection is philosophical: scholars have claimed that we cannot consistently ascribe to Plato the ideas that are in it. Here we find a great deal of confusion, but also a serious worry. The confusion is expressed in a curious kind of Catch-22 reasoning in which the dialogue cannot possibly

---

dialogues (in a way echoed in, for example, Shorey); after insulting every aspect of the dialogue's form and content he concludes that after all the *Alcibiades* contains some fine parts worthy of Plato. He is the first of many scholars to entertain fantastic hypotheses such as that Plato wrote parts of it; wrote a dialogue spoiled by somebody else; improved someone else's inferior dialogue, and so on. The desperation of these moves suggests that the basic problem is inability to make sense of the dialogue as a whole in terms of some leading theme.

14. Wilamowitz objected to κρήγυος (111e); he is adequately met by Friedländer (2) 6–11. De Strycker, 104, lists some words in the dialogue "which Plato seems to have systematically avoided" (however are we to know?). On p. 115 he complains of twelve uses of συμφέρειν which are "absolute" (without complement in genitive or dative). He admits that there is a parallel in the *Laws* (746c); and we can see why there is no problem in the *Alcibiades* either from 114a6–b2. There, Socrates says that he is precisely concerned with what is συμφέροντα in general, *not* with what is συμφέροντα *for* anyone. (De Strycker's objection is typical of many which come solely from a mechanical word-count, and disappear when the content of the dialogue is taken seriously.) Clark says that the last third can be ascribed to middle-period Plato on several stylistic tests, but not the first two-thirds, which she ascribes to a pupil. But the differences can all be accounted for by stylistic shifts appropriate to the content. In any case, the dialogue is not long enough for tests based on, e.g., frequency of particles, to be conclusive.

15. Objections have been made to the statements about Sparta and Persia; they certainly fit the early fourth century better than the dramatic date, but that is not an argument against Platonic authorship. (See Friedländer [2], 11–14, 52–56.) Vlastos claims that it is inconsistent with Plato's dignified portrayal of Zeno as a philosopher in the *Parmenides* to portray him as a sophist teaching for pay (119a1–6); this seems at best inconclusive. He claims that the figure of 100 minae is unrealistically high; but surely the large figure is put in, like the 150 minae at *Hippias Major* 282d–e, to shock the audience, not to indicate an average charge. Vlastos also contrasts the favorable picture of the education of the Persian crown prince (121c–122a) with the hostile picture of Cyrus' education at *Laws* 694c–695b; but this misses, I think, the ironical character of the "Persian speech" (see below, n. 22).

16. On the history of claims *pro* and *con* authenticity, see Heidel; Friedländer (2) and (4), 2:348–349, n.1; most recently, Thesleff, 215–217.

Self-knowledge 115

win. Some of the ideas and arguments in the dialogue have clear analogues in other Platonic works.[17] These are taken to show that the dialogue is, in Heidel's words, "too Platonic" to be Plato's. But it also contains passages of great originality whch have no analogue in any other dialogue; and these are taken, often by the very same scholars, to show that the dialogue is too un-Platonic to be Plato's. *Both* its similarities to, *and* its differences from, the rest of the Platonic corpus show that it is not authentic. With these rules, proving inauthenticity is naturally an easy game. Once the rules are made fair, virtually all of the case for inauthenticity drops away. But the confused objections often conceal a serious worry. The *Alcibiades* has been thought by many to be philosophically a mess; it seems to consist of a string of unconnected parts with no obvious directing theme. This paper is intended as the beginning of an attempt to trace such a theme in the concept of self-knowledge.

When a work is not standardly in the canon, we do find when we read it that it may not, initially, sound Platonic because our ideas of what is "Platonic" come from reading the accepted canon. The circularity here is obvious enough, but the circle takes some breaking into.[18] The best way to begin is, I think, to assume, heuristically, that the *Alcibiades* and *Lovers* are by Plato, and see what that achieves. If it proves illuminating about themes in the Platonic corpus, as I shall argue it does, then that is a reason for taking seriously Plato's authorship of these works. For it is only by a series of such attempts, and critical appraisals of them, that we can make progress in understanding a major work like the *Alcibiades*; and then and not before is the time to judge whether it is "worthy" of Plato.

The *Alcibiades* begins with a dramatic confrontation between Socrates and the twenty-year-old Alcibiades (123d) as he is about to

---

17. The appeal to *technē* or skill for cognitive respectability is widespread enough. Connections have always been noted with the discussion of self-knowledge in the *Charmides*, which will be picked up below; though in fact the *Charmides'* discussion as a whole moves in a rather different direction. Alcibiades' claim that he picked up morality the way he picked up his native language (110c–111a) recalls *Protagoras* 327e–328a. The argument about justice and advantage recalls the *Gorgias*; see n. 21. Common also in the early dialogues are Socrates' insistence on the importance of question and answer for committing the interlocutor to a serious and truthful answer (112d–113b); his claim that the worst kind of ignorance is pretension to knowledge (117b–118c); and his insistence on the teachability of knowledge (and thus of virtue if virtue is knowledge) with Pericles as counterexample (118d–e; cf. *Protagoras* 319e–320b).

18. Paul Woodruff has recently done just this for the *Hippias Major*, in his excellent translation and commentary. He deals thoroughly with the opponents of the dialogue's authenticity, while realizing that the best approach is simply to read the dialogue philosophically. His work is a model of what I hope to do some day for the *Alcibiades*.

come forward in public to begin a political career (105a–b). In a way familiar from many early dialogues, Socrates takes down his arrogance by showing him that he is proposing to teach others on matters about which he is himself grossly ignorant. For (106c–107a) the subjects he has learned in school, and so does know about, are not relevant to politics, and (107b–108e) on specific matters what people need is not his amateur view but that of the expert. Alcibiades thinks that he can direct the Athenians on what is generally "better"; Socrates pushes him into equating "better" with "juster,"[19] and then shows him that he has no real idea of what justice and injustice are (109e–113c). His confidence in the intuitive judgments he has picked up from his environment is unfounded; for people disagree over what is just, and Alcibiades is unequipped with any kind of deeper account that would enable him to resolve these disagreements.[20] Alcibiades tries to shrug off the problem (113a) by charging that people never do in fact deliberate about what is just or not (they find that obvious) but rather about what is prudent or profitable. After unkindly pointing out that Alcibiades is in the same state over prudence as he was over justice (113d–114b) Socrates shows him, in an argument analogous to one in the *Gorgias*,[21] that he cannot sustain his commonsense belief that justice differs from expediency (114b–116e). Alcibiades is shaken into admitting that he is ignorant while falsely assuming knowledge (116e–119a), but he cheers himself with the thought that at least his ignorance is no worse than that of the other politicians at Athens, and that he is thus bound to succeed because his natural advantages are so much greater than theirs (119b). Socrates in a long speech sharply urges him to measure himself rather against the rulers of Sparta and Persia, whose resources and power he details

---

19. Cf. 108d–109c. In spite of frequent use of "calling" (or "naming"—ὀνομάζειν) it is clear that Plato is not concerned with questions of meaning, but with what the correct reference is; so Socrates' move here is not outrageous: it merely clarifies what Alcibiades confusedly had in mind.

20. Socrates' objection here is weakly based. He moves straight from conflict between intuitions to the conclusion that intuitions should be distrusted, claiming (111b) that "those who know" should agree and not dispute, without considering the questions of whether ethical dispute either can or should be resolved. The argument here does not take the familiar form of claiming that ethical disagreement will lead to our calling the same thing or action both F and –F, although this form of argument is used later (115b–c).

21. The argument makes crucial use of the concepts of καλόν / αἰσχρόν. Alcibiades is forced to admit that all δίκαια actions are καλά (without resistance, 115a) and then that all καλά actions are ἀγαθά (with resistance, 115a–116a). But ἀγαθά things are expedient (taken as obvious, 116d). Compare the argument against Polus in the *Gorgias* at 474 c ff. where Socrates forces an unwilling Polus to admit that what is καλόν / αἰσχρόν is ἀγαθόν / κακόν.

(119c–124b). At this point Alcibiades finally collapses, admitting that Socrates is right; and for the rest of the dialogue they cooperate in helping Alcibiades "take care" (ἐπιμελεῖν) in improving his sorry state.

So far we have had a pattern familiar in other early dialogues; but there are some striking features peculiar to the *Alcibiades*. Firstly, why is Alcibiades faulted for his ignorance of what happens in Sparta and Persia? Socrates has shown, as usual, that his interlocutor is "ignorant" in that he lacks any intellectual backing for his intuitive judgments on important matters; even if they are right he cannot defend them because he cannot articulate adequate reasons for them. This is "ignorance" of a rather special kind; it has nothing in common with everyday ignorance of fact, and Socrates is not usually interested in whether his interlocutors are well informed.[22]

Secondly, once Alcibiades admits that he needs to learn, we return abruptly to the theme of politics, and an unexpected dilemma is thrust on us (124d–127d). Alcibiades desires excellence in "good counsel," εὐβουλία, the general ability to organize and manage one's own and others' affairs. To have this requires knowing what is the basis for good government and good organization in a state. He makes the promising suggestion that this is friendship, φιλία, where by this is understood unanimity and accord—ὁμονοία—among the citizens;[23] and he accepts that this will come about when all citizens "do their own"—τὰ αὑτῶν πράττουσι (127b).[24] Surprisingly, Socrates retorts that these two notions are actually in conflict: for insofar as people mind *their own* concerns they have no basis for agreement with others. Alcibiades reluctantly agrees and his suggestion founders; but the reader is left wondering why. Socrates' claim here is based on an assumption that his own examples clearly show to be wrong: that knowing about your own concerns *excludes* knowing enough about others'

---

22. We should of course not be too naively literal about Socrates' speech. It idealizes the Spartan and Persian royal education in a way which is, knowingly and ironically, not "true to the facts," and it is plausible that we have here a semiserious sketch of the education of an ideal philosopher-ruler. Nonetheless, what it brings home to Alcibiades is his ignorance of a certain kind of fact, as opposed to "Socratic ignorance," i.e., inability to give a reasoned defence of his intuitive views.

23. Aristotle takes this suggestion seriously in his discussions of φιλία, in a way suggesting that he had read the *Alcibiades* (*EN* 1167a22–b16). If the *Magna Moralia* is by Aristotle, we have another indication, since 1213a16–24 are a clear reference to the famous "mirror" passage at the end of the dialogue.

24. Cf. *Charmides*, 161b, where the suggestion clearly comes from Critias. As in the *Alcibiades*, the interpretation given of it seems deliberately trivial, and the objections inconclusive. Plato clearly found the current uses made of the idea unsatisfactory, but not the idea itself, which rises to prominence in the *Republic* as part of Plato's own (highly theoretical and redefined) account of the basic virtues of soul and state.

to reach agreement on shared issues. Unanimity between husband and wife, for example, is impossible, and hence friendship, since women's tasks have nothing in common with men's. This is pessimistic even for ancient Athens; the conclusion is in fact clearly outrageous, and it is hard to believe that Socrates is actually committed to it. With hindsight, we cannot help thinking of the way in which social harmony and "doing one's own" fit together in the *Republic*; but we cannot safely read in any of those thoughts here. Rather, it is best to take Socrates' claim here not as conclusive, but as marking a demand for more investigation by Alcibiades (and possibly also by Socrates himself; we cannot determine) of the two notions of political harmony and of "doing one's own" and their relationship. As such, the demand is reasonable, but what is it doing here?

Thirdly, when in the last section of the dialogue Alcibiades is finally told positively how to go about "caring for himself" he is given the surprising suggestion that he should seek self-knowledge; he should obey Apollo's command, "know yourself" (129a). The theme of self-knowledge is developed in ways to which we shall return, but for the moment we should note that it does not seem at all clear why *self*-knowledge should be the answer to Alcibiades' problems. He, and we, might well agree that by now he has been shown to be pretty ignorant; but, given what we have seen in the first, negative part of the dialogue, it would seem more appropriate for him to get clearer about justice and prudence through practicing Socratic dialectic—not to mention learning some Spartan and Persian history. How can *self*-knowledge help?

These three puzzling features have played a large role in nineteenth- and twentieth-century scholars' unwillingness to treat the *Alcibiades* as Platonic. They are troublesome both individually and in their apparent lack of internal connection; the dialogue seems to fall apart into a series of unconnected episodes. In fact, it is self-knowledge that provides the key and thus enables us to read the dialogue as having a higher degree of philosophical unity than is often thought. But self-knowledge is not an intuitively clear notion, and it may be helpful to come at it first through the claim, twice made in the dialogue, that self-knowledge is the virtue of *sōphrosunē* (131b, 133c). Given this (unargued) claim, reflection on *sōphrosunē* may help us understand the role of self-knowledge.

Sōphrosunē is a quality recognized by the Greeks as a virtue, and indeed after Plato's *Republic* standardly treated as one of the "four cardinal virtues," but it is notoriously difficult for us to specify, in our terms, just what this virtue *is*. It is often translated "temperance" or "moderation," but these capture only one aspect of the virtue; it is sometimes suggested that "soundness of mind" would be more appropriate.[25] Helen North's great study makes it clear that, at least up to the time of Plato, *sōphrosunē* was thought of as a single quality covering an area which we would divide between two rather different concepts. One is that of self-knowledge; the other, that of self-*control*, understood as control of one's desires, ability to harness or suppress one's immediate impulses in the service of one's reasoned plans. It seems clear that in ordinary speech "*sōphrosunē*" was used in a way that is bound to seem to us indeterminate: it was used of what we would call self-knowledge and of what we would call self-control without much reflection on what gave the concept its unity. (Indeed this problem appears to have troubled the Greeks rather little: it is we who have the problem articulating to ourselves the possible basis for regarding this concept as a unified one.)

Philosophers who use the concept in a more reflective way tend to stress one or other aspect—self-control or self-knowledge—more, and it seems clear that ordinary usage could accommodate this without strain.[26] Indeed, we can see Plato himself, in different contexts, developing both these aspects. Thus in the *Gorgias* (491d) Socrates is asked to explain the concept of "ruling oneself" and answers, "Nothing fancy—just what most people mean: being *sōphrōn* and in control of oneself, ruling the pleasures and desires in oneself."[27] However, Plato also says in the *Timaeus* (72a) that "it is a good saying, and an old one, that doing and knowing your own matters and yourself befits only the *sōphrōn*"; and in the *Sophist* we find quite casually (230d) the statement that "the best and most *sōphrōn* state is to be purged of ignorance by elenchus."[28] Thus both self-control and self-knowledge are intuitively acceptable interpretations of *sōphrosunē*, and both are available to a philosopher trying to analyze the concept. It is not, then, shocking or outlandish to find, as we do find in the *Alcibiades* (131b,

---

25. As by C. Taylor: see pp. 85–86, 121–124. He stresses that self-control is not to the fore in the *Protagoras* and *Charmides*, but does not stress the self-knowledge aspect.

26. Heraclitus stresses self-knowledge (this is further discussed below); Democritus, on the other hand, is interested only in the aspect of self-control and moderation.

27. In the *Republic*, 430e–431b, this order of exposition is reversed: *sōphrosunē* is explained *via* the notion of self-control. But here we have Plato's own highly theoretical account, not an appeal to common sense.

28. Here I diverge from North, who sees a progression in Plato from *sōphrosunē* as self-knowledge to *sōphrosunē* as self-control, a progression she characterizes as a move from Socratic to Platonic ideas. She does not take account of the difficulty raised for this interpretation by the fact that we find uncompromising conjunctions of *sōphrosunē* and self-knowledge in late dialogues. I suggest that Plato did not have to choose one exclusively and later change his mind in favor of the other.

133c), *Lovers* (138a), and *Charmides* (164c–165b) the suggestion casually thrown out that *sōphrosunē* is self-knowledge; it is just as intuitively available an interpretation of *sōphrosunē* as is self-control. (By the time of Aristotle's *Nicomachean Ethics*, this is obviously no longer the case.)

Still, we cannot progress until we look more closely at two points: What is the status of the claim that self-knowledge is *sōphrosunē* (and, of course, the claim that *sōphrosunē* is self-knowledge)? And what kind of self-knowledge is in question here?

The claim that self-knowledge is *sōphrosunē* is, I think, exactly what it seems to be: a statement of identity. (And thus it does not differ from the claim that *sōphrosunē* is self-knowledge.) It is just like other implausible-sounding identity claims in the early dialogues, like the claim that all the virtues are really one: it is not a claim about identity of meaning, since Plato is perfectly aware that as we use words, "self-knowledge" and "*sōphrosunē*" have some divergent uses, so that the claim that self-knowledge is *sōphrosunē* sounds paradoxical. Despite this, Plato believes that it is one and the same item to which these words correctly refer; in the present case it will simply be a state of the agent. The state that makes it true that an agent has the major virtue of *sōphrosunē* will simply be that state of him which is his having self-knowledge. This does not deny the existence, or the relevance, of self-control, but it does make it secondary in one's possession of the virtue; for it will not be what the virtue is, but will be a consequence of having it. The actions we call self-controlled are brought about by, and explained by, the virtue of *sōphrosunē*, but they are not what that virtue consists in; what it is, is self-knowledge. It is very natural for us to put this in terms of essence: the Socratic view will then be that *sōphrosunē* is essentially self-knowledge, while self-control will be among the manifestations in action of this state, but will not be what the state essentially is.[29] It is easy to see why the interpretation of *sōphrosunē* as self-knowledge is more congenial to Socrates (and indeed to other intellectuals like Critias) than is its interpretation as self-control. For, once one goes beyond just accepting as a blank fact the way that *sōphrosunē* covers both these phenomena and starts asking which of them is primary (which it is that *sōphrosunē really* is) then it will seem much more plausible to see self-control as a phenomenon of behavior which can be explained by a state of the agent that is self-knowledge,

---

29. It might be objected that, while this may be the status which the claim has *for Socrates*, surely his interlocutors would not agree? However, while they might not have in mind the explicitly reflective thought that "*sōphrosunē* is self-knowledge" is an identity statement, nonetheless, they would not need much prodding to accept this as a true account of what they do accept, namely that self-knowledge is part of the nature of *sōphrosunē* in a way that self-control is not. (I sketch briefly why a moderately reflective person would be ready to accept this.)

than it will be to see self-knowledge as a phenomenon of behavior explicable by a state of the agent that is self-control.[30] Why this should be so, is a deep and puzzling fact, and one might, on a deep level, query it (why *should* knowledge seem to be more of the essence of a virtue than behavior?) but it is a move that readily recommends itself; and the Socratic claim that *sōphrosunē* is self-knowledge can easily be seen as the kind of claim a reflective person would readily make, once the question arose of making sense of the uses of "*sōphrosunē*."

But what is this self-knowledge? One form it does *not* take is the modern concern with self-knowledge as knowledge of the individual personality. We are inclined to make this the paradigm of self-knowledge, and hence to think that deeper knowledge of oneself is to be attained by means like thinking over one's past actions or by techniques like psychoanalysis. But it is clear that in the ancient world the individual personality was not, in this connection, the relevant self to know.[31] What is relevant is knowing myself in the sense of knowing my place in society, knowing who I am and where I stand in relation to others.[32] The self-knowledge that is *sōphrosunē* has nothing to do with my subconscious and everything to do with what F. H. Bradley called "my station and its duties." We can see this quite clearly in the link made, by both Alcibiades in the *Alcibiades* and Critias in the *Charmides*, between *sōphrosunē* and each person's "doing their own"—τὰ αὐτῶν πράττειν. The connection is clear: a proper conception of who and what I am is at the same time a proper conception of my station and its duties, of what I may and may not appropriately do. As Xenophon puts it (*Memorabilia* IV 11 26–29), those who know themselves know what is suitable (ἐπιτήδειον) for themselves, and discern what they can and cannot do. Lack of self-knowledge thus exposes a person to the social penalties of ridicule and contempt (cf. Plato *Philebus*, 48c–49c). As in Bradley, knowledge of who I am already presupposes a correct appraisal of my relations to others. And, again as in Bradley, there are conservative implications: self-knowledge is conceived of as revealing, not an excitingly indeterminate set of possibilities but an already specified social role. It is no accident that *sōphrosunē* tends to appear, in the words of a commentator on the *Charmides*, as "the vir-

---

30. In the *Republic* (430e–431b) Plato finds difficulty in characterizing self-control as a single state of an agent.

31. Cf. C. Gill's forthcoming book on character and personality in the ancient world, especially ch. 1 on the individualistic sense of "personality."

32. Cf. Wilkins, chs. 2, 3, and 4. Interesting here is Xenophon, *Memorabilia*, IV 11, 24ff—indeed in many ways the whole of IV, 11 can be seen as a parallel treatment, though a much more superficial one, of the theme of the *Alcibiades*: Socrates gets a young man to follow him towards the study of philosophy by showing him the lack of self-knowledge which lies at the basis of his ignorance of politics.

tue of old age, of women, and indeed of all who behave in a way appropriate to their station in life."[33] The conservative implications are not always to the fore, but the root idea is nearly always visible: self-knowledge is knowledge of oneself in relation to others. Thus, a correct conception of myself is far from being revealed by scrutiny of my individual personality, for it requires a correct conception of my role in society, among others, and what this is, does not depend entirely on me—it is an objective matter. As we shall see, this is the aspect of the ordinary notion that Plato takes up and which we find him trying to give a deeper account of: the idea that my knowledge of myself is not simply up to me in the way I ordinarily might assume, but depends on knowledge that takes me beyond interest in my individual personality. This idea turns out to have a deep appeal for Plato.

Self-knowledge, then, is an objective rather than a personal and subjective matter. And it is readily taken to be the essence of the major virtue of *sōphrosunē*, a virtue that manifests itself in a variety of ways, including self-control. How does all this help us to understand the three striking features of the *Alcibiades* to which I drew attention, and their mutual connections?

Firstly, why is Alcibiades faulted not only for his "Socratic ignorance" of justice and prudence, but also for his common or garden ignorance of Sparta and Persia? We should note that he is not faulted for any old ignorance here: he is faulted for ignorance of what is relevant to his conception of his present self and his future ambitions. Socrates earlier (105b–c) reminded him of his hopes of conquering all of Greece and Persia; now he points out that he is going back on those ambitions if he regards Athenian politicians as his true rivals and fails to be interested in the rulers of Sparta and Persia, who are his true opponents. Socrates rubs the point in by detailing Spartan and Persian wealth and power, but clearly he is not reporting mildly interesting facts, but showing Alcibiades what he ought to know if he is to retain a true notion of himself, his capacities, and his aims. Ignorance of Persia matters to Alcibiades because of what it reveals of his ignorance of himself. That this is the point of the long speech is stated clearly enough at the end (124a–b): "Does it not seem disgraceful that the enemies' womenfolk have a better idea of us than we do about ourselves, as to what we should be (οἵους χρὴ ὄντας) to attack them? My friend, trust me and the Delphic inscription, 'Know yourself':

---

33. Tuckey, p. 6; cf. p. 9. Cf. Taylor, p. 85, who talks of *sōphrosunē* "in the sense of that soundness of mind which makes a man accept his proper role in society and pay due regard to the rights of others." The last clause signals an aspect of *sōphrosunē* which will be stressed below.

these are your rivals, not the ones you think." Alcibiades has, then, been shown to be ignorant of himself, of who and what he really is.[34] It is not surprising that this is the point at which he finally capitulates to Socrates; nor that, at the end of the dialogue, self-knowledge is presented as what he really needs.

What, however, of the fact that as soon as Alcibiades has become convinced of his ignorance of himself and has resolved to do something about it, the discussion is at once apparently side-tracked to a discussion of political agreement and of "doing one's own"? Why not go directly from confession of self-ignorance to the need for self-knowledge? In fact, we are not derailed from the theme of self-knowledge here, as can be seen from a little reflection on the notion of self-knowledge as knowing one's place.

In order to know who I am in the sense of knowing my place—my station and its duties—I need to know what my role is among others, and thus I need to know what their role is with respect to me in order to know what my role is with respect to them. If I am, for instance, a free Athenian citizen, then knowing who I am and what is appropriate for me will involve knowing, among other things, that I may expect certain sorts of deference from slaves but not from free men, and may treat slaves, but not free men, in certain ways: this is knowing my place. But knowing this is just knowing what is due to, and due from, slaves and free citizens; and knowing this is just knowing what is the right, and what the wrong, way, to treat slaves and free citizens. So if I act like a tyrant and treat free citizens as slaves, this will be a failure in self-knowledge insofar as it is a presumptuous failure to know my place among equals; but it will also be a failure to give others their due. And the failure to know my place and the failure to treat others properly are easily, and plausibly, regarded as the *same* failure, as a lack of the *same* knowledge. If self-knowledge is regarded as knowledge of the individual personality, it is easy to see how one might have it independently of having a sense of justice. But where self-knowledge is thought of as knowing one's place, one cannot know one's self without also thereby knowing what is due to and from others; in any given case I cannot separate knowledge of what is due to me from knowledge of what is due to others.

So it can easily come to seem natural to regard the virtue of *sōphrosunē*, interpreted as rightly understanding one's place, as being the same virtue as the virtue of justice, giving others what is due to them.

---

34. The speech is therefore far from being a digression loaded down with irrelevant learning, as is sometimes claimed—e.g., by Dönt (2), who ignores the clear reference to self-knowledge at the end of the speech.

So Alcibiades has not been side-tracked. He is ignorant of himself, and also ignorant of how rightly to adjust the claims of others. These are not unrelated because they are, as we have seen, the *same* failure. Socrates is merely making explicit the fact that Alcibiades' ignorance of himself brings with it ignorance of how others should be treated, and a tendency to repeat slogans without understanding them. Further, it is clearly indicated that in acquiring self-knowledge he will thereby acquire knowledge of the due claims of others; at the end of the dialogue, after accepting the lengthy recommendation to seek self-knowledge, he declares that he will from now on practice justice (135e); it goes without saying that in knowing who he truly is he will thereby know how to treat others properly.[35]

In the *Alcibiades* Socrates does not say outright that *sōphrosunē* is justice. (He could be said to imply as much, though, when he claims at 133e that ignorance of self implies ignorance of one's concerns, that this implies ignorance of others' concerns, and that this in turn implies ignorance of political concerns.) In the *Lovers* we do find, at 137b–139a, a brief but clear and definite statement of the positive claim, that *sōphrosunē*, thought of as being essentially self-knowledge, is the same as justice.

The passage comes after the main discussion in the *Lovers*, and has the character of an appendix to the main argument. Perhaps it puts its claims too high to call it an *argument*: despite the frequent inferential particles, what we find is a series of unargued claims. But what the passage lacks in argumentative force it gains as a witness of the intuitive acceptability of ideas that may not seem as obvious to us.

Rightly punishing, says Socrates, is one and the same skill as making the objects of punishment (whether horses, dogs, or men) better. In social matters this is justice. Rightly punishing is the same as distinguishing the good from the bad. If you don't know the good from the bad in the case of the kind of thing you yourself are, then you don't know what you yourself are. This ignorance of self is lack of *sōphrosunē*. Self-knowledge, then, is *sōphrosunē*. So the Delphic injunction, "Know yourself," means that you should practice *sōphrosunē* and justice. Since rightly punishing, and distinguishing the good from the

---

35. There are two complications that I pass over here, since they do not affect what I want to claim. (1) Alcibiades is treated throughout not just as a citizen but as a potential *ruler*—hence justice will for him involve *organizing* others' lives. See also notes 36 and 38, and cf. Sprague on Plato's early concern with the philosopher-ruler. (2) Socrates makes further, very extensive claims for the nature of just rule (134c–135c) which are not justified by anything in the dialogue; they need for their justification something like the theory of soul and state in the *Republic*, especially the claim that those weak in reason should be slaves to the reason in others.

bad, are done by the same skill, justice and *sōphrosunē* are the same thing (ταὐτὸν ἄρ' ἐστι καὶ δικαιοσύνη καὶ σωφροσύνη [138b]).[36]

This passage has been one of the main reasons for the athetizing of the *Lovers*: scholars have been scandalized by what they have seen as a farrago of concepts thrown confusedly together.[37] But at this point in the argument it should be clear that the passage, though indeed abrupt, makes good sense: there is a perfectly intelligible connection between *sōphrosunē*, self-knowledge, and justice which makes their abrupt identification here understandable. It is one that emerges also in two passages in the *Charmides* where the social implications of *sōphrosunē* are stressed (171e–172a, 173a–d). If individuals have *sōphrosunē*, we are told, then the social whole, whether household or state, will be well ordered. All will excel in their sphere of competence, and there will be harmony, because no one will try to take over another's.[38] We see here very clearly how and why the idea that *sōphrosunē* is self-knowledge appeals to conservatives like Critias. The just ordering of society is conceived of as simply being a matter of everyone's knowing, and keeping to, their place.[39]

We have found, then, that self-knowledge in the sense relevant to the *Alcibiades*, *Lovers*, and *Charmides* is in an important way at the opposite pole from a concentration on the individual personality and its unique and subjective point of view. Self-knowledge as the essence of *sōphrosunē*, as a knowledge of my place, is the same virtue as justice, the virtue leading me to give others their due. It thus presupposes a correct appreciation of my relations to others and theirs to me. And this is something objective in the sense that to get this knowledge I may have to put in some intellectual effort; it is not paradoxical if I lack it (a conservative like Critias would doubtless say that in a democracy most people lack self-knowledge, because they are wrong about what is and is not due to them), and others can put me right. To the extent that we find these points surprising, we are being tempted to

---

36. As in the *Alcibiades*, Socrates goes on to stress that this is the virtue of the *ruler*, hence various types of ruler and organizer are identified.

37. Cf. Souilhé, p. 108, "Est-ce Platon qui aurait . . . identifié, sans la moindre distinction, sagesse, justice, gouvernement de la maison, gouvernement des cités . . . ? S'il rapprochait dans une même formule les deux termes σωφροσύνη et δικαιοσύνη, il avait soin, du moins, de ne pas les confondre."

38. Again the stress is on *sōphrosunē* as the virtue that *organizes* and directs society rightly; it is made clear at 171e that people will not be allowed to overstep the boundaries of their competence.

39. There is only the most superficial resemblance to Plato's own account of social harmony in the *Republic*; Plato has so redefined the virtues in accordance with his theory of soul and state that what looks like the same language has very different implications.

think that self-knowledge must be knowledge of the individual personality; for about that it is more plausible to think that others cannot (normally) put me right, and that it is a kind of knowledge (normally) immediately present to me in the sense that I do not have to go looking for it. We should not, of course, conclude that the ancients were not interested in this kind of knowledge of one's personality; but it seems clear that they did not take this to be the kind of self-knowledge that could be identified with a virtue, such as *sōphrosunē* is always taken to be. One interesting corollary of this is that *sōphrosunē* conceived of as self-knowledge is not a personal virtue as it is if it is thought of as being essentially self-control; it does not chiefly, or only, benefit myself.[40]

However, even if it can be identified with justice, self-knowledge ought to remain recognizably *self*-knowledge, if it is not to be redefined out of all recognition; and this brings us to the *Alcibiades*' third striking feature: the recommendation at the end of the dialogue that Alcibiades make a start on all his deficiencies by knowing himself. We have been shown that he lacks self-knowledge, and thereby lacks *sōphrosunē*, and thereby lacks justice. At the end, he is told to acquire self-knowledge and thereby *sōphrosunē* and justice, but not in quite the way we expect from what has gone before. Rather, Plato, in one of his most original and interesting passages, develops the notion of self-knowledge in its own right, in a way that has had continuing appeal even to people who fail to notice any of the conceptual connections hitherto assumed between it and *sōphrosunē* and justice. (Indeed, most discussions of this passage take its treatment of self-knowledge in isolation from any connections to either justice or *sōphrosunē*, thereby encouraging the impression that there is no real thematic unity to the dialogue.) *Sōphrosunē*, understood as self-knowledge, is the same virtue as justice; but at the end of the *Alcibiades* it is not *sōphrosunē* or justice that is singled out for special discussion, but self-knowledge; and this points up something of note about the special status that self-knowledge has in this dialogue. As we have seen, *sōphrosunē* and justice can readily be seen as the same virtue with an inner and an outer aspect; but in the *Alcibiades* the inner aspect comes first. Alcibiades will

---

40. Whereas if *sōphrosunē* is conceived of basically as self-*control* then it does look like this kind of "executive" virtue, useful for me because it enables me to carry out my plans and exercise the other virtues; by the time of Aristotle's *Nicomachean Ethics* this is clearly what *sōphrosunē* has become. The *Magna Moralia* stresses the self-contained nature of *sōphrosunē* at 1193b14–5. Cf. North (1), p. 207: "For Aristotle, *sōphrosunē* never means 'moderation in government,' nor does it ever have an organic relation to the State. As the *Rhetoric* reveals, it is hard for Aristotle to conceive of *sōphrosunē* as a social virtue."

come to practice justice by coming to know himself; self-knowledge seems here to be the prior aspect of this two-sided virtue as least in the sense of being the point of entry for someone wanting to be virtuous. It is being shown to lack self-knowledge that stings Alcibiades into losing his arrogance and seeing the need to change; self-knowledge seems to be the road to beginning the practice of justice.

A contrast appears here with Plato's later attitude, in the *Republic*, to the relation of individual and social virtue. The assumption of the *Alcibiades* is that the individual should get straight about himself in order to be right about what is due to others. The just state will be, so to speak, the sum of individuals each of which has properly gone about knowing himself. In the *Republic*, however, we are told that we cannot start by knowing the individual: we cannot understand the individual's nature and virtues without first seeing them written in the "larger letters" of the state.[41] Of the terms in the equation, justice has come to interest Plato a lot more than *sōphrosunē*, and correspondingly his interest in self-knowledge lessens; in the later dialogues we find only a few passing remarks.

Self-knowledge, then, is what unifies the dialogue; and we find in it (and in parts of the *Lovers* and *Charmides*) a connected set of ideas. Self-knowledge is important; it is in fact the essence of the major virtue of *sōphrosunē*. Self-knowledge is knowledge of one's proper place and role: thus, it is also the essence of justice, the virtue of giving others their due. Self-knowledge is thus far from being an interest in my individual personality; it is something objective, something which I might quite well lack, and which it constitutes virtue to have attained.

Dramatically, the young Alcibiades is the perfect subject for Socrates' lesson. We believe that he genuinely wants to be virtuous; and historical hindsight shows how difficult self-knowledge, and thereby *sōphrosunē* and justice, are to obtain. But, Alcibiades apart, I think it is worth showing that this connected set of ideas, or at least a recognizable analogue of it, can be found in Heraclitus.

Plutarch (*adversus Colotem* 20) tells us that Heraclitus said, "I went in search of myself" (fr. 101 DK) and thought that the most divine of the inscriptions at Delphi was the one "Know yourself." We find further interest in self-knowledge in frs. 113, "Thinking ($\phi\rho o\nu\varepsilon\hat{\iota}\nu$) is common to all" and 116, "It belongs to all men to know themselves and *sōphronein*." Heraclitus is not only interested in self-knowledge, he accepts that it may have to be searched for; my self may be hard to find, it may

---

41. The contrast should not be exaggerated, and can be seen as a difference of emphasis; we can plausibly see the *Republic* as taking seriously what is implied by the *Alcibiades*' account of the relation of self-knowledge to justice.

be something I am wrong about. And he accepts that there is at least a close connection between self-knowledge and *sōphrosunē*.[42] Most significant is fr. 112: "*Sōphronein* is the greatest excellence and wisdom, to act and speak what is true, grasping things according to their nature."[43] Here *sōphrosunē* appears as the basic virtue, and also as being wisdom. So it involves not only self-knowledge and thus searching for oneself, but also turns out to be wisdom, which Heraclitus here characterizes as grasping the way things really and truly are by nature. (As we shall see, Plato also makes this connection: self-knowledge is ultimately the highest kind of knowledge that there is.) It is clear enough from other fragments (e.g., 2, 114, 44, 78, 32, 67) that for Heraclitus wisdom consists in a grasp of how things are, which will include, but not stop at, the way they appear to us humans. Wisdom grasps the Logos, the "account" common to everything; we attain wisdom by ceasing to fix attention on what is peculiar to each of us and by coming to grasp what is common to all. This understanding will include knowledge of what is just; for justice is likewise part of what is common to all, and not dependent on any particular or partial point of view. "Speaking with understanding they must hold fast to what is common to all, as a city holds to its laws and even more firmly. For all human laws are nourished by one, the divine one. . . ." (fr. 114) The person who achieves *sōphrosunē* and self-knowledge thus also achieves understanding of what is objectively the case, the Logos or rational basis of the world-order. As Kahn puts it, "For Heracleitus . . . the deepest structure of the self will be recognized as co-extensive with the universe in general and the political community in particular. Men may live as if they had a private world of thinking and planning, but the *logos* of the world order, like the law of the city, is common to all. . . . So true self-knowledge will coincide with knowledge of the cosmic order, and true self-assertion will mean holding fast to what is shared by all."[44]

It would, of course, be foolish to compare Heraclitean fragments at all closely with something as different as a Platonic dialogue, and some large differences are obvious: Heraclitus insists, as Plato here does not, that justice is part of the wider Logos which is the rational structure of the whole universe. (We find such ideas in the *Gorgias* and

42. Heraclitus "is . . . the first writer to make explicit the link that Homer implied between *sōphrosunē* and self-knowledge," North (1), 26.
43. σωφρονεῖν ἀρετὴ μεγίστη καὶ σοφίη, ἀληθέα λέγειν καὶ ποιεῖν κατὰ φύσιν ἐπαίοντας. I agree with Kahn (pp. 120–123) that the syntactical ambiguity should be left unresolved; it is part of Heraclitus' characteristic "linguistic density" (pp. 87–95), as is the difficult notion of "doing what is true" (p. 122).
44. Kahn, p. 14. Cf. also pp. 116–123, 251–252.

most fully in the *Republic*, but not in the *Alcibiades*, though we shall find Plato there introducing the germ of such ideas.) Still, the similarities are striking enough for us to say that, if we accept that Plato wrote the *Alcibiades* and *Lovers* as well as the *Charmides*, we can find, in early Plato, a development of ideas already taken up by Heraclitus. And it is of interest that his treatment of these ideas in his early works is actually closer to Heraclitus than it is to his own treatment of them in the middle dialogues. By the time we get to the *Republic* justice has taken over from *sōphrosunē* as the major virtue. It, not *sōphrosunē*, forms the basis of all the virtues (insofar as it gives both soul and state the structure without which the other virtues cannot develop)[45] and it, not *sōphrosunē*, is the virtue whose development leads to the wisdom that is a grasp of the objective way the world really is.

Of these three dialogues, the *Alcibiades* is the most interesting, because in it we can see Plato developing the notion of self-knowledge in a philosophically ambitious way. We have seen that, in a way surprising to us, self-knowledge has figured as the essence of the virtues of *sōphrosunē* and justice; and that for both Heraclitus and Plato this was possible because self-knowledge, at least insofar as it can be taken to be a virtue, is not thought of as knowledge of what is personal and unique to me, my own personality, but goes beyond this and requires a true conception of how I stand among others, and thus is knowledge that I might lack and others might have. At the end of the *Alcibiades* we find Plato taking a step similar to Heraclitus': he takes self-knowledge to involve not just social facts, but, at the deepest level, facts about objective reality as a whole. What attracts him is clearly the idea that there is a knowledge of myself which is not knowledge of the individual embodied person; knowledge of the "real" or "true" self turns out to be very different from what one intuitively thinks of as knowledge of self. Plato takes to its limit the idea of the "true self" implicit in the idea that self-knowledge is knowledge of how one stands among others, and thus involves a true conception of the world in which one lives.

As often, Plato begins by moving attention from the externals of action to the agent's inner state, and does this in terms of body and soul (128a ff). When Socrates and Alcibiades are conversing, he insists, the communication is between not their bodies but their souls; so the true Alcibiades, the self he should come to know, is not his body but his soul. (And, he adds, he is Alcibiades' only true lover, because he loves

---

45. The *Gorgias* seems transitional here. *Sōphrosunē* does appear, at 506–507, as the basic virtue, and it plays a structural role, but (1) it here appears as self-control, rather than self-knowledge, and (2) perhaps, as a result, it is not at all clear how it does or can form the cognitive basis of all the virtues.

his soul and not his perishable body. Here again is a theme found in Heraclitus, who stresses the soul [frs. 107, 45, 115, 118] and says that corpses, the mere body without the soul, should just be flung out [fr. 96].)

In itself, the idea that I am my soul rather than my body can be interpreted in different ways, not all of which involve downgrading the body; it all depends on what the soul/body relation is taken to be. Here we find, without warning, a sharply dualist conception. A person, Socrates says, is not his body, because he *uses* his body, as a craftsman uses his tools.[46] What uses, and so rules, the body can only be the soul. The person therefore is the soul. The body cannot take any part in ruling itself, so the person cannot be soul-and-body in any combination (129b–130c). The person is therefore the soul alone; Alcibiades in seeking to know himself must seek to know only his soul, not his body.

This drastic conclusion is not forced on us by the reflection that I am not my body; it is forced on us by the assumption that the soul/body relation ("using" or "ruling") relates things of totally distinct kinds: only souls can "rule," only bodies can be "ruled." Plato offers no argument for this counter-intuitive assumption. It is worth noting that when Cicero echoes this passage in the *Tusculan Disputations*, he does so without taking over the drastic conclusion, staying fairly open as to what the soul/body relation is.

Why does Plato insist that I am only my soul, that the body plays no part at all in what I am? In the *Alcibiades* this is not defended. (And it may be that Plato saw no need for defense; but I doubt this. In the *Phaedo* he assumes without argument that there are souls, but feels the need to argue at length that they are different in kind from bodies.) But although he has no good argument here, Plato does have a reason for insisting that only the soul, and not the body, is the self. For, as we have seen, Plato is here developing the implications for the self of the idea that self-knowledge is something objective, something which goes beyond what is individual and personal. It is only to be expected that the real self, the self I know when I have self-knowledge, should turn out not to be in any intuitive sense individual or peculiar to me. My body is certainly individual to me; but if my body is no part of what I really am, perhaps what I really am—my real self—is not individual to me in the way that my body is. Perhaps my

---

46. Thus the body is external to the "real" self; cf. the *Gorgias* myth where bodies are presented as external to souls the way clothes are external to bodies (523c–525a). In the *Alcibiades* the idea is introduced awkwardly at 129b–c: Socrates is talking; talking is using speech; using in general implies that user and thing used are distinct.

real self, far from being my individual embodied personality, is something that does not differ among embodied individuals. Greek does not have words that correspond at all closely to our "personal" and "impersonal," but it is tempting to see in Plato's concern to exclude the body from the real self, a concern to show that the real self is impersonal. Such a concern is not explicitly voiced here; but there are two very broad hints that this is what is in Plato's mind. For Socrates says (130 c–d) that the present discussion is only provisional, and that if it were followed through rigorously it would tell us about what he calls "the self itself," αὐτὸ τὸ αὐτό (129b, 130c–d). What the "self-itself" is, is obscure and some scholars find here a reference to the "Theory" of Forms, because Plato often refers to Forms by the phrase αὐτὸ τὸ . . . , but his use of the phrase is not limited to Forms, and any reference here to the "theory" would be wildly out of place. I incline to think that the Neoplatonists were more on the right lines in finding here a reference to a "rational soul" which is the true self and is not individual to each person.[47] My true self will not just be my soul (which, for all that has actually been shown in the passage might be individual to me) but soul conceived of impersonally, a "self-itself" or impersonal self which, like a Form, is the same in all of its instances.[48] Neoplatonist interpretation of Plato can be notoriously overimaginative, but here it is rather plausible that Plato is pointing towards the idea that my true self is not just my soul but impersonal soul: my real self, if you like, is just the self-itself, and is not *my* self in any intuitive sense at all, since it is just as much your real self as mine.

Plato points to this idea rather unmistakably; but he does not spell it out for us. But in any case the impersonality of the true self emerges anyway from the following passage, the most famous in the dialogue. An eye, to see itself, needs a mirror and can find one in another eye, especially its "best part," the pupil.[49] So a soul knows itself by "looking into" another soul, especially its "best part," wisdom. This is the most divine part of the soul, and a person looking at it will recognize all that is divine, which is God and wisdom,[50] and this is the truest knowledge of self (132d–133c). There follow a few lines which reinforce this

---

47. Cf. Olympiodorus, 203–204 for Proclus' and Damascius' views (similar on the relevant point) and 209–210 for his own: "αὐτὸ τὸ αὐτό" καλεῖ τὴν λογικὴν ψυχὴν τὴν μὴ χρωμένην ὀργάνῳ τῷ σώματι ἢ τῷ ἐν σώματι ζῆν, οἷον τὸν καθαρτικὸν ἢ τὸν θεωρητικόν · "αὐτό" δὲ τὴν λογικὴν ψυχὴν τὴν προσχρωμένην ὀργάνῳ τοῖς πάθεσι καὶ τῷ σώματι, τούτεστι τὴν πολιτικὴν ψυχήν.

48. Allen's interpretation seems to me basically right, except that he is too quick to infer that an argument for something with Form-like characteristics is a reference to a "theory" of Forms, and also to infer that Forms are universals.

49. On complications on this point, see Brunschwig.

50. The words "God and wisdom" have been suspected (Olympiodorus omits them)

point: the best mirror is God, and looking at God is the truest knowledge of self. These lines have been suspected, and with good reason; for one thing, they do not occur in any of our manuscript traditions, turn up only in extended quotations of the passage by Eusebius and Stobaeus, and contain several oddities.[51] But whether they are by Plato or not, they merely underline what is there already: knowing one's real self is knowing God, where God is of course not a person, but is just what is ultimately real, however that is to be otherwise characterized. This is not, for a Greek, a far-fetched idea; indeed, it too figures in Heraclitus, who identifies the objective *logos* that wisdom grasps with God, though he is careful to detach this from popular religion (frs. 32, 67).

Plato's image of the eye mirrored in another eye is a very striking one, so striking that it is hard not to surrender to its intuitive appeal rather than pressing for a satisfactory interpretation of it.[52] In fact, like most of Plato's famous images, it contains several difficulties. The eye needs another *eye*, something like itself; if we ask what corresponds to this in the case of knowledge, the obvious answer is the give-and-take of dialectic, the testing of one's beliefs by others which Plato always finds so crucial. But what the other eye does is to mirror: it gives back what is already there; mirroring looks like an image for the puzzling aspect of self-knowledge which we might call its reflexivity,

---

and some scholars emend θεόν to θεάν, to keep God out of our souls; but this is both unwarranted and ludicrous.

51. In Stobaeus the passage begins as well as ends with "And we agreed that knowing oneself was *sophrosune*"; and if this is a genuine passage, and this the original version, we can see how the whole chunk could drop out by dittography. But it could equally well signal a clumsy insertion at some point. Some scholars, e.g., Dönt (1), Wiggers, claim that 134d5 refers back to this passage, but this is not compelling. The passage twice contains the word ἐνόπτρον, not otherwise found in Plato, who in his frequent references to mirrors always uses κάτοπτρον. The grammar of Socrates' second long sentence is hard to construe. Further, the suspected passage spoils the metaphor. We were told that to see itself an eye should look at another eye (as seems reasonable in a culture with metal mirrors which would not give as clear a reflection of the eye as another eye would). Analogously, a soul should look at another soul, and *there* see God. But now we are abruptly told that God is a better and clearer mirror, just as there are better mirrors than the eye for an eye. So looking at God is now different from looking at the mirror in another soul. God thus seems to be both outside and inside the soul. It is tempting to see the passage as the work of a late pagan, or Christian writer, concerned to save Plato from the view that God is in our own souls, and hurriedly bringing God in as something external to us. Favrelle concludes that the passage is inauthentic.

52. Contrast the superficially similar image of eyes mirroring eyes at *Phaedrus* 255d–e (though the differences scarcely show, as Dönt (1) supposes, that the *Alcibiades* cannot be by Plato!) In the *Phaedrus* the lover sees the counter-*eros* to his own in his lover's eyes, and his own vision is infected by it, as though he had caught ophthalmia. This tasteless conceit has little in common with the *Alcibiades'* attempt to use mirroring as an image for the gaining of self-knowledge.

the fact that it is a finding-out about something which is already in our possession. Further, neither the eye nor the mirror helps us to understand what is most controversial here; namely the way that self-knowledge, which we pre-philosophically begin by thinking of as knowledge of an individual, turns out to be no such thing. Rather it turns out to be knowledge of the self itself, the precisely nonpersonal self, which is called divine and God because these are, for a Greek, attributes of what is most truly objective. But, difficulties apart, the general direction of this passage and the preceding one is clear enough. Self-knowledge is not of the paradigmatically subjective, the embodied individual; it is of the paradigmatically objective, so that the true self turns out to be God, the ultimate reality.

This line of thought, that my true self is not what it appears to be—personal, subjective, and individual—but is *really* something impersonal, something in which what I think of as my individuality disappears, is a recurring line of thought in philosophy. It is a thought which, in both philosophy of mind and ethical philosophy, we find perennially tempting and perennially repulsive: we seem forced to it by some considerations and forced to reject it by others. It is recognizable in Heraclitus,[53] but it has not, since the last century, been ascribed to Plato because the *Alcibiades* has been doubted or rejected. I myself would find it disappointing if the *Alcibiades* had on other grounds to be rejected, because these thoughts are deep and interesting ones. They are also very difficult, however, and attempts even to state them clearly run into certain persistent and systematic difficulties. The ending of the *Alcibiades* does not develop them; it leaves them at the level of image and metaphor: the eye and the mirror, the divine in the soul. Plato has, we feel, like Heraclitus, left us with sayings which are deep but dark.

Plato's other treatment of self-knowledge, in the *Charmides*, is difficult in a different way: instead of profound hints it gives us tangled arguments with no obvious conclusion. Without doing more than touch on the *Charmides* I should like to suggest how some facts about its structure may prove illuminating about the *Alcibiades*.

53. There are other adumbrations earlier than Plato of the idea that the reason in us is God. Cf. Aristotle, *Protrepticus* fr. B110 Düring, 'ὁ νοῦς γὰρ ἡμῶν ὁ θεός', εἶθ' 'Ἑρμότιμος εἴτ' 'Ἀναξαγόρας εἶπε τοῦτο. The reference, however, may be added by Iamblichus, and possibly Aristotle was quoting a famous tag by Euripides, ὁ νοῦς γὰρ ἡμῶν ἐστιν ἐν ἑκάστῳ θεός (fr. 1018 Nauck²). Connections have been drawn between Euripides and Anaxagoras, cf. *Troades*, 884–886, ὦ γῆς ὄχημα κἀπὶ γῆς ἔχων ἕδραν, ὅστις ποτ' εἶ σύ, δυστόπαστος εἰδέναι, Ζεύς, εἴτ' ἀνάγκη φύσεος εἴτε νοῦς βροτῶν. . . . But interesting as the connections are, Euripides' dramatic purposes have nothing in common with what we know of Anaxagoras' use of νοῦς, and Plato is innovating brilliantly in linking the idea of God as the reason in us with *self*-knowledge.

The *Charmides* begins by discussing and abandoning various unsatisfactory definitions of *sōphrosunē*.[54] Eventually Critias, Socrates' main opponent, says that he is willing to abandon all that has gone before if it is recognized that *sōphrosunē* is self-knowledge in accordance with the Delphic inscription (164c–165b). We expect, then, to find a discussion of self-knowledge. But Critias surprises us by moving at once from knowledge of *oneself* (ἐπιστήμη ἑαυτοῦ) to knowledge of *itself* (ἐπιστήμη ἑαυτῆς); self-knowledge is forthwith identified with knowledge of knowledge. This is not just a casual slip, as 169e makes clear: there Critias says explicitly that just as the person with speed will be speedy, so the person who has knowledge of itself will have knowledge of himself.[55]

This switch has always been a *crux* in the interpretation of the dialogue.[56] Some commentators take the heroic course of holding that there is in fact no connection between these topics; they then have to face the conclusion either that Plato was so unintelligent that he failed to notice this, or that he did notice it but pointlessly went ahead anyway to try to make Critias look foolish. Most commentators think that there is in fact some connection between self-knowledge and knowledge of knowledge, and try to show in various ways how the latter illuminates the former. But there are problems with this: the discussion of knowledge of knowledge develops in some ways which seem to have nothing to do with self-knowledge. For one thing, ἐπιστήμη shifts, at least sometimes, from knowledge in the sense of cognitive state to mean "a body of knowledge" or "a science," and comes to be used in the plural.[57] For another, attention moves to the question of first- and second-order knowledge in general, and so to the question of whether one can have knowledge of *another's* knowledge, not just of one's own. The discussion of knowledge of knowledge has in fact acquired a life of its own, and come to replace the promised discussion of self-knowledge.

---

54. *Sōphrosunē* as self-control does not explicitly appear, but it does appear implicitly, in the immense dramatic stress laid on Socrates' self-control, both in battle before the dialogue opens, and, within the dialogue, when sexually tempted by Charmides' body. Plato seems to be indicating that self-control is involved in *sōphrosunē*, but is not a candidate for being its defining essence.

55. We could make the transition less abrupt by filling in a step: knowledge of myself-knowledge of what I know-knowledge of knowledge-knowledge of itself. But (as Dyson points out) this is to reverse the order of Plato's steps; he considers knowledge of what I know only after the transition has been made and does not seem to be relying on it to make the transition plausible.

56. Cf. Tuckey, 33–37, and Appendices I and III. See also Santas, 119–120 and n. 12; Dyson, 103–106; Witte, 110 n. 58; Martens, 40–45; Ebert, 65–7.

57. 170c; cf. Tuckey, 58–59.

Why does Plato do this? There is, of course, no reason why we must be able to answer this question; but the ending of the *Alcibiades* prompts at least a suggestion. As we have seen, in the *Charmides* Plato retains for self-knowledge much of the role it has in the *Alcibiades* and *Lovers*: it is the basis of *sōphrosunē* and justice, and thus of great importance for virtue. But self-knowledge demands some explication; and Plato may have come to think that there was nothing he could say, apart from hints and metaphor, to explain self-knowledge as knowledge which has for its object the elusive true or real self. In the *Charmides* the quest for the self as object of self-knowledge is replaced by the more manageable and clearly articulable discussion of knowledge that has knowledge as its object.

This is of course speculation, but there is a less speculative way in which the results of the *Charmides* are relevant to the *Alcibiades*. For the *Charmides* contains a battery of arguments designed to show that there is something wrong, and basically so, with the idea of a kind of knowledge that has only knowledge as its object. Most of these arguments are not very good, and we will not go into them here, but they share an assumption that is significant. Socrates brings, in many different guises, the objection that knowledge must have a subject-matter distinct from itself. Knowledge of knowledge peters out because there is no way of interpreting it as knowledge *of* something in the way Socrates requires; and it is clear that the requirement can only be met if knowledge is conceived of as a relation between a subject and a distinct object, existing separately from the knower. This demand on knowledge, that its subject-matter exist separately from the knowing subject, is one which is very visible in the middle dialogues, where the preferred model of knowledge is mathematics, and it is one of the main features of what we mean by "platonism" as a philosophical position. The demand plays a role, though an unobtrusive one, in many of the passages where Plato establishes Forms and mathematical objects as objects of knowledge. Here we find a further reason for the demise of self-knowledge as a central concern for Plato. For the more he thinks of knowledge on the model of something like mathematics, the less he will be able to accept self-knowledge as genuinely being *knowledge*. The self is not the required kind of *distinct* object that knowledge, given this model, requires. The end of the *Charmides* (in part, for other things are going on there too) chronicles Plato's struggles to retain the notion of self-knowledge as a philosophically comprehensible one, and they are losing struggles; every attempt to explain knowledge of self as knowledge that has itself as object fades because Plato, given the way he now thinks of knowledge, can no longer even make philosophical sense of them. And as the notion of self-*knowledge* becomes problematic, it drops out of Plato's major discussions of *sōphrosunē* and loses its role as the basis for all the virtues.

I have suggested that in his early dialogues Plato was more drawn than is commonly thought to ideas that had already interested Heraclitus: *sōphrosunē* is the basic virtue; self-knowledge, properly understood, is knowledge of what is impersonal and is most truly real. This does not, of course, alter the fact that by the time of the middle dialogues, especially the *Republic*, Plato's concerns are what they have traditionally been thought of as being: the basic virtue is justice, the model of knowledge is mathematics. Still, I think that it is of value to recover, and to give due stress to, these earlier ideas for two reasons. One is that they are themselves interesting and have philosophical depth. The other is that the more familiar later ideas now appear, not as mere assumptions—as ideas that, so to speak, merely happened to appeal to Plato—but as responses to earlier thoughts and to the difficulties implicit in working through those thoughts.

BIBLIOGRAPHY

Adam, R. "Ueber Echtheit und Abfassungszeit des platonischen *Alcibiades* 1," *Archiv für Geschichte der Philosophie* 14 (1901): 40–65.

Allen, R. E. "Note on *Alcibiades* 1, 129b1," *American Journal of Philology* 83 (1962): 187–190.

Bluck, R. S. "The Origin of the *Greater Alcibiades*," *Classical Quarterly* NS 3 (1953): 46–52.

Bos, C. A. *Interpretatie, vaderschap en datierung van de Alcibiades Maior,* Culemborg, 1970.

Boyancé, P. "Cicéron et le *Premier Alcibiade*," *Revue des Études Latines* 41 (1963): 210–229.

Brunschwig, J. "Sur quelques emplois d'ὄψις," *Zetesis*, Album for E. de Strycker, 24–39.

Carlini, A. (1) "Studi sul testo della quarta tetralogia platonica," *Studi Italiani di Filologia Classica* 34 (1962): 169–89.

(2) "Alcuni dialoghi pseudo-Platonici e l'Accademia di Arcesilao," *Annali della Scuola Normale Superiore di Pisa,* 31 (1962): 33–63.

Clark, P. M. "The *Greater Alcibiades,*" *Classical Quarterly* NS 5 (1955): 231–240.

Courcelle, P. "Cicéron et le précepte delphique," *Giornale Italiano di Filologia* 21 (1969): 109–120.

Croiset, M. *Platon, oeuvres complètes,* tome 1, Paris 1959, 47–59 (introduction to the *Alcibiades*).

Dillon, J. "Harpocration's *Commentary on Plato*: fragments of a Middle Platonic commentary," *California Studies in Classical Antiquity* 4 (1971): 125–146.

Dönt, E. (1) "'Vorneuplatonisches' im *Grossen Alkibiades,*" *Wiener Studien* 77 (1964): 37–51.

(2) "Die Stellung der Exkurse in den pseudo-platonischen Dialogen," *Wiener Studien* 76 (1963): 27–51.
Dyson, M. "Some problems concerning knowledge in Plato's *Charmides*," *Phronesis* 19 (1974): 102–111.
Ebert, T. *Meinung und Wissen in der Philosophie Platons*: Untersuchungen zum "Charmides," "Menon" and "Staat," Berlin 1974.
Favrelle, G. *Eusèbe de Césarée: La Préparation Évangélique, Livre XI*, tr. and ed., Paris, 1982 (Sources Chrétiennes 292).
Friedländer, P. (1) *Der Grosse Alkibiades*: ein Weg zu Plato. Bonn, 1921.
(2) *Der Grosse Alkibiades*: kritische Erörterungen. Bonn, 1923.
(3) "Socrates enters Rome," *American Journal of Philology* 66 (1945): 337–351.
(4) *Plato*, vols. 1–3, tr. H. Meyerhoff, New York, 1958, 1964, 1969. Vol. 2, 231–243.
Heidel, W. A. *Pseudo-platonica*, Baltimore 1896, reprinted New York, 1976.
Iamblichus. *Fragments of commentaries on Plato's dialogues*, tr. and ed. J. Dillon, Leiden, 1973.
Isnardi, M. "Note al dialogo pseudo-platonico *Anterastae*," *La Parola del Passato* 9 (1954): 137–143.
Kahn, C. H. *The Art and Thought of Heracleitus*, Cambridge, Eng. 1979.
Martens, E. *Das selbstbezügliche Wissen in Platons Charmides*, Munich 1973.
Motte, A. "Pour l'authenticité du *Premier Alcibiade*," *L'antiquité classique* 30 (1961): 5–32.
North, H. (1) *Sophrosune*, Ithaca, 1966.
(2) *From Myth to Icon*, Ithaca, 1979.
Olympiodorus. *Commentary on the First Alcibiades*, ed. L. G. Westerink. Amsterdam, 1956.
Pépin, J. (1) "Que l'homme n'est rien d'autre que son âme: observations sur la tradition du *Premier Alcibiade*," *Revue des Études Grecques* 82 (1969): 56–70.
(2) *Idées grecques sur l'homme et sur dieu*. Paris 1971, part 1.
Proclus. *Commentary on the First Alcibiades*, ed. L. G. Westerink. Amsterdam, 1954.
Commentary on Alcibiades 1, translation and commentary by W. O'Neill. The Hague, 1965.
Santas, G. "Socrates at Work on Virtue and Knowledge in Plato's *Charmides*" in *Exegesis and Argument*, ed. E. Lee, A. Mourelatos, R. Rorty. New York, 1973 (*Phronesis* Supplement 1).
Schleiermacher, F. *Introductions to the dialogues of Plato*, tr. W. Dobson. Cambridge, 1836; reprinted New York, 1973.
Souilhé, J. *Platon: oeuvres complètes*, tome XIII 2ᵉ partie, Paris 1962, 105–112 (introduction to the *Lovers*).
Sprague, R. K. *Plato's Philosopher-King*. South Carolina, 1976.
de Strycker, E. "L'authenticité du premier *Alcibiade*," *Les études classiques* 11 (1942): 135–151, also printed as ch. 13 of Bidez, J, *Eos*, ou Platon et l'Orient. Brussels, 1945, 101–125.
Taylor, C. C. W. *Plato's Protagoras*. Oxford, 1976 (Clarendon Plato Series).
Thesleff, H. *Studies in Platonic chronology*, *Commentationes Humanarum Litterarum*, 70 (Helsinki, 1982): 214–217.
Tuckey, T. G. *Plato's Charmides*, Cambridge, Eng., 1951.
Vlastos, G. "Plato's Testimony concerning Zeno of Elea," *Journal of Hellenic Studies* 95 (1973): 136–72, especially the Appendix (155–161).

Wiggers, R. "Zum grossen *Alcibiades*, 132a–133c," *Philologisches Wochenschrift* 52 (1932): n. 25 col. 700–703.
Wilkins, E. G. *"Know Thyself" in Greek and Latin Literature*. Chicago, 1917; reprinted New York and London, 1979.
Witte, B. *Die Wissenschaft vom Guten und Bösen*: Interpretationen zu Platons *Charmides*. Berlin, 1970.
Woodruff, P. Plato's *Hippias Major*: translation and commentary, Indiana, 1983.

St. Hugh's College, Oxford

6 RATIONAL PRUDENCE IN PLATO'S GORGIAS

NICHOLAS P. WHITE

I would like to offer a new way of reading the *Gorgias*. As it is generally taken, the dialogue seems to claim to prove much more than it possibly can and appears to rely on rhetoric to cover up bad argument. But this is because it has not been read correctly.

One must begin by distinguishing between what Plato believed and what he took himself in a given work to have demonstrated. Mention the *Gorgias* and most readers will think of the theses that one is always made better off by acting justly than by acting unjustly, that doing injustice is worse than suffering it, and that if one does injustice one is made better off by paying just penalty than by going unpunished. All of these are theses about justice. That Plato believed them there is no doubt. That he thought he had supported them to some extent in the *Gorgias* is also clear. But that he thought he had fully demonstrated them there is, I think, false. Instead, I shall try to show, he took himself to have demonstrated important things about another virtue, temperance or *sōphrosunē*, and about what I shall call rational prudence. He thought that these things had to be established before he could prove—as he later tried to do in the *Republic*—his theses about justice. The establishment of these things about rational prudence is what he took the work of the argument of the *Gorgias* to be. They are, moreover, what is philosophically most fruitful in the dialogue.

There are several ideas that will be focused on in what follows. The first and most important is the one just mentioned, that the dialogue firmly purports to prove only certain things about rational prudence and only prepares the way for the proof of the theses about justice that it enunciates. The second idea, companion to the first, is that Plato's main opponent in the dialogue, Callicles, advocates a very extreme position, not merely against justice or against those aspects of temperance that have to do with social morality and one's relations to others, but against any and all restrictions of one's present desires, even those aiming at one's own future well-being. I maintain that only when Plato's opposition is taken in this way do his own claims for his arguments make sense. What he claims to show is that no one is really willing consistently to reject all temperance, in the sense of all rational prudence in the planning of the satisfaction of one's desires (in a very broad sense of "desire"). The third idea to keep in mind, in order to articulate the second one clearly, is the distinction between two different notions of well-being, that of pleasure proper and that of the satisfaction of desire, both of which have played roles in discussions of hedonism and utilitarianism over the last century. Philosophers often confuse them, though Plato, as we shall see, did not. The word "pleasure" is often used loosely to cover either one. I shall argue that in *Gorgias* (unlike the *Protagoras*, among other works), Plato uses that word, and has both Socrates and Callicles use it, in the sense of desire satisfaction. Again, I shall argue, only when this fact is understood do Plato's arguments against Callicles make sense. The fourth leading idea of the interpretation I shall advance is that when Plato argues for the desirability of rational prudence, he is arguing that it is desirable both for a person's well-being, that is, for that person to be well off or to have a life that is good for him, and also for a person to *be* good or excellent, that is, to have virtue. These two aspects of a desirable life are not explicitly distinguished by Plato (as they often are not explicitly distinguished in Greek ethics), but they do have different roles in different arguments in the *Gorgias*.

I

Let us begin by considering Callicles' position. It is crucial to realize that, as he says quite explicitly, he officially rejects any and all forms of temperance, not merely those that have to do with ordinary social morality and justice vis-a-vis others (491d–e, 492c, 493c–d, 494a–b). Of course he *does* reject the aspects of temperance that *are* parts of ordinary morality, as is well known from his espousal of what he thinks of as "natural" justice (482e–484c), and this fact makes commentators think that they have to attend only to these aspects. But the passages just cited show clearly that he extends his rejection of temperance to all other aspects as well, and that his opposition to ordinary morality and the temperance essential to it is simply a corollary of his rejection of temperance in all its forms.[1] Thus, he is not dismissing simply the

1. As Helen F. North remarks, in her *Sophrosyne* (Ithaca, 1966), p. 90, the virtue of *sōphrosynē* can be divided into two types, one serving society, and the other being self-

control or modification of desire that is necessary for giving others their due or getting along with them in some social or cooperative situation. Rather, he makes it abundantly clear that he rejects any and all restrictions that a person might place on the satisfaction of his desires at any time (491e–492a). Socrates of course embarrasses him with the consequences of this rejection, as we shall see, but is able to do so only because the rejection is so sweeping.

Callicles' view grows naturally from the claims that Gorgias makes early in the work and no doubt represent what Plato thought was the natural tendency of the thought and activity of rhetoricians like him. This fact has not always been clear to commentators. For example, Grote says with very uncharacteristic lack of perception that the *Gorgias* dialogue is "almost three dialogues, connected by a loose thread."[2] But the thread is sturdy, and easy to see once one recognizes Callicles' view for what it is. Gorgias has a two-part advertisement for rhetoric as he teaches it: *a*) that skill in rhetoric is an unqualified good for anyone who acquires it, and *b*) that it is so precisely because it gives its possessor the power to obtain *anything that he wants* (448c, 452a, d, 456a, c, 466b, e).[3] Notice that the claim is that rhetoric enables one to satisfy *any* desire *that one happens to have*, not just one's enlightened or informed or prudent or rational or otherwise idealized or selected desires. Part of Gorgias's reason for saying this is that he wants to disclaim responsibility for what his students do with the rhetoric that he teaches them (456c–457c). But it is equally clearly implied that the good that they derive from his teaching is not in any way dependent on their having from him any particular instructions about how to use it. Their capacity to benefit from it comes entirely from themselves, that is, from the wants that they bring with them.

---

interested prudence. Callicles rejects both of these. In *Merit and Responsibility* (Oxford, 1960), A. W. H. Adkins speaks of some of the virtues as "quiet virtues" and some of them as "cooperative virtues." Unfortunately, he does not seem consistently to draw a distinction between these two classifications (p. 36), so as to say clearly that one type of *sōphrosynē* is cooperative and the other type is not (both of them presumably being "quiet"), but the point does come through (pp. 246–247).

2. George Grote, *Plato and the Other Companions of Socrates*, new ed. (London, 1888), 2:317. In his edition of the *Gorgias* (Oxford, 1959), E. R. Dodds, for example, frequently emphasizes Polus' view grows out of Gorgias' view, and Callicles' view grows out of Gorgias', though not in the way discussed here (on Polus, see below, sec. VII).

3. The theme of power ($δύναμις$) and ability ($δύνασθαι$ and cognates), which is at 466b sqq. linked directly to being able to do what one wants, is a kind of leitmotif throughout the dialogue (e.g., 447c2, 449b1, e5, 452e7, 455d7, 456a5, 460a2, 466b6, 483d2, 508a7, 509d–510a, 469e–470a, 468d–3, 513a, 514a, 522c, 525d, 526d–e). The theme of wanting and desire is sounded at the start of the work ($βούλεσθαι$, 447b3, 7, c1; $ἐπιθυμεῖν$, b4; $ἐθέλειν$, 69; $δοκεῖ$, b2, in the same sense in which it is prominent at 466e2 in contrast with $βούλεσθαι$).

After Polus has developed Gorgias' idea to a certain point, beyond which he is unwilling to advocate it consistently (482d), Callicles pursues it by trying to develop the connection between a) and b) that is central to Gorgias' advertisement: that something can be an unqualified good precisely because it enables the satisfaction of whatever desire one happens to have. Callicles takes the consequence of this notion to be that any restriction of a desire must be inimical to one's good. Hence his opposition to temperance.

As North has shown, rejection of the desirability of temperance is not confined to Plato's Callicles.[4] Though traditionally *sōphrosunē* had been regarded as a virtue and a desirable trait, there was in the fifth century a trend in the other direction. In Euripides and Aristophanes, for example, we see signs of a rejection of temperance much like that by Callicles, and it seems evident, as North says, that it was this trend that Plato was attacking in the *Gorgias*.[5] Not surprisingly, he gave the trend a fuller and clearer articulation than we see in any other writing of the time, but the basic idea was not one that he made up simply to attack, or to use in attacking rhetoricians like Gorgias.

II

Let us now turn to the way in which the notion of satisfaction of desire figures in Callicles' view. To begin with, we may look at a contrast, made visible in modern discussions of utilitarianism and associated issues in economics, between two notions of well-being. One is a notion close to that of satisfaction of desire. It is contrasted with an older notion, employed by Mill and Sidgwick, of quantity of pleasure or (in a broadly hedonistic sense) happiness.[6] Under that notion, one's well-being is measured as the net sum of one's pleasure over time, with pain counted as negative pleasure. It is crucial on this conception that one be thought to be able to add the quantity of pleasure experienced over one period of time to the quantity experienced over another.

---

4. See North, "A Period of Opposition to *Sophrosyne* in Greek Thought," *Transactions of the American Philological Association*, 78 (1947): 1–17, and *Sophrosyne*, chs. 2–3, and Adkins, pp. 246–247. Surprisingly, *sōphrosunē* is almost totally ignored by E. R. Dodds, *The Greeks and the Irrational* (Berkeley, 1951), and is likewise insufficiently attended to in his commentary on the *Gorgias*.

5. North, *Sophrosyne*, pp. 159–165, as well as *From Myth to Icon* (Ithaca, 1979), pp. 105–106.

6. For a discussion of these ideas in the development of utilitarianism, see Richard B. Brandt, "Two Concepts of Utility," Harlan B. Miller and William H. Williams, eds., *The Limits of Utilitarianism* (Minneapolis, 1982), pp. 169–185; and Allan Gibbard, "Interpersonal Comparisons: Preference, Good, and the Intrinsic Reward of a Life," J. Elster and

Thus, given a measurement of quantities of pleasure experienced over certain relatively short periods, the quantity experienced over long periods, even a whole lifetime, becomes a well-defined notion and can be argued to represent one's degree of well-being over whatever period. It is easy to see that in the later part of the *Protagoras* (348c–362a) Plato is operating with a notion of pleasure like this (see esp. 355e–357b). Quantities of pleasure, it is assumed, can be added to and subtracted from each other, regardless of the times at which they are experienced (356a–b), and their sum is an objectively determinable quantity, not relative to its appearance from the point of view from which it is calculated or judged (356d–357a).

The other notion of well-being that figures in these discussions is that of preference satisfaction. It differs from the ordinary notion of desire satisfaction in two main ways. First, "satisfaction" here is not taken to connote any subjective feeling, but simply signifies that the desired state of affairs obtains, whether or not one knows that it does, and whether or not one feels pleasure at the thought that it does. In this sense, your preference that your spouse be faithful is satisfied if and only if he or she is faithful, regardless of your subjective state of knowledge or feeling. This feature of the modern notion is mostly irrelevant to Callicles' position. Second, preference satisfaction is not a matter of the occurrence of a state that is desired in isolation, but of the occurrence of a state that is placed somewhere in a *ranking*. In the degenerate (and for most purposes oversimplified) case, a state of affairs can be said to be desired merely in the sense that its obtaining is preferred to its not obtaining. In general, ranked alternatives are more numerous and more complex. For describing Callicles' view, the simple two-alternative case is usually adequate, though it is a good idea to keep the more general idea in mind. In any case, a preference ranking puts prospective states of affairs in order of preferredness, and one considers a person's preferences satisfied to the degree that a more highly ranked state is realized.

If one wants a notion of well-being that fits with the idea that temperance and prudent planning are to be rejected, then it seems more natural to adopt the desire satisfaction view than quantitative hedonism. That is so, at any rate, if one's pleasures are regarded, as we have seen the *Protagoras* does regard them, as (*a*) objectively measurable independently of their temporal position relative to the time of mea-

---

A. Hyllan, eds., *The Foundations of Social Choice Theory* (Cambridge University Press, forthcoming). Gibbard's paper gives a brief historical sketch of the role of these ideas.

surement, and as (*b*) having an objective value likewise independent of the temporal standpoint from which they are viewed.[7] That is, if your future pleasures can be objectively measured in size against your present ones, and their respective values are independent of temporal position, then it seems unreasonable, just as the *Protagoras* insists (356a–c), not to let future pleasures figure in one's deliberations just as much as present ones. But doing that requires prudent planning, and possibly the tempering or sacrificing of some possible present satisfactions for the sake of larger ones in the future. The conclusion could be avoided by denying that (*a*) and (*b*) hold of an individual's pleasures, but this denial in and of itself does not seem attractive.[8] Without it, we seem impelled to admit intertemporal comparison of pleasures, and of the values of pleasures, of one and the same person, and thus the reasonableness of one kind of prudent planning.

As is well known, inter*personal* comparisons of pleasures and their values have seemed to most philosophers far more problematical, and that is the main reason why modern economists and most modern utilitarians have rejected quantitative hedonism as an account of well-being suitable for discussions of social well-being. For our purposes in discussing the *Gorgias*, however, we can sidestep this issue.

The notion of preference satisfaction, on the other hand, seems more amenable to Callicles' unfavorable attitude toward temperance. Given two preference rankings even of the same set of options, there is no clear way to get anything like their "sum," which could represent the somehow combined ranking of which they are both equally weighty constituents. For one thing, the "strength" of one's present preference for B over A may be greater or less, it seems natural to say, than the "strength" of one's later preference for A over B. But preference rankings themselves take no account of "strength," but only of the order in which options are placed. Those thinkers who prefer this notion to quantitative hedonism generally do so because they deny the possibility of objective interpersonal measurement of pleasure, and they take the same attitude toward measurement of strength of preference, as well as anything else that is needed for straightforward aggregation of preference rankings analogous to calculation of sums of

---

7. By the "value" of the pleasure here I mean not the number assigned to it to measure how much pleasure it consists in, but rather the measurement of how much *good* a given quantity of pleasure amounts to. For example, the *Protagoras* operates on the assumption that the degree of goodness of a state of affairs is proportional to the amount of pleasure it contains (351b–e, 353e; whether Plato accepts this assumption there is another matter, which has consequences too complex to be treated here).

8. Still, it is a possible view. It is related to the considerations touched on in secs. IV and VII, esp. with reference to Nagel and Parfit (cf. n. 36).

pleasure under quantitative hedonism.[9] This is why it seems so difficult to know how to aggregate the preferences of individuals to get a reasonable ranking representing social well-being. But—and here is the important point for our purposes—it seems equally difficult to combine preference rankings even when one is talking about different rankings made by the same individual at different times.[10] Inevitably, it seems, individuals' preferences change over time. At this moment, Jones prefers that he spend the summer reading the *Metaphysics* in Greek rather than improving his tennis. By July it will be the other way around. If we stick to preferences alone as our guide, how do we provide for his overall well-being if our only options are to give him either a Greek lexicon or a raquet but not both?[11] Without going back to something like quantitative hedonism, there seems to be no way to "sum" the two rankings. The only other possibility seems to be to choose one of the rankings as constituting his well-being, and let the others go.[12]

This is where the idea fits itself to Callicles' rejection of temperance.[13] Once a selection is made of a particular time, which is to be such that the satisfaction of the preferences one has then are to constitute one's well-being, then one is insulated from considering, in combination with it, varying sets of preferences that one has at other

9. See esp. Gibbard.
10. See Brandt, pp. 169–185, and Gibbard, passim.
11. Things become even worse when we reckon in the fact that we have preferences about what our preferences should be, and these too change over time so as to produce further conflicts.
12. Of course, in the case where one supposes oneself to have a group of individual preference rankings, and wishes somehow to get a social preference ranking for the group, this way out seems unacceptable—which is why social choice theory has its work cut out for it. Still, some philosophers are willing to use interpersonal comparisons along with the notion of preference; see, e.g., John C. Harsanyi, "Morality and the Theory of Rational Behavior," Amartya Sen and Bernard Williams, eds., *Utilitarianism and Beyond* (Cambridge, Eng., 1982), pp. 39–62, esp. pp. 49–52. But far too many issues arise than can be mentioned here, even if we restrict ourselves to individual well-being and leave aside social well-being. (In this connection I would argue that Plato almost *totally* ignores social well-being in the *Gorgias* and takes it up only in the *Republic*; cf. sec. VI and Grote, p. 349.)
13. Most commentators assimilate pleasure and desire satisfaction without attention to the relevant distinctions. See, e.g., A. W. H. Adkins, *From the Many to the One* (Ithaca, 1970), p. 115; North, *From Myth to Icon*, p. 159. In *Plato, Gorgias* (Oxford, 1979), Irwin makes numerous observations about pleasure and desire and their interrelations, but does not hit on the point that seems to me essential to understanding Callicles' position. Grote begins to see it (pp. 350–357), and realizes that whereas the *Protagoras* attends to the "calculable" element of well-being, "in the *Gorgias*, no mention is made of future or distant pleasures and pains: the calculable element is represented only by immediate pleasure or pain" (p. 354); but he thinks this is a sign of the sketchiness of the *Gorgias*, not seeing that it is rather the result of the *concept of well-being* that Plato has chosen to attack there.

times, because there is no clear way for the combination to be made. There are no easy systematic compromises to be made among distinct preference rankings, as there are, under quantitative hedonism, among pleasures obtainable at different times. Now it is quite clear how Callicles thinks you should pick the desires whose satisfaction shall constitute your well-being: they are the desires that you have *now* (494c–e, 492e–492a).[14] In a sense, this choice does not seem arbitrary—not now. But the point is this, that whereas it seemed unreasonable to select present pleasures to be maximized with no account taken of future pleasures, it seems less patently unreasonable to select present desires as the ones to be satisfied, regardless of what future desires may be. For it seems relatively sensible to aggregate pleasures intertemporally, but not to aggregate preference rankings. So Callicles avoids any suggestion of the kind of quantitative hedonism of the *Protagoras*, and never treats pleasure as something accumulable over time. On the contrary, as we shall see more fully as we go along, his notion of pleasure is incompatible with such an idea, and Plato's arguments against him make no sense if taken as directed against it.

It is easy to confuse the view that one's well-being consists in satisfaction of present desire with a kind of sensualism that says that well-being consists in satisfying sensual desires, and so it is important that Plato takes pains to distinguish Callicles from the sensualist. The confusion is easy because sensual desires are often felt as particularly insistent and tend to block out thoughts of prudence. But Callicles disgustedly disavows the suggested comparison of himself to the itch-scratcher (494c–d). Of course, he recognizes that he is committed to saying that someone who desires to scratch is best off if he does so (494d) but he makes plain that it was not sensualism as such that he was espousing.

Once again we can see how Plato could have thought of this view as naturally arising from Gorgias' manner of presenting himself to the public. Gorgias holds that you will inevitably be made better off by learning rhetoric because it enables you to get what you want. Although he has not reasoned the matter through fully, he obviously holds that if you are thinking of learning rhetoric, there is no time like the present. He suggests no planning for any particular period of one's life. Perhaps it is relevant here that Callicles sneers at philosophy

---

14. Some pertinent observations about *sōphrosynē* are to be found in K. J. Dover, *Greek Popular Morality in the Time of Plato and Aristotle* (Berkeley and Los Angeles, 1974), esp. pp. 119–122, 225, making the connection between that concept and "the overcoming of the impulse to immediate or short-term pleasure or gain" (p. 119) and "rational foresight" (p. 121).

as something whose value is restricted to only a certain immature stage of life (485a–b). No such temporal restrictions are part of Gorgias' advertisement for rhetoric. Plato, on the other hand, holds that the value of philosophy is unrestricted as to time and place, and even holds, in the *Phaedo* and the *Republic* as well as in the *Gorgias*, that its value extends even beyond one's lifetime (whereas Callicles holds, against Socrates' disagreement in 511b–c, that the longer one lives the better off one can be).

III

By seeing what Plato's line of attack against Callicles is we can confirm that Callicles' position is as I have described it and understand why Plato confronts himself with such an opponent.

I said earlier that Plato's arguments concern the desirability of rational prudence both for the sake of one's well-being and for the sake of one's being good. In this section I shall treat arguments relevant mainly to the former, and take up in the next section arguments directed mainly to the latter.

First of all we should notice the main weakness in Callicles' position, since this is in fact where Plato attacks. To succeed, Callicles' view must contain a defensible account of well-being. Given that it employs an account of it as desire satisfaction, and in particular as the satisfaction of present desires, it must be able to show that the selection of *those* satisfactions is in some sense reasonable. Plato attacks at this point. He shows us a Callicles who is unwilling to uphold this selection consistently, because he feels constantly impelled to make evaluative judgments that involve a concern for states of affairs, in particular states of oneself, different from and conflicting with the kind of restricted satisfaction of present desires that his official view identifies with well-being.

From the point of view that most of us seem to take toward ourselves and our well-being, in at least our most reflective moments, Callicles' position seems unreasonable. Certainly it seems unreasonable if we think of it as aiming to make a *nonarbitrary* selection of satisfactions to constitute well-being. As I have said, there is a way in which satisfaction of present desires can seem, *now*, nonarbitrary. But when we raise the issue reflectively we are usually trying to raise it from a time-transcendent viewpoint. From that viewpoint there seems to be nothing special to recommend the preferences of one time over those of another as a guide to the person's well-being. If we think of the desires that a person has at a time as the desires belonging to a particular temporal stage of the person, then the idea is that there is nothing special to recommend one stage as the sole representative, through its preferences, of the well-being of the whole, continuing person.

It is open to a philosopher at this point to deny that one can or should take such a transtemporal viewpoint, or else to deny that one can or should regard oneself as a being extended into future time. Some philosophers have pursued this line of thought.[15] Plato, in fact, was one of them (as we can see, for example, in *Symposium* 207e–208b).[16] In the *Gorgias*, however, he neither pursues it himself nor allows Callicles to use it as a defense. Instead, Plato uses the fact that Callicles does regard himself as a temporally continuing being, whose future condition is of concern to his present self (and in general whose subsequent condition is of concern to himself at any given time), to induce him to contradict his official view, that well-being is present satisfaction of present desire and that temperance is to be rejected, and to accept the view that at least some prudent planning for the future is desirable.

Plato's argument against Callicles begins in an important way, before Callicles intervened, in the conversation with Polus. Polus has also developed Gorgias' original advertisement by saying, about as loosely as Callicles does, that being well off is satisfying your desires (466b–c). Then in 467c–468c, in the guise of a terminological point about the usage of the verb "to want" (βούλεσθαι), Plato has Socrates place an entering wedge. Socrates persuades Polus that if one wants A for the sake of B, then one should properly be said to want B, not A. I think that Plato cast the point as a terminological one to show that people like Polus and Callicles really do hold a certain substantive belief about desire and well-being that they might not own up to if they were on their guard, but the device worked so well that Plato's commentators have not caught on any better than Polus and Callicles did. For what is really going on here is that Socrates is illustrating an important piece of intertemporal structure in our desires. The point is that the value to us of the satisfaction of some of our desires is dependent on the later satisfaction of others. This may seem a minor point,

---

15. In "Personal Identity," Derek Parfit argues against the determinateness of one's identity through time in a way that would, if successful, undermine the reasonableness of this time-transcendent viewpoint. See also the reply to Parfit by John Perry and Parfit's response in A. O. Rorty, ed., *The Identities of Persons* (Berkeley and Los Angeles, 1976), pp. 67–90, 91–107.

16. Plato's views on *certain* aspects of identity through time are similar to Parfit's; note *Symp*. 207e–208b and cf. my "Aristotle on Sameness and Oneness," *Philosophical Review*, 80 (1971): 177–197.

and it does to Polus, but it is one of the lynchpins of Plato's argument. When A is wanted because it will or may lead to B in the future, one's reason for pursuing A must rest on the belief that one's interest in B will persist until it is actually forthcoming. This does not yet introduce temperance in any very full-blooded sense, but it does introduce the idea of planning, for what one's desires will be at some time other than now. Socrates' next move is to propose using the word "good" for those things for whose sake other things are done (to simplify a bit). Very significantly, this claim, unlike anything else that Polus has to say, is taken over directly by Callicles without any announcement (499e–500a). The important thing again is not the terminological claim, but the fact that Callicles is conceding that evaluations can depend on consideration of times other than the present.[17]

Understanding the issue between Plato and Callicles enables us, next, to make sense of Plato's argument that there can be no skill or *technē* concerned with pleasure (500a–501c). Laboring under the impression that Plato is here dealing with the same quantitative hedonist's notion of pleasure that is in play in the *Protagoras*, commentators have understandably thought that Plato's argument is preposterous. For in spite of what he maintains here, there seems to be no reason why there should not be a systematic procedure for allowing a person to maximize the quantity of pleasure he accumulates over a given period of time.[18] Things fall into place, though, when we understand the argument to involve Callicles' notion of pleasure.

To do this fully, though, we have to take a further step in interpreting that notion. So far, I have talked as though Callicles' rejection of temperance and planning of satisfactions extends merely to insisting that one be concerned only with satisfying the desires that one has now. But Callicles carries his rejection of temperance even further than this. He maintains that one's pleasure and well-being at a given time is proportional to the amount of desire satisfaction *that is taking place at that time*. As he puts it, "living pleasantly is . . . having as much as possible flowing in" (494b). This is different from saying that a life is *in toto* pleasant in proportion to the total amount of "inflowing" that has occurred in it. Callicles may believe this, too, but his point throughout this passage is simply about one's well-being at a time, and its dependence, not just on the satisfaction of the desires one has then (though it is dependent on them too, since Callicles emphasizes in

---

17. Notice that the distinction in 499 between good and bad pleasures is not at all a distinction between *morally* good and bad pleasures, in a sense involving social morality.
18. See for example Irwin, pp. 208–209.

491e–492a, d, that satisfaction requires a present desire), but on the satisfaction that is occurring then.

This is why there can be no *technē* concerned with pleasure in Callicles' sense. The crucial point is that by a *technē* of pleasure, Plato says he means a *technē* of pleasure *alone*, without any concern with whether a pleasure is good or bad (500b, 501b). By a good pleasure, he has explained (in 499d, harking back to the discussion with Polus in 467e–468c), he means a pleasure that is beneficial, in the sense of production of some good.[19] So a *technē* of pleasure alone, in the strict sense, would ignore any further effects that a pleasure might have. Why would such an enterprise necessarily be only a "knack," as Plato claims, and not a *technē* after all? Because pleasure has here in effect been defined to be, as we have just seen, the satisfaction occurring at a particular time. Given the fact that desires of different times can conflict with each other, the increasing of "inflow" taking place now will only by sheer luck be conducive to or even compatible with the increasing of "inflow" taking place at any later time. The notion of pleasure under which Plato is working does not make room for the aggregating of satisfactions at different times, or trading those of one time against those of another so that the total satisfaction over the whole period might be maximized. For this reason there is no role here for a *technē* that would take account of the effects, positive or negative, of present satisfactions on those of subsequent times. On this understanding, then, Plato's argument makes quite reasonable sense.

In 495e–497d, Plato offers one of two arguments (the other to be taken up in sec. IV) against Callicles' identification of pleasure with the good. This argument too can be understood once we know what both are taking "pleasure" to mean. To desire, Callicles says, is to have a certain lack, which is painful (496c–d). Pleasure occurs when this lack is being filled, and is over when the filling is. But since the lack is still painful even while being filled, therefore pleasure can occur simultaneously with pain. On Callicles' identification of pleasure and the good, Socrates says, it ought to be the case that the occurrence of good can be simultaneous with that of bad. But, Socrates maintains with Callicles' agreement, this is not so, because a man's being well off and his being badly off do not occur simultaneously (496b–c). So, they conclude, the good and pleasure cannot be identical.

19. There is some awkwardness of terminology here, because Plato has not developed the terminology for a clear distinction between the intrinsically and the extrinsically good. Some see that distinction in *Rep.* II, but see my paper, "The Classification of Goods is Plato's *Republic*," forthcoming in the *Journal of the History of Philosophy*.

Gorgias   151

At first sight, this seems a thoroughly unsatisfactory argument. Callicles might reply, among other things, that if he is right in his identification, then granted his account of what pleasure is, it turns out that being well and badly off can be simultaneous after all. For just as I can have pleasure and pain together, so I can have some goods and some evils together, too.[20]

But Plato is making a point about Callicles' concepts of good and pleasure, maintaining that they are not identical. Callicles is plainly thinking of pleasures here as exclusively associated with present satisfactions of occurrent desires. No possibility of pleasures without attendant desires is contemplated. Such pleasures are perfectly possible on other hedonist views, and indeed Plato introduces them in other works.[21] It can legitimately be said, however, to be part of Callicles' concept of pleasure, as we have seen, that pleasure occurs only through and accompanied by the satisfaction of a contemporaneous desire. If desire is conceptually identical with pain, as Callicles appears to make it, then it is part of the concept of pleasure that it always is simultaneously with pain. The point is made plain at the end of the argument, in 497c–d (the earlier part, at 496e–497a, says only that pleasure *can* occur simultaneously with pain on Callicles' view). On the other hand, it is evidently no part of Callicles' concept of well-being that it can occur only with being badly off. Indeed, Callicles seems to allow that it is part of these two concepts that they are contraries, and cannot occur together (496b–c, e–497a). I doubt that Plato is holding that there are no intermediate degrees between being fully well off and being fully badly off, or that there is no such notion as being partly well off and partly badly off. His point, rather, is that there *is* a concept of being fully well off, and a concept of being fully badly off, and that *these* two things are incompatible. But on *his* concept of pleasure as the satisfaction of a desire that one has at the time, there can be *no* such thing as being fully in a state of pleasure, since all pleasure must be associated with the simultaneous pain of the desire (though 496c–d clearly allows a state of being fully in pain, i.e., a desire not currently being satisfied). Quite obviously, the clarification of Plato's argument once again depends on seeing the special character of Callicles' notion of pleasure, which Plato is here examining to the exclusion of other conceptions of it.

20. See Irwin, p. 202.
21. For example, at *Phileb.* 51e he notes that pleasures of smell can occur without attendant painful desires (cf. 51a–52b).

IV

In the arguments examined in the previous section, Plato attempts to show that a person who is well off must have at least some sort of rational prudence in the satisfaction of desires. Now we shall turn to the arguments by which he tries to show that a person who is good or excellent, i.e., who has virtue or *aretē*, must likewise be in some degree prudent. Once again he will present us with a Callicles who is unwilling to maintain a consistent opposition to prudent planning, because he will not refrain from ascribing goodness to people by some criterion other than merely their satisfaction of present desire.

The crucial argument for the present issue is the other of Plato's two arguments against identifying the good with pleasure (in Callicles' sense), in 497e–499b. Callicles has maintained that pleasure (in his sense) is the good. But he also admits here that a good man is good "by the presence of goods" (498d with 492d). So it should follow on his view that the man who is best is the one with the most pleasure. Socrates, however, gets Callicles to concede that as a matter of fact, brave men sometimes have less pleasure than cowards, and fools less than wise men (497e–498c). All it takes is Callicles' admission that the wise and the brave are good while fools and cowards are bad, to seal him into a contradiction.

Although from our point of view it might appear that Callicles' fatal mistake was to agree that good men are good by the presence of goods, it seems clear that Plato does not here envision the possibility of Callicles' giving this premise up, but rather portrays both him and Socrates as accepting it as obvious. We, of course, are used to the notion that the moral assessment of a person is overriding, as an assessment of the person himself, even while we are inclined to admit that a morally good person may, at least conceivably, not be the person who is best off or has the greatest well-being. Though this is a larger topic than I can treat fully here, I do not think that the Greeks were at all used to the idea that any overriding assessment of a person, moral or otherwise, could be thus out of kilter with how well off the person was. Although I think that Plato thought that in very exceptional circumstances, the two evaluations might fail to be proportional to each other, most of the time he ignores this possibility, and clearly is doing so in the *Gorgias*.[22] Without any demur by Socrates, Callicles says twice that a person is good by possessing what is good (492d, 498d), and

---

22. The possibility is actualized, I believe, in Book VII of the *Republic*; see my *Companion to Plato's Republic* (Indianapolis, 1980) pp. 46–48, 190–196, and "The Rulers' Choice," forthcoming in the *Archiv für Geschichte der Philosophie*.

Socrates relies on the same assumptions in an argument of his own (506d). Plato shows no sign of thinking that there is any sort of pun involved in saying that we are good by the possession of the good, or of trying to get us to see that this is a mistake (certainly he neither perpetrates nor warns against the mistake of saying that we are pleasant by the possession of pleasure—cf. 506d). So this is not the nub of the issue between Plato and Callicles.

So of the elements of Callicles' position that lead him to contradiction in this argument, the important one seems to be his concession that someone who is brave or wise is therefore better than a coward or a fool, or in other words, that bravery and wisdom are virtues or excellences.

As I have emphasized, it would be a mistake to think that Callicles is being pictured as here inconsistently willing to buy into a part of standard morality, in particular, justice. Nothing in the argument depends on regarding the bravery or wisdom in question as having to do with morality or one's dealings with, or obligations toward other people. Indeed, the example in 498a–c seems clearly to have to do with the prudence related to one's own well-being. So the inconsistency in which Callicles finds himself has nothing in particular to do with moral assessments of character in the relevant sense.

The important question to ask here, though, is why there need be any conflict for Callicles between saying that pleasure is the good and saying that bravery and wisdom are virtues. True, sometimes brave or wise men get less pleasure than cowardly or foolish ones, but surely Callicles would wish to say that in general the brave and the wise are more able to procure pleasure for themselves, so that their excellence consists not quite in the possession of pleasure at a given moment, but in their overall *capacity* to possess it.[23] So why does Plato not have Callicles defend himself in this way? It seems to me that any interpretation ought to be able to answer this question. In particular, it ought to be able to explain why, when Socrates points out that a coward may sometimes have more pleasure than a wise man (498b–c), Callicles does not reply, "Of course if you compare them at a particular moment, Socrates, the coward may have more pleasure than the brave man and so be better than he is; but the appropriate comparison to make is of longer stretches of their lives, and if you do this, you will find that in the overwhelming majority of cases, a brave man will be able to accumulate more pleasure than the coward."

Now it is clear from what we have already seen why Callicles does

23. Cf. Irwin; p. 203.

not adopt any such argument against Socrates. For his idea that pleasure is the good does not involve saying that the person who is best off is he who has accumulated that greatest total amount of pleasure over a period of time. And that is why in the present passage the argument is restricted entirely to comparisons of the brave man and the coward, and of the wise man and the fool, at particular moments, and nothing at all is said about their accumulations of pleasures and pains over extended periods. Callicles' notion of the man who is well off is that of the man who is enjoying himself and so well off *now* (cf. 492c, 491e), and the present argument involves declaring that equivalent to the notion of the man who is good or excellent now.

But, of course, Callicles also finds it irresistible to make assessments of people's character that conflict with this his official view. That is, he regards bravery and wisdom as virtues or excellences, construed as persisting traits of people that have reference to their capacities to deal with situations courageously and intelligently. As he makes clear that he understands (491b, 490a), they are traits that have value in affecting conditions in the future and make people, in his phrase, "capable of fulfilling what they intend" (491b). The theme of the ability to do what one intends is derived from Gorgias' idea that rhetoric provides one with "power" ($\delta\acute{\upsilon}\nu\alpha\mu\iota\varsigma$) and enables one to bring about what one wants. Gorgias and Polus have both suggested also that rhetorical power is a splendid ($\kappa\alpha\lambda\acute{o}\nu$) thing and that a person who has it deserves admiration (449a, 462c, 463b–c).

Callicles' difficulty, then, arises from the fact that he admires and calls good two types of people, those who are enjoying themselves now, and those who have traits that generally lead to enjoyment. What Socrates does is simply to make clear to him that these two types are distinct. Accordingly, Callicles cannot think that in admiring a person who has the resources of wisdom and bravery, he is adopting an attitude concerned merely with the present condition of the admired person. Rather, his attitude involves favorable judgments about capacities to deal with future contingencies both by planning (wisdom) and by coping with difficulties in carrying out those plans (courage and wisdom). When he is pressed, he adheres to these judgments, at the expense of denying his original official view—that being well off, and therefore good, has nothing to do with concern for the future.

V

Before considering how the arguments so far described are related to the rest of the *Gorgias*, let us dwell briefly on why Plato makes Callicles react as he does to the conflicts in his position. Callicles holds officially that being well off and being good are matters of one's state at the present moment to which prudent concern for one's future is irrelevant. But under questioning from Socrates he is pictured as also believing, inconsistently with his official view, that concern for the future is crucially relevant to both sorts of evaluations. When the conflict is brought home to him, he seems to be made to abandon his official view in favor of the other beliefs that he has held alongside them. Why? Why does Socrates not, as he sometimes does, simply point out the inconsistency and exhort Callicles to work it out? Alternatively, why does Plato not have Callicles stick to his official view and develop or alter the rest of his views to accord with it?

A full examination of these questions would require a lengthy discussion of Platonic dialectic and *elenchus*, but it is pertinent to present concerns to suggest the following.[24] It seems to me that Plato's line of thought here is similar to views that he expresses in later works about the notion of goodness, views closely related to certain of his metaphysical and epistemological positions. I would cite as examples his claim in the *Theaetetus* that considerations of goodness involve considerations of past and present in relation to the future (186a–b), and also his idea in the *Republic* that bare desire or $\dot{\epsilon}\pi\iota\theta\nu\mu\iota\alpha$ or craving, as I would translate the word there, is not directed at the good, but only at a certain object regardless of its goodness (437d–439a).[25] Part of the latter point, I suspect, is the idea that a craving involves no thought to future benefit. Without hazarding a guess as to how fully Plato had developed metaphysical support for these ideas when he wrote the *Gorgias*, I would suggest that the work already contains the view that goodness is not a property applicable to things at particular moments, but is rather a kind of global property that must be attributed to longer temporal stretches of things.

So in refraining from pursuing his official view in a single-minded and radical way, Callicles is adhering to what Plato thought was a deep fact about our evaluative notions, the inarticulate understanding of which he sometimes compares to memory.[26] Plato does sometimes

---

24. The larger issue concerning *elenchus* arises from the fact that Plato does not show an inconsistency *within* Callicles' doctrine of what well-being and excellence are, *provided* that that doctrine is taken narrowly, to include only those things that he wants to make part of what I have been calling his "official" view. Rather, Plato shows an inconsistency *between* that view *and* certain other evaluations that Callicles wishes to make. See esp. Richard Robinson, *Plato's Earlier Dialectic*, 2d ed. (Oxford, 1953), passim, esp. pp. 29–32. I think it likely, though, that Plato would regard the distinction just made between the two kinds of inconsistency as in some way artificial.

25. Cf. my *Companion to Plato's Republic*, pp. 124–125.

26. In the *Meno* and the *Phaedo*, esp. at *Phdo.* 72ff.

confront himself with opponents who are more radical than Callicles is, but if we wish that he had made Callicles stick to his guns more firmly, we can at least understand how extreme a view he had been adopting, in trying to reject completely all prudence and concern for times other than the present. And if we do that, we can understand how it would have seemed to Plato that a person would not be able to sustain that rejection, but would irresistibly be drawn to conflicting evaluations, implying concern with other times, in a way reflective of what Plato took to be the objectively correct notion of goodness.[27]

VI

I want next to explain how I think Plato's arguments against Callicles fit with the rest of the *Gorgias*, particularly the parts dealing with justice, and also why Plato thought it worthwhile to argue against Callicles' position.

It seems to me that the reasonable thing to say about the first of these matters can be summarized as follows. First, as I said at the outset, although Plato asserts in the *Gorgias* that in various ways justice is a desirable trait to have and to act on, he does not purport to demonstrate this within the dialogue. Rather, he claims to demonstrate that temperance of a certain kind is desirable (and actually provides good reason, given certain sensible assumptions about our concern for our future selves, for thinking this is so). In addition, however, he regards this demonstration as a necessary preliminary to a further argument, for the contention that justice too is desirable. That further argument is given not in the *Gorgias* but in the *Republic*.

To begin to see the grounds for this account, let us now turn to the later parts of the *Gorgias*, which are usually the parts most closely attended to but which I have been trying to deemphasize. These parts make up most of the discussion of justice and just action, especially from 505c to the end of the work. In my view, once Plato has completed the negative task of refuting Callicles' own view, which is the major argumentative task of the work, what he then does is only to state his positive position as forcefully and dramatically as he can, and to give rough sketches of his grounds for holding it, without, as I said, giving anything like a full argument.

It seems to me, as it has seemed to other commentators, that 505c marks a significant boundary within the dialogue, whose philosophical point the present interpretation allows us to understand. It ends

---

27. For some more remarks on this notion of goodness, see my "Rulers' Choice."

Gorgias 157

the part where Plato claims to refute Callicles' rejection of prudent planning. Plato accords this refutation a particularly robust status, claiming that agreement between Socrates and Callicles "will possess the goal of truth" (487e). Part of what Plato means by this must be that because Callicles and Socrates are so far apart in their fundamental inclinations about these issues, and because Callicles has no motivation to hide or soften his position (cf. 482c–d, 487b), what they can agree on will be true. As we saw in the previous section, Plato regards an unwillingness to accept the value of prudent planning as objectively absurd, not merely likely to appear absurd to particular people. But I do not think that he accords the same status to most of what is said after 505c. For this is the point where, as is well known, Callicles bows out of the discussion and Socrates for a time conducts it himself (506c–509c). I think that this turn of events is significant, because Socrates had said only that *agreement* between himself and Callicles would attain truth (487e). This clearly does not imply that everything to come is proved to be true, and seems to me rather pointedly to suggest that where agreement is not forthcoming things are less firmly established than they might be. And when he says later on, in 508e–509a, that what he has just said is tied down by arguments "of iron and adamant," he adds the equally pointed qualification, "at least as it appears so far" (ὡς γοῦν ἂν δόξειεν οὑτωσί), which is more than a little like the *Mikado* chorus' wish, "Long life to you, till then." For following 505c most of what is said is not agreed to by Callicles, and I take Plato to be indicating, quite correctly, that those passages contain material that he cannot claim firmly to have established.[28]

It fits this picture that after 505c we do find a couple of brief passages where Callicles does return and act as genuine interlocutor, giving his assent to statements by Socrates that he accepts. But, significantly, these passages stick to claims that *would* be acceptable to him, and that do not go much farther than what he has already agreed to. One is 509c–511c. This concerns an issue of prudent strategy, of the sort that Callicles has now admitted that he accepts. The question is how to keep from doing injustice and from having injustice done to one. Socrates believes that one will wish to avoid the former, and says that he has shown Polus that no one wants to commit injustice (509e; cf. 480d–e). Callicles, though he does not say where he thinks that reasoning went wrong, indicates clearly that he does not accept its alleged conclusion. But he does genuinely join the following discussion,

28. Irwin, p. 219, suggests that after 505c "the interlocutor's role shrinks ... because he realizes that he has not worked out adequate grounds for all his claims," but he does not elaborate.

in 510a sqq., about the best strategy for preventing injustice to oneself. But this discussion is aborted without agreement in 511c. Socrates then takes off on his own again, and henceforth Callicles makes no substantial philosophical concessions to him, and except for such issues as whether Pericles left the Athenians better than he found them (515c–516d), his responses are not made to indicate agreement (see esp. 513d–514a). In 522c–e it is clear that he has *not* accepted that refraining from injustice is always better than committing it, and at the beginning of the final myth that illustrates this view, at 523a, Socrates acknowledges explicitly that Callicles will not accept its truth. I conclude, therefore, that the points made in this last quarter of the dialogue are not claimed to be demonstrated or to have the same status as the points argued in the earlier part. The later points, although Plato assuredly is convinced of them, have not been established for us; the earlier points have been.

As soon as Callicles has quit the conversation in 505c, Socrates himself takes over the role of his own interlocutor, and proceeds to convince himself by a very poor argument that it is desirable to be just. He does this by building on Callicles' admission that it is desirable to be temperate, and trying to show that if one is temperate then one will be just. The argument for the entailment of justice by temperance is so defective, however, that we can easily see why Plato does not present it as an argument that convinces Callicles or any other real interlocutor. The argument is this: that if one is temperate, one will do "fitting things" ($\pi\rho o\sigma\acute{\eta}\kappa o\nu\tau\alpha$) to both gods and men; that fitting things to gods and men are respectively just and pious things; and so as someone who does these things, a temperate person will be both pious and just (506c–507b).

It is hard to believe that Plato thought that this argument is adequate as it stands.[29] For one thing, it contains no reason to think that the actions of a temperate person, even though they might be admitted to be "fitting" in some sense, are so in a sense that entails that they are just. Moreover given the complete lack of any explanation of this "fittingness," it seems hardly possible that Plato should have thought that he had established this entailment. The argument itself merely says that a soul that is temperate (506e–507a) and pursues pleasure for the sake of good (506c–d), as Plato earlier convinced Callicles is what it ought prudently to do (500a), must be structured or ordered ($\tau\epsilon\tau\alpha\gamma\mu\acute{\epsilon}\nu o\nu$, $\kappa\epsilon\kappa o\sigma\mu\eta\mu\acute{\epsilon}\nu o\nu$, 506d–e). But Plato has not shown that a temperate soul is ordered in any sense entailing that it acts justly (or,

---

29. For some criticism see Irwin, p. 220.

fittingly in a sense entailing justice). He has indeed argued, in 503e–505b, that temperance is better for the soul than intemperance (505b) and also makes it better (505a–b). He has argued this by claiming (504a–b) that when the practitioner of a skill or *technē* makes something well, he does it by proceeding not "at random" (εἰκῇ) but by producing in it some structure (τάξις) or order (κόσμος). Although Plato says in passing that order in the soul is justice (504d), he makes nothing further of the point, and his conclusion is only that temperance is good for a person, not that justice is (505b). Moreover the operative sense of "order" is defined only by its contrast to randomness (503e–504a), not by anything guaranteeing its connection with justice.[30] The idea is rather to articulate the point, by this time already won from Callicles (which is why he is at this juncture so acquiescent), that one is best off planning one's satisfactions rationally than by simply satisfying desires randomly from moment to moment. So there is no basis either provided or claimed here for the step in 506c–507b from temperance via "fitting" action to justice.

Aside from failing to establish the entailment of justice by temperance, the argument in 506c–507b is inadequate in another way that would surely have been obvious to Plato. It is the assumption that he requires in 507a–b that a person who does just and pious things must himself be just and pious. This is the sort of inference from the character of a person's actions to the quality of his soul that is firmly rejected in the *Phaedo* (68d–69a), where the person who merely acts correctly without the proper state of soul is condemned.[31]

I think it is important that the inadequacies of this argument are made good in the *Republic*. For one thing, that work contains an elaborate scheme, expounded especially in Books IV and VIII–IX, for trying to link a person's actions with the state of his soul, and to show under what conditions just actions manifest justice in the soul. For another thing, the *Republic* refuses to proceed on the basis of an insecure understanding of what actions are just, as the *Gorgias*' present argument does proceed with the notion of "fitting" action. Instead, it adopts a special approach to the whole problem of defining justice, by first defining it in its application to a soul and a city, and only then explaining what a just action is (*Rep.* IV, esp. 443e). In Plato's view at

30. Adkins, *Merit and Responsibility*, p. 274.
31. Cf. Irwin, pp. 221–222, where he is unable, like other commentators, to find any satisfactory explanation of why Plato should depart here from his fixed view. Instead of trying to press for explanations of how Plato might have viewed these arguments as sufficient to establish his stated views about the advantageousness of justice, I am of course arguing that it makes much more sense of the dialogue to realize that Plato did not so view them.

the time of the *Republic*, the argument of the *Gorgias* evidently contained some large gaps. Although I do not know whether at the time of the *Gorgias* Plato yet saw the shape of the arguments that he would offer in the *Republic* for saying that it is advantageous to be just, it is in any case impossible for me to believe that when he wrote the *Gorgias* he regarded its argument for that proposition as even close to cogent. It seems too blatantly incomplete and, as we have seen, his warnings against treating it as decisive seem plain.[32]

VII

But if it is accepted that the *Gorgias* does not claim to demonstrate Plato's point about the desirability of justice, but only his claim about the desirability of temperance, as against Callicles' complete rejection of prudence or rational planning, the question still remains why Plato thought it worthwhile to confront an opponent like Callicles, rather than turning his attention forthwith to the issue about justice.

The most obvious answer to this question is that before one tries to show why a person should be concerned with other people or with institutions like cities in the way that is required by justice, it is necessary to clear away first the idea that one should be concerned with nothing but satisfying one's own present desires. It is not worth much time arguing for being just if one is assailed by people who pooh-pooh the value of any kind of rational planning of satisfactions even if it is restricted to one's own well-being. This fact is shown by Socrates' conversation with Polus, whose position in the dialogue we are now finally in a position to understand. As Terence Irwin notes, the concept of justice is prominent in that conversation, and the real focus on temperance comes in the exchange with Callicles.[33] But as Callicles insists and Socrates does not deny, the argument against Polus, and in favor of the superiority of justice to injustice, was inconclusive. Callicles means to bring the discussion down to brass tacks, and not to flinch from maintaining the position that he thinks Polus was too weak to defend successfully (482c–e). He says that Polus should have been willing to say that doing injustice is less shameful than suffering it, and he goes on to draw his famous contrast between natural and conventional justice, holding that natural justice permits the strong to possess all that they are capable of possessing (483b–c, 490a). This declara-

---

32. For some observations about the way in which the *Republic* extends the line of thought of the *Gorgias*, see North, *From Myth to Icon*, pp. 100ff., esp. pp. 105–106; *Sophrosyne*, pp. 163–164; and above, n. 12.

33. Irwin, p. 221.

tion can easily mislead one into thinking that the subsequent discussion with Callicles aims to prove precisely what the earlier conversation with Polus attempted to show, that one is better off by being just. But this is not so. At 490a the conversation takes a crucial turn, when Callicles says that in his view, natural justice dictates that the man who is better should rule over others. From that point Socrates turns to the question who the "better" men are, and when Callicles reveals his belief that a man cannot be well off or good if he is "enslaved to anything whatsoever" (491e), and that by nature one who lives rightly should have appetites as large as possible and never restrain them (491e–492a, d–e), we are immediately embarked on a discussion of temperance, which does not end until Callicles abdicates his role as interlocutor, and Socrates reintroduces justice in the conversation with himself that we have already examined (506–507).

So the course of the dialogue shows Plato retreating from an argument over justice, and dealing first with Callicles' rejection of temperance, which underlies Callicles' rejection of justice as conventionally conceived. People like Polus can be convinced of the value of justice, but only by a superficial argument, because they are not willing to come out and say what Callicles' more thoroughgoing case against justice rests on, namely the view that any sort of temperance is undesirable, whether it has directly to do with justice or not.[34] In sum, then, Plato believes that he must deal with Callicles' position before any treatment of justice can be satisfactorily completed. No doubt he was stimulated to take up the issue by the presence, noted earlier, of fifth-century figures who denied all value to *sōphrosunē*, in combination with what he took to be the clear tendency of Gorgias' advertisements for rhetoric. The discussion with Callicles provided the vehicle for doing so.

But there is also a philosophically deeper account of why Plato confronts Callicles' view before dealing directly with justice. It is a line of thought that finds expression in the views of recent philosophers like Nagel and Parfit,[35] according to which concern for other people is taken to be in certain ways analogous to concern for other moments of one's own life than the present, and that one who has the latter has no good reason not to have the former as well. This suggests that if ir-

---

34. This is not to say that all denials of the value of being just were or must be based on a rejection of temperance. In Book I of the *Republic*, the rejection of justice is espoused by Thrasymachus in a way which, while it bears certain resemblances to Callicles' position, is nevertheless importantly different.

35. See Thomas Nagel, *The Possibility of Altruism* (Oxford, 1970), and Parfit, pp. 26–27.

rationality is thought to attach to taking an interest only in one's present and not in other times of one's own existence, then much the same irrationality ought to be seen in taking an interest only in one's own self and not in any larger whole. I believe that this suggestion reflects Plato's thinking fairly accurately.[36] On his view, I believe, understanding why it is desirable to impose some kind of order on one's own satisfactions over time is the first step to understanding why it is desirable to see order imposed on such larger wholes as cities, and moreover the two notions have fundamentally the same character. The *Gorgias* adumbrates this analogy clearly, I suggest, but tries itself to take only the first step.

University of Michigan

36. For some further remarks on this matter, see my "Rulers' Choice."

7 PLATONIC PROVOCATIONS:
Reflections on the Soul and the Good in the *Republic**

MITCHELL MILLER

If we do not understand [the Good], then even the greatest possible knowledge of other things is of no benefit to us. (505a)

The aim of this reflection is to explore the nexus of notoriously obscure notions that lies at the center of Plato's *Republic*. Anything like a complete discussion would be impossible in this short space. What I hope to do instead is to offer the initial sketch of a unified response to these perennial questions: What does Plato intend by his notion "the Good"? How does the properly metaphysical understanding of the forms and the Good fulfill the search for justice in the soul? And what, in light of this, is the ethical and political value of philosophical education as Plato understands it?

I. SOCRATIC AND PLATONIC PROVOCATIONS

To let these matters come to focus within the context and intention of the dialogue, it is best to begin with some observations on the way, to put it vaguely to begin with, the *Republic* "works." We get help from a strange source. In his eulogy to Socrates in the *Symposium*, Alcibiades offers this characterization of Socrates' "arguments" (λόγοι): like the songs of the satyr Marsyas, "whoever plays them, from an absolute virtuoso to a twopenny-halfpenny flute girl, [they] will still have a magic power, and by virtue of their own divinity they will show which of us are fit subjects for the rites of initiation (215c)."[1] The *Re-*

---

*This essay formulates ideas first presented in a symposium on Plato at Vassar College and in a lecture at Yale University. I am grateful to Michael Anderson, Jennifer Church, Charles Griswold, Drew Hyland, and David Lachterman for their critical comments on earlier drafts. I also owe special thanks to Ellen Handel for extraordinary help in completing the final version.

1. I have only slightly revised Michael Joyce's translation, *Plato's Symposium or the*

public, I suggest, is an extraordinary medley of such songs—and, most importantly, on two distinct, though coordinated, levels. First of all, there is a striking sequence of provocations *within* the dramatic action of the dialogue: time and again, Socrates offers his partner arguments whose real point appears to be to elicit a demand—often from someone in the audience who has been quiet until then—for deeper inquiry; thus Socrates awakens in his interlocutors, if not always a fully philosophical potency, at the least a genuine concern with philosophical proposals. Such provocations structure the phased ascent from Book I to Books II–IV to Books V–VII,[2] as well as the coming and going of interlocutors within each phase.[3] To illustrate by citing only the most conspicuous instances:[4] (i) by his rebuttal of Cephalus, Socrates provokes Cephalus' son Polemarchus to step in to defend the conventional notion of justice as "rendering to each his due" (331d ff.); (ii) by his subsequent interpretation of this to prohibit harming even one's enemies, he provokes Thrasymachus, there to sell himself as a teacher of political rhetoric, to burst in with a real-political defense of might as right (336b ff.); (iii) by refutations that defeat Thrasymachus more in word than substance,[5] he then provokes Glaucon

---

Drinking Party (London, 1935), reprinted in E. Hamilton and H. Cairns' edition of *Plato, Collected Dialogues* (New York, 1961).

2. A full discussion of the dramatic structure of the *Republic* would of course include a thoroughgoing analysis of the dramatic setting, especially as this is sketched in the opening pages of the dialogue, and it would of course require an account of Books VIII–IX and X as parts within the whole. Both go beyond the scope of this essay, which is intended as a contribution to, not an attempt at, that larger discussion. For some general remarks on the structural rhythm of dialogue form and on its final third part, in particular, see the preface to my *The Philosopher in Plato's Statesman* (The Hague, 1980).

3. Other middle dialogues that are structured in this way are the *Gorgias*, in which Socrates' strategy of provocation becomes an explicit topic at 482c ff., and the *Phaedo*.

4. For other instances, see, in particular, Socrates' extended and exaggerated praise of the rustic ways of the city of producers and the interruption (note ὑπολαβών, 372c) it incites from Glaucon at 372a ff.; his sweeping denial of anything private to the rulers and the interruption (note, again, ὑπολαβών) it incites from Adimantus at 416d–417b and 419a; and his extended recourse to a string of superlatives in describing the philosopher and the reaction it provokes in Adimantus at 484b–487a and 487b–d.

5. In particular, Socrates' key distinction between the arts of shepherding and money-making, decisive for the whole series of arguments he offers at 338c–347a, invites the cynical interpretation that the ruler practices his art as a means for succeeding in the distinct art of money-making; thus Socrates, while defeating Thrasymachus' formulation, does not defeat the latter's basic point. Again, Socrates' argument at 348b–350c leaves itself open to being interpreted as contradicting his earlier denial that the just man ever harms anyone (335d, e); a key premise is that the just man does try to "get the better of," πλεονεκτεῖν, the unjust man, and this expression implies aggrandizement at another's expense. And again, Socrates' argument at 351a–352b, when it shows that even a band of thieves derives its power from the justice with which its members treat one another, implies that justice is of value as a means for successful injustice.

and Adimantus to demand a deeper, more adequate defense of justice "for its own sake" (357a ff.); (iv) by his conspicuous failure to explicate his notion that the guardians "share women and children in common" (423e–434a), Socrates arouses the whole company to require him to explicate the notions of the equality of female with male and of the abolition of private families (449a ff.); (v) by *these* very notions, in turn, he provokes Glaucon, in particular, to insist (471c ff.) that he show how such a city might ever be actualized[6]—that is, in effect, that he offer the paradoxical notion of the philosopher-king (473c ff.);[7] and, finally, (vi) by this very notion, he provokes *himself* to object to the inadequacy of the account of the soul and its education that he has offered so far (502e, 504b ff.)—and, so, to present the distinctively philosophical idea of the "conversion" of the soul to the forms and the Good (518c ff.). Now, all of this Marsyan singing is aimed at Glaucon, Adimantus, and the other interlocutors. By provoking them to ask to go deeper, even at the expense of all that is familiar to them, Socrates' arguments motivate and structure their own self-initiation into philosophy. There is, however, a second level of provocation and initiation as well: precisely by Socrates' exchange with his interlocutors, *Plato* challenges *us*, the listeners outside the dialogue.[8] Moreover, the coordination of these levels is precise. It is, specifically, just where (as, for example, in [vi] above) the interlocutors fail to respond to Socrates, just where, that is, they prove not to be "fit subjects for divine initiation," that we are both most severely tested and most pointedly invited to show our fitness. In this sense, even as we witness Socrates' examination of his partners and, as witnesses, take their measure, the dialogue is examining us and taking our mea-

---

6. Note in particular how Socrates, having originally announced and postponed the question whether such a city might ever be actualized (457d–458b), first stalls for a while (464c–466c), then recalls the question (466d), only to resume stalling (466e–471b)—all, evidently to provoke Glaucon's impatient interruption and insistence on facing the question directly at 471c.

7. Such a city depends on its rulers, and the denial of all private property, the equality of the sexes in their qualifications to rule, and the abolition of the private family create, as tacit requirements for the rulers, indifference to wealth, sexual identity, and lineage. Who in the Greek world but the philosopher—exemplified especially, of course, by Socrates himself—meets these requirements? Thus the question of how to actualize the just city leads directly to the notion of the philosopher-king. See p. 174 below.

8. By "Socratic" I mean only to refer to the *persona* Socrates and the action *within* the drama of the dialogues. The historical relation of the actual Socrates and Plato is not at issue here. (Indeed, it seems to me in principle beyond the reach of interpretation. See E. Havelock, "The Socratic Problem: Some Second Thoughts," in J. Anton and A. Preus, eds., *Essays in Greek Philosophy*, 2 (Albany, 1983): 147–173.)

sure; its deepest function, if I am right, is to provoke us, to move us beneath and beyond its own explicit content into philosophical insight of our own.

In the list just given, I identified six major moments of Socratic provocation. What, then, are the major moments of *Platonic* provocation, the major points at which, by the interlocutors' failure, we are invited to inquire more deeply? I identify three: (i) When Polemarchus and Adimantus object at the outset of Book V and, again, when Glaucon objects at 471c ff., they all seem to have lost track of the point of the reflection on the just city; whereas Socrates initially proposed this reflection as a heuristic means of gaining insight into the just soul (369a, b) and, indeed, even after he later expresses serious misgivings about its adequacy for this (435d), the young men are absorbed almost exclusively by the work of political construction. It falls to us, then, to remember the original project and search out the reasons for Socrates' misgivings. (ii) In response to his own objection at 504b, Socrates introduces "the Idea of the Good" as "the greatest object of study" (505a); then, however, he insists that they "dismiss for the time being the question of what the Good itself is—for it seems to me that to reach what I now hold about it is beyond our present impetus (ὁρμὴν)" (506e), and he substitutes, instead, his images of the sun and the divided line and the cave. *That* these are images becomes striking precisely as we begin to understand them. All three announce the order of being that is prior to the physical-sensible—and yet rely on the physical-sensible to do so. At the close of his account of the stages of philosophical education, Socrates gives Glaucon an indirect explanation for the necessity of this procedure; at the same time, Plato seems to challenge us to overcome this necessity. Refusing to give an account of "the power of dialectic" (532d), Socrates says: "You would no longer be able to follow, my dear Glaucon—it is not that I am not eager [to go ahead]—for you would no longer be seeing an image of what we are discussing but, rather, the truth itself, or so it seems to me." (533a) Both in these lines and, generally, in the tension between form and content in the three images, we are challenged to overcome Glaucon's reliance upon imagery and the limitations it imposes on Socrates in order, in turn, to appropriate what Glaucon cannot—the genuine Socratic insight into the forms and, especially, the Good. (iii) At 519d ff. and again at 540a ff., Socrates puts the figure of the philosopher back into the political context of the just city. At 519d ff., Socrates tells Glaucon that once the philosopher has "seen" the Good "sufficiently," he must be required "to go down again to the prisoners in the cave" in order to "care for and guard them." At 540a ff., he declares how, at the age of fifty,

those who have survived the tests and have excelled in everything, both in deeds and in studies, must at last be led to the goal. And once, having lifted up the beams of their souls (τὴν τῆς ψυχῆς αὐγὴν) and looked upon that which provides light for everything, they have seen the Good itself, each in turn must be required (ἀναγκαστέον), taking it as a model, to bring order to the city and other individuals (ἰδιώτας) and themselves for the rest of their lives. For the most part they spend their time in philosophy, but each when his turn comes drudges in politics and rules for the city's sake, doing this not as something splendid (καλόν τι) but as something necessary. And thus always educating other like men (ἄλλους . . . τοιούτους) and leaving them behind in their place as guardians of the city, they go off to dwell in the Isles of the Blessed.

Glaucon, like Adimantus much earlier (419a), objects: Socrates seems to make the philosophers, the paradigmatically just men, "live a worse life when [by keeping to themselves and their studies] they could live a better" (519d). Socrates' reply, even while it satisfies Glaucon, should move us to raise further questions. If we grant that he is right to be concerned with the happiness not of a select few but, rather, of all the citizens together (519e ff.) and that only a city governed by those "least eager to rule" will be free of internal faction (520c–521b), still we should want to learn more about the philosopher's disinterest. On the one hand, what does it suggest about the type of soul that Socrates puts forth as the paradigm of justice? If the philosopher does not want to take up the responsibility of "caring for and guarding" others, and if he does take it up only in an act of self-sacrifice, has Socrates really presented an alternative to the selfishness that Thrasymachus proclaimed as universal at the outset (especially 338d ff.)? However distinct in their actions, *at the level of inclination* the philosopher would seem convergent with the tyrant, and justice, as he embodies it, would seem to come only at the cost of his happiness. On the other hand, such a convergence would leave the central dramatic fact of the *Republic*, Socrates' presence in the Piraeus, a striking mystery. There is a conspicuous tension between what Socrates *says* at 519d ff. and 540a ff. and what he *does* in initiating and extending the inquiry in the first place; it is, if anything, with a characteristic zest that he himself has "descended" into the Piraeus (327a), seeking out others who are "like" him by his provocations and "educating" them (540b).[9] In contrast

---

9. Is the point of the opening by-play at 327b ff. that Socrates is forced, against his will, to remain in the Piraeus? On this reading, that scene portrays the necessity, for the

to the too quickly satisfied Glaucon, we should remain puzzled and ponder this tension. Is Socrates' description of the philosopher veiled or ironic? Is there anything in what Socrates says about the philosopher that, properly understood and developed, could both undercut the appearance of inner selfishness and explain the extraordinary generosity of Socrates' own political-educative practice?

In the following sections we shall take up each of these Platonic provocations. Our aim shall be to let the provocations themselves lead us. Although the three sets of issues are, initially, apparently discrete, they will turn out to be closely interrelated, and the reflections they occasion will give us the elements for an understanding of the unspoken vision that lies at the heart of the *Republic* as a whole.

II. PROBLEMS IN THE ANALOGY OF CITY TO SOUL

"If you wish, first let us investigate what justice is in cities. Then afterwards let us consider it, in turn, in the individual, examining the likeness of the larger in the form of the smaller."

"What you say seems sound to me," he said.

"Well then, if we should witness in theory a city come into being, would we also see its justice come into being, and its injustice?"

"Probably, yes."

"And as the process went on, could we hope to see what we are searching for more easily?" (369a–b)

Given the explicitly tentative and heuristic nature of Socrates' initial proposal of the analogy of justice in the city to justice in the soul, it is

---

survival of philosophy, of some compromise between the philosopher and the many. See, e.g., Allan Bloom's commentary in *The Republic of Plato* (New York, 1968), pp. 310–312. Much of this reading is interesting and persuasive. In particular, it is sensitive to Plato's depiction of the rise of commercial culture and the attendant erosion of aristocratic values. But it is very implausible that Socrates does not want to remain. Note that he makes no effort to "persuade" Polemarchus against forcing him to stay; on the contrary, he encourages Polemarchus by showing interest in the torch race (328a). Moreover, as narrator he makes a point of reporting Polemarchus' mention of the prospect of later "conversation" (διαλεξόμεθα, 328a) with "many of the young." Most basically, however, this is just the battle—the effort to generate, in the youth, a spiritual resistance to Piraean values—that Socrates joins with such zeal on so many occasions; one thinks especially of the *Gorgias*, the *Symposium*, the *Meno*, and the *Protagoras*. If anything, his making a show to Polemarchus of "hurrying off on [his] way back to town" (Polemarchus' words, 337b) may be designed to provoke the latter to come after him. (Compare the ruse of his late arrival at Agathon's party in the *Symposium*.) If so, this would be, as an opening dramatization, Plato's forewarning of Socrates' strategy throughout.

striking that later, when it comes time to look from the city to the soul, Glaucon seems to have granted the analogy the status of a positive truth. Thus when at 434c Socrates sums up the account of justice in the city, Glaucon gives his unreserved endorsement (434d); that Socrates must reply by reminding Glaucon that they have yet to "apply" this account to individuals (434d–435a) shows that Glaucon has no misgivings about the analogy. What is more, Glaucon is content simply to ignore the misgivings that Socrates goes on to declare he himself does have:

"But know well, Glaucon, that in my opinion we shall never get a precise grasp [of the inner order of the soul] by following methods of the sort we are now using in the argument. There is another longer and fuller path which leads to that. Perhaps, however, we can proceed in a way that is worthy of our statements and investigations so far."

"Mustn't we be content with that?" he said. "It would be enough for me at present." (435c–d)

Again at the close of Book IV when Socrates sums up the results the analogy has yielded, Glaucon shows the same complacency, failing to respond to Socrates' ironic indication of problems: when, for instance, Socrates calls the notion of justice derived from the city "a kind of phantom (*eidolon ti*) of justice" (443c), he merely agrees; and when Socrates confirms the claim to "have found the just man and city and what justice really is in them" by saying, "I don't suppose we seem to be completely deceived"[10] (444a), Glaucon gives an almost comically hearty "By Zeus, no indeed!" This persistent lack of discernment is not really surprising. Socrates first proposed the analogy as a heuristic strategy precisely because Glaucon, Adimantus, and the others are, above all, men of the city. They are unaccustomed to the reflexive examination of the interior which their own demand for a defense of justice "for its own sake" requires. It is thus in character that their various objections all bear exclusively on Socrates' just city. To go back to Socrates' telling simile, they suffer a myopia that keeps them from "reading the small letters" (368d) of the soul. Unable to "see" (ἰδεῖν, 369a) the soul except in terms of the city, they are bound to the analogy. Thus it falls to us, noting Socrates' own unease, to pursue its grounds by just the critical "examining" of the "likeness" which he originally called for.

We should establish the context by a synopsis of the well-known basic

---

10. οὐκ ἄν πάνυ τι οἶμαι δόξαιμεν ψεύδεσθαι. Bloom, pp. 310–312, and Grube, *Plato's Republic* (Indianapolis, 1974), both take ψεύδεσθαι as "to lie." Thus Bloom, in particular, accentuates the irony almost to the point of sarcasm: "I don't suppose we'd seem to be telling an utter lie."

structures. The city, first of all, is found to have three major parts, the class of producers and tradesmen, the warrior guardians, and the rulers; their names bespeak their functions: producing material goods, war-making and peace-keeping, and ruling. In the good exercise of these functions, finally, the four virtues come to light. Wisdom, consisting in giving "good counsel" concerning the city as a whole, belongs to the rulers; courage, consisting in unshakable true opinion about what is to be feared and what is not to be feared, belongs to the warrior guardians; temperance, since both the pursuit of material goods and the use of force need be kept within the limits set by the "good counsel" of the rulers, consists in letting "the better" rule and belongs to producers, warriors, and rulers alike. Justice, finally, is the precondition for temperance, the principle of distinction which the harmony achieved by temperance presupposes: it is τὸ τὰ αὑτοῦ πράττειν (433a), "minding one's own business," or, less idiomatically and more elaborately, ἡ τοῦ οἰκείου τε καὶ ἑαυτοῦ ἕξις τε καὶ πρᾶξις (433e–434a), "having and doing what is proper to oneself and is one's own." If each part of the city holds to this and, so, does not interfere with the work of any other, then in each case the work will be well done; and this assures, in turn, that when the producers and warriors defer to the rulers as "the better," the city as a whole will be well ruled and harmonious. Now, once all of this is established, it remains to apply it to the soul. The application reveals the soul as, firstly, tripartite like the city, with its appetites corresponding to the producers, its "spiritedness" (θυμός) corresponding to the warrior guardians, and its "thinking part" (τὸ λογιστικόν) corresponding to the rulers. Given these correspondences, the virtues seem also to carry over from city to soul. Wisdom, consisting in the "knowledge of what is beneficial for each part and the whole community of these three parts" (442c), belongs to the thinking part; courage, the steadfast conviction of what is and is not to be feared, belongs to spiritedness; temperance, consisting in the agreement to let the better part rule, belongs equally to the appetites and spiritedness, which thereby accept the governance of the thinking part, and to the thinking part, which accepts the task of ruling. Justice, in turn, emerges once again as "minding one's own business" (443b and c); and as before, it is because no part—now, however, of the soul—interferes in the work of any other that, given their shared temperance, the whole is well ruled and harmonious.

If, now, we follow Socrates' instruction to "examine" this "likeness" critically, at least two major difficulties come to light. They are distinct but coordinated. The first is implicit in the general strategy of looking at the soul as an analogue to the city; the second is a consequence of the notion of justice that the strategy yields. If we pursue them, we find ourselves led, step by step, into new terrain.

(i) The first difficulty has a double aspect. (a) To begin with, by the strategy of analogy Socrates manages to change the basic context of the whole inquiry. When Glaucon and Adimantus insist on a defense of justice "for its own sake," they mean to focus on the intrinsic benefit of being just in distinction from the social rewards of appearing to be just. What justice itself is, however, they presume themselves to know from the outset; essentially, they accept the conventional notion of self-restraint, of not trying to "get the better" of one's fellows when not provoked to do so, that Socrates defends against Thrasymachus (cf. especially 349bff.). (See, e.g. 360b, d, and 366a.) Conceived this way, justice is social and external; it is a character of one's actions toward others. By beginning with the city, Socrates seems at first to respond in their terms, for justice is present in the city as the principle that regulates the way each man treats his fellow citizens. Precisely because of this focus on the relations internal to the city, however, the shift from city to soul brings justice into view as a regulative principle for relations *internal to the soul*, and so leaves the social context altogether.[11] (b) The point is not, of course, that the new intrapsychic conception of justice has no social implications. Just what these are, however, is in fact obscure. Socrates appears to acknowledge this (as well as to use it to force us to concentrate all the harder on the intrapsychic) when he pauses at 442d ff. to "reassure" Glaucon that the new "justice hasn't in any way been redefined (ἀπαμβλύνεται) so as to seem, now, to be something different from what it was seen to be in the city" (442d). His means of "reassurance" is to ask Glaucon whether the newly conceived just soul would commit any of the acts—sacrilege, theft, breach of oaths and agreements, etcetera—which the latter had earlier taken as clear cases of injustice. With each of Glau-

---

11. As Gregory Vlastos points out in his "Justice and Happiness in the *Republic*," in Vlastos, ed., *Plato* (Garden City, N.Y., 1971), 2:86–87, the key here is a shift from the sense "justice" has as a "relational predicate" naturally applied to individuals (this is what Glaucon and Adimantus have in mind at the start) to the sense it has as a "one-place group-predicate" (this is the sense Socrates introduces by his analysis of justice in terms of the city's whole-part structure). But whereas Vlastos sees an unwitting "equivocation" that vitiates Socrates' argument, I see an intentional play whose purpose is to disclose a terrain otherwise hidden. It would be presumptuous to do more than acknowledge the deep difference in ways of reading this represents. Vlastos honors one side of Plato (and of philosophy in general) by his press for argumentative rigor in the dialogues; the essay cited is a powerful example. The cost, however, may be the obscuring of what I have called the provocative function of Platonic argument; key psychagogic movements are brought to light as, instead, logical errors to be repaired by reconstructions that avoid the need for shifts of basic context.

con's denials (442e–443a), however, we can only ask: why not? That is, what is there to keep the wise, daring, and well ordered—that is, inwardly just—individual from outward actions that, judged by the conventional standards implicit in Socrates' list, would be unjust?[12] The difficulty becomes all the more pressing when we recall that the newly emerging just soul is thought on the analogy of a city which, though just in its internal relations, is a violent aggressor against its neighbors; the very need for a warrior class, we recall, stemmed from the city's act of "cutting off a piece of [its] neighbors' land" (373d) in order to possess surplus wealth. Seen in this light, Socrates' analogy risks not simply dissociating but, even worse, opposing the new intrapsychic and the conventional social conceptions of justice. If this is to be avoided, we must understand more about the new conception than Socrates has so far disclosed. What is there *internal to the soul*, we must ask, that will make the inwardly just individual not a particularly effective aggressor against his fellow citizens but, on the contrary, one who will take his place amongst them with self-restraint and responsibility?

(ii) Is the soul really like the city in the first place, however? Oddly, the conception of justice that the analogy yields serves to expose, in retrospect, an important problem with the analogy. So long as we restrict our focus to a city with a class defined by its function or work of ruling, it will be self-evidently just for this class to rule; for justice is "minding one's own business" and ruling is, by definition, the "own business" of this class. When, however, we turn from city to soul and, correlatively, from the rulers to the thinking part, the situation is suddenly not so self-evident. The "own business" of "the thinking part" should be (to follow the homonymy of "rulers" and "ruling") to *think*, and it is hardly obvious that thinking, in and of itself, will coincide with the practical work of caring for the needs and proper limitation of the appetites and spiritedness. At the very least, thinking is distinct

---

12. This is in essence the question raised by David Sachs in his widely discussed "A Fallacy in Plato's *Republic*," *Philosophical Review* 72 (1963): 141–158, and much of the rest of my discussion constitutes a reply. But it should be clear in advance that there is an ineliminable ambiguity in the idea of judging actions by the conventional (or vulgar) standards (τὰ φορτικά, 442e). Who is to judge? And by reference to the spirit or the letter? If the many are to judge, the spirit may well be lost in the letter, and—to take the obvious example—no less than Socrates' own deeds in the course of this conversation with the young may appear indictable as "betrayal" of his city (442e) and "neglect of the gods" (443a). Thus the discovery of what keeps the inwardly just soul from unjust actions towards his fellows will not guarantee that the actions he does commit may not nonetheless appear to violate conventional standards. This is an issue that Plato treats generally in exploring the problematic relation between the being and appearance of the philosopher and of the statesman in the *Sophist* and *Statesman*, and I have discussed it in my *The Philosopher in Plato's* Statesman, especially chaps. I and IVd.

from the business of ruling the other parts of the soul.[13] Once this distinction becomes apparent, however, it becomes unclear why the work of ruling the other parts of the soul is not a violation, rather than an imperative, of justice. Insofar as it may be contrasted with thinking, ruling appears not as the "own" or "proper business" of the thinking part but, rather, as a reaching beyond its "own business" to attend to that of the other two parts of the soul. It might seem that Socrates' new notion of temperance—letting the better rule—can reverse these consequences. In truth, it only refocuses the basic question. Now that the thinking part can no longer be simply identified by reference to the work of ruling, it needs to be shown both that and how it truly is the better of the three parts. This, however, requires that we first understand it in its "own proper" nature and work, that is, in the thinking by which it comes to its "knowledge," and just such understanding is *blocked in advance* so long as we simply presume the truth of the analogy. If, that is, we conceive the thinking part from the beginning as ruling, we deny ourselves the occasion to investigate what, in its "own"-most activity of thinking, first makes it well suited to rule. Thus we come to an ironic state of affairs: the analogy of city to soul, it turns out, has concealed as much as it has revealed of the soul; now, precisely in order to pursue the notion of justice which reflection on the city has produced, we need to suspend that reflection and turn directly to the inner life of the thinking part of the soul.

On both counts, then, the analogy of city and soul leads us away from the context of the city. Even while Glaucon and the others, "seeing" only the city and not the soul, miss this and (to his ironic dismay) make Socrates go back to his elliptical comments on the "sharing" of women and children, we find ourselves pursuing Plato first from the social context to the interior of the soul and, secondly, from the "sociality" or "other-directed" life of the thinking part to *its* interior. Thus Plato manages to provoke us to ask for deeper inquiry. In what does the "own" and "proper" activity of the thinking part—that is, thinking itself—consist? Given this, why (if at all) should the thinking part rule the soul as a whole? And, even granting that it should,

13. Note the key passage at 442c, in which the soul is called "wise because of that small part which ruled in him and declared these things [i.e., instructions about what is and is not to be feared, to the spirited part of the soul], which has in itself the knowledge of what is beneficial for each part and the whole community of these parts." Though Socrates declares that the thinking part rules, it is not *by virtue of* its wisdom that it does so but, as his next speech (442c–d) declares, by virtue of the whole soul's temperance. Its wisdom consists only in its having the "knowledge" of what benefits each part, not in its doing the work of regulating the other parts on the basis of that knowledge.

why (if at all) will such a just soul make for a just life towards others, much less a life devoted to giving "good counsel" and entitled to rule in society?

III. THE OBSCURITY OF THE GOOD

That Socrates' dismay is indeed ironic becomes clear from his response to the demand to go back to the issue of women and children. Seizing on what (he says) he earlier sought to avoid, Socrates develops the notions of the equality of male and female and of the abolition of the private family. Such "sharing" amounts to purging from the idea of political leadership the qualifications of manliness and noble lineage, and this runs so deeply counter to Greek heritage that it seems to make Socrates' just city utterly implausible and impossible to actualize. Evidently, this is just what Socrates intends. To Glaucon's impatient question, how could such a city ever be made actual? (471c–e), Socrates responds by designating the one life-praxis that is genuinely disinterested in the contingencies of body and social prestige—philosophy. Of course, his famous assertion that the actualization of the just city requires the philosopher-king really only heightens the political implausibility of his proposal. But this too seems to be what Socrates intends. Glaucon and the others can now pursue their interest in his city only by demanding an explication of the nature of the philosopher, and it is here, finally, that Socrates sees the one true hope for an alternative to Thrasymachean self-seeking.

With these developments, the Socratic and Platonic levels of provocation converge, only to diverge again. On the one hand, Socrates' politically oriented interlocutors, aroused by the three waves of paradox (457b ff., 472a, 473c), and we, aroused by the difficulties in the analogy of the city to soul, now have joint occasion to explore the "proper" activity of the thinking part of the soul. On the other hand, thinking is least other-directed, most concentrated on what is "its own," when it is devoted to the "greatest object of study," the "form of the Good" (505a); yet it is just this, as we noted earlier, that Socrates declares "beyond our present impetus" (506e) because Glaucon and the others "would no longer be able to follow" (533a). Thus provoked, we must part company with them, searching beneath the surface of Socrates' presentation for a more adequate grasp of the Good.

As before, it is best to begin by synopsizing what Socrates makes explicit. The two key passages are his presentations of the similes of the sun (507a–509c) and the divided line (509d–511e).

507a–509c: Socrates begins by recalling the earlier agreement (at

475e–480a) that the forms—the beautiful itself or the Good itself, for example, each of which is one and is titled "that which is"—are to be distinguished from their many participants; whereas the forms are the proper subject matter for "intellection" (νοεῖσθαι), the many participants are subject matter for "sight" (507a–b). He then proposes that the Good plays epistemic and ontic causal roles "in the intelligible" (ἐν τῷ νοητῷ) precisely analogous to those which the sun plays "in the visible" (ἐν τῷ ὁρατῷ). As the sun provides the light which makes things visible and, so, empowers the eye to see them, so the Good gives to the objects of knowledge—that is, presumably, the forms—"the truth" (τὴν ἀλήθειαν) which first lets them be knowable and, so, empowers the soul to know them. It is important to note here that when he matches "truth" with light in the simile, Socrates characterizes it not as a property of the relation of the intellect and its object but, rather, as the precondition for such a relation; like light "in the visible," truth is what first lets the object-to-be present itself to, and so become object for, the intellect. It is as source for this precondition, in turn, that the Good plays an epistemic causal role. In addition, Socrates goes on, as the sun is the source of "the generation and growth and nourishment" of things, so the Good is the source of "the being" (τὸ εἶναί τε καὶ τὴν οὐσίαν) of the objects of knowledge—again, presumably, the forms. This is its ontic causal role. Thus the Good is responsible for the being known and the being itself, as such, of what is known.

509d–511e: Once this is established, Socrates turns to the distinction between "the intelligible" and "the visible" and offers the figure of the divided line to explicate their relation. He proceeds by three steps. First, he distinguishes within "the visible" between sensible images (shadows, reflections, and the like) and the physical things of which they are images. Second, he makes use of this distinction, familiar in ordinary experience, to disclose the unfamiliar relation, hidden in ordinary experience, between things and forms: the objects of "opinion"—that is, natural and artifactual individuals—relate to the objects of "knowledge"—that is, forms—analogously as, within "the visible" or "opinable," likenesses relate to that of which they are likenesses. Finally, he distinguishes "the intelligible" or "knowable" into two sections. On the one hand, there is a sort of "reasoning" (διάνοια) typical of geometry; although the geometer's subject matter is forms, in his ordinary practice he relies on sensible things (drawn figures, for instance) to serve as images, and he takes his most basic notions for granted as "evident to everyone" (παντὶ φανερῶν, 510d), treating them as "premises" (ὑποθέσεις, 510c) and giving no direct account of them.

On the other hand, there is the pure and critical "thinking" (νόησις) proper to philosophical dialectic; the dialectician dispenses with images, making use only of forms, and he treats what the geometer takes as premises as, instead, "springboards" for further inquiry, seeking their ultimate foundation. Thus Socrates sorts out the initial two types, "the visible" and "the intelligible," into a series of four: the awareness which has mere sensible images as its objects, the "trust"-ful (πίστις) or unsceptical perception of physical things, the "reasoning" typified by geometry, and the "thinking" typified by dialectic.

Socrates' similes work, in a sense, in two directions. As a first introduction to the notion of the purely intelligible, they are vivid and clarifying expositions of what is strange in terms of what is familiar. As we reflect upon them, however, we will also be struck by the provocative irony of this procedure; even as Socrates brings the strange down to the level of the familiar, he also incites us, by a series of coordinated problems, to re-ascend to the strange.

To begin with the simile of the sun: By first introducing the Good as "the greatest object of study" (504d ff.), then by his arguments showing that it is neither knowledge nor pleasure (505b ff.), Socrates raises and heightens the question, what *is* the Good? By his simile, however, he addresses the altogether different question, what does the Good *do*? Since the work that something does—its causal power—is a consequence of what it is, this is a provocative shift; like the geometers he goes on to criticize, Socrates appears to take what is basic for granted and to start, instead, from what really first follows from it.[14] The effect of this should be to awaken a "dialectical" resistance in us; we will want to reverse Socrates' procedure, treating his account of what the Good causes as a "springboard" for just the inquiry he appears to drop. What must the Good *be*, we will ask, if by virtue of this it is to do the work of causing the being and the intelligibility of the forms? So soon as we raise this question, however, two further problems with the simile present themselves. First, Socrates tells us next to nothing about what the forms are; indeed, after beginning by recalling the results of the earlier account at 475e–480a, he does not even mention them explicitly by name again. But we can hardly understand what in the nature of the Good qualifies it to cause the being and intelligibility of the forms if we do not first understand what this "being" comes to and how, in it, the forms are "intelligible." Secondly, there is the tension we

---

14. For an illustration of such presumption in the ordinary routines of geometrical practice, see *Meno* 82a ff., together with R. M. Hare's comments in "Plato and the Mathematicians," in R. Bambrough, ed., *New Essays on Plato and Aristotle* (New York, 1965), pp. 24–27.

noted earlier between the form and the content of the simile itself. If we do not discover this for ourselves, Socrates' objection to the geometer's reliance on sensible images should alert us to it. What the simile reveals, on the one hand, is an order of being distinct from and somehow prior to sensible things; the way it makes this revelation, on the other hand, is by representing that order in terms of the relations between sensible things. Thus the content of the simile stands in tension with its mode. If we accept the simile as true, then we need to dispense with simile itself, reformulating our insight "without making use of anything visible at all, but proceeding by means of forms" (511c). We therefore come to the divided line passage with a complex task: to win a nonimagistic understanding of what the forms are, in their "being" and "intelligibility," in order, in turn, to understand what the Good is, such that it can be cause of these.

On first inspection, Socrates' presentation of the divided line appears only to reproduce the difficulties of the simile of the sun. Not only does he not explicate the Good—he does not even mention it. And though he does now turn explicitly to the forms, he interprets them by yet another sensible simile: sensible things relate to forms as shadows and reflections relate to the sensible things they are shadows and reflections of; thus things are like sensible images, and forms are like the originals or models 'imaged.' The strength of the simile is the clarity with which it expresses the notion of the responsibility of one sort of entity for the very being and recognizability of another. It is familiar to us from ordinary experience that shadows and reflections are—and, too, that we immediately recognize them as—what they are only by virtue of an essential relation to something both different in kind and prior. This very reliance on ordinary experience, however, also makes the simile dangerous. As with the simile of the sun, so here the content of Socrates' thought stands in tension with his mode of thinking. To suggest the insubstantiality of sensible things in relation to forms, he must appeal to our everyday "trust" in their substantiality in relation to shadows and reflections; to introduce us to the status of forms as models for things, he invites us first to think of things as models for forms. As before, therefore, the final effect of the simile is to challenge us to rethink it, to reappropriate its content in a nonimagistic way.

At just this point, however, Socrates offers something new and, potentially, decisively helpful. In his third step, he contrasts mathematical thinking with philosophical dialectic. Ironically, one of the major defects of the ordinary practice of geometry—its reliance on images—makes it a timely means beyond imagistic thinking and towards the possibility of a more adequate grasp of the forms. Socrates stresses how geometers "use as images" just the sort of sensible things that, within "the visible," are "imitated" by shadows and reflections (510b); thus they "mold" three-dimensional structures and "draw" real figures (510e). At the same time, they "know" that the true referents of their thinking are not these but, rather, the forms—for instance, "the square itself" and "the diagonal itself" (510d)—that these merely "resemble" (ἔοικε, 510d). To be sure, this may be no more than tacit, practical "knowledge"; insofar as they do not step back to reflect explicitly on it, the geometers fall short of dialectic.[15] If, however, we now let Socrates' criticism move us to step back, we can recognize the crucial philosophical notion to which geometry bears witness. By the nature of its concepts, geometry makes peculiarly clear the inappropriateness of thinking the forms imagistically: the exactitude of these concepts makes conspicuous the *imperfection* of every physical representation of geometrical form.[16] Socrates will later point this out

---

15. Plato appears to offer a general presentation of this danger in his portrayal of the geometer Theodorus in the *Theaetetus*. For the way in which his antipathy for "abstract inquiries" (165a) keeps his mathematical insight from becoming knowledge in the Platonic sense, note especially 147d.

16. In "Plato on the Imperfection of the Sensible World," *American Philosophical Quarterly* 12 (1975): 105–117, Alexander Nehamas argues against the traditional reading that takes sensibles, in general, to fall short of their forms by virtue of their being only approximately what their forms are exactly. He argues, instead, that forms are "essentially" what sensible particulars, since they "possess their properties only in an incomplete manner," are only "accidentally" (p. 116). Thus, the imperfection of particular equals would consist not in their not actually being equals but, rather, in their being "equal only to some things and not to others," while the form "equality is always equal" (p. 116). On the one hand, Nehamas' reading, although it is directed primarily to the *Phaedo*, provides a much better interpretation of *Republic* 475e–480a than does the traditional reading. After all, in what sense is a beautiful thing only "approximately" beautiful? The mathematical notions of exactitude and approximation simply do not apply to many sorts of form and instance. How, then, has the traditional reading arisen and taken hold in the first place? It would seem that it is an inappropriate generalization from what Plato has Socrates say about geometrical forms in *Republic*, VI–VII, especially at 529d ff. There (as quoted in my text) Socrates says explicitly that celestial phenomena, though "the most exact of visible things," still "fall short of true beings"; this is easily taken to imply that it is in respect of exactness that all visible things fall short of forms. The proper correction, I think, is to point out that (as Socrates' formulation at 530b—also quoted in my text—seems to indicate) the inexactness that makes celestial motions imperfect should itself be interpreted as a case of possessing properties "incompletely" and "accidentally": for the motion of a star to "deviate" at certain points from perfectly circular form is for it both to be circular (when projected from the non-deviant points through which it passes) and not to be circular (when projected from the points at which it "deviates"). Having said this in agreement with Nehamas, one should also say, in behalf of the (now refocused) tradition, that the contrast of exact and approximate is, as a species of the more general contrast of perfect and imperfect, particularly important at a certain stage of philosophical education. The thought of the perfectly beautiful, for instance, does not in itself force us beyond the sensible as a frame of reference; because beauty characterizes the sensible, it is easy (indeed, all too

when, discussing the educational value of astronomy, he stresses that even the heavens, "the most beautiful and the most exact (ἀκριβέ-στατα) of visible things, fall far short of true beings" (529d); just as "a man versed in geometry" would regard it as "absurd" to "examine" even the very best physical drawings "with any serious hope of finding in them the truth about equals or doubles or any other ratio" (529e), so "a real astronomer" (530a) would "consider it bizarre to believe that [celestial phenomena], since they are corporeal and visible, are always the same and do not deviate at all anywhere" (530b). Since such imperfection is a manifest feature of *every* physical representation, it is also manifest, conversely, that *the forms—precisely as, in each case, "the perfect" with respect to some geometrical character—cannot be or be thought as sensible things.* This negative insight, in turn, clears the way for a newly radical interpretation of the notion of the function of the forms as originals or models. Since it is now evident that "the square itself," for instance, cannot itself be a square thing,[17] there can be no question of imagining that one "looks," in any sense requiring an image for an object, from the former to the latter or *vice versa.* Nonetheless, the geometer is able to "mold" and to "draw" his various sensible representations of "the square itself." To do this, it would seem, he must have "the square itself" in mind from the outset, as the principle of design according to which he constructs his sensible representations.[18] It would also be the basis for his recognition of the figures others construct; that a certain range of drawings, however rough and ready, immediately present themselves as squares, indicates that the form is present from the beginning, serving as the criterion for the

---

easy) to fail to realize that we must now "convert" (518c) to "something" essentially nonsensible. With the notion of "the square itself," on the other hand, it is clear and striking that we cannot be referring to anything sensible in kind. This makes mathematical studies a timely occasion for philosophical reflection on the difference in kind between forms and sensibles, and the traditional reading, so far as it brings this out, is well oriented.

17. As already indicated in n. 16, geometrical examples have particular power. In terms of contemporary analysis of Plato, we might say that they enable us to distinguish a possible implication of self-predication that Plato consistently objects to—namely, thinking the forms as if they were spatially determinate beings—from self-predication itself; "the square itself," as perfectly square, *both* cannot be spatial (and so cannot be an instance or specimen of squareness) *and* is self-predicative. For a lucid formulation of the purely logical notion of self-predication this requires, see Alexander Nehamas, "Self-Predication and Plato's Theory of Forms," *American Philosophical Quarterly* 16 (1979): 93–103.

18. Thus, geometrical construction would make vivid the sense in which the form of a thing is (to borrow from the *Gorgias*) that principle of "order appropriate to [a thing]" that, "present in it, makes it good" (506e). For a statement of this same idea after the *Republic,* see (under the interpretation of "the One" in hypothesis III as a thing's defining form) *Parmenides* 158b–d.

geometer's spontaneous perceptual identifications. Forms function as originals or models, therefore, in the sense that, as a priori principles of structure for sensibles, they first enable these latter to be—and enable us to recognize them for—what they are.

Needless to say, there is much more that needs to be explicated before we will have given anything like a full articulation of the theory of forms.[19] Nonetheless, we have won the basis for a first response to the complex task implied by the simile of the sun. The key is the concept of perfection. Because of the way it leads thinking beyond the sensible, it puts us in position to give a nonimagistic account of what the forms are, in their distinctive being and intelligibility; the implications of this account, in turn, serve as a "springboard" back to the prior question of the nature of the Good. (i) *The being of the forms*: To generalize from the geometrical cases, each form just *is* "the perfect" with regard to—or the perfection of—some definite character. Hence, it is that character καθ 'αὐτό, "itself as it is in accordance with itself alone." To see this is to grasp the sense and the necessity of Socrates' earlier characterization of the form as τὸ παντελῶς ὄν, "what is [what it is][20] fully" or "all-completely" (477a). As the perfection of a character, a form cannot be lacking in that character in any possible respect; it will be what it is "fully," with no restriction by any contrary or privative character. This, in turn, brings out the necessity for the difference in kind that Socrates ascribes to forms in making them the originals in

---

19. In fact, the *Republic* connects with the *Parmenides* in a way evidently designed to introduce such a full articulation in the latter dialogue. The pointedly Parmenidean accounts of the forms as "beings" (with no admixture of non-being) and as "ones" at the close of Book V and again in Book X suggest that the elder Socrates has benefited deeply from the exchange which, according to a Platonic fiction in the *Theaetetus* and the *Parmenides*, he had as a young man with Parmenides. When, accordingly, we trace "back" to the *Parmenides*, we find Parmenides, not limited by an unprepared and not-yet-philosophical audience (136d–137b) as the elder Socrates is in the *Republic*, providing guidance for a conceptual explication of the doctrine of forms. By setting aside the simile of likeness/original and distinguishing the precise senses of "is" and "being" proper to forms and to things, Parmenides leads, in the hypotheses, just the "conversion" of soul from things to forms for which the elder Socrates, given his audience, can only call in *Republic*. By connecting these dialogues in this complex way, Plato offers two beginnings—the *Republic* for thoughtful men still immersed in the everyday, the *Parmenides* for those who have made the first beginning—in understanding the forms. I have attempted to spell this out in detail in my *Plato's* Parmenides, *the "Conversion" of the Soul*, Princeton University Press, forthcoming.

20. Since the "all-complete" way in which, e.g., the Beautiful "is" is set into specific contrast with the partial way in which any beautiful thing "is beautiful" (479a), I take it that ὄν at 477a points back to a grammatically predicative use of ἔστι. Thus Socrates' talk of the "being" of the forms refers not to their existence, as such, but rather to their self-relation, that is, to the way in which each *is* itself, or *is* καθ' αὐτό ("in accordance with itself alone").

his second simile.[21] Like shadows and reflections, sensible things are essentially dependent on a medium; to be a sensible thing is to be both spatially and temporally determinate and, as such, essentially subject to shifting spatial perspectives, to the changing phases of a history, and (at least for all terrestrial particulars) to eventual nonexistence. Such conditionedness gives rise to various respects in which the thing in question will lack the very characters that in other respects it has. As the perfections of these characters, the forms must therefore be different in kind from sensible things; they must transcend all spatial and temporal determinateness, being placeless and timeless. (ii) *The intelligibility of the forms*: Likewise, the intelligibility of the forms cannot be assimilated to that of their instances. Since it is only in—or strictly, as—their proper forms that characters present themselves perfectly, it is only as their forms that characters are παντελῶς γνωστόν, "fully knowable" (477a); hence the forms are the proper and preeminent objects of knowledge. The notion of "object" here, however, requires a distinction. As the geometrical case makes clear, we grasp forms for what they are when, stepping back from sensible objects, we reflect on what we have judged or recognized these to be. This suggests that

---

21. For powerful argument that Plato asserts between forms and their participants a difference not in kind but only in degree, see Gregory Vlastos, "Degrees of Reality in Plato" (in his *Platonic Studies*, [Princeton, 1973], pp. 58–75). By setting the participants into analogy only with what are distinctively "insubstantial images," however, Plato in the second simile does suggest difference in kind. (For the distinction between "insubstantial" and "substantial images," see Edward Lee, "On the Metaphysics of the Image in Plato's *Timaeus*," *Monist*, 50 (1966): 341–368, especially p. 353.) It is possible, of course, that Plato is inconsistent in the *Republic*. To argue this, we would oppose to the second simile's assertion of difference in kind a number of other passages' apparent assertion of difference in degree—e.g., the comparison of the "being" of participants and forms at 475e–480a, the setting of participants into analogy with "substantial images" in the allegory of the cave and again in the account of μίμησις in Book X, and the characterization of forms as μᾶλλον ὄντα, "more real," than their participants at 515d. On the other hand, it is also possible that Plato's talk of difference in degree is only a way of introducing the forms to minds long and deeply accustomed to thinking only of sensible things. How else than by comparison with the familiar can the radically strange be presented? On this possible line of interpretation we would need to distinguish two stages of philosophical formulation: that which is appropriate to the effort to break beyond the familiar, and that which, presupposing the success of that effort, is appropriate to the new context, no longer strange, that we have come to grasp. (For a distinction of this kind, see Lee, "Reason and Rotation: Circular Movement as the Model of Mind (Nous) in the Later Plato," in W. H. Werkmeister, ed., *Facets of Plato's Philosophy* [Amsterdam, 1976], pp. 70–102, especially pp. 90–93.) Plato's major effort to shift from the first to the second sort of formulation occurs, I will argue elsewhere (see n. 19), in the *Parmenides*. If, however, he already has the shift in view as the future task implied by the present of the *Republic*, then, since in the *Parmenides* he distinguishes form and participant as different in kind, the simile in the divided line passage may be interpreted as representing his deepest insight, truest to his conception of the forms, in the *Republic*.

forms are given to be known in two different ways. On the one hand, by trying to bring into focus that perfection that sensibles can present only in certain limited respects, we aim at explicit knowledge of the form; here the form is, as a distinct and explicit object, the goal of inquiry. The reflection by which we inquire, however, is itself first possible only if the perceptions upon which we reflect are already guided by the presence of the form. It is only by a tacit and implicit reference to the perfect that recognition of sensibles for what they imperfectly are is possible, and it is this tacit reference that reflection aims to bring into focus. Here the form is not the goal so much as the enabling condition for inquiry.[22] (iii) *The nature of the Good*: Since it is by virtue of what the Good is that it is fit to be cause of the being and intelligibility of the forms, these reflections already imply a first specification of its nature. Just insofar as each form is the perfection of some one character, it is an instance of perfection itself; moreover, its intelligibility as a perfection presupposes the prior intelligibility of perfection itself. The nature of the Good, therefore, must be just this, perfection itself; the Good will be "the perfect" *as such*.[23] Note the remarkable self-consistency this gives the doctrine of forms as a whole. As each one form (the perfection of some one character) is responsible for what limited being and intelligibility its many sensible instances have, so the Good ("the perfect itself") is responsible for the "full" being and intelligibility of the many forms; likewise, as each sensible represents its form imperfectly, so each one form "imperfectly" instantiates the Good. This analogy must be qualified on two key points. First, the sort

22. These reflections appear to capture the epistemological point of the ἀνάμνησις myth. It is not just that inquiry has as its object that which, necessarily in some nonobjectifying way, the mind already "knows." Also, the inner connection between sense-perception and the knowledge of forms now becomes clearer; in particular, it becomes evident why we can trust our perceptual identifications to remind us of the right forms—these identifications are intrinsically dependent upon, as deriving their orientation from, a nonperceptual tacit grasp of these very forms.

23. At this point my account dovetails in different respects with—and so binds together within itself—valuable reflections on the Good offered by Gerasimos Santas in "The Form of the Good in Plato's *Republic*," in *Essays in Ancient Greek Philosophy* 2:232–263 and R. M. Hare, pp. 24–36 (and underscored by N. White, *Plato on Knowledge and Reality* [Indianapolis, 1976], p. 101, n. 57). Hare observes how, for Plato, for a circle to "(really) be a circle" is for it to be "a good or perfect circle"; this is why, Hare argues, Plato thought of the Good as "the source of the being and reality of the circle— and of everything else likewise . . ." (p. 36). Santas makes an extended argument for why the form of the Good should be responsible for the "ideal attributes" asserted of the forms at *Symposium* 211a–b and *Republic* 475e–480a (pp. 235–252), that is, for the various characters implied by the placelessness and timelessness of the being of the forms. By interpreting the Good as "perfection itself," I mean to show what the nature of the Good's goodness is, such that it is "proper" (p. 236) to it that it give rise to the placeless and timeless—that is, "ideal"—"being and reality" of the forms.

of imperfection that applies to forms is *only* analogous, not identical, with that proper to sensibles. Since, as a perfection, a form cannot be a physical existent, it cannot fall short of the Good in any way sourced in spatial or temporal determinateness. Rather, it is because of its proper determinateness as the particular form that it is, that each form falls short. To reappropriate Socrates' language at 475e–480a: because each form *is* the perfection of some *one* character and *is not* the perfection of any other, it is only a limited instance, making only a partial presentation, of the Good. Second, the Good itself both does and does not transcend this determinateness. Here the distinction we drew with regard to the intelligibility of the forms applies, so to speak, at a higher level. On the one hand, Socrates insists that the Good can be made the object of reflective inquiry and "distinguished from all the other [forms]" (534b); but this is to single it out as a determinate being, as the perfection of some *one* character and *not* of any other. On the other hand, when we recognize that this character is just perfection itself,[24] it becomes evident that the Good must also transcend this determinateness. Like "the square itself" with regard to the drawn squares that we recognize in perception, the Good as perfection itself is already tacitly in play in our reflective inquiry, enabling us to recognize each of the various forms for what it is, and in this presence it can no more be reduced to the status of these forms than "the square itself" can be reduced to the status of the drawn squares. This is the sense in which it is "beyond being," that is, the being-what-it-is of each of the forms, "exceeding it in dignity of age and in power" (509b). Note, moreover, that insofar as—in making precisely this last observation—we distinguish the Good for what it is from the other forms, it must bear this relation of transcendence to itself. Like the sun, it cannot be "seen" except by virtue of the "light" that it itself provides; as perfection itself, it is already in play in—as that, tacit reference to which enables—our recognition of it *as* perfection itself. This is why, by contrast with the other forms, it is "unhypothetical" (511b); for its being and intelligibility it presupposes nothing other than itself.

IV. THE PARADOX OF SOCRATES' PRESENCE

These reflections carry us a significant part of the way towards meeting the second Platonic provocation, the challenge to appropri-

---

24. That is, for the Good to be "the perfect" as such is for it to be, as a form, a perfection. But of what? Of perfection itself. The Good is therefore perfectly perfect or, again, the most perfect perfection. The twofold consequence of this is developed below. First, it is a necessary condition for the Good's *both* being that from which "all" (cf. τοῦ

ate for ourselves the genuine Socratic insight into the Good. Moreover, since the Good and the forms are the "proper" concern for philosophical thinking, they also help us to continue our response to the first provocation, the challenge to "see into" the activity of the thinking part of the soul. At the same time, however, they seem incomplete and, on an important count, even unhelpful. In responding to the first provocation, we asked what real connection, if any, there is between thinking and the work of ruling, both within the soul and in the relation of the thinker to others in the city. The interpretation of the Good as perfection itself suggests, at best, why an accomplished philosophical mind might *qualify* one to rule. Both within (in the thinking part's relation to the appetites and spiritedness) and without (in the thinker's relation to nonphilosophers), understanding of the Good and the forms yields the fullest understanding of particulars as well; the accomplished thinker will therefore appreciate the objects of his own appetites and passions and the interests of his fellow citizens better, in each case, than these latter themselves do. (Socrates gives a version of this point at 520b–c and plays on it in many places.) Still, to be qualified to rule is quite different from being genuinely inclined or moved to do so; moreover, it is not yet clear how the desire to apply one's understanding in the work of ruling guarantees that one will strive to rule justly. If anything, these problems appear only more difficult in light of our reflections so far. If at first the Good had the look of moral significance, our present conception of its nature appears to lack this altogether. Perfection itself is constitutive as much for the form of injustice as for that of justice (475e ff.)[25] and, again, as much for "the square itself" and "the diagonal itself" (510d) as for either injustice or justice. Indeed, if we accept Socrates' account of justice as "minding one's own business," it is hard to see any inner link between what this means for the philosopher—a life devoted to reflective inquiry into perfection itself and its instances—and what it means in the context of the city—a life of self-restraint and social responsibility.

παντος, 511b7) the forms derive their "being" as forms *and* being itself one of these forms. (See the close of section III.) Second, it will also turn out that, properly explicated, it is a sufficient condition for the Good's being that from which "all" the forms derive their "being" as forms. (See section IV.)

25. One merit of interpreting the Good as perfection itself is that it allows us to make sense of the several striking passages in which Plato has Socrates refer to forms for vices, for instance, injustice and the bad (*Republic* 475e) and impiety (*Euthyphro* 5d, 6d). These may be understood as, in each case, the perfection of a character, even while the relevant character is a kind of moral deficiency in the person or act, etcetera, to which it belongs; if they are understood this way, they will be no less instances of perfection itself than the forms for the virtues that are their opposites. For a brief discussion of this, see White, *A Companion to Plato's Republic* (Indianapolis, 1979), p. 41.

That this difficulty presents itself here should not, however, be surprising. This is, in essence, just the substance of the third Platonic provocation, at 519d ff. and 540a ff. Socrates says that the philosopher descends to the "drudgery" and "necessity" of ruling only "for the city's sake"—not, by implication, for his own. But if this is so, we observed earlier, then the self-sacrifice of the philosopher-king's descent really masks just another variation on the split, accepted as a fact of nature by Thrasymachus, between self-interest and the interests of others. However admirable for setting aside what he desires for himself for the sake of the city, the philosopher will still be one victimized by internal faction. On the level of genuine inclination, he will represent only a variant of the all-too-familiar selfishness that makes the notion of the value of justice "for its own sake" seem so problematic; Socrates' defense of this notion, in turn, will continue to be, as in Book I, insubstantial.

With an eye to deepening our responses to the first two provocations, we should now turn to the third. As we also observed earlier, Socrates seems to contradict what he *says* by what he *does*.[26] The philosopher *par excellence*, he has spent his life going down into the cave—whether this be the marketplace, a Callias' or an Agathon's house, or the Piraeus—and seeking out his "likes" by relentless pro-

---

26. Discussions of the philosopher's motivation in face of the task of ruling generally focus exclusively on the express argument of the *Republic* (what Socrates says), ignoring its dramatic dimension and the portrait of Socrates as the exemplary philosopher that this contains. (On the importance of this portrait for understanding the moral psychology of the middle dialogues, see Charles Kahn, "Plato on the Unity of the Virtues," in W. H. Werkmeister, ed., *Facets of Plato's Philosophy*, pp. 21–39.) This portrait should bear on the issue in a number of basic ways. (i) The image of the philosopher as primarily contemplative and disinclined towards practical activity, when it is considered together with the portrait of Socrates, begins to look one-sided. Socrates is, of course, contemplative; his famous trance on the way to Agathon's party (*Symposium* 174d ff., see also 220c ff.) is a striking dramatic symbol of this. But Socrates chooses not to remain outside; he emerges from contemplation in order to join the party and play his characteristic role of critic and teacher. (ii) Moreover, there is no intimation that he sacrifices himself, acting against his own personal preference or interest for the sake of the distinct interests of others, in turning from contemplation to practical activity. (iii) Especially in light of Socrates' own description of his activity as "the practice of politics and the true political art" (*Gorgias* 521d, see also *Apology* 30e ff.), the portrait of Socrates should broaden our sense of what Plato intends by the notion of "ruling." Plato has in mind not just or even primarily the official tasks of government but, more generally, participation in the essentially social work of forming the character of the community as a whole. As his brief description at 540b confirms, to "rule" is, in essence, "to bring order to the city" by "education." (iv) Neither the activity of "ruling" in this sense nor the inner unity of the philosopher's psyche in giving himself over to this activity presupposes, as its enabling context, the actuality of the just city envisaged in Books II–IV. Socrates devotes himself to "bringing order" to Athens, and he does so with a passion and involvement that belie the image of the philosopher as "required" to act against his own personal self-interest.

vocative elenchus.[27] Moreover, Plato has him elsewhere call this educative work "the practice of politics and the true political art" (*Gorgias* 521d). Yet nothing external has either "compelled" or enticed him to this extraordinary generosity.[28] On the contrary, Plato portrays him as exceptional for his indifference to the praise and censure alike of his peers. His life thus bespeaks an *inner* source of motivation which, in the *Republic* at least, he chooses not to describe in the depiction of the philosopher that he gives to Glaucon. What is this inner source? Why, moreover, does he choose to keep silent about it?

Different kinds of indications suggest that we must think further about the Good.[29] Consider, in particular, the convergence of these three: (i) When Socrates tells Glaucon that the philosopher takes up the task of ruling "not as something splendid" (οὐχ ὡς καλόν τι, 540b), he undercuts the traditional image of the καλοκαγαθός, the heroic leader whose goodness (-αγαθος) consists in the strength for deeds that are grand and impressive to behold (καλο-). By denying that politics is anything "splendid" in itself, Socrates rules out the look of nobility and the recognition it brings as the philosopher's motivation for ruling. This leaves open the very notion that Socrates' life seems to

27. See, in this context, *Gorgias* 486d. That Socrates often seeks his "likes" amongst those seemingly most opposed to philosophy is explained by his remarks to Adimantus at *Republic* 489e ff. Those most vigorous and capable of greatness will almost inevitably be seduced by the cult of praise and honor away from philosophy and into the pursuit of political power. Callicles, Alcibiades, and Charmides are cases in point.

28. A recurrent theme in Alcibiades' "eulogy" of Socrates in the *Symposium* is the latter's freedom from needs, sexual, social, and material alike. As "unique" (221c) as this makes Socrates, however, it is only the surface of the mystery of his character. To go further, one must ask: *why*—and especially if eros stems from neediness, as Socrates argues—*is he moved* to devote his energies to Alcibiades? In the *Symposium* this question should turn the reader's attention back to Diotima's speech. At 210d she describes the φιλοσοφία of the one on the verge of "seeing" Beauty itself as ἄφθονος, "unjealous" or "generous" or (following Suzy Groden's translation) "fruitful." As Groden's translation suggests, this generosity is to be connected with the power of generation; but note how, when Diotima turns explicitly to this in her closing lines at 212a, she leaves inexplicit just what it is that, by making Beauty itself "visible," permits it, in turn, to inspire the thinker to become generative. Does ᾧ at 212a3 refer to the Good?

29. Other approaches to the question of the philosopher's motivation that focus on the Good are Raphael Demos, "A Fallacy in Plato's *Republic?*" in Vlastos, ed., *Plato* 2: 52–56; John Cooper, "The Psychology of Justice in Plato," *American Philosophical Quarterly* 14 (1977): 151–157; and Nicholas White, *A Companion to Plato's Republic*, especially Introduction, Section 4, and pp. 190–196. All three stress the universality or unqualified character of the Good and find in this the key to why the philosopher who knows the Good will want to realize not just his own good but the good throughout the world, the good for everyone. So far as it goes, this seems correct; but in specifying the kind of action that knowing the Good motivates, it jumps over the question of what, in this knowing, causes it to be motivating *of action* in the first place. (Note, however, White's "inclination" to reject this as a question, p. 49, and his speculative reflections on the Platonic conception of the soul, p. 195.)

attest, an inner motivation stemming from inner experience. (ii) *The major moment* of such experience that Socrates declines to go into with Glaucon, we have seen, is the experience of the Good. Within the constraints imposed by the limitations of the *personae* of the drama, Socrates must decline; Glaucon and the others have not yet embarked on the philosophical education, in particular the study of mathematics, that is necessary to get free of a reliance on imagery. That Plato, in turn, chooses such *personae* in the first place is part of his strategy of 'Marsyan' provocation: by having Socrates remain silent, he moves us to try to recover Socrates' experience of the Good for ourselves. (iii) That this should be our focus appears to be confirmed by a series of important reflections Socrates makes on motivation and μίμησις.[30] In his reformation of traditional poetry and music in Books II–III, Socrates' main concern is to eliminate various images of gods and heroes and various literary and musical modes that will be bad influences on the young souls of future guardians. The presupposition underlying all of his analysis is that the soul, impressed by these images and modes, will "assimilate itself" (ἐνδύεται, 377b) to them, taking on within itself the dispositions they express. Gods and heroes are models, so it is natural for the soul, presented with images of them, to take on the traits that these images embody. This is especially so when poetry is written in the "imitative" mode (392d), for this requires of those engaged in recitation, whether as performers or enthralled audience, that they "form themselves according to and fit themselves into the moulds of" (396d–e) the character-types the poetry presents. Now, the philosopher is a "lover" not of the "sights and sounds" provided by traditional poetry but, rather, of the inner spectacle of the forms (474c ff.); as different as his object is, however, he too is drawn to emulate it. As Socrates says at 500c, "he imitates (μιμεῖσθαι) and, as

---

30. Socrates' comments on μίμησις in Books II–III and the extension of the notion to describe the philosopher's response to experience of the forms (500c) and, in particular, of the Good take on a new forcefulness if, following H. Koller's horizon-setting *Die Mimesis in der Antike* (Bern, 1954), we make the external notion of μίμησις as *nachahmen* or "imitate" (to wit, copying one existent thing by making another that resembles it in appearance) secondary to the richer notion of μίμησις as *darstellen* or "exhibit" (to wit, giving expressive form to . . . , bodying . . . forth as . . .). Koller recovers this latter sense by discovering and reflecting on the fact that, for the Greeks, dance and musical performance are types of μίμησις prior to painting and its pursuit of likeness. In music and dance, μίμησις refers to the way the performer gives his body over as the medium in which the substance of the music is expressed and given form as melody and gesture. Here the performer—to bring out the sense of Plato's expression at *Republic* 377b— "assimilates himself" to that substance, becoming in his own being as performer an expression of it. In the following paragraphs I will be exploring the possibility that an analogously mimetic relation holds between the Good and the philosopher's soul.

much as possible, fashions himself after the model of (ἀφομοιοῦσθαι) [the forms]. Do you suppose one can keep company with what one admires without imitating it in one's own person?" Since, in turn, it is the Good that, of all the forms, is "the greatest object of study" (505a) for the philosopher, it is the Good, most of all, that he will "assimilate himself" to. "Keeping company with" it by means of persistent reflective inquiry into the perfections of various characters and into perfection itself, he will come to constitute, by his own character and comportment, a kind of analogue in the context of human being to the nature of the Good.

These observations bring us back once more to the question of the nature of the Good. Once again we are given a work—a causal power—of the Good and must use it as a "springboard" for inquiry into what the Good is. Now, however, the work is not ontological and epistemological so much as it is existential and ethical. What is it, we must ask, in the nature of perfection itself such that the philosopher—that is, Socrates as the exemplary philosopher—will be moved by the inner spectacle of it to his extraordinary generosity?

On reflection, it becomes evident that we must develop and deepen our preceding interpretation of the Good as perfection if we are to answer this question. On two related counts, "the perfect itself" as a model for μίμησις would seem likely to give rise to the philosophers Socrates talks about rather than to the philosopher he himself is—that is, to thinkers who are free of "envy and ill will" (500c) only because, having discovered something beyond the physical and social, they have little interest in the concerns of the human everyday. First of all, our interpretation so far leaves particularly obscure just that ontological aspect of the Good that would seem most relevant to the existential account we are seeking. If it is Socrates' generosity, his great-spirited interest in human affairs, that is an analogue to the Good, then the aspect of the nature of the Good most important to consider would be its "generosity" in giving rise to the other forms and, through this, to sensibles. Our interpretation in section III has indeed shown what the Good must be, and what the forms must be, if forms and sensibles, respectively, are to be instantiations; but it has not shown why there should be instantiations in the first place. We have shown about the nature of the Good only what is necessary, not what is sufficient, for it to be cause of the being and intelligibility of the forms and sensibles. This limitation is a reflection of the mathematical context from which we generalized. To grasp the forms as the referents of exact concepts is to make the concrete instances of the forms—in particular, the geometer's inexact physical representations—dispensable and, however subjectively useful, objectively unnecessary. Our whole stress is on the way the forms transcend, and in their own being are indifferent to the existence of, sensible particulars. As we have seen, this is of crucial value to the thinker who is trying to make the "conversion" of mind from sensibles to the Good—at the same time, however, it leaves quite mysterious what in the Good might move the same thinker to descend again, to a new interest in sensibles. Secondly (and this really just focuses the first count), the very nature of "the perfect itself"—as it emerges in the mathematical context—seems almost pointedly unhelpful. "The square itself," for instance, is that which, as perfectly square, lacks nothing of squareness; this is why it cannot be a square thing but, instead, just is squareness itself, "as it is in accordance with itself alone" (καθ' αὐτό). Perfection here comes to light as the lack of any deficiency in being such-and-such; "the perfect" will therefore be that which, being in no way needy, is "fully" (παντελῶς) sufficient to itself. Why would such a nature give rise to other forms and, through this, to sensibles? Correlatively, why wouldn't the philosopher, "assimilating himself" to such self-sufficiency as a spiritual model, live a life of inner detachment from others?

As so often in the *Republic*, putting the difficulty in the sharpest possible focus is itself the beginning of a way through. Our questions naturally provoke counterquestions. Does such detachment constitute the best expression of self-sufficiency? Or, to compress this into the relevant paradox, does that sort of self-sufficiency express the most perfect perfection? As we ponder this, the text of the *Republic* offers two striking figures. The first is political and occurs at 371e ff. By his first description of the just city, Socrates provokes Glaucon to object:[31] a city that produces all that it needs *and nothing more*, which is, therefore, materially self-sufficient and so "complete" (τελέα), is really a "city of pigs" (372d) and not yet fully human. By the development he gives to Glaucon's objection, Socrates shows that the political sphere can provide only ambiguous evidence for the distinction Glaucon wants to make; surplus wealth requires the violent expropriation of neighboring lands, and this, setting the city against its neighbors and introducing internal faction, undercuts self-sufficiency. Nonetheless, Socrates accepts the distinction itself: having just enough and having more than enough are distinct forms of self-sufficiency, and in proportion as this "more" exceeds what is "enough," having more than enough is a higher form. If, now, we ask how this bears on the Good,

---

31. Recall n. 4, above.

the second striking figure, Socrates' simile of the sun, presents itself—and in an aspect that the mathematical context of our earlier reflections gave us no occasion to exploit. The sun is a precise figure for that which, needing nothing other than itself to be itself, has, as it were, more than enough of itself. Nor does it hoard this surplus; rather, as if by a generous treasurer, this is "paid out" (ταμιευομένην) in a sort of "overflow" (ἐπίρρυτον) as the light which enables sight (508b) and nourishes all living things (509b). Thus, the sun is precisely not "detached" from what is other than it; on the contrary, *in being itself it gives of itself unstintingly*, dispensing the light by which everything else can grow and become. To extend this now to the Good: for it to be itself as "the perfect itself" is for it to be what it is as "fully" or perfectly as possible, and this is for it to suffice to itself in the form of having more than enough of itself. From its very nature, therefore, the Good gives of itself. This essential "generosity" suffices for it to be cause of the forms (including itself) and of sensibles; it gives to the forms the perfection that each, to be itself, must have in its properly determinate way; and since each form thereby instantiates the Good, they too will be "generous," giving to sensibles the characters that these, to be themselves, must have in their properly determinate ways.

That this recaptures, at least in outline, the vision of the heart of the *Republic* seems indirectly attested by the way it responds to the three Platonic provocations. In making explicit the inner experience Socrates chooses to withhold from Glaucon, we open up for ourselves the "own"-most activity of the thinking part of the soul; and since this is the experience of the Good, we continue to deepen our penetration of Socrates' similes; finally, once we have penetrated to the present depth, we can see (in terms of the first provocation) the internal connection between thinking and ruling or (in terms of the third) why Socrates, the exemplary thinker, gives of himself so generously to others. Thinking comes most fully into its "own" when, by "dialectical" reflection on its own foundations, it "springs" (cf. ὁρμάς, 511b) "back to the source of the whole" (ἐπὶ τὴν τοῦ παντὸς ἀρχὴν, 511b), that is, to the ultimate atemporal arisal, from "beyond being," of the being and intelligibility of the forms. Here the Good shows itself to be perfection itself and, *as* perfection itself, the spontaneous gift of itself;[32] thus philosophical

---

32. In the *Timaeus*, where Plato has not Socrates but a physical cosmologist present a "likely story" (29c–d) of not the "formal" but the "efficient" causal beginnings of the cosmos, we are given the following remarkable account of the demiurge's motivation in fashioning the world: "He was good, and the good can never have jealousy (φθόνος) of anything. And being free from jealousy, he desired that all things should be as like himself as they could be." (29e–30a) In a similar vein, in the *Statesman* the Eleatic stranger

thinking culminates in an appreciation of the fundamental fact of the *givenness* of the determinate intelligibility of the world.³³ That the Good moves Socrates to his extraordinary generosity should now begin to make sense. In his repeated descents "into the cave," Socrates "assimilates himself" to the content of the experience that is most of all his "own"; "imitating and fashioning himself after the model of" the Good, he gives of himself to others, seeking to enable in them, as fully as they are capable of it, the same insight that moves him. Here the motif of μίμησις expresses a deeply internal connection between soul and the Good. In the very passage at 540a ff. in which Socrates chooses to keep silent on the philosopher's motives for descent, he indicates this in a striking way by referring to the soul as an αὐγή, a "beam of sunlight." If thinking is what is most of all "proper" to the philosopher's soul, the Good, in turn, is both the ultimate guide and the highest goal of thinking; in coming to the Good, therefore, the philosopher comes back to the basis of his own being. In this light, it is only fitting that Socrates chooses to "take the Good as a model" and, as a consequence, gives himself over to the task of ruling, that is, of "bringing order to the city and other individuals and himself." He is only, as it were, "being what he is," expressing in his deeds what he has come to know as his own substance. This is why, finally, his proposal of the philosopher as the just man does, after all, pose a radical alternative to Thrasymachean selfishness. If the surface meaning at 540a–b seems to praise the soul that overpowers its own selfish inclinations by accepting the need for self-sacrifice, beneath the surface he undercuts the static antithesis between self and other, inclination and duty, that this would imply. The thinker does indeed withdraw from others, and from his own physical and social dimensions, as he struggles to make

---

offers a mythical description of the "age of Cronus" when "the god" cared directly for the well-being of the cosmos; in that age, he says, the earth gave men "fruit without stint," καρποὺς ἀφθόνους (272a)—that is, unjealously, without begrudging anything. If we read the second passage against the background of the association of divinity with goodness in the *Republic* (379b ff.), then it stands with the first as a linking, albeit in myth, of the good, freedom from jealousy, and the generous giving-of-self. The passages on the Good in *Republic* VI–VII, by contrast, are provocation to think this nexus directly, free of mythic imagery.

33. Cf. Edward Lee's penetrating remarks on the sense in which Platonism is "realism," in "Plato on Negation and Not-Being in the *Sophist*," *Philosophical Review* 81 (1972): 276ff., n. 14. Lee closes that note by saying, "for [Plato] the central fact—or wonder—in reality is precisely such determinacy of nature, which, rightly understood, encompasses all that there is to say and know" (p. 277). I would add that wonder, since it is precisely opposite to taking for granted, is the appropriate mode for appreciating the givenness, as *giv*enness, of the forms. If I am right, Socrates' elliptical remarks on the Good in the *Republic* point back to the experience of coming to just this appreciation or wonder as the root of genuine φιλοσοφία.

the "conversion" of mind from sensibles to forms; the culmination of this process in the spectacle of the Good, however, motivates his return.[34] As Socrates' generosity displays, being true to one's "own" selfhood turns out to imply the gift of oneself to others.[35]

V. POSTSCRIPT: THE GOOD AND PLATONIC DIALOGUE

In closing, it is worth noting how these reflections illumine not only Socrates' presence in the Piraeus but also Plato's very presentation of it. If we were correct at the very outset to take our bearings towards Socratic discourse from Alcibiades' remark in the *Symposium*, then its essence—as, of course, Plato represents it[36]—is provocation towards deeper inquiry. And if, further, we were correct to distinguish between two levels of provocation in the *Republic*, the Socratic and the Platonic, then we may here be glimpsing one of the major respects in which Plato makes himself a true heir to Socrates. To put this in terms of the words Plato gives to Socrates at 540b, Plato tacitly claims to be one of those "like" men whom Socrates discovered and "educated" and "left behind in [his] place as guardian of the city." The dialogues

---

34. On this reading, therefore, we would not do justice to the philosopher's motivation to rule by characterizing it as egoistic or as unselfish or, indeed, as a coincidence of interest and duty. In different ways, the first two positions sustain the distinction between what I want just for myself and what I recognize others require, whether by seeing securing the second as instrumental to securing the first (see, e.g., the subtle version of this offered by Thomas Brickhouse, "The Paradox of the Philosophers' Rule," *Apeiron* 15 [1981]: 1–9) or by seeing the philosopher as willing to sacrifice something of the first in order to secure the second (an element qualifiedly present in White's account, p. 195). The third position, as it is usually maintained, preserves the distinction in principle but argues that, in the just city constructed in Books II–IV, there is no difference in content; the impetus for this position is given by what Socrates says at 412d ff. As observed in n. 26 above, however, Socrates himself lives and acts as he does in the far-from-just setting of Athens. What is decisive is not the contingent fact of the condition of his city but, rather—to recall a phrase from Vlastos, "Justice and Happiness in the *Republic*," as cited in n. 11—the "moral" "energizing" that results from his "unique intellectual experience" (p. 93).

35. Two remarkable studies by L. A. Kosman—"Platonic Love" (in *Facets of Plato's Philosophy*, pp. 53–69) and "Charmides' First Definition: Sophrosyne as Quietness" (in *Essays in Greek Philosophy* 2: 203–216)—have encouraged me to try to think into the extraordinary integrity that Plato puts before us in the *persona* of Socrates. The experience of the Good would be, on my understanding of it, that which unites the "two loves," of self and of other, that Kosman connects in the first essay (especially p. 66). The mimetic moment of that experience, in turn, is what makes the Socrates of the dialogues a "master," not a "journeyman"—that is, one who is "effortlessly" great-spirited, not willfully self-controlled—in his ethical disposition, as Kosman draws this distinction in the second essay (especially pp. 213–216).

36. As Havelock shows (above n. 8) with new forcefulness, the "Socrates" to whom Plato claims to be heir is impossible to distinguish from Plato's own creation in the dialogues. Recognizing this, however, should not prevent us from studying the figure of Socrates in the dialogues as a way of learning about Plato's self-understanding.

would be his own distinctive way of practicing Socratic guardianship. Our study points to the possible depth of this $\mu\acute{\iota}\mu\eta\sigma\iota\varsigma$. Socrates' generosity, we have seen, mimes the Good in its abundance. It is a distinctive mark of Socrates' teaching that he takes care not to eclipse the "original" by its "image." Because he recognizes that thinking itself belongs—like a "beam" to the sun—to the Good, he knows that he himself is not the source but only, at best, an occasion for the arisal of insight in others. This is why he claims only to be a "midwife" (*Theaetetus* 149a ff.) and why, in one of the most striking aspects of his generosity, he often holds back at key moments, leaving his companions to have for themselves, as their "own," the insights he has prepared. Dialogue form, in turn, incorporates all of this within its own larger structure of provocation. The new elements it adds are the timely failure of Socrates' companions, as a way of giving us, as *our* "own," the insights they miss, and the constant portrayal of Socrates' generosity as a mimetic clue to what there is to be "seen." But this is to say that Plato too holds back; thus dialogue form is itself on a second level a mimetic clue. As a mode of provocation, it is itself generous in just the Socratic way that it depicts.

Vassar College

8 PLATO'S UNNATURAL TELEOLOGY
JAMES G. LENNOX

In a number of later dialogues, Plato contrasts two sorts of accounts for features of the natural world.[1] One would account for the pattern of the visible world's changes by invoking chance, spontaneity, or blind necessity, *and nothing else*, as the responsible force. The other insists that an intelligent maker or craftsman is the truly responsible agent. Plato encapsulates the former well in these lines from the *Laws*:

Fire, water, earth and air, all of them they say are by nature and chance, while none of them is by craft. And again, the bodies made from these, earth, sun, moon and stars they say have come to be due to these [nature and chance], being entirely without soul. Each one, moving about among each of the others by chance of its power, hot to cold, dry to moist, soft to hard, and all whatsoever have been blended by the blending of opposites according to chance from necessity, by which has been concocted a harmony which is somehow fitting. (889b1–7)

He has the Athenian endorse the latter view three pages later:

And so judgement and foresight, wisdom, art and law would be prior to hard and soft, heavy and light; and the great and primary works and actions just because they are primary, would be those of art; those of nature and nature herself—this very thing which they mis-name—would be secondary, having its origin from art and intelligence.

The idea of the "natural" world as *unnatural*, as the product of a *technē*, is a stable feature of Plato's later thought and had momentous

---

*The first half of this paper was delivered to the *APA* Pacific Division meeting in 1981. An earlier version of the whole was read at The Catholic University of America, November 1983, and at the Princeton Ancient Philosophy Colloquium, December 1983. The final rewriting benefited from many discussions and suggestions on those occasions, most especially from David Furley's commentary at Princeton. I have also been helped by the written comments of Alexander Nehamas and Joan Kung; and from discussions with Anne Carson, Mary Louise Gill, Areyh Kosman, and Deborah Roberts. The penultimate draft was written while enjoying the varied pleasures of a junior fellowship at the *Center for Hellenic Studies*.

1. *Sph.* 265c–266c; *Lg.* X, 889a–890a; *Phlb.* 28d–e, *Ti.* 46c–47c; 68e–69d.

consequences for the history of natural philosophy.[2] Robert Boyle, a leader among the British "mechanical philosophers" of the seventeenth century, looked back self-consciously to Plato in his *Disquisition on the Final Causes of Natural Things*: "The provident Δημιουργός wisely suited the fabric of the parts to the uses, that were to be made of them: as a mechanic employs another contrivance of his wheels, pinions, etc., when he is to grind corn with a mill."[3]

The world viewed as the product of a good and benevolent craftsman was one of two aspects of Darwin's formal education at Christ College, Cambridge which he looked back upon with approval (the other also had Greek roots, Euclidean geometry). Indeed, as one traces the numerous versions of Darwin's argument for natural selection, from its first formulation in the late 1830s through the last edition of the *Origin*, one sees a palpable struggle to free himself from the implications of this picture.

The tradition begins in a familiar passage in the *Phaedo*, and so shall we. In it, Plato provides two models of explanation which he clearly feels are preferable to those put forward by the "natural investigators." One of these types of explanation is teleological in nature; the other uses forms as *aitia* of coming to be and being. The *Phaedo* self-consciously announces Socrates' failure to develop the former, and to integrate it in any way with the latter. During Plato's middle and later period there is a persistent exploration of a model of skillful craftsmanship, a major theme in the *Gorgias, Cratylus, Republic X, Timaeus Statesman, Sophist*, and *Philebus*.[4] The central question of the second half of this paper is this: to what extent, and in what ways, do these explorations help Plato develop a more integrated theory of scientific explanation?

I

In an allegedly autobiographical digression, Socrates tells of his initial enthusiasm for, and ultimate rejection of, certain attempts to provide explanations of generation and destruction. These accounts had

---

2. David Gallop, *Plato's Phaedo* (Oxford, Clarendon Press, 1975), p. 175; G. Vlastos, *Plato's Universe* (University of Washington Press, 1975), p. 97. Both these authors overstate the extent to which the "mechanical philosophers" of the seventeenth century reject Plato's vision. That the universe as a whole was a rationally designed artifact was seldom in doubt before the nineteenth century.

3. Robert Boyle, *A Disquisition about the Final Causes of Natural Things*, in *The Works of the Honorable Robert Boyle*, Vol. 5, ed. Thomas Birch (London, 1688), p. 409.

4. Cf. R. S. Brumbaugh, "Plato's Relation to the Arts and Crafts," in *Facets of Plato's Philosophy*, ed. W. H. Werkmeister (*Phronesis*, Supplementary Vol. 3, Van Gorcum, Assen, 1976), pp. 40–52.

consequences that left him confused even about things he had once thought he understood. At this point he reports, "I now rashly adopt a different method, a jumble of my own, and in no way incline toward the other" (97b6–7, Gallop trans.).[5]

Socrates appears about to introduce the safe (100d8, e1) but simpleminded (100d3–4) form of explanation, which, however, is not introduced until 99b4. What interferes is an apparently parenthetical discussion of Anaxagoras, which puts off the presentation of the method of explanation by hypothesized forms for two pages.[6]

I want to look carefully within the parentheses with two primary questions in mind. What can this passage tell us about Plato's views on what a fully adequate account of a feature of the natural world should look like? Second, what is the significance of the placement and style of this passage for an evaluation of other discussions of teleological explanations in the Platonic corpus?

Professor Frede has pointed out that this passage exploits a distinction, integral to the moral/legal contexts in which it arose, between τὸ αἴτιον, the agent responsible for a state of affairs, and ἡ αἰτία, that in virtue of which the agent is responsible, which may be called the reason why.[7] In legal contexts, this would be the distinction between the accused and the basis of the accusation. The doctrine attributed to Anaxagoras is that intelligence is the agent responsible for orderly arrangement and all else.[8] But at 97c6ff., discovery of the reason why each thing comes to be, is, or passes away as it is or does is said to depend on discovery of why that particular arrangement is *best*. Like-

---

5. John Burnet, *Plato's Phaedo* (Oxford University Press, 1911), p. 108, claimed his ideas on the *deuteros plous* were in agreement with W. J. Goodrich, "On *Phaedo* 96a–102a and on the δεύτερος πλοῦς 99d," *Classical Review*, 17 (1903): 381–385; 18 (1904): 5–11. However, Goodrich convincingly links Socrates' disparaging remarks concerning his own method of explanation to the hoped for teleology of 97b8–99b2, and so unlike Burnet saw no irony in this remark.

6. There are four pieces of evidence that indicate that the sense of intrusion of the Anaxagorean discussion is intentional. (i) The use of the present at 97b6 generates anticipation that Socrates' random method will be discussed immediately. (ii) The discussion of the *deuteros plous* is re-introduced at the end of our passage. To quote Goodrich, "Ἔνδοξε τοίνυν μοι κ.τ.λ. . . . (99d4) links back immediately where the narrative had previously broken off, at 97b8 . . . ." (Goodrich [1903], p. 382). (iii) The problems that had led to Socrates' dissatisfaction with natural science, discussed just prior to the Anaxagorean excursus, are shown to be resolved by the *deuteros plous* (100e5–103c4), but are not mentioned from 97b–99e. (iv) As I will discuss in detail shortly, the sorts of *explanantia* focused on in this passage are in striking contrast to those on either side of it.

7. Michael Frede, "The Original Notion of Cause" in *Doubt and Dogmatism: Studies in Hellenistic Epistemology*, ed. M. Schofield, M. Burnyeat, and J. Barnes (Oxford, 1980), pp. 217–249, esp. 222–223.

8. *Phd.* 97c1–2: νοῦς ἐστιν ὁ διακοσμῶν τε καὶ πάντων αἴτιος. Compare Aristotle, *Met.* A 984b15–17: νοῦν . . . τὸν αἴτιον τοῦ κόσμου καὶ τῆς τάξεως. . . .

wise, Socrates had hopes that after Anaxagoras had said whether (πότερον) the earth was flat or spherical,[9] he would set out in detail the *aitia* and the *anagkē* of it, which would be a matter of showing that it is better to be this sort of thing (97d8–e3; cf 98b1–4, 99c5–7). Throughout *Phd.* 97–99 intelligence is the responsible agent, while a certain state of affairs' being good (better, best) is said to be the reason why the agent brings that state of affairs about. Further, accounts that make reference to intelligence and the good are contrasted with "mechanical" explanations—the former provide the true explanation, though their ability to bring about appropriate states of affairs is dependent on the operations of the relevant physical processes.[10]

The operative presupposition that accounts for this distinction comes out clearly in the following comment, revealing to us the nature of Socratic expectations for Anaxagorean *Nous*: "For I never supposed that someone who said these things to be ordered by intelligence would offer any other cause for them than that these things are best just as they are." (98a7–b1) Let me encapsulate Socrates' presupposition in the following formula:

P   If intelligence bestowes a certain order on something, that thing has that order *because* its having that order is best.[11]

What this hypothetical formulation is intended to stress is the conceptual link in Socrates' thinking between intelligent agency and the explanatory efficacy of goodness. Only intelligent agents bring about certain states of affairs *because* they are good, though good states of affairs may arise by chance. Aristotle encapsulates the point neatly in a fragment of the *Protrepticus*: ". . . something good might come about by chance; but in respect of chance, and insofar as it results from chance, it is not good." (Fr. 11)

Aristotle, like Plato, will only allow the good outcome of a process to explain it if that good outcome was somehow responsible for the process. They differ, of course, over the issue of whether an intelligent agent is the only sort of agent that can initiate changes for the sake of a goal. But they agree, I would argue, that some such agency must be involved if explanations by reference to the goodness of the outcome are to be legitimate.[12]

9. For problems with translating στρογγύλη in the *Phaedo*, cf. J. S. Morrison, "The Shape of the Earth in Plato's *Phaedo*," *Phronesis* 4 (1959): 101–119.
10. *Phd.* 98c5–99d4.
11. The pattern of this formulation, though not its content, was suggested by Larry Wright's *Teleological Explanations* (University of California Press, Los Angeles, 1976).
12. Cf. *Met.* Z.7, 1032a12–13, a25–32; *Ph.* II.5, 196b23–26, II 8, 199a3–8; *Part. An.* I.1, 639b15–21. The story is complex. Plato in *Laws X* discusses those he opposes as

P maintains the τὸ αἴτιον /ἡ αἰτία distinction in the following way. Intelligence, conceived of as productive of a certain state of affairs, is its αἴτιον. That state of affairs, *identified as best*, and therefore as the outcome desired by intelligence, is the αἰτία—the reason why—for that production.

Confirmation that *P* adequately captures Socratic presuppositions on this subject comes from an examination of his distinction between true causes and the things without which they wouldn't be such. Socrates chooses a timely example to explain the distinction. Why does he remain in Athens, though he is about to die? It isn't a matter of constraint—he could easily flee.[13] Nor is it simply a matter of pointing out that, given the way his bones and sinews are arranged, he could hardly do anything else. No—he has an opinion that remaining is *good*, and he has chosen to remain because it is good that he do so.

Socrates' characterization of the "careless" account of his actions also stresses the role of both intelligence and "what is best" in the prefered account.

If someone were to say that without having such bones and sinews and whatever else I have I would not be able to act on my judgements, he would speak truly; but to say that I do what I do *because* of these things, and do these things with intelligence, but not by means of the desire for what is best, would be an extremely careless account. (99a5–b1)

Commentators regularly note the carelessness Socrates finds in saying "*because* of bones etc." and "*with* intelligence."[14] But they ignore the fact that Socrates is drawing it to our attention that these accounts fail to make reference to the desire for what is best. But the above remarks stress its importance. In fact, that those who offer the careless account leave this out altogether may explain why they are so careless as to reverse the true order of priority between intelligence and physical systems. By leaving out of account what is best, they ignore the fact that intelligence is intentional; and thus they will fail to realize that the crucial agency involved in bringing about *this* state of affairs (i.e., the one that is best) is not the physical processes involved, but intelligence.

This passage is not, of course, putting forth a theory about human

---

holding that the cosmos is due to nature and chance rather than to intelligence and craft. Ultimately, however, as Joan Kung reminds me, Plato wishes to insist that if φύσις refers to what is primary and an ἀρχή, then it is soul and intelligence that are φύσις and *their* products that are φύσει (cf. 892c). Aristotle treats φύσις as *sui generis*, refusing to range either intelligence and craft on the one hand, or chance and spontaneity on the other, with it.

13. As is made clear at *Cri.* 53b3ff; cf. *Phd.* 99a1–2.
14. E.g., Burnet, p. 106; Gallop, p. 175.

action per se, but rather a perfectly general thesis about causal attribution. This is made clear as Socrates goes on to note that various theories of why the earth came to be and remains where it is make the same error of taking the physical preconditions of its becoming or remaining where it is to be the actual cause. Later, in a craftily hypothetical mode, Socrates claims to have been persuaded that *if* the earth is a sphere and in the heaven's center, *then* the mere uniformity of the heavens would insure its remaining.[15] Such an account in no sense *competes* with the teleological; rather, it provides the appropriate answer to the question, by what means does intelligence accomplish this good?

The radical discontinuity between the Anaxagorean excursis and the rest of the exploration of the *aitia* of generation and destruction is clear, and clearly self-conscious.[16] At the same time, there is no obvious shift in philosophical motivation. The entire discussion in 96a6–106c9, where its results are applied to the issue of the soul's immortality, is governed by the requirement that a general examination of the reason for coming to be and passing away (ὅλως γὰρ δεῖ περὶ γενέσεως καὶ φθορᾶς τὴν αἰτίαν διαπραγματεύσασθαι—95e9–96a1) be carried out. Throughout, Socrates is concerned with answers to the very general question, why (διὰ τί) does each thing come to be pass away and exist (96a9–10). To have such an answer is to know what's really responsible for each thing (εἰδέναι τὰς αἰτίας ἑκάστου—96a9). It is this knowledge he pursues in natural investigation (96c7–97b7)[17], in the book of Anaxagoras (97b8–99c6)[18] and in the idea of form-participation (99d1–105c11).[19] There is no hint that the question has changed, nor that different types of answers will be required either for different domains or for different questions. The sort of *aitia* hoped for in Anaxagoras, and those which occupy Socrates' attention from 100a onward, both attempt to substitute for, and avoid basic

---

15. Vlastos (1975), p. 30, wrongly claims that "he [Plato] reproaches them [the *physiologoi*] for deciding such a question as whether the earth is flat or round without first asking which of the two would be the "better" (97e)." This reverses the order clearly recommended in the text: ... καί μοι φράσειν πρῶτον μὲν πότερον ἡ γῆ πλατεῖά ἐστιν ἢ στρογγύλη, ἐπειδὴ δὲ φράσειεν, ἐπεκδιηγήσεσθαι τὴν αἰτίαν καὶ τὴν ἀνάγκην. Indeed, the πρῶτον μὲν πότερον ... ἐπειδὴ δὲ ... τὴν αἰτίαν, could hardly be more emphatic.

16. Cf. note 6 above, for the evidence.

17. Indeed the discussion has in a general way been about how to account for generation and destruction from 70d7. 71a10's πάντα οὕτω γίγνεται, ἐξ'ἐναντίων τὰ ἐναντία πράγματα, is referred to at 103a4 when Socrates notes that it doesn't contradict the idea that opposites *themselves* don't come to be from their opposites.

18. *Phd.* 97c6–7: εἰ οὖν τις βούλοιτο τὴν αἰτίαν εὑρεῖν περὶ ἑκάστου ὅπῃ γίγνεται ἢ ἀπόλλυται ἢ ἔστι. ...

19. 102e3–103b5.

problems of, explanations provided either by common sense or by the "natural investigators." Both lay out stringent, though different, Socratic constraints on what can legitimately be said to be responsible for a state of affairs.[20] Both provide preferred responses to *dia ti* questions. And most importantly, the method which makes use of hypothesized forms is introduced as a "second best voyage in search of the αἰτία" (99d1)[21] implying a single search for adequate explanations in general.[22]

Thus we are left with a continuous background of explanatory concerns and motives, yet two radically different accounts of explanation each with its own claims to superiority. Faced with this fact, commentators have tended to polarize around two extreme positions. At one extreme is the view that the teleological parenthesis is of no significance to the rest of the dialogue; on this view, Socrates' claim that the hypothetical use of the theory of forms is a "second best" is a bit of characteristic irony.[23]

20. In the discussion of teleological explanation, purely mechanical accounts are held to state only the means for accomplishing various ends; such accounts fail to discriminate between various ends achievable by these means because they fail to inquire why the ends achieved are good (98b7–99c5). In the discussion of explanation *via* participation in hypothesized forms various common sense explanations are criticized on three grounds, summarized by David Gallop (1975), p. 186, as follows:

(i) No opposite, F, can count as the "reason" for a thing's having a property, if its opposite, G, can also give rise to that property (97a7–b3).

(ii) Nothing can count as a "reason" for a thing's having a property, if its opposite, G, can also give rise to that property (101a6–8).

(iii) A "reason" for a thing's having a property F, cannot itself be characterized by the opposite of that property, G. (101a8–b2).

21. On the meaning of *deuteros plous* in this context I am following Goodrich (1903), (1904), and Hackforth *Plato's Phaedo*, (Cambridge University Press, 1955), p. 127, note 5. I have not been convinced by K. M. W. Shipton "A good second best: *Phaedo* 99bff." *Phronesis* 24 (1979): 33–53, that the issue here is whether Socrates can acquire a "divinely revealed" and therefore certain account or whether he must proceed "hypothetically." The reference of τῆς τοιαύτης αἰτίας at 99c7 is clearly to the good achieved by intelligence. It is *this* sort of explanation Socrates failed either to discover himself or learn from another, and compared to which what he goes on to state is a *deuteros plous*. On the other hand, the other uses of this term in Plato (*Phlb.* 19c1–2, *Plt* 300c4) do not *merely* imply a more laborious means to the same good (*pace* Kenneth Dorter, *Plato's Phaedo, An Interpretation*, [Toronto, 1982], p. 125), but a considerably more modest approach to a subject. The explanation of each thing's coming to be, being or ceasing to be F by means of its coming to be, being or ceasing to be related to what truly is F is a *deuteros plous* with respect to the epistemic desires of 97b–99c in just this way.

22. It is thus distressing that virtually every discussion of the passage focuses either on 96a–97c/100a–105, or on 97c–99d, as a glance at the various discussions referred to in these notes shows.

23. Cf. Gregory Vlastos, "Reasons and Causes in the *Phaedo*," *Philosophical Review* 78 (1969): 291–325; E. Burge, "The Ideas as *Aitiai* in the *Phaedo*," *Phronesis* 10 (1971): 1–13; Burnet (1911), pp. 103, 108.

Opposed to this are attempts to find, hidden away in the *deuteros plous*, teleological explanations of some sort.[24] Neither strategy works. There is no evidence for the latter position.[25] Against the former, one needs to consider the following facts in the context of the characteristic care taken by Plato over the structure of a dialogue. First, the philosophical intelligence of the Anaxagorean excursis, in combination with Socrates' impassioned expression of the need and importance of explanations which make use of intelligence motivated by the good, speaks for its importance. Second, the intrusiveness of the passage appears clearly intentional. Third, even as Socrates "takes to the oars," he criticizes those who say nothing about "the good or binding, that genuinely does bind and hold things together." And, with hindsight, of course, we know that the developed use of the theory of forms for various philosophical purposes did not lessen the importance of teleological explanations in Plato's system.

I propose to take at face value both the continuity of concern to find a general explanation for the world of generated things throughout, and the clearly flagged intrusiveness of the Anaxagorean discussion. Once one does so, very natural *comparative* questions arise, questions concerning the relative virtues and shortcomings of various forms of explanation.

There is, for example, a clear preference for intentional/teleological explanations in certain explanatory contexts. Repeatedly (97c2, c5, 98a7, 98b1–5, 98c1, 99c1, 99c5–6) Socrates formulates his vision of a noetic *aitia* as an explanation for the *order* (ὁ κόσμος) that we find in the world. *Noũs* is an *ordering* cause, and chooses a certain order because it is best. This is not in itself surprising, in that this was just the role Anaxagoras himself claimed for Intelligence. Yet, no such concern is in evidence during the discussion of the safe, simple explanations which explain something's coming to be beautiful (καλόν) by participation in τὸ αὐτὸ καλόν. And this would appear to be an inevitable shortcoming of the safe form of explanation. The appearance of an order and pattern in the world's comings and goings is left inexplic-

---

24. Cf. Damascius I, para. 417–418, in L. G. Westerink, *The Greek Commentaries on Plato's Phaedo*, Vol. II, (New York, 1977); R. S. Bluck "ὑπόθεσις in the *Phaedo* and Platonic Dialectic," *Phronesis* 2 (1957): 21–31.

25. Those who take this approach typically read the ideas on explanation of *Republic* VI–VII or the *Timaeus* into the passage. Gallop (1975), p. 191, is properly cautious, as is Julia Annas, "Aristotle on Inefficient Causes," *Philosophical Quarterly* 32 (1982): 311–326, esp. p. 318. Gallop himself interprets Socrates' enigmatic reference to God and the form of life (pp. 220–221) to suggest a form-explanation as a replacement for Anaxagorean teleology. While this is ingenious, it throws his earlier caution to the winds.

able. Or, to put it in a manner Aristotle was fond of, given the theory of form-explanation in the *Phaedo*, we will *still* need a theory of why things come to have the features they do as and when they do.²⁶

It remains true throughout Plato's philosophic life, in dialogues as diverse as the *Republic, Timaeus, Philebus,* and *Laws*, that intelligence is invoked to explain the *order* and *unity* in a potentially disordered and dis-integrated world. This is one clue to the centrality of craftsmanship as a metaphor for divine intelligence.

Another curious difference between the two sorts of explanations presented here can be brought out by following a clue quietly dropped by Socrates early in the discussion of form participation explanation.

When Socrates turns to the *deuteros plous*, he seeks agreement from his interlocutors that certain things exist *auto kath' hauto*. Among these things he includes "good" (100b6). This is not surprising, of course. This passage relies on the easy agreement obtained at 65d6 for the theory of forms, and καλόν and ἀγαθόν were among the forms mentioned there as well. But immediately after discussion of a theory in which the goodness of a state of affairs was said to be its *aitia*, a theory reluctantly abandoned by Socrates, the use of the good to exemplify the *deuteros plous* has curious implications. Here is a theory in which the good, or alternately participation in it, is once more said to be an *aitia*. It is instructive to see why Socrates (rightly) doesn't see this as a substitute for his preferred teleology.

What can be explained about a thing by citing its participation in the good itself on its own? Only this, that it happens to be good. But Socrates had much grander hopes for a theory which used Νοῦς bringing about various arrangements because they were good. In each case, goodness ought to account, not only for the *goodness* of a state of affairs, but *also* for that state of affairs itself—that is, we ought to be able to say, citing its goodness, why intelligence brought *that* about (e.g., brought it about that the earth is a spherical thing.)

By comparing the two examples Socrates has given us of how the good can be an *aitia*, we have isolated a crucial ingredient in the intentional/teleological accounts. Explaining by goodness is not just one more explanation of a feature (namely goodness) possessed by a number of particulars: it is a way of explaining why particulars possess

---

26. Compare *Phd.* 100d6-7, 102c2 with Aristotle, *Met.* A 991b3, *Met.* Z 1034a2-5, *Gen. et Corr.* B. 335b7-24. An effective reply to the claim (in G. Vlastos, "Reasons and Causes in the *Phaedo*" *Philosophical Rev.* 78 [1969]) that Aristotle has misunderstood Plato in these criticisms is to be found in Annas (1982).

the *other* features they do. We may wonder, then, whether Plato ever considered form participation as an adequate account of why a particular or sort of particular can be said to have some feature or other.

Now the issue of how goodness is related to other features of the world is one which Plato explores from a variety of directions. The *Republic's* analogy between the sun and the good is one such exploration,[27] the *Philebus* in its entirety is another. Whether these explorations constitute a linear development or are mutually consistent I am not prepared to say. But they all in their way deal with the issues that arise when the Anaxagorean excursis and the *deuteros plous* are treated as components of a single discussion of explanation.

I wish to consider the *Timaeus* as another such exploration. Its affinities to the Anaxagorean component of the *Phaedo* have been noted since ancient times, at least in a general way: a craftsman uses his intelligence in order to produce a good κόσμος.

But with a more fine-grained picture of the *Phaedo's* account of explanation, a richer understanding of this relationship is available to us. In particular, the *Timaeus* appears to develop a theory of explanation in which the distinction between forms and the world of perceptible particulars is an aspect of an intentional/teleological account of the world. The πρῶτος and δεύτερος πλοῦς have been united. If this appearance is not deceptive, such unification must entail an account of "good intentions" explanations and how they relate to an account of the perceptible world in terms of separate forms. Many questions are opened up: what has happened to the distinction between true causes and the means of their operating? Are forms, Intelligence and the good *all aitia*? What is the nature of the good the demiurge is seeking to achieve? Behind these questions, I shall argue, is one basic one: Why did Anaxagoras' *Nous* become a divine *craftsman* in Plato's later thought? A reasonably detailed answer to this last question goes a long way toward explaining the differences between the account of scientific explanation in the *Phaedo* and in the *Timaeus*.

II. HUMAN CRAFTSMEN

The *Cratylus* considers the giving of appropriate names to be a craft. The good rhetorician is, according to the *Gorgias*, just like other

---

27. For excellent discussions of which, cf. Gerasimos Santas, "The Form of the Good in Plato's *Republic*," in J. P. Anton, A. Preus, eds., *Essays in Ancient Greek Philosophy* (Albany: SUNY Press, 1983) pp. 232–263; Nicholas P. White, *A Companion to Plato's Republic*, (Indianapolis, 1979) pp. 171–181.

craftsmen (503e1). The maker of good laws is a practitioner of statecraft, a craft parallel in many ways to weaving (*Statesman*, passim). And, as we've seen, the divine intelligence which is responsible for our world having the character it does is also a craftsman (*R* VII 530a6, X 596c4, *Lg.* X 889–906, *Ti.* passim, *Phlb.* 26e5, *Sph.* 262b5–c4). The *Republic* is already toying with the idea that the natural world is the product of a craftsman;[28] and the later dialogues consider it wrongheaded to treat the products of nature as anything other than *craft* products. Looking carefully at what Plato imagines to be involved in the production of a craft product is thus an integral part of understanding his philosophy of nature.

As a focal text, we can do no better than this characterization of the craftsman in the *Gorgias*:

Come now, the good man who speaks with a view to the best, surely he won't speak at random, but will look to something? He will be like all other craftsmen; each of them selects and applies his efforts looking to his own work (βλέποντες πρὸς τὸ αὐτῶν ἔργον), not at random, but so that what he produces will acquire some form. Look for instance if you like, at painters, builders, shipwrights, all other craftsmen—whichever one you like; see how each of them arranges in a structure whatever he arranges, and compels one thing to be fitting and suitable to another, until he composes the whole thing arranged in a structure and order (503d6–504a1; Irwin trans., with modifications).

This protean passage makes note of five distinctive features of the craftsman's activity.

1. Craftsmen proceed by looking to a paradigm, an εἶδος, an ἰδέα or ἔργον.[29] Indeed, to use the language of paradigm and likeness or imitation is simply to use the natural language of craftsmanship. But lest we imagine the image of "looking to" as pictorial, it is relevant to recall that the ὃ ἔστιν k locution *is* substitutable for any of the above names of the craftsman's intensional object. The requirement that a craftsman look to a paradigm insures that his activity is, as the above passage stresses, orderly rather than random. It does not by itself insure

---

28. With the reference at 530a6 the strangely playful wording of *R.* X has more force. It remains true, however, that the latter discussion is ambiguous: 596b9–10 says, "For surely none of the craftsmen craft the idea itself; for how could he?" but then asks what such a craftsman would be called (596b12). In the same vein, 596e5–9 suggests this craftsman is the one referred to at 530a6, but then hints that only a person with a mirror could produce all natural things, and only in the sense of producing *images* of them. But then the form of the craft product is reintroduced as perhaps the work of a god at 597b5, again with some hesitancy (ἣν φαῖμεν ἄν, ὡς ἐγῷμαι, θεὸν ἐργάσασθαι). Finally, at 597c1–d1 Socrates seems straightforwardly to assume such a diety.

29. Typically, βλέπειν πρός; e.g., *Grg.* 503d8, 504d5; *Cra.* 389a5, c5, c7, d6, 390e; *R.* V 472a4–7, *R.* X 596b7, *Ti.* 28ab.

that his actions produce the best possible product: the *Cratylus* warns against using a faulty paradigm (389b1–3), and the Demiurge of the *Timaeus* fortunately looked to a timeless rather than a changing paradigm (28a6–b2).

2. There is no suggestion that such copies or imitations would arise *without* the activity of the craftsman. Nor is it suggested that the form or paradigm of the craft product is an *aitia* of its likenesses, copies or imitations. Within this model—that is, when the dialogues recount a discussion of craftsmanship—the language of communion and participation to describe the relationship between what-k-is and the many (sorts of) k's is absent. The *Cratylus* likes "placing the form in the materials" (389c1, 389c6–7, 389c9, 389d9–6, 389e1–3, 390b1–2, 390e3–4); above, we have the craftsman placing, sometimes compelling, things into proper order, which entails having a certain form (εἶδός τι). In every case, being like a form is not something which just happens; it is the result of a goal-directed productive activity. Interestingly, the goal is never to make a good copy: making a good copy is a means to accomplishing some (other) good.

3. If a craftsman must *look to* a paradigm (which may simply mean that he must know *what it is* that he is making), so must he *work with* materials. Becoming a likeness of a form is not like becoming warm through being acted on by a very hot object; it is a matter of materials being structured, organized, and arranged. An unorganized, disintegrated plurality is compelled to become "a whole thing arranged with structure and order." In fact the quoted passage introduces a section of the *Gorgias* in which Socrates suggests that just as it is the physician's task to restore or maintain τάξις and κόσμος in the body, so it is the good rhetorician's task to restore or maintain τάξις and κόσμος in the soul (504a3–e4).

This element of the craft model recalls that it was in contexts where the order that prevailed in nature required explanation that Socrates found the idea that Intelligence was its αἴτιον and the goodness of that order its αἰτία so compelling. Socrates spoke reprovingly of those who forgot that "the good and binding truly does bind and hold things together" (99c5–6). This reproach echoes throughout the *Republic*. At 462b1–2 we are told that the greatest good for a state (whatever it turns out to be) "binds it together and makes it one (ὃ ἂν συνδῇ τε καὶ ποιῇ μίαν), its greatest evil is whatever fractures it and makes it many instead of one (ὃ ἂν αὐτὴν διασπᾷ καὶ ποιῇ πολλὰς ἀντὶ μιᾶς)." The breakdown of the good *polis* begins when it becomes two rather than one (551d5). The fact that justice is each part of a state or soul doing what is naturally its own is always a theory about the harmonious order achieved by a soul or *polis* being just.³⁰

4. This speaks (briefly) to the issue of the nature of the *ordering* materials receive. But it is equally central to craftsmanship that it is constrained by the fact that it is an activity of ordering *materials*, and these materials are a given, in two distinct ways. First, the nature of the craft product constrains the *choice* of appropriate materials: knives must cut; making them of soft or crumbly material won't do. Second, whatever material is used has a nature of its own: the craftsman cannot do anything he likes with his material, but only what it is capable of being compelled to do. *The Cratylus* compares the namegiver to a smith or a carpenter. If one is to produce names, awls, or shuttles, one must use letters, iron or wood (whether Greek or foreign is not relevant). If one is given letters, iron or wood, only certain sorts of copies can be made. (387e–390b5) In neither case need we imagine that the given determines a *unique* choice; but it *constrains* the craftsman's choices and actions considerably.

5. Finally, Socratic discussions of craftsmanship present a curiously ambiguous attitude toward the good intended by the craftsman's work. This ambiguity results from a distinction which periodically emerges within the craft model between the person who *directs* or *oversees* production and the producer himself. The maker of a shuttle produces an instrument for the weaving of other things; it is the *weaver* who will know what a good shuttle ought to be like, and will use this knowledge to guide the actions of the carpenter. In such cases, the user of the instrument is said to have knowledge of what a good instrument consists in and to direct the builder (*R.* X 601e–602a, *Crat.* 390b–d).³¹

---

30. These passages, which all suggest the good is a unity achieved through mathematical bonds, are a clue to the relevance of the increasingly mathematical course of study recommended in *R.* VII to grasping the nature of the good. In a variety of Platonic texts it is suggested that goodness for a plurality is to be found in the principles which bind it into a unity, principles of proportion (ἀναλογία) and commensurability (συμμετρία) or measure (μέτρον). The same language appears in the *Statesman's* characterization of statecraft (308c–311a) and the *Timaeus'* characterization of the Demiurge's work (32b, 69c). Such passages make it less surprising that, as Aristoxenus relates, Aristotle reported that Plato's lecture "On the Good" turned out to be a discussion of arithmetic, geometry, and astronomy, culminating in the claim that τὸ πέρας ὅτι ἀγαθόν ἐστιν ἕν (Aristoxenus, *Elementa harmonica* 2: 30–31). Cf. Konrad Gaiser, "Plato's Enigmatic Lecture 'On the Good'," *Phronesis* 25 (1980): 5–37; John Cooper, "The Psychology of Justice in Plato," *American Philosophical Quarterly* 14 (1977): 151–157, esp. 155. The development of this section of this paper owes much to suggestions by David Furley and Joan Kung.

31. A related but somewhat different distinction is drawn in the *Statesman* between

The idea that the good achieved by craftsmen is instrumental is at times subordinated to a quite different notion of goodness, one which "faces in the other direction," so to speak. The very existence of the craft product, because it represents the triumph of order, unity, proportionality, and harmony over their opposites in a given domain is viewed as a good in itself. In the passage with which we began, for example, the usefulness of the craft product is not discussed, for the production of a good soul, the focus of the discussion, is not measured by its instrumentality but simply by the unity and harmonious order of its parts. This counterentropic concept of goodness is relative to the random, uncoordinated dis-integration that would exist in the absence of the goal-directed intelligence of the craftsman—relative perhaps to that world of universal flux which, surprisingly, the world we live in is not.[32]

III. DIVINE CRAFTSMEN

It is not news that the *Timaeus* fulfills the fondest wishes of the Socrates of *Phaedo* 97–99. But while this is often noted in a general way, the comparison between the hope and the fulfillment is seldom looked at in detail. I now propose to do just that. The first order of business is to establish that *Phaedo* principle *P* is in place, and to explore the rich theory of causality in the *Timaeus* against the background of the *Phaedo*. Then I wish to explore in some detail the influence of the model of craftsmanship just discussed on the role of intelligence in the *Timaeus*.

Timaeus opens his portion of the feast being served up to Socrates by stating the reason why (δι' ἥντινα αἰτίαν) the framer of the entire universe (τὸ πᾶν) did so.

---

the overseer of a craft such as weaving or governing and those who supply the materials necessary for weaving. Cf. *Plt.* 281a–e, 287d; and compare Aristotle, *EN* I.2, 1094a26–1094b11.

32. Aristotle's claim that Plato's desire to separate forms from particulars grew out of the influence of Heraclitus and Cratylus and their doctrine of radical flux has been used to shed light on the development of Plato's thought by Terry Irwin, "Plato's Heracliteanism," *Philosophical Quarterly* 27 (1977): 1–13; and R. W. Jordan, *Plato's Arguments for Forms, Proceedings of the Cambridge Philological Society* (Cambridge, 1983). *Tht.* 179d3–183b7 and *Cra.* 439d–440 indicate Plato's concern with this doctrine, and it is common to suggest that Plato may have held some such view of the physical world. I believe that, at least from the *Timaeus* onward, Plato's view could be stated counterfactually as follows: If the physical world were not the product of a good and efficacious craftsman, it would be as the friends of flux describe it. The initial description of the Receptacle prior to divine craftsmanship is remarkably like the account of the flux doctrine in the *Theaetetus*, but it is important to recall that that passage does *not* describe the physical world as it actually is.

For the god, wishing all things to be good and nothing to be bad in so far as possible, took over everything which was visible—not at rest but moving in a discordant and disorderly manner—and led it from disorder to order, judging this to be in all respects better. (30a2–5)

The explanatory role of the good to be achieved by a state of affairs coming about is no longer expressed in the language of αἰτία. The αἴτιον/αἰτία distinction is reserved for the divine craftsman and the necessary motions of materials or for propositional accounts of their respective causal functions. The typical explanation has it that the divine craftsman uses or persuades various unintelligent cooperative materials to bring about a certain state of affairs, *in order that* some good is achieved, or *for the sake of* some good.[33] Thus the divine craftsman of the *Timaeus* acts with intelligence, and what is thus brought about does so *because* that state of affairs is good—the best, given the possibilities. Which is to say, *Phaedo* principle *P* is at the heart of Timaeus' plausible story about the cosmic likeness of the Living Thing Itself.

Whereas the aetiological role of the good in the *Timaeus* is virtually always expressed by prepositional phrases or final clauses expressing purpose, there are two sorts of causal agents reference to which is taken to be essential to a fully adequate explanation of any stable feature of the world. At 68e7–8 these explanations are referred to as the divine *aitia*, which makes reference to intelligence or the craftsmen of beautiful and good things as a cause (46e4, 48a2), and the necessary *aitia*, which makes reference to whatever produces in a random and disorderly fashion in the absence of the divine *aitia* (46c7, d1, e6, 76d6). The latter are cooperative causes (συναίτια, συμμεταίτια), used (46c9, 76c6) and ruled through persuasion (48a2) by the former.

The compatibility of these two "agencies" and the consistency of the idea of a "necessity" which can be ruled and persuaded and which is equated with chance when not so ruled was persuasively argued some years ago by Cornford, followed by Morrow, and others. The brilliant Epilogue to *Plato's Cosmology* reveals the extent to which such ideas were a legacy bequeathed to Plato rather than inventions of his own.

But Cornford, in attempting to avoid the idealism of earlier accounts of this distinction, was misled into positing two *realms* in the cosmology of the *Timaeus* corresponding to this distinction, and Vlastos

---

33. ἵνα and ὅπως with final clauses used at 32a1, 33a2, 38b6, 38c4, 39b2, 5, 39d9, 40a2, 41c3, 47b6, 69e3, 70b3, c7, d3, e5, 71b3, 74b4, e5, 77a4, c8, e3, e6; ἕνεκα at 39d7, 47a1, c5, 74a7, 75d6, 76d1, d7; χάριν at 33c1, 72b7, 72c2, 75e1; διὰ τὴν αἰτίαν at 33a6, 38d7, 40b4. Notice the virtual absence of these expressions from *Ti.* 49–69.

has recently followed.[34] These authors both imagine that the Demiurge had a better world than the one actually produced in mind, that the inherent powers of the world's basic constituents were recalcitrant, that the Demiurge was thus forced to compromise with his ideals, and as a consequence this world has an irreducible realm where necessity reigns, unpersuaded by intelligence.

The first premise in this argument is crucial, for it determines what will count as evidence for the others. If one postulates a world quite different from our own as the Demiurge's goal, then the world we see necessarily falls short, and one might look to the distinction between the two αἴτια as an account of this.

But in none of the statements of the Demiurge's aims is any goal mentioned other than to bring the maximum order and perfection possible to the materials at hand. And it is consistently maintained that this is achieved.

The central portion of Timaeus' story, concerning what occurs of necessity, drops copious hints that necessity is an aspect of every part of the Demiurge's construction and that within that construction it is always a servant of intelligent ends.

First, the random flux described in the language of chance and disorder is explicitly described as what the Receptacle, *absent intelligence*, would be like (48b, 53b, 69b). This suggests that, even as an account of the physical world, Plato could not buy the ontology of radical flux described at *Tht.* 179–83 and *Cra.* 440. It is rather an ontology of a world uncontrolled by intelligence working for the good.

Second, "the productions of necessity" rely throughout on intelligent design. Only the random traces of the elements would occur in the absence of intelligent design, but much, much more than that is described at 46a–c and 53c–68d.

Finally, the description of the necessary powers and properties of the physical world as *sunaitia* is a give-away.

The necessary causes in the *Timaeus* are *always* the inherent necessities possessed by the materials at hand, used or persuaded by divine intelligence "to lead (ἄγειν) the greatest part of the things that come to be to the best" (48a3). It is important to stress that it is the material necessities that are the subject of ἄγειν here. The role of intelligence is clearly circumscribed. Plato does not conceive of intelligence as superimposing *other* sorts of activities on a recalcitrant matter with its own—intelligence uses those very material powers, insuring that they shall *work together* for the best result.

---

34. F. M. Cornford, *Plato's Cosmology* (London: Routledge and Kegan Paul, 1937), pp. 173–175; Vlastos (1975), pp. 28–30.

When our creator made our heads shaggy with hair, he used the aforementioned causes (αἰτίοις), while reasoning that this rather than flesh ought to be the covering around the brain for the sake of protection (ἕνεκα ἀσφαλείας). . . . (76c5–d1)

Among "the aforementioned causes" is the necessary behavior of thin skin when acted on by the heat and moisture necessarily emanating from the brain. "Nail was crafted by these agents (τοῖς συναιτίοις), but due to the most responsible reasoning (τῇ αἰτιωτάτῃ διανοίᾳ) for the sake of (ἕνεκα) the fashioning of the things which were to be later." (76d6–8) Here then are the necessary results of drying on a compound of sinew, skin, and bone.

Such passages indicate clearly that a συναίτια is the physical *agency by means of which* intelligence achieves good ends. Plato doesn't conceive of *nous* superimposing other kinds of activity on those of matter, but as insuring certain specific interactions will take place among all those possible, namely, just those which will cooperatively produce the best possible cosmos. His model is of a reasonable counsel who accomplishes his ends by *persuading* various agencies to operate cooperatively, according to a plan, for some end.

These explanations recall the relationship between the master weaver (and by analogy the statesman) and the subordinate craftsmen in the *Statesman* who are referred to as τὰ συναίτια (281d11–e10). They are described as "that without whose attendance the ruler of each of the arts would never produce" (281e2–4), words which again recall the *Phaedo's* notion of "that without which the cause would not be a cause." The statesman, and the true weaver, act by directing and commanding their subordinates.[35] This image, perhaps borrowed from the world of craftsmanship, captures well the nature of the relationship between reason and "necessity." Viewed independently of the *guidance* and *coordination* of intelligence these active materials are "wandering" causes (48a7), producing in a disorderly manner whatever chances to occur (46e5). Without intelligence, only fleeting traces of the four elements would appear, and then only by chance (69b5–c2). But *they* are capable of being persuaded to produce the best order possible (46c7–8; 48a1–4). To call them *sunaitia* is to describe them as operating and interacting according to a plan which is, however, not their own, much like the *productive* craftsmen are guided in their work by the *directive* craftsmen.

The chief methodological message of the *Timaeus* is that, of any feature of the physical world we must ask two distinct questions, and seek

---

35. *Plt.* 281a–e; 287d.

out two distinct "becauses": (i) What are the physical interactions required to produce this result? (ii) What is the good for the sake of which these physical processes are *cooperating* to produce this result?

> ... he (the demiurge) made use of causes of this sort as subservient, while he himself contrived the good in all things that come to be. We must accordingly distinguish two kinds of causal account, the necessary and the divine. (68e4–7)

> We must speak of both kinds of causes but separate those which, with intelligence, are craftsmen of fine and good things, from those which in the absence of foresight, produce their sundry effects at random and without order. (46e3–6)

The *Timaeus* recommends that *we*, as far as possible, distinguish these two sorts of explanation. But this is a recommendation concerning how best to understand the world, not an account of distinct aspects of the world's makeup. These passages do *not* picture a layer of the operations of the world where necessity is unconstrained, nor does it distinguish, as Prof. Vlastos suggests, between triumphs of "pure teleology" and compromises between teleology and necessity. Precisely, it characterizes a world which, at every level of structure, is the product of necessary physical interactions ordered and coordinated for the sake of some good.

The *Timaeus* thus develops the teleology of the *Phaedo* in rich and complex ways. In contrast with the *Phaedo*, however, the *Timaeus* never describes *forms* as causes. This, and the introduction of a third element in Plato's ontology, the Receptacle, are directly attributable to Plato's use of the image of divine craftsmanship, an image absent from the *Phaedo*.

A common image used by commentators to characterize the Receptacle in the *Timaeus*, though not one used by Plato, is the image of the mirror.[36] The things which come to be are images of the forms, reflected in the Receptacle. This image is dangerously misleading, for it ignores the fact that anything which has a stable enough existence to be named at all is *constructed* by intelligence (69b3–c2). Thus there is no sense in which the world we perceive is due to simple reflection. Plato *does* describe a precosmic activity in the Receptacle (52d2–53c2; 69b5–c3), which involves mere chance occurrences of traces (ἴχνη, 53b2) and characters (52d6) of the four elements. This suggests that,

---

36. Cf. R. E. Allen, "Participation and Predication in Plato's Middle Dialogues," in *Studies in Plato's Metaphysics*, ed. R. E. Allen, (London: Routledge and Kegan Paul, 1965) pp. 55–58; Cornford (1937), p. 181; Kenneth M. Sayre, *Plato's Late Ontology: A Riddle Resolved*, (Princeton University Press, 1983) p. 249. Indeed all three writers talk as if 52c discusses the Receptacle as a mirror. It doesn't; *R. X*, 596c, uses the notion of mirror images, but with reference to the relationship between images and their imitations.

without intelligent guidance the receptacle may, somehow, participate in the two basic sorts of triangles out of which the elements are constructed.[37] But what is crucial for Plato is that the world is *not* such an indeterminant and nameless flux, though if intelligence were not present it would be. In so far as "space" has the character of the rational, ensouled mathematically structured and stable organization that it does, it is due to intelligent persuasion.

Participation, then, understood as a relation between copy and paradigm in virtue of which the copy may bear the name of the paradigm, is not something which occurs independently of an intelligent agent aiming to achieve some good.[38] Thus the explanation of some feature of our world in terms of its likeness to a paradigm is, in the *Timaeus*, only an aspect of the nature of intelligent production, not worthy of independent identification as a cause. As we were led to expect by our brief look at Plato's human craftsmen, paradigms within a craft model are not *aitia*.

But again, everything which comes to be does so from necessity by some cause (ὑπ' αἰτίου τινός); for in all cases it is impossible for there to be a generation apart from a cause. Now, whenever the craftsman, looking to (βλέπων . . . , πρὸς . . .) that which is always the same[39] and using some such paradigm,

---

37. It is startling that the standard English commentaries on the *Timaeus* don't really face the issue of the nature of the basic elements which the craftsman encounters in the Receptacle. The triangles themselves are never explicitly said to be constructed—earth, air, fire, and water are constructed from them by god (53b), or traces or *pathē* of this chance to occur (52d, 53b, 69b–c). On the other hand, forms of earth, air, fire and water—accounts of their stereometric configurations, perhaps—are mentioned, but *not* forms of the two basic triangles used in the god's stereometry. Plato leaves us with the material for two inferences, and I can't see any obvious means of deciding between them. The first, suggested by Mary Louise Gill at the *Princeton Ancient Philosophy Colloquium* on "Plato's Natural Philosophy" in "Matter and Flux in Plato's *Timaeus*" is that the triangles are the basic physical constituents of the Receptacle. Gill does not discuss the possibility of there being permanent images of Forms of the Right Angle Scalene and Isosceles Triangles. There are difficulties with either view. On the one hand, no such forms are mentioned. On the other hand, the radically indeterminate and unmeasured nature of the pre-crafted contents of the Receptacle is difficult to reconcile with the view that it is replete with geometrical objects.

In either case it remains true that all those *gignomena* for which forms are mentioned are *constructed out of basic elements*. This view of the physical world, furthermore, is detachable from the mythic imagery of the *Timaeus*, for it is mentioned in virtually *all* later dialogues.

38. Thus Plato himself seems to have answered Aristotle's critique of form-participation explanations in the *Phaedo* (discussed in note 26 above). He accepts the view that without the activity of a goal-directed agent, participation will not provide an account of coming-to-be. The Demiurge is a response to such complaints. Cf. Annas (1982), pp. 313, 315.

39. Taking the ἀεί in πρὸς τὸ κατὰ ταὐτὰ ἔχον βλέπων ἀεί with ἔχον rather than βλέπων in light of 29a1–7, where τὸ κατὰ ταὐτὰ καὶ ὡσαύτως ἔχον (29a1) is the equivalent of τὸ ἀίδιον (29a3–a5).

fashions (ἀπεργάζασθαι) the *idea* and capacity of it, everything thus completed is from necessity beautiful (καλόν). But whenever he looks to a generated thing, using a generated paradigm, what is thus completed is not beautiful. (28a4–b1)

Out of an extensive list of questions this passage raises, the one I wish to focus on is why it is stressed that the craft product will only be καλόν if the divine craftsman uses a changeless model.[40] This is not justified in our passage, and on a certain interpretation of what it is the craftsman hopes to achieve, it is unjustifiable. For if he simply wants to make a living thing, and has no desire to make it changeless, why should it matter whether the paradigm is changeless?

The same question can be raised about arguments that the copy must be single and unique (30c2–31b3), that air and water are needed to make the body one and insoluable (31b4–33b1), that all movements but one are to be removed from it (34a2–6), that it be made if not eternal without qualification, at least an everlasting likeness (37b6–d8). As David Keyt has noted, such arguments seem to confuse copying the form of *living thing* with copying *the form* of living thing, *qua* form. Any paradigm has properties *qua* paradigm that it is "mad" to instantiate in one's copy—houses, as copies of blue prints, should not be made of blue paper.[41]

The consistent stress of the above arguments in the *Timaeus* on producing a copy with these "formal" features make us doubtful that such a criticism understands Plato's motives. The assumption of this criticism is that the goal of the Demiurge is to produce a living being (or living beings). This assumption is false. What the Demiurge aims to do, as we've seen, is to bestow maximum unity, order, and persistence on his materials, because this is, in itself, *good* for those materials. The *means* of achieving this is to copy the form of Living Thing in these materials. Reconsidered in this light, the Demiurge is, at least from an economic point of view, sane.

One can achieve *this* sort of goodness only by looking to the changeless paradigm, for only it truly instantiates those features you strive for in your model. Your copy must be, if possible, unique (μονογενής)[42] for a number of related reasons, all given by Plato.

---

40. As Cornford notes (p. 27), the background is likely the distinction between true producers and mere imitators in *R*. X, 597–598. Another use of this distinction in the *Timaeus* is Plato's reference to the created gods, who base their mortal constructions on the Demiurge's created model, as *imitators* of his work.

41. David Keyt, "The Mad Craftsman of *Timaeus*," *Philosophical Review* 80 (1971): 230–235; for criticisms in a similar vein, cf. Santas (1983), Richard Mohr, "What Plato's Demiurge Does" (unpublished).

42. μονογενής: cf. Parmenides, fragment VIII: ὡς ἀγένητον ἐὸν καὶ ἀνωλεθρόν ἐστιν/οὖλον μουνογενές τε καὶ ἀτρεμὲς ἠδὲ τελεστόν.

First, the form of living things is pictured as a genus/species hierarchy (30c5–6, 39e3–40a7). If the god made two animals, each would be a μέρος and thus a copy of one *sort* of living thing, but not a copy of Living Thing itself. "Now we must never suppose the maker composed the world of those things which are in the form of parts—for nothing akin to the incomplete could ever come to be beautiful—but of that of which the other animals, individually and by kinds, are parts. . . ." (30c3–6) Thus Plato views making "two or a plurality" of living things as akin to making copies of subkinds of Living Thing. But an obvious alternative view seems possible—why could the craftsman not work with many distinct parcels of material, providing each parcel with copies of *all* the living things, and therefore a complete copy in the relevant respect. Plato's response to this alternative is parallel to his response to supposing that there are two *forms* of Living Thing. On what grounds do we claim that more than one copy has been produced? Each of these "parcels of material" contains the same four kinds of living thing, under the same (generic) kind. If there were two islands that possessed the same four species of the genus finch, no biologist would argue that we had two finch kinds and eight distinct species.

A response to this argument carries me to my next point. One might say that Plato has to admit the possibility that a good craftsman could construct two animals, at least in so far as they are spatially differentiated, even if they are of one kind.[43] But this is false, because a good craftsman is out to unify and organize his material to the greatest extent possible, and this would not be accomplished by the construction of two formally identical but materially distinct universes. It must never be forgotten that the materials of *this* craftsman make up the *entire* visible flux. If it can become one, unified, bound together whole, it will be better than if it remains to whatever extent a plurality.

Which introduces a third reason for the Demiurge's monomania—a composite body, if acted on from without, can be destroyed. An antidote to this possibility is to produce one, self-contained physical system, as the Demiurge is craftily aware. (33a–b)[44]

Briefly consider the other Demiurgic activities, remembering that the goal of the informing process is not in the first instance to make a

---

43. This response was suggested to me by a comment from Richard Perry during the Princeton Colloquium; cf. his "The Unique World of the *Timaeus*," *JHP* 17.1 (1979): 1–10. I agree with Perry that the Demiurge's primary concern is to craft an orderly and harmonious perceptible world. But I believe the argument set forth here allows *that* without requiring us to abandon the standard account of the Living Thing Itself embracing its four *genē* as something like a relation between kind and subkinds.

44. Cf. 32c5–33b1.

living thing, but to provide maximum unity and harmonious structure (mathematically conceived throughout) to the visible and tangible world. Take the puzzling account of why the world body consists of just the four elements. Fire and earth are introduced as implications of our world's visibility and tangibility. Air and water, however, are provided with a very different explanation. "But two things alone cannot be satisfactorily united without a third; for there must be some bond (δεσμός) between them, drawing them together. And of all bonds the best is that which makes itself and the terms it connects a unity in the fullest sense (μάλιστα ἓν ποιῇ) and this is naturally effected best by a proportion (ἀναλογία)." (31b8–c4) The three dimensional nature of the cosmos requires a four-term proportion and thus (with some work), air and water are explained.[45]

Notice that two goods are effected by the creation of precisely four elements. One is that the visible and tangible plurality becomes a *unity*; the second is that it becomes *indissoluble* (ἄλυτον), except by the one who bound it together. This is the beginnings of a world that is as far from the randomly shifting flux of the *Theaetetus* and *Cratylus* as a physical world can be. Behind the world revealed to us by our sense organs is an organization and stability which is due to intelligent production of the good.

Again the craftsman, while he cannot turn what is by nature created into something eternal, can, and does, endow it with an orderly and simple change "revolving according to number, an imitation of eternity" (37d–e). Likewise, as we've seen, the mathematical structure it embodies allows it to be indestructible. It is self-sufficient (68e), and possessed of every sort of measure, order and harmonious proportion (30a, 68b–d). In this way each aspect of the cosmos possesses a *summetria* both relative to itself and to everything else (69d2–5).[46] Finally, while he cannot remove the world of becoming from the realm of change altogether, he does his best. "He caused it to turn uniformly in the same place and within its own limits and made it revolve round and round; he took from it all the other six motions and gave it no part in their wanderings." (34a2–6)

The constant stress, then, on the creation of as Parmenidean a universe as possible is not a mistake—or if it is, it derives from a mistaken

---

45. For an interesting conjecture on the mathematical background to the passage, cf. Cornford (1937), pp. 45–52.

46. Cf. the interesting account of συμμετρία in R. VII in A. D. P. Mourelatos, "Plato's 'Real Astronomy': *Republic* 527d–531d" in J. P. Anton, ed., *Science and the Sciences in Plato* (New York, Eides, 1980), pp. 33–73. In particular, the important discussions of the parallel between R. 530a–b and Ti. 69b3–5, pp. 39–40 and 56–58.

theory of goodness. Given the conception of the good that is operative, and given the goodness of the Demiurge (which we dare not deny!), his activities as characterized in the *Timaeus* are as we should expect.

Where does this concept of goodness as a mathematical ordering and unifying of a diverse plurality come from? We have seen it as a natural feature of the craft model. But the notion of order and unity is given a very precise meaning in the *Timaeus*. An ordering and unifying of elements is here achieved by creating relations of proportionality and commensurability among them and their changes.[47] And this is carried through in the production of mortals by the created, imitating gods[48] and in the transformations undergone by the solids which constitute earth, air, fire, and water. Plato did not have to invent the idea of a mathematical account of any of these domains. But for him that such accounts were possible itself required explanation. He accounted for the underlying measurability of the *cosmos* by identifying that measurability with the good aimed for by a divine craftsman.

It is this mathematical version of counterentropic goodness which the Demiurge seeks to achieve by his actions and is perhaps most explicitly articulated in the following comment of Socrates near the close of the *Philebus*: "[Surely no one is ignorant of this] that every compound which does not in any way partake of measure and the nature of proportion necessarily destroys both the mixture and first of all itself. . . ." (*Phlb.* 64d 9–11) Rather, you end up with, in the inspired translation of Hackforth "a miserable mass of unmixed messiness" [64e 2–3]. This is the δύναμις of the good [64e5] found in the nature of the beautiful, in that beauty and excellence turn out to be a matter of measure and proportion.[49]

Likewise, in a quiet reference to the *demiurgos* of the heavens in the *Republic* (530a3–b4), we are told that it is the astronomer that focuses on the nature of the συμμετρία which the heavenly movements exemplify as well as physical bodies can, that may hit on the nature of the beautiful and the good (531c5).

And indeed, apprehension of *this* good is the teleological explanation why our eyes interact with the physical world as they do.

But for our part, let us speak of eyesight as the cause (αἰτία) of this benefit, for the sake of these things:[50] the god invented and gave us vision in order

---

47. Cf. *Ti.* 73c1, 74c5, 85c5, 86c5, 87c–d, 90a2.
48. Cf. *Ti.*, 59a1, 62a3, 64d9, 66b1, 66d3, 67c7.
49. Compare, *R.* VII: 529e3–530b1; Aristotle, *Met.* M.3, 1078a36–1078b6.
50. Following Cornford (1937) on 47b5–6; cf. p. 158, note 2.

that (ἵνα) we might observe the circuits of intelligence in the heavens and apply them to the circuits of our own thought, which are akin to them, the orderly to the disorderly; thus by learning from them and taking part in correct calculations in accordance with nature, and imitating the completely stable circuits of the divine, we might stabilize the wanderings in ourselves. (47b5–c4)

Notice that sight is the αἰτία of the good which results, *and* that we have eyesight *because* (ἵνα) of the good which results. Vision is the mechanism by means of which we may discover the good. But this is not an end in itself. We are provided with vision in order that we might get our souls in shape. The Demiurge aims at this, of course, because we are a part of the visible world he wishes to be good.

University of Pittsburgh

9 THE PRIMACY OF ΟΥΣΙΑ:
Aristotle's Debt to Plato

DANIEL DEVEREUX

In this essay I shall attempt to clarify some of Aristotle's early views concerning the nature of being and substance. My approach will be based on the assumption, shared by many students of Aristotle today, that to see how Aristotle's thought develops, in these crucial areas at least, we must compare his views with those of Plato. Two of the best known exponents of this approach to the study of Aristotle's metaphysics are Werner Jaeger and G. E. L. Owen. On a very general level, one might say that, according to Jaeger's interpretation, Aristotle begins at Platonic starting points and gradually develops a position which is, in most essential respects, quite different from Plato's. Owen, on the other hand, has tried to show that Aristotle's relationship to Plato is much more complex: that in relation to some issues Aristotle starts from a position antithetical to Plato's and eventually arrives at views much more in harmony with those of his mentor. A good example is the development of Aristotle's conception of metaphysics as a science of being in general. According to Owen, in his early works Aristotle associates the idea of a general science of being with Platonic dialectic, and argues that such a science is impossible; there can only be departmental sciences, sciences dealing with specific kinds of entities. Later, in the central books of the *Metaphysics*, he seems to be much more sympathetic towards the Platonic project and describes his own inquiry as a science of being in general.

Owen suggests that the reason for this surprising reversal was Aristotle's discovery that the categories of being exemplify the relationship he labels "focal meaning." As a result of this discovery Aristotle came to see that there was a unity in the concept of being that had earlier

---

*Versions of this paper were read at the University of Aix-en-Provence, California State University at Long Beach, and The Catholic University of America. I am grateful to those who raised questions and gave me helpful advice along the way, especially to Didier Pralon, Peter McCormick, Daniel Graham and Al Spangler.

escaped his notice. It was this new-found unity that led him to change his mind and "reinstate" the science of being in general.

I shall begin my discussion by focussing on the early stage of Owen's developmental story, i.e., the stage prior to the so-called "discovery." I believe this part of Owen's account is open to question on two important points. In the first place, Owen claims that the notion of focal meaning was first discovered in Plato's Academy, and was used by Aristotle, though sparingly, in his earliest works. A closer look at the evidence will show that Aristotle deserves the credit for discovering focal meaning, and that this notion does not appear in his earliest works. Secondly, Owen believes that the differentiation of the categories goes hand in hand with the distinction of the various senses of "being" or "existence"; i.e., the term "being" or "existence" is ambiguous, having different senses corresponding to the different categories. We might call this the "categorial ambiguity" of being. We shall find that this idea of the categorial ambiguity of being is not linked to the differentiation of the categories in the earliest works, and that in fact there is little evidence that Aristotle believed in the categorial ambiguity of being at this stage.

These two negative conclusions will lead directly to the central question of the essay: How does Aristotle understand the relation between substance and the other kinds of being in his earliest works? I will try to show that there are important parallels between this relation and the relation, as Aristotle understood it, between Platonic forms and their participants. As Aristotle sees it, a form is the first or primary member of a synonymous set, and this, as we shall see, is exactly how he understood the relationship between substance, the primary kind of being, and the other forms of being. His view of what qualifies as a primary kind of being is of course poles apart from Plato's, but his conception of the way in which such beings are primary is deeply indebted to Platonic notions.

I

In his polemic against the Platonic form of the good in the *Eudemian Ethics* Aristotle contends that, just as there cannot be a science of the good in general, so also there cannot be a science of being in general.[1] The apparent rejection of a general science of being contrasts sharply with well-known passages in the *Metaphysics* in which Aristotle argues in favor of such a science.[2] Harold Cherniss was one of the few

1. 1217b 25–35.
2. 1003a 21–b 19, 1045b 27–32, 1060b 31–1061a 10, 1061b 11–17. Owen refers to

scholars before Owen to pay any attention to this discrepancy. He seems to have thought that the passage in the *Eudemian Ethics* could not have been written by Aristotle and that the work as a whole was probably written by a disciple.[3]

Owen points out, however, that this passage is not an isolated instance; there are several passages in the logical works which also seem to be critical of the idea of a general science of being. The target of all of these passages, according to Owen, is the Platonic science of dialectic.[4] In the *Republic* Plato describes dialectic as a master science that concerns itself exclusively with being as opposed to becoming, and whose aim is to explain the nature of reality as such.[5] Owen believes that Aristotle's rejection of such a science is related to his view that the term *being* is ambiguous, having diverse significations corresponding to the different categories. Put somewhat differently, being, the sum total of what exists, does not constitute a single genus. Given the requirement, set forth in the *Posterior Analytics*,[6] that the subject matter of a science must form a unified genus, the conclusion seems inescapable: there can be no science of being in general. Thus certain characteristic doctrines of the logical works lead directly to the conclusion formulated in the *Eudemian Ethics*. Not only is there no hint of the possibility of a science of being in general in the logical works: there is no *room* for such a science.[7]

Owen's hypothesis is that the *Eudemian Ethics* and the logical works were written at an early stage in Aristotle's career, before he had worked out his own conception of a science of being *qua* being.[8] In this early period Aristotle was familiar with the type of systematic ambiguity which Owen calls "focal meaning," but he had not yet thought of applying it to the categories of being. He had distinguished the different senses of being corresponding to the different categories, but saw no connecting links among them, and thus no underlying unity.

VI 1 1026a 29–32 as a further instance of the use of focal meaning to justify a general science of being, but as far as I can see Aristotle's conception of a "science of being *qua* being" in VI 1 does not involve the application of focal meaning to the categories of being; see "Logic and Metaphysics in Some Earlier Works of Aristotle," *Aristotle and Plato in the Mid-Fourth Century*, eds. I. Düring and G. E. L. Owen (Göteborg, 1960), 168. Owen's paper has been reprinted in *Articles on Aristotle, v. 3, Metaphysics*, eds. J. Barnes, M. Schofield, R. Sorabji (New York, 1979).

3. *Aristotle's Criticism of Plato and the Academy* (New York, 1962), 238, n. 143 and 360, n. 269.
4. Owen, "Logic and Metaphysics," 168, 175–179.
5. Cf. 511b–c, 533b–534a.
6. See, e.g., 74b 24–26, 75a 28–31, 75a 38–b20, 76a 11–12.
7. "Logic and Metaphysics," 175.
8. Owen, 164.

Later on, according to Owen's hypothesis, Aristotle came to see that there was a systematic unity among the different significations of being; one signification, being as substance, was logically primary and served as a focal point for all the others. With this newfound unity, Aristotle saw a way of circumventing his earlier objections to a general science of being; and this is what we find him doing in the *Metaphysics*, in those passages in which he argues that even though being is not univocal, there is sufficient unity in the concept for a single science of being *qua* being.

Owen thinks that the type of systematic ambiguity he calls "focal meaning" was discovered in the Academy and was used by the Platonists in at least one important argument for the existence of forms.[9] Aristotle inherited this semantic notion from the Academy, but used it only infrequently in the logical works and seems to have attached little importance to it at this stage.[10] The breakthrough comes when he sees a way of applying the notion of focal meaning to the relationship between substance and the other categories.

Owen's interpretation has been attacked on several fronts. Some critics have attempted to show that already in the *Eudemian Ethics* Aristotle sees the relationship between substance and the other categories in terms of focal meaning, and that his rejection of a general science of being is only apparent.[11] Others have argued that various passages in the *Organon* indicate that Aristotle, at the time of writing these works, had already conceived the idea of a general science of being which is set forth in the *Metaphysics*.[12] Some of my remarks will have a direct bearing on these claims and will go some way towards showing that parts of Owen's general view are defensible. However, my main interest at this point is the question of the provenance of the notion of focal meaning, and here I think Owen's account needs to be modified. I will try to show that focal meaning does not appear at all in the logical works making up the *Organon*, and that there is no clear evidence that it was used in the Academy.

Let us begin by noting a puzzling feature of Owen's discussion of the *Topics*.[13] The business of distinguishing different senses of terms and

9. Owen, 182–185.
10. Owen, 174–175.
11. See, e.g., E. Berti, "Unité et multiplicité du bien selon EE I 8", in *Untersuchungen zur Eudemischen Ethik*, eds. P. Moraux and D. Harlfinger (Berlin, 1970); H. Flashar, "The Critique of Plato's Theory of Ideas in Aristotle's Ethics," in *Articles on Aristotle, v. 2, Ethics and Politics*, eds. J. Barnes, M. Schofield, R. Sorabji (New York, 1977); W. Leszl, *Logic and Metaphysics in Aristotle* (Padua, 1970), 530–538.
12. See Leszl.
13. "Logic and Metaphysics," 173–174.

different semantic relations is an important and recurrent theme of this work. Owen points out that there are a number of passages in which one is surprised to find no mention or use of the notion of focal meaning. For instance, the term *healthy*, which is Aristotle's favorite illustration of focal meaning in later works, is here treated as a simple case of homonymy; there is no suggestion that one signification of the term is primary and logically prior to the others.[14] Again, in a passage in which Aristotle gives a list of different semantic relations, we find mention of synonymy, homonymy and, as a third possibility, "metaphor."[15] This would obviously be an appropriate place to include some reference to focal meaning; if we assume that the notion was familiar to Aristotle, it is difficult to see why he omitted it from his list. In fact, the notion of focal meaning seems to be completely absent from the *Topics*.[16]

Owen cites these passages as evidence that Aristotle attached little importance to focal meaning in his early works. Actually, however, they lead one to wonder whether Aristotle was familiar with the notion at this time. Owen himself seems to have been puzzled about the complete absence of focal meaning from the *Topics*,[17] but he thought Aristotle must have known of it at this time because the notion appears in other works from the same period and was already discussed in the Academy. Let us, then, look at the evidence for these claims.

Surprisingly, Owen cites only one passage from the *Organon* as a clear example of the use of focal meaning.[18] The passage occurs in the discussion of quantity in the *Categories*. It deserves a careful look since some of the ideas in it will be important later in our discussion.

---

14. Owen says (174) that in such passages as 106a 4–8, 107b 6–12 we find materials for the focal meaning relation, but they are "unused"; in other words, Aristotle has not yet seen that these cases involve focal meaning. In his recent article, "Homonymy in Aristotle," (*Review of Metaphysics* (1981) 523–544), T. Irwin cites these same passages as evidence that Aristotle did recognize focal meaning in the *Topics*: "The healthy is spoken of in many ways—sometimes as what produces health, sometimes as what preserves it, and so on; all the definitions mention health," (526). However, in the passages cited Aristotle does not mention that the different definitions include the term "health," nor does he point out that they are unified in this way. Owen's characterization of the passages seems closer to the truth.

15. 139b 32–140a 17.

16. It is pretty clear that this is what Owen believes, although he does not say so; he does not cite any passages in the *Topics* as clear instances of the use or mention of focal meaning. It is perhaps not surprising that some have mistakenly thought that Owen was arguing that Aristotle had not developed his theory of focal meaning at the time of writing the *Topics*; see E. de Strycker, "Concepts-clés et terminologie dans les livres ii à vii des *Topiques*," in *Aristotle on Dialectic*, ed. G. E. L. Owen (Oxford, 1968), 153.

17. ". . . it is at least as likely that Aristotle had not yet evolved the general 'doctrine' [of focal meaning] for which Robin was looking." (174)

18. Owen mentions (175) as a more doubtful case the two uses of "substance" at *Cat.*

Strictly and primarily (κυρίως) only the things just mentioned are quantities; all the other things are only quantities derivatively (κατὰ συμβεβηκός). For it is with these in view that we call the others quantities: e.g. the white thing is called large in virtue of its surface being large, and the action is called long because of the time being long. . . . These things are not called quantities in virtue of themselves (καθ' αὑτό).[19]

There are clear parallels between this passage and those in which Aristotle spells out the notion of focal meaning. In his favorite example of focal meaning, the predicate "healthy" is applied primarily to a physical organism and secondarily to types of food or climate.[20] So also in this passage the predicate "large" applies primarily to a surface and secondarily to a white thing. But there is a crucial difference that Owen seems to overlook: Aristotle does not say or imply that the predicate "large" (or "long") has different significations depending on whether it is applied to "surface" or to "white thing."[21] Moreover, such a claim seems extremely implausible. Consider the following statements: (a) "This blackboard is large," and (b) "The surface of this blackboard is large." Surely one would not want to say that "large" has different meanings or significations in these two statements. Consider, by contrast, the use of "healthy" in "This body is healthy" and "This food is healthy." Here we *would* give different explanations of what "healthy" means in each statement: the predicate clearly does have different significations.

Fortunately, there is no compelling reason to attribute this implausible claim to Aristotle; as mentioned before, there is no indication in

---

2b 29–37; here Aristotle distinguishes between primary and secondary substances, pointing out that the latter deserve to be called "substances" since they reveal what the primary substances are. There is no suggestion that the definition or account of primary substances is somehow present in that of the secondary substances, and this is presumably why Owen considers it a "doubtful" case. Instead, there seems to be a set of criteria associated with the term "substance," and an entity will be called a "substance" in virtue of satisfying one or more of these criteria; those entities which satisfy the most, or the most important, criteria will be called "primary" substances.

19. 5a 38–b 4; cf. *Met.* 1020a 14–32 for a somewhat more refined version of this passage.

20. See, e.g., *Met.* 1003a 34–b 14.

21. Irwin (526) accepts Owen's reading of this passage. He claims that Aristotle is making a distinction between primary and secondary quantities, and that "these are quantities in different ways, with different definitions; but the definitions of the secondary will mention the primary." Thus quantities will be "connected homonyms"; i.e., they will exemplify the focal meaning relation. The crucial question is whether or not Aristotle supposes that, e.g., "large" has different senses or definitions as applied to "surface" and "white thing." Irwin does not cite any evidence for his claim, apart from the contrast between primary and secondary which is quite compatible with the denial that "large" has different definitions. One might also wonder, in a skeptical vein, what the different definitions would look like.

The Primacy of ΟΥΣΙΑ 225

the passage quoted that he thinks of the predicate *large* as having different significations in the two cases. What we have here is an instance of what Aristotle calls "synonymy": the account (λόγος) of what "large" means in each of the two statements would be the same.

The passage we have been discussing is closely related to a group of passages in which we find a distinction between a strict or primary subject of a predicate and derivative or secondary subjects of the same predicate. For instance, in the *Topics* Aristotle mentions that the predicate "having angles equal to two right angles" applies to the subject "triangle" καθ' αὑτό and applies κατὰ συμβεβηκός to a particular type of triangle like an equilateral triangle, for it is in virtue of its being a triangle and not an equilateral triangle that it has this attribute.[22] Another example from the *Topics* is the predicate "colored" as applied to body and surface of a body. Surface is said to be the "primary" subject since it is in virtue of its surface being colored that we can speak of a body as colored.[23] In all of these passages there is no suggestion that the predicate has different significations when applied to primary and secondary subjects.

The notion of a primary subject of a predicate has a special importance in the *Posterior Analytics*. One of the essential conditions stipulated for a scientific demonstration is that a predicate must be demonstrated of its primary subject. Aristotle again uses the example of "having angles equal to two right angles": if in our proof we demonstrate this predicate of an isosceles or equilateral triangle, we will not have a genuine scientific demonstration for we will not have demonstrated the predicate of its primary subject, triangle.[24]

The passage from the *Categories* cited by Owen turns out not to involve the notion of focal meaning at all, but instead the distinction between primary and secondary subjects of a predicate. In such cases the predicate has the same signification in its different applications and thus exemplifies the semantic relation of synonymy. The upshot is that we have not found any clear evidence of the notion of focal meaning in Aristotle's logical works. As far as I have been able to tell, the notion is completely absent from the *Organon*.[25] And since there

22. 110b 21–25; cf. *Anal. Post.* 74a 25–32.
23. 134b 10–13; cf. 131b 33–36, 134a 22–25, *Met.* 1022a 16–17 and 29–31, *Phys.* 248b 21–23. Some other passages in which the same distinction is found are: *Top.* 129b 18–21, 134a 18–25, 134a 32–34, 145a 28–32, 147b 28–33, *Cat.* 6b 36–7a 5, 7a 18–22, *Anal. Post.* 73b 33–74a 3, 74a 35–b 4.
24. 73b 33–74a 3.
25. Owen believes the notion is also to be found in another early work, the *Protrepticus* ("Logic and Metaphysics," 183–184). Without going into questions concerning the date of composition and authenticity of this work, I might point out that it is quite

are places where its absence is conspicuous, the explanation would seem to be that Aristotle had not yet discovered the notion.

But what about Owen's claim that focal meaning was discovered and used in the Academy? The evidence offered for the claim is again a single passage, this time from Aristotle's treatise *On Ideas* (Περὶ ἰδεῶν).[26] This passage contains Aristotle's report of an argument apparently used by members of the Academy to establish the existence of forms. The argument is full of problems, and it will not be possible to discuss it in any great detail; in any case, something short of a detailed analysis will be enough to raise reasonable doubts about Owen's claim that focal meaning is employed in the argument.

Let us begin by noting a puzzling inconsistency in Owen's account of how the Platonist understood the relationship between forms and their participants.[27] He says in several places that the Platonists conceived of the form as "the first of a synonymous set," and that the predicate corresponding to the form had the same signification whether applied to the form or to its participants.[28] Further, the form was thought to be naturally but not logically prior to its participants. In other words, the only sort of priority forms have is priority of existence: participants depend on forms for their existence, but not vice versa. Forms are not prior in definition or in some other fashion that would constitute logical priority.

This way of understanding the Platonists' position does not sit very comfortably with Owen's claim that, in the argument from the Περὶ ἰδεῶν, the application of the form-predicate to the form itself and to its participants is to be understood in terms of the focal meaning rela-

---

doubtful whether the example cited is a case of focal meaning. Two senses of "perceive" and "live" are distinguished, corresponding to the distinction between potentiality and actuality, and one sense is said to be prior to the other. This sort of distinction is found in many passages in Aristotle's works (see the passages cited by Düring in *Aristotle's Protrepticus* [Göteborg, 1961], 245–246), but is never, to my knowledge, classified under the rubric of focal meaning. The reason, presumably, is that the relationship between the different senses is not the same: we do not have a case where the definition of one sense is included (or referred to) in the other, but not vice versa.

26. "Logic and Metaphysics," 185–186; "A Proof in the *Peri Ideōn*," *Journal of Hellenic Studies* (1957), 103–111. The argument is also discussed in G. Fine, "Aristotle and the More Accurate Arguments," in *Language and Logos*, eds. M. Schofield and M. Nussbaum (Cambridge, 1982), 155–177, esp. 169–173; C. J. Rowe, "The Proof from Relatives in the *Peri Ideōn*: Further Reconsideration," *Phronesis* (1979), 270–281; R. Barford, "A Proof from the *Peri Ideōn* Revisited," *Phronesis* (1976), 198–219; W. Leszl, *Il 'De Ideis' Di Aristotle e la Teoria Platonica Delle Idee* (Florence, 1975), 185–224.

27. Or, more precisely, Owen's account of *Aristotle's reports* of the Platonists' understanding. Owen seems to assume, as I will for the time being, that Aristotle's reports give us an accurate picture of positions held in the Academy. I shall return to this question towards the end of the paper.

28. "Logic and Metaphysics," 172, 174, 182.

tion. For the focal meaning relation, as Owen indicates, involves a kind of logical priority. The signification of the predicate in the focal case is contained in the significations of the predicate in the secondary cases, but not vice versa; in other words, the definition of the focal case stands on its own while the definitions of the secondary significations must appeal to the focal case.

Now either the Platonic doctrine involved (at some point in its development) focal meaning and thereby involved the logical priority of the form vis-à-vis its participants, or the priority of the form was natural and not logical and focal meaning was not part of the doctrine: we cannot have it both ways.[29] I believe a close look at the argument in the Περὶ ἰδεῶν will convince us that the latter alternative is correct, i.e., that focal meaning played no role in the Platonists' conception of the relation between a form and its participants.

The argument is specifically designed to prove the existence of ideas or forms of relatives, and it uses the idea of Equality as a representative example.[30] In the first stage, the Platonist distinguishes three cases in which a predicate can be applied to a subject nonambiguously (μὴ ὁμωνύμως). Consider, for instance, the predicate *man*.

(1) As applied to an individual man, the subject is strictly or exactly what the predicate signifies.
(2) When the predicate is applied to an image or likeness of an individual man, the subject is not strictly or exactly what the predicate signifies.
(3) A third case is when the predicate is applied to a group of things including both individual men and their images or likenesses.[31]

According to the Platonist, the predicate *man* is applied nonambiguously in all three types of cases.

The next stage of the argument introduces the idea of equality, and poses the following question: When we apply the predicate *equal* to things in this world, is this a predication of the first, the second, or the third type?[32] In other words, are we applying the predicate to things which *are* strictly what the predicate signifies, or to things which are only images or likenesses of these, or to a combination of these? The Platonist then tries to show by elimination that when we call things in

---

29. A third possibility will be discussed below; see n. 81.
30. Alexander Aphrodisiensis, *In Aristotelis Metaphysica Commentaria*, ed. M. Hayduck (Berlin, 1881), 82, 11–83, 17; reprinted in W. D. Ross, *Aristotelis Fragmenta Selecta* (Oxford, 1960), 124–125.
31. Alexander, 82, 11–83, 6.
32. Actually the predicate is "equal itself." The more precise wording, although important for the argument, is not essential for our purposes.

this world "equal," this is a predication of the second type: it applies exclusively to things that are images or likenesses of things that are strictly what the predicate signifies. The first type of predication is eliminated because the definition of equality does not apply *strictly* to any sensible instance of equality; because of the imperfection of sensible things, and the fact that they are in constant flux, they always fall short of strict equality. The third type of predication is eliminated on the ground that no sensible instance of equality has a greater claim than any other to be considered a paradigm or model. So the Platonist draws the conclusion that there must be something apart from the equal things in this world which is their model or original and which is exactly that which the predicate signifies. This is of course the form or idea of Equality.

Owen points out that in the illustrations of the first and second types of predication, the predicate *man* seems to have different definitions or λόγοι.[33] When applied to an individual man, it signifies the definition of man, or whatever it is to be a human being; when applied to an image or portrait, it signifies a *likeness* of whatever it is to be a human being. Owen regards the relationship between the two cases to be essentially the same as focal meaning, or πρὸς ἕν predication. For instance, in the standard case of focal meaning the predicate *healthy* as applied to an organism signifies whatever it is to be healthy; as applied to a type of food, it signifies that which *promotes* or *contributes to* whatever it is to be healthy. There are different definitions in each case, one being central or logically prior to the other. Because of the link between the definitions or λόγοι, the different predications are not regarded as instances of simple ambiguity or homonymy.

We find the same relationship, according to Owen, between the different applications of the predicate *equal* in the course of the argument. As applied to the form, it signifies the definition or whatever it is to be equal. When applied to sensible instances, the predicate signifies not the simple definition but the definition qualified in a certain way: "equal in respect to length," or "equal in relation to such and such an object."[34] Owen contends that when the Platonist says that the definition of equality does not apply "strictly" or ἀκριβῶς to any sensible instance, what he means by the term ἀκριβῶς is "without qualification"; the definition applies without qualification to the form, but only with qualification to sensible instances of the form.[35] So here again we see one central signification of the predicate, and various

33. "A Proof," 104.
34. Ibid., 109.
35. Ibid., n. 37.

secondary senses, all of which contain the central one. And this, says Owen, is the same semantic relation that Aristotle elsewhere labels "focal meaning" or πρὸς ἕν predication.

However, there are certain features of the argument which might lead us to wonder whether Aristotle saw it this way. In most of the passages where we find the notion of focal meaning it is presented as a third possibility, intermediate between synonymy and "simple" homonymy. Moreover, in most if not all places where we find focal meaning, we also find the expression πρὸς ἕν ("towards one" or "in relation to one"). But in the argument from the Περὶ ἰδεῶν we do not find this expression, nor do we find any mention of a third possibility, an intermediate between synonymy and simple homonymy.[36]

But considerations of this sort are not decisive. One might easily argue that the notion of focal meaning is appealed to in the passage even if it is not formally introduced or referred to in the usual ways. However, there are other, stronger, reasons for doubting that the notion is to be found in this passage. Crucial to Owen's case is the translation of the term ἀκριβῶς. The usual translation of this adverb is "strictly," "precisely," or "exactly." Owen thinks that in this passage the word has a somewhat different sense and should be translated as "without qualification."[37] This is a crucial point because if we understand the adverb in the standard way, there is no implication that the *logos* or definition of "equal" will vary depending on whether the predicate is applied to the form or to sensible instances of the form. If the Platonist is saying that "the definition of equality does not apply *exactly* or *precisely* to any sensible instance of equality," we will naturally understand him to be making the point that the form has a kind of clarity and exactness that sensible objects lack, and not the point that some qualification must be added to the definition so that it will fit a particular instance.

While it is true, as Owen points out, that the adjective ἀκριβής is sometimes used by Aristotle to mean "simple" and "without extra determinants," there do not seem to be any cases, apart from this disputed passage, where Aristotle uses the adverb ἀκριβῶς to mean

---

36. It is also interesting to note that the use of ὁμωνύμως in this argument is different from Aristotle's typical use of the term. For Aristotle, if two things are called F ὁμωνύμως, they are both properly and correctly called F. However, when it is said in this argument that "equal itself" (ἴσον αὐτό) is applied ὁμωνύμως to things in this world, what is meant is that things in this world are not properly described as "equal itself." There are a few passages where Aristotle uses ὁμωνύμως in this way; e.g., *Part. An.* 640b 35–641a 3 (a painted eye is not really an eye, but only ὁμωνύμως an eye). Irwin calls these "spurious homonyms"; see "Homonymy," 527–529.

37. "A Proof," 109, n. 37.

"without qualification." Owen does not cite any other examples, and I have not been able to find any.[38] And even if there were evidence that ἀκριβῶς sometimes means "without qualification," the context in which it occurs does not seem very congenial to this translation. According to the Platonist, at least part of the reason why the definition cannot apply ἀκριβῶς to any sensible instance is the indefiniteness of sensible objects and the fact that they are in constant flux.[39] The contrast is between the clarity and exactness of the form and the lack of these qualities in sensible objects.

Thus a crucial argument for Owen's interpretation seems to be based on a mistranslation of the term ἀκριβῶς. Once we restore the standard translation, which seems more plausible in the context, there is no suggestion that the predicate *equal* has different significations when applied to the form on the one hand and to sensible instances on the other. It seems much more likely that, in the Platonist's view, the predicate is being used synonymously in these different applications.

So far we have been examining Owen's claims about the second phase of the argument, and we have not considered the first phase in which the three types of nonambiguous predication are set forth. Owen thinks that here too we find evidence of the notion of focal meaning insofar as the predicate *man* is regarded as having different significations as applied first to some individual man and second to an image or likeness of a man; in the first case it signifies what it is to be a man whereas in the second case it signifies a likeness of this.[40] Since the first signification is referred to in the second, but not vice versa, the first is logically prior to the second, and the example thus seems to fit the criteria for focal meaning.

The different uses of the predicate *man* are clearly meant to illustrate the relationship between a form and its participants; the participants in a form are related to the form in the same sort of way that an image or likeness is related to its model. Now if the different uses of

---

38. See Bonitz, *Index*, 28a 39–46.

39. οὔτε τὰ ἀληθῶς ἴσα σημαίνομεν. κινεῖται γὰρ τὸ ποσὸν ἐν τοῖς αἰσθητοῖς καὶ μεταβάλλει συνεχῶς καὶ οὐκ ἔστιν ἀφωρισμένον. (Alexander, 83, 8–10). Owen describes this passage as a "rider," and argues that it has no role in the argument ("A Proof," 109). This is related to his claim that this argument "isolates one strand" of the theory of forms, i.e., the contrast between complete and incomplete predicates, and "ignores" the mutability of the sensible world—a later extension of the theory. These are obviously large issues which go beyond the scope of this paper. It does seem to me that this part of Owen's discussion is not very convincing. The argument from the Περὶ ἰδεῶν contains what we find throughout the middle dialogues: the mutability thesis side-by-side with the contrast between complete and incomplete predicates, and no attempt to explain how these fit together. (Owen fails to note the following "early" references to the mutability thesis: *Phd.* 78 c–e, 79e–80b, *R.* 485b, 508d, 525c.)

40. "A Proof," 104.

the predicate *man* count as a case of focal meaning, then we might as well say that focal meaning (and the kind of logical priority it involves) is found in all those passages in the dialogues in which Plato speaks of sensible particulars resembling forms and being "called after" them.[41] For in these passages Plato is also maintaining that predicates apply strictly and primarily to forms, and that they are applied to sensible particulars only insofar as these resemble the forms. But Owen apparently thinks it would be a mistake to see focal meaning in these passages. He says that although the form F is that by reference to which other things are called F, this does not imply for the Platonist that the definition of the predicate *F* differs when it is applied to the form and when it is applied to the participant.[42] Even though the predicate applies strictly and primarily to the form, and only by way of resemblance to the participant, these different uses of the predicate are regarded as synonymous, the predicate having the same signification throughout.

It seems to me that what Owen says here is right. There are no signs that Plato, in speaking of particulars being "called after" forms, was thinking of the kind of logical priority that is involved in focal meaning. What he seems to have had in mind is not so much a distinction between different significations of the same predicate as a distinction between different types of *subject* to which the same predicate can be applied. A given predicate applies first to something primary, the form, and then to other things in virtue of their relationship to the form; it has the same signification whether applied to a primary or secondary subject. This, of course, is the same idea we encountered earlier in the *Categories*: the predicate *large* applies to "surface" as a primary subject and to "white object" as a secondary subject; *large* means the same thing in each application.[43]

Assuming this is the correct way of understanding the Platonist's talk of particulars being "called after" the form, and his use of the relation between an original and its copies to explain the relation between forms and their participants, we have no basis for saying that focal meaning is involved in the different applications of the predicate

---

41. See, e.g, *Phd.* 102b, 103b; cf. 78d–e with *Prm.* 130e.
42. "Logic and Metaphysics," 172, 174, 182.
43. See "Logic and Metaphysics," 174: "This simple treatment takes on a special significance in his attacks on the Ideas, for he recognises that the Platonists' use of the prefix αὐτό or ὅ ἐστιν, 'absolute' or 'what (really) is,' is just such an attempt to pick out the Idea as the primary subject of a predicate; yet here too he does not suppose that such a prefix entails any variation in the *logos*, the definition of the predicate." The passages Owen has in mind are listed on 172, n. 5; cf. also *Met.* 997b 5–12, *Top.* 162a 26–34.

man in the first part of the argument from the Περὶ ἰδεῶν. The point of this example is to illustrate the standard Platonic view of the relationship between forms and particulars, and Owen himself holds that focal meaning plays no role in this view.

So far we have reached two negative conclusions. The notion of focal meaning does not appear in any of Aristotle's early logical works, and there is no evidence that it was discovered and used by members of the Academy. Our results suggest that Aristotle deserves the credit for discovering this important notion; his rather careful explanation of the focal meaning relation in the discussion of friendship in the *Eudemian Ethics* may be an indication that he is introducing it for the first time in this passage.[44] Whether or not this is true, it seems clear that the concept of focal meaning was not inherited by Aristotle from the Academy and used, though infrequently, in his early works. It was his discovery, and one which he made only after he had written the *Organon*.[45]

II

I now want to turn to another part of Aristotle's conception of a general metaphysics, and try to show that it too is absent from his early works. There are three different notions which, when combined, provide the foundations for Aristotle's unified science of being: (i) the doctrine of the categories of being; i.e., the idea that the totality of what exists can be divided into a relatively small number of ultimate

---

44. Cf. Owen, "Logic and Metaphysics," 182: ". . . and the *Eudemian* version is probably the first and clearest exposition of focal meaning in the Corpus."

45. The fact that focal meaning is used and explained in the *Eudemian Ethics* but is not applied to being provides some support for Owen's view that there was a period in which Aristotle had the notion but did not see its full import for his metaphysics. It is also worth noting that our suggested revision of Owen's account of the provenance of focal meaning eliminates a problem which he struggled with in the final section of "Logic and Metaphysics." In Aristotle's criticisms of the Platonic theory of ideas, both in the *Metaphysics* and elsewhere, he operates with a simply dichotomy between homonymy and synonymy. He offers the Platonist a choice: either the form is synonymous with its participants or it is homonymous; either way there are insuperable problems. He never gives them the benefit of the third alternative, focal meaning—an alternative that would allow the Platonist to defend his theory against many of Aristotle's objections. (However, it seems to me that if the Platonist tried to defend the theory by making use of focal meaning, he would only lay himself open to new and equally powerful objections.) This poses a dilemma for Owen, given his view that the concept of focal meaning was actually used by members of the Academy in arguing for the theory of ideas. It looks as if Aristotle's treatment of his opponent's position is either grossly negligent or dishonest. However, if the concept of focal meaning was his own discovery, and was not used by the Platonist at all, the dilemma disappears.

categories;[46] (ii) the "categorial ambiguity" of being, i.e., the idea that the term *being* is ambiguous, having diverse significations corresponding to the ultimate categories; and (iii) the idea that the categorial ambiguity of being falls under the rubric of focal meaning; in other words, one of the significations of being, being as substance, is logically prior to the others and ties them all together so as to form a kind of unity.

According to Owen's account, the first two ideas, the distinction of the categories of being and the categorial ambiguity of the term *being*, are found throughout Aristotle's works, from the earliest to the latest. It is the third idea that is the relative latecomer, the idea of applying the notion of focal meaning to the different significations of being. This idea is found only in the mature works, and it provides Aristotle with the key to a general science of being. Owen seems to have assumed (as have most scholars) that the first two ideas are two sides of the same coin; i.e., that the division of being into a number of ultimate categories is at the same time a distinction of irreducibly different significations of the term *being*.[47] This is a natural assumption to make, since in the later works the two ideas are often mentioned together.[48] However, when we look at the references to the doctrine of the categories in the early works, it is not at all clear that the two ideas are linked. In fact, the categorial ambiguity of being seems to be completely absent from these works.

Let's first consider the *Categories* itself. Although the work begins with a distinction between homonymy and synonymy, it is striking that nowhere in the work is there any mention of the homonymy of being: there is no suggestion that the term *being* or *on* has different significations as applied to substance, quantity, quality, and so forth.[49] It might

---

46. Michael Frede has argued that it is a mistake to think of Aristotle's categories as the ultimate genera of what exists; see "Categories in Aristotle" in *Studies in Aristotle*, ed. D. J. O'Meara (Washington, D.C., 1981), 1–24. He tries to show that according to Aristotle's technical use of the term κατηγορία it designates a kind of predication, not a kind of entity. There are ten categories, just as there are ten ultimate genera of entities (in the *Categories*, and *Topics*), and though the two sets are related they do not coincide. It is interesting to note (in support of Frede's contentions) that where we find unambiguous references to the ultimate genera of entities in the *Topics*, they are referred to as "divisions," not as κατηγορίαι; see, e.g., 120b 36–121a 9; cf. 166b 14. Although Frede may be right about Aristotle's usage in the *Topics*, it seems clear that in other works "categories" refer to ultimate genera of existing things; e.g., *EN* 1096a 23–29, *Met.* 1068a 8–11. Gen. et Corr. 319a 11–12. I will therefore follow (one) traditional usage of "category" as designating an ultimate genus of entities.

47. An exception is M. Woods, *Aristotle's Eudemian Ethics* (Oxford, 1982), 70–71.

48. *EE* 1217b 25–30, *EN* 1096a 23–28, *Met.* 1017a 22–27, 1026a 33–b 1, etc.

49. Irwin (525) believes that 1a 20–b 6 shows that Aristotle recognized a kind of homonymy of being. This is the passage in which he divides entities into four types:

be thought that the two ideas were so closely linked in Aristotle's mind that he saw no reason to mention the ambiguity of being. But this begins to look quite dubious once we extend our search beyond the *Categories* to such works as the *Topics, Sophistical Refutations,* and the *Posterior Analytics.* In the *Topics* there are of course many passages that discuss homonymy, and many examples of homonymous terms are cited. But nowhere is it suggested that being (ὄν) might be homonymous. In fact, there are several passages which, if anything, suggest the contrary. For instance, at IV 1 121a 14–19, Aristotle points out that if something is posited as the genus of being, it will turn out that the species will partake of the genus, for being is predicated of everything that is, and therefore its definition (λόγος) will be predicated as well. The argument here seems to depend on the assumption that being has a single λόγος or definition. In other places, Aristotle considers possible definitions of being, and does not even mention the possibility that being does not admit of a single definition.[50] Of course, he may be speaking with the vulgar in these passages, but in view of the many examples of homonymy discussed in the *Topics* it is surprising to find that there is not even a hint of the possible homonymy of being.

Another pertinent passage is at IV 5 127a 26–38. Aristotle here considers the possibility of positing being as a genus. One might have expected the answer that there is no single genus of being since the term has different significations corresponding to the different categories. Aristotle *does* say that being cannot be a genus, but the reason he gives has nothing to do with homonymy. The problem with positing being as a genus is that we would have the impossible result that it would be coextensive with one of its species. For unity would be a species of being, and unity, like being, is predicated of everything. The lesson to be drawn is that terms like being and unity which can be predicated of everything cannot be posited as genera.[51] Aristotle's argument in no way implies that being is homonymous.

---

some are said of a subject, some are in a subject, some are both said of and in a subject, and some are neither said of nor in a subject. According to Irwin, this passage indicates that "different types of beings are connected homonyms, since the definitions of all mention a subject by reference to which the other beings are defined." If we do in fact have a recognition of the homonymy of being in this passage, it is clearly not categorial homonymy: the different significations do not correspond to the different categories. But in any case there are strong reasons for doubting Irwin's claim. Not only does Aristotle not mention homonymy in this context—he does not use any terms such as "signify" (σημαίνω) which would indicate that he sees himself not only distinguishing four types of entities but also distinguishing four different significations of being.

50. 146a 21–33, 139a 4–8.

51. In *Met.* 998b 17–27 and 1059b 27–34 Aristotle rejects the thesis that being (or unity) constitutes a genus for somewhat different reasons, but not because of the hom-

The Primacy of ΟΥΣΙΑ   235

In the *Sophistical Refutations* there are several passages in which Aristotle makes passing reference to the question whether "being" and "one" have different senses.[52] Though he does not explicitly commit himself on the question, it seems pretty clear that he thinks being *does* have different senses. However, we should not infer from this that Aristotle is thinking that being has different senses corresponding to the different categories. For this kind of homonymy is only one of several kinds he might be thinking of; other examples would be the difference between "being in potency" and "being in actuality," and the use of "being" to mean "true."[53] These too are cases in which the term *being* can mean different things in different uses, and these types of ambiguity are not tied to the doctrine of the categories. Indeed, contextual considerations make it unlikely that Aristotle was thinking of categorial ambiguity in these passages.[54]

In the *Posterior Analytics*, the doctrine of the categories of being is occasionally appealed to, but there is no sign of categorial ambiguity.[55] In each of the works mentioned the categories of being play an important role, and yet there is no explicit commitment to the idea that being is ambiguous with respect to the categories. It is possible, of course, that Aristotle had already formulated the idea, and for various reasons saw fit not to mention it in these works. But this seems unlikely; after all, the categorial ambiguity of being is frequently mentioned in the later works, in a variety of contexts: why should there be no mention of it in the early works, if the doctrine were already formulated?

It might be objected that there is at least one passage in the *Topics*

---

onymy of being; cf. *Top.* 140a 23–30. The thesis is also rejected in *Soph. El.* 172a 13–15, *Anal. Post.* 88b 1–3, 92b 14, but no reasons are given.

52. 169a 24–25, 170b 21–24, 182b 22–27. All of these passages seem to be parentheses.

53. See, e.g., *Met.* 1017a 31–b 2, *De Int.* 23a 7–11, a 21–26; cf. *Top.* 146b 13–19, 106b 13–20.

54. In *Soph. El.* 169a 22–25, Aristotle refers to certain instances of homonymy which are difficult to detect, e.g., being and unity; this passage obviously implies that being is not only a πολλαχῶς λεγόμενον but is also homonymous. But the kind of homonymy Aristotle has in mind here is probably not categorial ambiguity, for later in the same chapter (169a 30–b 2) he discusses fallacies which involve conflating items from different categories, and these are not treated under the rubric of homonymy; cf. 170a 12–19 and 178a 4–179a 10 (at 178a 23–27 Aristotle indicates that the cases under discussion are not cases of homonymy).

55. 83a 21–23, 83b 14–17, 85b 15–21, 88b 1–3. The *De Int.* contains nothing relevant to the categorial ambiguity of being. It is only in the *Prior Analytics* that we first encounter the notion, and even here it is not explicitly stated that *being* has as many significations as there are categories; cf. 49a 6–9 with 48b 2–4. There is a good deal of evidence that the *Anal. Prior.* is the latest of the works making up the *Organon*. See, e.g., J. Barnes, "Proof and the Syllogism," in *Aristotle on Science: The Posterior Analytics*, ed.

which clearly commits Aristotle to the view that being has different significations corresponding to the different categories. This is the passage in I 15 in which the term *good* is shown to be homonymous.[56] Aristotle begins with the general suggestion that we should check to see if "the kinds of predications [or "categories"] corresponding to the term" (τὰ γένη τῶν κατὰ τοὔνομα κατηγοριῶν) are the same in all cases; if not, the term will be homonymous. He then illustrates this with the term *good*: the good in food is what produces pleasure; in medicine what produces health; in the soul being of a certain quality, e.g., temperate; good in the case of time will be the opportune, and so forth. It has been pointed out that this passage closely parallels the passages in the ethical treatises in which Aristotle claims that good, like being, has as many senses as there are categories.[57] If this passage maintains that a term such as *good* is homonymous if it is predicated in different categories, then it looks as if *being* must be homonymous in the same way as *good*, for it is surely predicated in all of the different categories (as we saw earlier, being is predicated of everything). The passage seems to have the clear implication that being is ambiguous with respect to the categories, and it is difficult to believe that Aristotle was unaware of this.

However, the parallel with the passages in the ethical treatises is misleading. This passage is not maintaining that *good* has different senses corresponding to the different categories. Two of the examples of different senses ("productive of pleasure" and "productive of health") actually fall within the same category. If these are two "kinds of κατηγοριῶν," the term κατηγοριῶν cannot mean categories. The expression must mean "kinds of predications," and there will be different kinds of predication just in case there are different accounts of what a term means in its different applications. Thus there can be, as in this passage, different kinds of predication falling within a single category, but also the same kind of predication in different categories; e.g., "good," meaning "of a certain quality," could be predicated not only of substances but of qualities, quantities, and so forth.[58] So the passage is not maintaining that a term is homonymous if it is predicated in different categories, but rather if it is used to make different

---

E. Berti (Padua, 1981), 17–59; also J. Brunschwig, "L'objet et la structure des *Seconds Analytiques* d'après Aristote," in the same volume, 61–96.

56. 107a 3–12. J. L. Ackrill discusses this passage in "Aristotle on 'Good' and the Categories," in *Articles on Aristotle, v. 2. Ethics and Politics*, eds. J. Barnes, M. Schofield, R. Sorabji (New York, 1977), 17–24; see esp. 21–22.

57. Ackrill, pp. 17–24.

58. This is apparently the way Aristotle *sometimes* understands the meaning of "good" in the *Topics*; cf. 121a 1–3, 124b 19–22.

kinds of predication; and the test will be whether or not different accounts of the meaning of the term can be given.[59] Even though being is predicated in all of the different categories, it will not be categorially homonymous unless there are different accounts of its meaning corresponding to the different categories; and the passage under consideration says nothing about this one way or the other.

But this answer invites a further objection. If we think of the distinction between substance and other kinds of entities in the *Categories*, it seems obvious that being, as applied to each, will be used to make different kinds of predication. The being of a quality or quantity is derivative in that such an entity can only exist insofar as it inheres in an underlying subject, a substance. The being of a substance, however, is nonderivative; it does not depend on something else for its existence. When being is predicated of a substance and a nonsubstance, it seems clear that there will be different accounts of what *being* means in each case. By Aristotle's own criteria of homonymy, *being* will be homonymous at least with respect to substance and other types of entities. And yet there is no clear evidence that Aristotle saw it this way. In fact, the relevant passages in the early works seem to point in the opposite direction: they suggest that Aristotle did not recognize any ambiguity in the term *being* as applied to entities in different categories.

We may recall a somewhat similar point in our earlier discussion of the Platonist's views.[60] The Platonist holds that the predicate *F* applies to the corresponding form in virtue of the very nature of that form, whereas it applies to the form's participants in virtue of their being related to the form in a certain way—they are called *F* insofar as they resemble the form. The predicate applies to the participants derivatively, to the form nonderivatively. Given this difference in the way the predicate applies to the two kinds of entities, one might naturally suppose that, according to the Platonist, the predicate has a different signification in each case. Yet, according to Aristotle's reports, this is not how the Platonist saw the matter: the predicate *F* was viewed as synonymous with respect to the form and its participants. More generally, whenever a predicate is applied to things derivatively and nonderivatively, it is applied to those things synonymously.

I believe Aristotle in his early works is still operating within this Platonic framework. He holds that substances are primary and self-subsistent beings, and that the being of nonsubstances is derivative and parasitic on that of substances. And because he accepts the Pla-

---

59. Cf. Ackrill, 21.
60. See above, pp. 230–231.

tonic view of the nature of derivative and nonderivative predication, he holds that being applies to substances and nonsubstances synonymously. He may have had his own reasons for adhering to the Platonic view. He claims in several places in the early works that in order to make comparisons of things with respect to a certain predicate, the predicate must apply to those things synonymously.[61] If, for instance, one wants to say that one thing is "more F" than another, the predicate F must apply to both synonymously. What this implies is that if one wants to compare entities in general and say that one kind of entity is primary with respect to its being, one must hold that being is synonymous in relation to all of these entities. And Aristotle does, of course, want to designate one type of entity as primary: he follows the Platonists in using the term οὐσία as an honorific label for those entities he picks out as primary. It is thus understandable that he should hold that *being* is synonymous with respect to the categories.

My suggestion, in short, is that Aristotle's early conception of the primacy of substance is an adaptation of the Platonic understanding of how predicates apply to forms and particulars, respectively. In the remainder of the paper I will try to specify in greater detail what is involved in this suggestion, and at the same time attempt to give it the sort of textual support it needs.

III

Let us look first at a couple of distinctions Aristotle makes in the *Posterior Analytics*. The first distinction is a crucial one for his theory of scientific demonstration. He says that some attributes are καθ' αὐτά or per se in relation to their subjects, while others are mere "accidents" or συμβεβηκότα.[62] The καθ' αὐτά attributes are those which are either elements in the definition of the subject, or whose definition includes the subject as an element. "Two-footed" in relation to "man" would be an example of the first type of καθ' αὐτά attribute: "odd" in relation to the subject "number" would be an example of the second type since the definition of "odd" will include a reference to "number."[63] Attributes which are accidents or συμβεβηκότα are simply those which do not have this sort of definitional connection with their subjects. For example, the attribute "musical" in relation to the subject

---

61. *Top.* 107b 13–18, *Cat.* 11a 12–13, *Phys.* 249a 3–8; later Aristotle softens this claim: cf. *EN* 1155b 14–16. This change may well be due to the introduction of focal meaning as an intermediate between synonymy and homonymy.
62. 73a 34–b 5.
63. Cf. 84a 12–17.

"man": a man may or may not be musical, and the term *man* does not figure in the definition of "musical."[64]

Immediately following this, Aristotle formulates another distinction, using the same terms καθ' αὑτά and συμβεβηκότα. In this case it is not attributes in relation to subjects which are said to be καθ' αὑτά or συμβεβηκότα, but entities taken by themselves.

> Further, that which is not said of something else as a subject—e.g., the 'walking' [thing] is something else [which is] walking, and the 'white' [thing is something else which is white]—but substance, and what signifies a 'this' are what they are not being something else. Those which are not [said] of a subject I call καθ' αὑτά, but those [said] of a subject "accidents", συμβεβηκότα.[65]

Crucial to this distinction is the contrast between things which are said of a subject and things which are not. Things which are not said of a subject are καθ' αὑτά, while things which *are* said of a subject are "accidents" or συμβεβηκότα. But what exactly are the things which are, and are not, said of a subject? Aristotle mentions "the walking thing" and "the white thing" as examples of things said of a subject. In a later chapter he says that nothing is simply white: the "white thing" is always something else that is white, e.g., a man or a stick.[66] White cannot "stand on its own"; it must inhere in something as a subject, and this

---

64. Cf. *Top.* 102b 4–9, *Cat.* 7a 25–39. There are several interesting differences between the *Top.* and the *Anal. Post.* in regard to the concept of a συμβεβηκός attribute. (i) The attribute "snub" would apparently be a συμβεβηκός according to the *Top.* account, but a καθ' αὑτό attribute according to the *Anal. Post.* (ii) The *Top.* seems to treat an attribute like "white" as a συμβεβηκός regardless of the sort of subject of which it is predicated, whereas the *Anal. Post.* is careful to specify that "white" is a συμβεβηκός in relation to "animal" (73b 4–5); presumably it would not be a συμβεβηκός in relation to "surface": see *Met.* 1022a 16–17, 29–32, 1029b 16–17, *Phys.* 248b 21–23. As we noted above (n. 23), there are passages in the *Top.* in which Aristotle recognizes that an attribute that would be classified as a συμβεβηκός has a special, logical, connection with one particular subject, but this view is not (yet) incorporated into his classification of the different types of attributes. (iii) "Having interior angles equal to two right angles" would be a συμβεβηκός of "triangle" according to the *Anal. Post.* (since it lacks a definitional tie), but not according to the *Top.* (since it belongs necessarily). Such attributes seem to fall outside the classification of predicables in the *Top.*, perhaps because the entire discussion is geared to definition rather than demonstrations (cf. J. Barnes, *Aristotle's Posterior Analytics* [Oxford, 1975], 115). The attribute in question belongs to "triangle" not only necessarily but καθ' αὑτό; it is in virtue of being a triangle (and not, e.g., an isosceles triangle) that the subject has this attribute. Thus Aristotle often refers to these attributes as συμβεβηκότα καθ' αὑτά (see, e.g 75b 1, 83b 20, 75a 18). This can be confusing since he also speaks of συμβεβηκότα as attributes which do not necessarily belong to their subjects: 74b 12, 75a 20–21, 31 (this usage of the term harks back to the *Top.*). Given this use, the expression συμβεβηκότα καθ' αὑτά seems self-contradictory. (Aristotle is aware of the possible confusion—cf. 75a 21–22.) For more on συμβεβηκότα καθ' αὑτά, see below, n. 75.

65. 73b 5–10.

66. 83a 25–32; cf. *Met.* 1088a 27–29.

will be a substance. The point is made several times that the underlying subjects are substances.⁶⁷ So the distinction Aristotle is making corresponds to the distinction between substance and the other categories. Substances are καθ' αὑτό entities; qualities, quantities, relations, etc. are all "accidents" or συμβεβηκότα.⁶⁸

Aristotle's choice of the term συμβεβηκότα as a designation of nonsubstance entities is puzzling. The root meaning of the word is related to the notion of what *happens* to be the case or what is coincidental; it is contrasted with what is necessarily the case, or at least what is usually, or "for the most part," the case.⁶⁹ The use of the term to designate attributes which may or may not belong to a given subject (as in the *Top.* and sometimes in the *Anal. Post.*), is in perfect accord with the basic meaning of the term. But why would Aristotle choose this term, in the second distinction, to designate items in nonsubstance categories?⁷⁰ He obviously does not mean that they may or may not inhere in their subjects or substances, for some of them will necessarily inhere.

We can make some progress towards a solution by noting that the two different uses of the term συμβεβηκότα are paralleled by two uses of the expression κατὰ συμβεβηκός (*per accidens*). According to the more common use of the expression, a subject has a certain attribute κατὰ συμβεβηκός if it has it neither necessarily nor essentially; it is the sort of attribute that a subject could easily lose, or might never have possessed, and still remain the same subject.⁷¹ The expression designates a particular *way* in which an attribute or description belongs to a subject; by a natural extension the term συμβεβηκός can be used to designate an attribute which is possessed in that way.

But there is another quite different use of the expression. For instance, in a passage from the *Topics* mentioned earlier, Aristotle says that the subject "equilateral triangle" possesses the property of having its interior angles sum to two right angles only κατὰ συμβεβηκός, while the subject "triangle" has the same property καθ' αὑτό.⁷² Ob-

---

67. 83a 24–32, 83b 17–24, 73b 5–10. In the *Cat.* Aristotle speaks of entities from nonsubstance categories as "subjects" (ὑποκείμενα) in relation to their species and genera, but in the *Anal. Post.* he seems to use the term exclusively for entities falling under the category of substance.

68. 83b 10–12; cf. *EN* 1096a 20–22.

69. See *Met.* 1026b 24–27, 1064b 30–1065a 2, 1025a 14–21.

70. A similar question could be posed in regard to the συμβεβηκότα καθ' αὑτά. It might seem more natural to classify these as a subset of the καθ αὑτά attributes: all καθ' αὑτά attributes belong to their subjects in virtue of what the subjects (or attributes) are; some are definitionally tied to their subjects, some are not. See below, n. 75.

71. See Bonitz, 714b 5 ff.

72. 110b 21–25; cf. 111a 2–6, *EN* 1159a 17–27, 1151a 35–b2, *Phys.* 195a 34–b 12. Bonitz seems to overlook this use.

viously he does not mean that an equilateral triangle could lack this property and still remain what it is; the property in question is a necessary attribute of all equilateral triangles. The idea is rather that the subject "equilateral triangle" has this property *derivatively*: it is in virtue of its being a triangle, not an *equilateral* triangle, that it has the property of possessing interior angles which sum to two right angles. It is the subject "triangle" which has this property in virtue of itself, καθ' αὐτό.

This use of the expression κατὰ συμβεβηκός involves a contrast between primary and derivative applications of a predicate. It is the same use which we found in the passage from the *Categories* discussed earlier.[73] The subject "white thing" has the property of largeness only κατὰ συμβεβηκός; what has the property primarily and καθ' αὐτό is the surface of the white thing. The notion of contingency is also present in this second use of κατὰ συμβεβηκός, but in a different way. It is not that the subject could lose the property and still remain the same subject, but rather that, e.g., with respect to the size of an object, its color is contingent but its surface is not; or with respect to the property of having interior angles sum to two right angles, being isosceles is contingent but being a triangle is not.[74]

As we noticed earlier, the first and more common use of the expression κατὰ συμβεβηκός is clearly related to the first use of the term συμβεβηκότα; both have to do with predicates that apply only contingently or coincidentally to their subjects. It also seems pretty clear that the second use of κατὰ συμβεβηκός underlies and explains Aristotle's choice of the term συμβεβηκότα to designate entities in nonsubstance categories.[75] In both we find the contrast between primary and derivative. Entities which are accidents or συμβεβηκότα are always said of subjects, and they have their being not in virtue of themselves but in virtue of their relationship to these subjects; entities which are καθ' αὐτά are not said of subjects and they have their being in virtue of themselves. In terms of their existence, the one type of entity is primary, the other is derivative; in other words, the predicate *existence* or *being* applies primarily and καθ' αὐτό to substance, and only derivatively or κατὰ συμβεβηκός to nonsubstances, just as the predicate

---

73. 5a 38–b 10; see above, pp. 224–225.
74. Cf. *Soph. El.* 168a 40–b 4.
75. We can derive a similar explanation of his use of the term in the expression συμβεβηκότα καθ' αὐτά. Since these attributes are demonstrable of their subjects, they inhere in their subjects not "directly" but through the middle term or terms used in the demonstration. So in a sense they too are derivative, even though they belong to their subjects in virtue of the nature of those subjects. It seems plausible to suppose that their derivative nature underlies Aristotle's choice of the term συμβεβηκότα.

large applies primarily to surface and only derivatively to "white thing."

We noticed earlier, in discussing the passage from the *Categories*, that Aristotle pretty clearly thought of the predicate *large* as having the same signification whether applied to "white thing" or to "surface." It applies to the first κατὰ συμβεβηκός and to the second καθ' αὑτό, but this is quite compatible with its being applied synonymously in each case. In fact, it seems that whenever these expressions are used to mark the distinction between derivative and nonderivative predication, the predicate applies synonymously. Thus the passage at *Anal. Post.* 73 b 5–10 provides some additional support for the claim that being is thought of as synonymous with respect to the categories in the early works.

If our hypothesis is on the right track, we would expect that when Aristotle arrives at the view that being is categorially ambiguous, he will drop the contrast between substance as that which has being καθ' αὑτά and nonsubstance as that which exists κατὰ συμβεβηκός, for this contrast presupposes the synonymous predication of being. This does seem to be true of the later works in which the categorial ambiguity thesis is clearly to be found. In the *Metaphysics*, for instance, the term συμβεβηκότα seems never to be used as a generic label for nonsubstances;[76] nowhere are nonsubstances said to exist κατὰ συμβεβηκός— in fact, in his discussion of the different types of ambiguity of the term *being* in Book V, Aristotle says that entities from *all* of the different categories can be said to exist καθ' αὑτό.[77] And when he refers to the entities that he considers primary, he no longer speaks of them as καθ' αὑτό.[78] He now describes the primacy of substance in terms of the focal meaning relation.[79]

---

76. In *Met* V 30, Aristotle sets out two meanings of συμβεβηκός. According to the first, an attribute is a συμβεβηκός if it belongs to a subject, but not necessarily. According to the second, an attribute is a συμβεβηκός if it belongs to a subject καθ' αὑτό but is not part of its essence; e.g., "having two right angles" in relation to "triangle." In other words, this second meaning of συμβεβηκός is equivalent to what is called a συμβεβηκὸς καθ' αὑτό in the *Anal. Post.* The various uses of the term throughout the *Met.* seem to fit one or the other of these two definitions. Nonsubstances are said to be συμβεβηκότα in *EN* 1096a 20–22, but Aristotle is here characterizing the Platonic view (see Alexander, 86, 8–10; 83, 33), which is parallel, as we shall see, to his own early view.

77. 1017a 22–24.

78. See, e.g., 1037a 5–7, a 27–b 4, 1030a 7–11. An apparent exception is in the discussion of whether each thing is identical with its essence in VII 6. Here he speaks of certain entities that are primary (πρῶτα) and καθ' αὑτά insofar as they do not have any natures or essences prior to them; 1031a 28–31, 1031b 11–14, 1032a 4–6. But it is clear that his attention is focused primarily if not exclusively on Platonic ideas (1031a 30–b 1), and he seems to be appealing to the Platonic usage of καθ' αὑτά, cf. *EN* 1096a 21 and Alexander, 83, 24–26 and 86, 7–10.

79. An objection to the general view I have been arguing for might be put as follows:

Let me summarize some of the points I have been arguing for so far. First of all, I have tried to show that Aristotle does not inherit the notion of focal meaning from the Academy; it is his discovery, and the discovery was not made until after the composition of the early logical works. Second, I argued that the doctrine of categorial ambiguity is another relative latecomer; again, we find no evidence of it in the earliest works. Third, I suggested that the way Aristotle understands the relationship between substance and the other categories in the *Posterior Analytics* shows why he did not accept the doctrine of categorial ambiguity in this early stage: being applies to substances καθ' αὑτό and to nonsubstances κατὰ συμβεβηκός, and it is a presupposition of this type of distinction that the predicate has the same signification in each case.

IV

The importance of this third point is that it enables us to see Aristotle's early view of substance and its relationship to Platonic doctrines in a new light. A number of interesting parallels have already been noted in passing. For instance, we pointed out a similarity between Plato's way of understanding how predicates apply to forms and particulars respectively and Aristotle's notion of a "primary subject" of a predicate. In the example discussed earlier, Aristotle says that the predicate *large* applies primarily or strictly to the subject "surface," and only derivatively or κατὰ συμβεβηκός to "white thing." This is not a distinction between different significations of the same predicate, but a distinction between different types of subject to which the same predicate can be applied. In general, a predicate *F* will apply to A as a primary subject and to B as secondary subject if it applies to B in virtue of its applying to A, and applies to A simply in virtue of itself.

We saw that this notion of a strict or primary subject of a predicate is referred to a number of times in the *Topics*, and takes on special importance in the *Posterior Analytics* in connection with the requirements

---

I have claimed that in the early works the concept of being is synonymous with respect to the categories; if so, why should Aristotle have any objection to a general science of being? If being is not regarded as categorially ambiguous, what then is the basis of the rejection of a general science of being? A proper answer to this objection would go beyond the scope of this paper. I might say, briefly and dogmatically, that it is not clear to me that Aristotle does rule out the possibility of a general science of being in his early works. In one passage (*Anal. Post.* 76a 16–25) he clearly rejects the possibility of a single master-science which demonstrates the first principles of the various departmental sciences; but this seems compatible with the idea of a general science of being, which in-for scientific demonstration. We also noted that Platonic forms are in effect primary subjects of predicates. Particulars which are called F are called so only derivatively; it is in virtue of their participation in the form that they have this predicate applied to them. The form F-ness, on the other hand, is called F simply in virtue of itself. The form is the primary subject of the predicate; the particulars are secondary subjects insofar as they are "called after" the form.[80] As Owen points out, it is not part of the Platonic view that the predicate has different significations in its different uses; the form is conceived of as the "first" or primary member of a "synonymous set," naturally but not logically prior to its participants.[81]

The Academy, it appears, used terminology similar to Aristotle's to mark the distinction between primary and secondary subjects of a predicate. Forms are classified as καθ' αὑτά entities, presumably because they are called whatever they are called in virtue of themselves and not in virtue of being related to something else; participants, on the other hand, are classed as πρός τι or "relative" entities insofar as they are "called after" forms and are called what they are in virtue of a relationship to a form. From Aristotle's reports, especially in the Περὶ ἰδεῶν, it looks as if this distinction was intended as a simple division of categories of being, and that entities in the first category, the καθ'

---

vestigates the nature of being *qua* being and the attributes which belong to it καθ' αὑτό. But obviously a careful investigation of a number of passages is needed in order to settle the question.

80. See above, n. 41.

81. "Logic and Metaphysics," 174. Passages giving some support to Owen's claims about Aristotle's understanding of the Platonic theory are: *Met.* 997b 6–8, 1040b 32–34, 1079b 3–11. One might question Owen's claim that the Platonists regarded the form as naturally, but not logically, prior to its participants. By "natural priority" here is meant priority of existence: if the destruction of A involves the consequent destruction of B, but not vice versa, then A is "naturally prior" to B. This sort of priority is attributed to the forms by Aristotle in *EE* 1217b 10–13; cf. 1218a 3–5. But in the same passage he also says that the form of the Good is the cause (αἰτία) by its presence of the goodness of other things, and that other things are only good "by participation" (κατὰ μετοχήν); 1217b 2–10. This pretty clearly implies that there is more to the priority of the form than priority of existence; the form is also prior in explanation (it is by looking to the form that we understand why its participants are F). It seems appropriate to call this a kind of logical priority, although it is clearly not the kind of logical priority involved in focal meaning. Turning to a somewhat different point, one might question the reliability of Aristotle's account of the Platonic theory of forms. Some commentators, for example, have contended that a predicate F has a different meaning or signification when applied to the form and its participants respectively (e.g., G. Vlastos, "The 'Third Man' Argument in the *Parmenides*," in *Studies in Plato's Metaphysics*, ed. R. E. Allen [New York, 1965], 253–254; R. E. Allen, "Participation and Predication in Plato's Middle Dialogues," in the same volume, 43–60). If they are right, then Aristotle's reports must be based on a misunderstanding of the theory. Whatever the merits of such a view, the

αὐτά entities, were called "substances" (οὐσίαι) by the Platonists.[82]

The Aristotelian counterparts of these technical terms and distinctions are particularly evident in the passages discussed earlier from the *Posterior Analytics*. In this work he makes a fundamental division between two classes of entities, those that are καθ' αὐτά and those he calls συμβεβηκότα. We saw that this particular use of the term συμβεβηκότα (accidents) is based on the idea that these things are spoken of as entities, not in virtue of themselves, but in virtue of their relationship to something else, i.e., in virtue of their inhering in something else as a subject. Even though the relationship is different in each case (inherence on the one hand, participation on the other), the Aristotelian concept of a συμβεβηκός entity is obviously closely related to the Academy's notion of a πρός τι or "relative" entity. The two relationships involve different ways of understanding the contrast between derivative and nonderivative entities. In fact, there is a formula that seems to bridge the gap between the two. The Platonist would agree with Aristotle that a primary entity is one that "is what it is without being something else."[83] The Platonist would say, for example, that the form White is white without being something else that is white, whereas any participant in the form will always be something else that is white: e.g., a man, a stick, a house. Aristotle argues that there is nothing that is white without being something else that is white,[84] but he holds at the same time that there are entities that are what they are without being something else, and these are for him the primary entities; e.g., Socrates is a man without being something else that is a man.[85]

Because, according to both views, a καθ' αὐτό entity is one that is in a certain way *non*derivative, it is defined through the negation of its correlate. In other words, a καθ' αὐτό entity for Aristotle is one that does *not* inhere in something else as subject, while for Plato it is one that is *not* what it is by virtue of being related to something else. Finally, in addition to these parallels, there is the fact that Aristotle uses the same term οὐσία or "substance" for those entities he regards as primary or καθ' αὐτά.

---

important point for our purposes is that Aristotle understood the Platonists to be claiming that the predicate was synonymous with respect to the form and its participants.

82. *EN* 1096a 17–23; cf. Alexander, 83, 24–26; 86, 7–10 (= Ross, *Aristotelis Fragmenta Selecta*, 125, 127); Simplicius, *Cat.* 63, 21–24.

83. *Met.* 987b 22–23; cf. 1031b 11–14 and *Anal. Post.* 93b 5–10.

84. *Anal. Post.* 83a 30–35.

85. This becomes more complicated when the matter-form distinction is brought into the picture; see R. Dancy, "On Some of Aristotle's Second Thoughts about Substances: Matter," *The Philosophical Review* 87 (1978): 372–413.

What all of this shows is exactly what we might have expected in any case: that Aristotle formulated his early view of the primacy of substance working within the framework of a set of distinctions and notions developed in the Academy. From the very beginning, he seems to have been a vigorous opponent of the theory of forms. But in articulating his own theory of being, he takes over certain ideas that were integral to the theory of forms and adapts them to suit his needs. Thus he takes the Platonic distinction between καθ' αὑτό and πρός τι entities and transforms it so as to fit his division between entities that are not said of subjects and those that are. And just as the Platonist regards the form as the first or primary member of a "synonymous set," so Aristotle regards substance as the first or primary member of a synonymous set of *types* of entities. That is, Aristotle's understanding of how the predicate *being* applies to the different categories is based on the Platonic view of how predicates apply to forms and their participants. Substance is the primary or proper subject of being; being applies to nonsubstances only secondarily or derivatively. Yet there is no variation in its signification; it applies synonymously to substances and nonsubstances alike. And thus, in relation to being, substance—like the Platonic form—is the primary member of a synonymous set.

Much more needs to be said about the views of Plato and the early Aristotle on the primacy of οὐσία. But perhaps we have at least shown that, in this area as in others, Aristotle owes much to Plato; his debts are deep even where his opposition seems most pronounced.

University of Virginia

10 PLOTINUS ON HOW SOUL ACTS ON BODY

DOMINIC O'MEARA

It is easy to be led in modern discussions of questions concerning mind and body to the conclusion that "Cartesian dualism" is unable to explain *how* mind could ever act on body, despite its claim that there is such action. This failure, it seems, leaves the Cartesian with a choice between withdrawing the claim that mind acts on body, or (better yet) abandoning entirely the substantial distinction between mind and body which is the source of the quandary. A notorious text in this regard is the following passage in a letter Descartes wrote towards the end of his life to his friend Princess Elizabeth:

> And I may say . . . that the question that your Majesty proposes seems to me the one that one can put with most justification, in view of the writings I have published. For there are two points [concerning soul] . . . one is that it thinks, the other that being united to the body the soul can act and suffer with it. I have said little or nothing about the second point and have tried only to make clear the first.[1]

This is hardly a confession of failure. But it is tempting enough to conclude that if Descartes had not, at this stage, explained how mind acted on body, it was because he could not. And if the little pineal gland is intended to mediate the reciprocal action between mind and body, it can hardly be said to convince.

In this paper I wish to discuss neither the extent to which modern versions of "Cartesian dualism" (and its supposed difficulties) are relevant to Descartes' own thought, nor how Descartes himself might deal with the question as to how mind acts on body.[2] My object rather is to

---

*I am greatly indebted to those who were kind enough to raise questions and make suggestions concerning various versions of this paper delivered at the universities of South Carolina and of Fribourg and at The Catholic University of America.

1. Letter CCCII, dated 21 May 1643 in C. Adam and P. Tannery, *Oeuvres de Descartes Correspondance* 3 (revised ed. Paris 1971): 664–665.
2. Cf. R. Richardson, "The 'Scandal' of Cartesian Interactionism," *Mind* 91 (1982): 20–37.

propose the elements of an answer to this question as these may be found in another "dualist," Plotinus. Even if difficulties emerge in the way Plotinus explains how soul acts on body, it will have been shown, I hope, that in his case at least "dualism" is not at a loss for explanation when it comes to this subject.

Although it seems obvious enough that Plotinus insists on making soul and body two radically different kinds of things,[3] my purpose to show how he explains soul's action on body may surprise in view of the conclusion to which Henry Blumenthal comes in his very valuable book on Plotinus' psychology to the effect that Plotinus "does not really explain how [soul] can act on [body]."[4] If this is taken to mean that Plotinus is unable to provide an explanation of how soul acts on body, then it points to a sort of Cartesian failure that casts doubt in consequence on Plotinus' distinction between soul and body and thus on a fundamental part of his philosophy. I hope to show that such a Cartesian failure is not to be imputed to Plotinus. If, on the other hand, Blumenthal means that there is no specific treatise or substantial body of text in Plotinus devoted to answering the question as to how soul acts on body, this is true enough: the answer will have to be pieced together from indications that he gives in various places in his work. Before doing this, however, it will be useful to recall by way of introduction some relevant themes in Plato and Aristotle and then to sketch briefly the way in which Plotinus distinguishes soul from body, so that the question of how soul acts on body in Plotinus may be approached along lines suggested by the distinction to which it relates.

I

For some time now contemporary discussion of the "mind-body" problem has inspired fruitful investigations into the subject in Greek philosophy. Aristotle has prevailed in this work as the champion of an appropriate position, a materialist or functionalist theory of the relation between soul and body.[5] The Stoics also seem promising.[6] Plato

---

3. This is I believe what is usually meant by "dualism" in this general context. The term is somewhat misleading however as a characterization of Plotinus' position; cf. A. M. Rich, "Body and Soul in Plotinus," *Journal of the History of Philosophy* 1 (1963): 2, 15.
4. *Plotinus' Psychology*, (The Hague 1971), pp. 138–139.
5. To name but a few: M. Nussbaum, *Aristotle's De motu animalium*, (Princeton 1978); E. Hartman, *Substance, Body and Soul*, (Princeton 1977). Against this see most recently H. Robinson, "Mind and Body in Aristotle," *Classical Quarterly* 28 (1978): 105–124; "Aristotelian Dualism," *Oxford Studies in Ancient Philosophy* 1 (1983): 123 ff.
6. Cf. A. A. Long, "Soul and Body in Stoicism," *Phronesis* 27 (1982): 34–57.

has attracted less attention than Aristotle in this regard, perhaps because he appears to subscribe to an extreme dualism of soul and body.[7] It has also been pointed out, however, that modern distinctions between mind and body (and the attendant difficulties) must not be confused with distinctions in antiquity between *soul* and body. Thus the philosophy of Plato or of Aristotle cannot be regarded simply as a stand-in for a contemporary dualist or perhaps functionalist position.[8] At the same time various distinctions and relations between soul and body are to be found in ancient thought which possess their own intrinsic interest. I would like to recall here some ideas that occur in Plato and Aristotle to the extent that they introduce major themes that Plotinus will exploit in his approach to the subject.

Much of the imagery and argument of Plato's *Phaedo* certainly suggests an extreme dualistic separation of soul from body: the soul is, as it were, emprisoned in the body, nailed to the body. By nature it is more at home in another realm: that of the simple, eternal, incorporeal. This otherworldly emphasis is balanced however by the constructive and permeating action exerted by the soul of the *Phaedrus* and the *Timaeus* in the moving, directing, and organizing of the world. This dynamic immanence of soul in body implies a much more intimate and extensive relation between soul and body than that to be found between mind and body in Descartes, for whom mind does not involve itself directly in the mechanical processes of the body. At the same time this immanence of Platonic soul is not achieved, it appears, at the price of abandoning the difference of nature separating soul from body. In the *Phaedrus* the soul gives movement to the body, but is for itself a principle of movement, or "self-mover." Hence, it is immortal and the body is not. And the description of the constitution of soul in the *Timaeus* does not suggest that it is confused in its nature with the body. Even in as late a dialogue as the *Philebus* Plato keeps the pleasures of soul and of the body separate while at the same time assuming extensive interaction and mixing of them. But how, if soul is of a different nature than the body, can it move or act on the body?

The nearest we can come it appears to an answer to this question in Plato is in a passage in the *Laws*:

---

7. Cf. however E. Ostenfeld, *Forms, Matter and Mind. Three Strands in Plato's Metaphysics*, (The Hague 1982); K. Dorter, *Plato's Phaedo*, (Toronto 1982), pp. 179 ff.

8. Cf. C. Kahn, "Sensation and Consciousness in Aristotle's Psychology," *Archiv für Geschichte der Philosophie* 48 (1966): 43–45; R. Sorabji, "Body and Soul in Aristotle," *Philosophy* 49 (1974): 63–84; Ostenfeld, pp. 153–155. (Kahn and Sorabji are reprinted in *Articles on Aristotle 4. Psychology and Aesthetics* ed. J. Barnes, M. Schofield, R. Sorabji [New York, 1979].)

Soul, then, by her own motions stirs all things in sky, earth, or sea—and the names of these motions are wish, reflection, foresight, counsel, judgement, true or false, pleasure, pain, hope, fear, hate, love—stirs them, I say, by these and whatever other kindred, or primary, motions there may be. They, in turn, bring in their train secondary and corporeal movements, and so guide all things to increase and decrease, disgregation and integration. . . . By these . . . when wisdom is her helper, she conducts (παιδαγωγεῖ) all things to the right and happy issue.[9]

It seems then that soul possesses activities or movements proper to itself and corresponding to its nature by means of which it guides or conducts the changes in corporeal nature. But how does this "conducting" work? Plato is using the image of the tutor, the παιδαγωγός, who directs his ward. But the ward can follow the tutor because he, like his tutor, has soul, whereas the corporeal, as that directed by soul, does not. The image is thus not very helpful. A little later Plato discusses the question of how soul directs the sun:

Either she dwells within this visible round body and conveys it hither and thither, as our soul carries us wherever we go; or, as some hold, she provides herself a body of her own, of fire, or it may be of air, and pushes body from without, forcibly, by body; or finally, she is herself entirely incorporeal, but guides the sun along its path by virtue of possessing some other prodigious and wonderful powers.[10]

The matter is left open in the *Laws*. And whatever option is chosen it seems to me we are still left with the problem of how *our* soul can be said to "carry" us wherever we go.[11]

In his *De anima* Aristotle clearly thought he had laid such problems to rest. Having brought out in Book I many of the difficulties in Platonic psychology, including the problem of how the heavens are moved (407b5–11), he introduces in Book II his conception of soul as the form or act of a particular kind of organized body. This eliminates, it appears, the problem of how soul is united to body, since this union is now that of form with matter in one substance, and the unity of form and matter in substance is not problematical. As for how soul acts on body, this question becomes a matter of determining the organizational principles and structures acting in particular bodies in the exercise of certain living functions. If Aristotle refers to the soul as the efficient cause of the body, as a principle of change in the body, as

---

9. *Lg.* X, 897a, trans. A. E. Taylor; cf. Ostenfeld, pp. 263 ff.
10. *Lg.* X, 898e–899a, trans. Taylor (slightly modified).
11. It has been pointed out that a problem more central in Plato than that of soul's action on body is that concerning soul's own motions and self-movement (cf. Ostenfeld, p. 267).

moving the body, we must not be misled into thinking of this as a matter of one substance acting on another. Take, for example, the *De motu animalium*, chapter 6. There Aristotle asks himself Princess Elizabeth's question: how does soul move the body (πῶς ἡ ψυχὴ κινεῖ τὸ σῶμα)? According to Aristotle it is an exterior object of desire that first moves the living body: the animal perceives the object, desires it, and this desire triggers a sequence of physiological changes that lead to the animal moving.

We see that those things which move the animal are calculation, imagination, choice, will, desire. And all these reduce to intellection and desire.[12]

Despite some similarities, the situation here is not to be confused with that described in the first passage I quoted from Plato's *Laws*: it is not the case that soul as a separate nature, by activities cognate to its proper nature, somehow gives rise to bodily changes. Rather there is a complicated sequence of changes, described in chapter 7, linking perception (itself a kind of change) to the moving of the limbs, which changes are the functioning of various components of the animal as a particular kind of physical organization or structure.

However much one might succeed in reading Aristotle in such a way as to banish the problem of how soul acts on body, there remain of course certain areas of Aristotelian philosophy—by no means peripheral ones—where a curious immaterial causality might be said to persist. The active (or "agent") intellect of *De anima* III, 5 is required, it appears, as an efficient cause for the actualization of our capacity (itself immaterial) to think. How the active intellect does this is anything but clear. Or rather it is clear that the usual model of efficient casuality, which involves bodily contact[13] and appears open to a materialist or functionalist interpretation, does not apply here. Furthermore all change in the world ultimately depends on the pure immaterial actuality of thought that is the unmoved mover of *Metaphysics* Λ. Although the unmoved mover acts as an object of love, as a "final" and not as an "efficient" cause, this occurs again independently of physical or local contact. There is no pushing or pulling in the function of the primary cause of all change. Such aspects of Aristotle's philosophy as those Plotinus will explore in his treatment of the question of soul's action on body.

12. *De motu animalium* 6, 700b17–19; cf. *De anima* I, 3, 406b24–25.
13. Cf. Sorabji, "Body and Soul," pp. 85–86.

II

Before approaching this subject, it will be useful to sketch briefly the lines along which Plotinus distinguishes between soul and body, for we may reasonably use this distinction as an appropriate context within which his views on soul's action on the body may be considered.

Plotinus' ideas on the distinction between soul and body can be found, for example, in *Ennead* IV, 7 [2], an early work in which he discusses the subject of immortality. In order to show that soul is immortal, he argues against those who identify soul with body. His opponents are the Stoics and Epicureans. Against both groups he marshalls an array of arguments—some of them fairly traditional[14]—organized so as to make the same general point I would summarize as follows. (i) Plotinus and his opponents agree that by soul is meant what is responsible for the life, or living functions, of a body. (ii) Yet the nature of body is such that it could not be responsible for such functions. (iii) Therefore soul is not body. I doubt very much if Plotinus' opponents would have found this attack effective, to the extent at least that they would not have agreed to the second premise because they would not have shared Plotinus' assumptions about the nature of body. But it is these assumptions and this second premise that are of interest to us here.

Roughly speaking, Plotinus thinks of bodies as masses, "lumps" (ὄγκοι), which have size or quantity and occupy discrete places. These masses are conglomerates, ultimately composed of the four Aristotelian elements (fire, air, earth, and water) which are themselves composites of matter and form. The conglomerate and composed nature of bodies points to their congenital behavior, which is to disintegrate, to break up into the constituent elements.[15]

If these characteristics of body are kept in mind, it becomes clear why they appear to rule out any claim that body might have to be a principle of life. Plotinus attempts to show this first by dealing with life considered in general.[16] He assumes that soul must possess life of itself, if it is to be the source of life (2, 5–6). He then argues that if soul is a body, a composite made up ultimately of the elements, one or other or all of the elements must have life of itself or of themselves.

---

14. Cf. E. Bréhier, *Plotin Ennéades* 4 (Paris 1927): 179–183; Blumenthal, pp. 9–11. In what follows I attempt to bring out the general argumentative *form* under which Plotinus subsumes the traditional *topoi*.

15. IV, 7, 1, 8–19; 2, 1–2; cf. 3, 19–30; IV, 2 [4], 11–17.

16. Plotinus follows the order of treatment of the *De anima*: soul as principle of life in general (IV, 7, 2–4, 21), soul as principle of particular living functions taken individually (IV, 7, 4, 21ff).

But the four Aristotelian elements do not have life of themselves (2, 7–15). If, on the other hand, soul is a composite of lifeless elements that possesses life *from* being put together, it cannot put itself together, nor can its elements, since they are not life-giving. So we must postulate something other than bodily composites and their elements which organizes them and gives them life (cf. 2, 22–25). But this is only to say that soul, as a life-giving principle, can neither be a body considered as a composite of elements nor a body considered as one or other of these elements.

Plotinus makes the same sort of point in relation to some of soul's specific living functions, which for him are roughly those listed by Aristotle in the *De anima*. Soul, as a principle first of motion and change, produces a wide variety of such motions and changes. But body is limited, in what it can do, by its specific qualities. How, then, could it be a principle of so many changes (4, 21–5, 2)? Further, we could not account for the stable identity entailed by the psychic functions of memory and recognition, if soul were body, since body is in a state of continual flux (5, 20–24). If one examines sense-perception as a specific psychic function, one sees that it must be one and the same principle that senses everything in the body.[17] One must suppose then that soul is present as a unity throughout the body (7, 26–27). But body is incapable of such a presence: to be present throughout, it must be fragmented and hence must lose its unity; to retain its unity, it cannot be spread throughout a body. Sense-perception as a psychic function presupposes, then, a mode of presence in body of which body itself is incapable. Hence, soul, as the principle of sense-perception, cannot be body.[18]

I might be permitted at this point to forego presenting Plotinus' other arguments against the corporeality of soul. Some of his arguments may not withstand close scrutiny. They would hardly have convinced his opponents.[19] Yet they do help to indicate his views on the distinction and relation between soul and body. Body is composite, quantitative, localized, limited in the changes it can undergo, incapable of self-organization. However the psychic functions of enlivening, moving, remembering, perceiving, presuppose a principle that has life of itself, can organize others, can produce many different changes,

---

17. 6, 3–15; for this in Aristotle cf. Kahn, "Sensation," pp. 54 ff.

18. I am expanding here the very compressed reasoning at 7, 26–28; cf. 5, 36–38; ch. 8²; and my article "The Problem of Omnipresence in Plotinus *Ennead* VI, 4–5: A Reply," *Dionysius* 4 (1980): 62–74.

19. On Plotinus' argument with the Stoics, cf. M. van Straaten, "On Plotinus IV, 7 [2], 8³," *Kephalaion. Studies . . . offered to C. J. de Vogel*, eds. J. Mansfeld and L. M. de Rijk (Assen 1975), pp. 168–169.

can remain identical and unified in itself and yet be present at the same time throughout a body. These properties of soul, which rule out for Plotinus the identification of soul as body, are also characteristic, one might note, of the Stoic divine principle or πνεῦμα, a dynamic force that pervades passive matter, organizes and enlivens it. Plotinus agrees, therefore, with the Stoics in calling for a cosmic organizing force. He disagrees with them, however, in that he denies that this force can be identified as body. Or rather the force that bodies exhibit depends on a psychic dynamism of another sort—thinking, perceiving, calculating, desiring—that indicates another kind of substance.[20] This claim will be explored further in the next section.

III

I believe I have presented enough evidence from *Ennead* IV, 7 to show not only that Plotinus distinguishes with some insistence between soul and body, but also that he holds soul to be extensively and actively involved in organizing and enlivening the corporeal world. *How* then does soul act on body? To answer this question, I propose taking one of the psychic functions, that is, from his viewpoint, one of the many ways in which soul acts on body. Among such functions we have already met in *Ennead* IV, 7 those of moving—which includes locomotion and growth—and sense-perception. Let us then take the function of growth as a test case, putting to ourselves the question "How does soul cause the body to grow?" as a starting-point and focus for our search in Plotinus for an answer to the general question of how soul acts on body.

To begin, I would like to return to Plotinus' polemic with materialism in IV, 7, since in that context he discusses soul as a cause of growth in a body. In chapter 5 he argues that if soul were both a body and the cause of growth in another body, it would need to grow itself in order to keep pace with that which it causes to grow.[21] Plotinus derives, however, from the necessity that the cause of growth itself grows an insurmountable dilemma (5, 14–20). He concludes from this, of course, that soul cannot be both a body and the cause of growth in a body. Whatever the fairness or cogency of the argument, we can notice in it an implicit distinction that is of some interest: if soul in causing growth in a body cannot grow itself, then the *action* whereby soul

---

20. IV, 7, 8¹, 1–9 (Henry-Schwyzer in their edition indicate the Plotinus is thinking here of the first passage from Plato's *Laws* quoted above.)
21. 5, 12–14; on the growth of the soul in Stoicism cf. Bréhier *ad loc.*, citing *Stoicorum veterum fragmenta* (=*SVF*) ed. J. von Arnim, Leipzig 1903, III, p. 251 (No. 50).

causes growth is not the same as that change, namely growth, which it provides. Thus soul's action on body must be distinguished carefully from the bodily changes this action produces. The significance of this distinction can be brought out by making the point that difficulties concerning how soul acts on body have to do in part with a confusion of soul's action with bodily change, a confusion that makes it hard to see how anything incorporeal such as soul could act. Indeed the point is made by Descartes when he introduces a distinction between psychic action and corporeal change in the letter quoted above.[22]

This distinction is made explicitly in one of Plotinus' later treatises, *Ennead* III, 6 [26]:

> For, of course, the growth-principle does not grow when it causes growth, nor increase when it causes increase, nor in general, when it causes motion, is it moved by that particular kind of motion (κίνησις) which it causes, but either it is not moved at all, or it is a different kind of motion and activity (ἐνέργεια). So, then, the actual nature of the form must be an activity, and produce by its presence.[23]

This passage stresses the difference between soul's action on body and the changes in body this action produces. But it also formulates more specifically the character of soul's action as contrasted with bodily change. Soul's action is itself either free of change, or it is characterized by a higher kind of change than bodily change, which in fact corresponds to the Aristotelian concept of unchanging activity (ἐνέργεια) or "actuality" as the Aristotelian term will be translated in what follows. Somehow, by its "presence"—whatever that is[24]—in body, this actuality which is soul brings about bodily change without itself changing. The bodily change itself, as Plotinus refers to it in the same chapter, is an Aristotelian change (κίνησις) taking place in a subject that undergoes or "suffers" (παθεῖν) the change as a result of some relation between it and the unchanging actuality that is soul.[25]

---

22. *Oeuvres*, ed. Adam-Tannery, III, pp. 665–667; cf. R. Richardson, pp. 22–24. The Stoics of course argued that only body could "touch" or affect body and thus that soul could not be incorporeal (*SVF* I, No. 518; II, Nos. 790–791). Cf. also Lucretius I, 304 and Sextus Empiricus, *Against the Physicists* I, 216–217.

23. III, 6, 4, 38–42 (Armstrong trans.).

24. Cf. the article referred to above note 18.

25. The debt to Aristotle is clear already in the key phrase of the passage just quoted, (nor) ". . . is it moved by that particular kind of motion which it causes," which is almost word for word what Aristotle says at *De anima* I, 3, 406a30–31. Aristotle uses the assumption that soul moves in the same way as the movements it causes to undermine the idea that soul moves; Plotinus denies the assumption, as he must, given Aristotle's argument, but attributes to soul another sort of movement than the corporeal kind considered by Aristotle. Compare Philoponus on the Aristotelian passage (*In de anima* ed. M. Hayduck (Berlin 1897), p. 106, 8 ff.).

Plotinus compares the situation to the playing of a stringed instrument: "For in the case of playing an instrument . . . it is not the tune which is affected [or suffers], but the string; the string, however, would not be played as it is, even if the player wished it, unless the tune directed it to be played thus."[26] This analogy successfully contrasts the change undergone by the string with the guiding tune which in itself remains as it is. However, the analogy also limps by introducing a separate agent, the player, between tune and strings, whereas the unchanging actuality of soul must itself be in some way the agent of bodily change.

To advance, it would be desirable to find in Plotinus more details on the distinction between soul's actuality and the bodily changes this actuality produces and more information, in particular, on the relation between these two in which the one is brought about by the other. This can be done by turning to an unlikely quarter, Plotinus' critique of Aristotle's categories in *Ennead* VI, 1 [42] and his attempt to formulate a new set of categories for the material world in *Ennead* VI, 3 [44]. *Enneads* VI, 1 and VI, 3 seem hardly the place to go for psychological theory and indeed these treatises are scarcely mentioned, for example, by Blumenthal in his book. However, it turns out that in criticizing Aristotle's categories of "action," or making (ποιεῖν), and "suffering" (πάσχειν) in VI, 1, 15–22, and in exploring his own new replacement for these, the category of change (κίνησις) in *Ennead* VI, 3, 21–23, Plotinus has frequent recourse to psychology in order to make his points. *Enneads* VI, 1 and VI, 3 are also, however, notoriously difficult works. Plotinus' position and line of argument are not always clear. Yet some ideas are put forward which are of particular relevance to us here and which can be paralleled in some measure in his other works.

In VI, 1, 15–23, Plotinus argues that the Aristotelian categories of action and suffering are subordinate to, and collapse into, a higher genus, actuality (ἐνέργεια). Actuality itself can be assimilated to change, κίνησις, since if we examine Aristotle's definition of change as "incomplete [or imperfect] actuality" (*Phys.* III, 2, 201b31–32), we find that the lack of completion refers not to the change itself, but to what is effected or perfected by the change. The change in itself is complete and perfect and thus actuality. Take the Aristotelian example of walking. When we are walking, the action is complete in itself at every instant that it takes place.[27] It can be incomplete, however,

---

26. III, 6, 4, 49–52 (Armstrong trans., slightly modified). The Pythagorean theory of soul as harmony or tune is already altered in this direction in IV, 7, 8⁴, 18–21.
27. VI, 1, 16, 1–8; Iamblichus says this is Stoic theory (*SVF* II, No. 498, quoted by

in respect to a certain distance to be traversed. Thus the walking is complete in itself, but incomplete *per accidens*, incomplete with respect to a given distance (16, 8–12). So Plotinus argues as he attempts to dissolve the Aristotelian distinction between change and actuality. One of the confusing things about this argument is the fact that elsewhere, for example in III, 6, (as we have seen), Plotinus adopts the Aristotelian distinction between change and actuality. It appears that here in VI, 1 he is separating change from *what* changes, i.e., what is changed, so that it becomes assimilated to actuality. His argument thus leads him to make the point that actuality and change are per se nonspatial, atemporal, and free of the characteristics of what they effect. Only *per accidens* are they temporal, bound by the features of what is effected by them. Thus, for example, walking is not visible per se, but visible *per accidens*, as the walking of feet, as the feet brought to walk by actuality.[28]

Plotinus' ideas in VI, 1 could be considered a rather unusual development of Aristotle's anti-Platonic position in the *De anima* that soul only changes *per accidens* and not per se when the body changes. Plotinus is developing Aristotle's position very much in what you might call a "dualist" spirit. The actuality or higher "unchanging change" that produces bodily changes is further isolated from such bodily changes: it is nontemporal, nonspatial, nonquantitative, free of the ontological hallmarks of the bodily changes it produces. These bodily changes, as Plotinus describes them in VI, 3, chapter 22, are orthodox Aristotelian changes: they are actualizations of a suitable substrate by a prior actuality.

Plotinus' further isolation in VI, 1 of actuality from the bodily change it produces will also lead us of course to insist even more on being informed of the relation whereby this production by actuality of bodily change takes place. On this point, I would like to draw attention to a passage in VI, 1, chapter 22:

Bréhier and Henry-Schwyzer *ad loc.*). Compare J. L. Ackrill, "Aristotle's Distinction between *energeia* and *kinesis*," *New Essays on Plato and Aristotle* ed. R. Bambrough (London 1965), pp. 131–136.

28. Cf. VI, 1, 16, 14–35 with VI, 3, 23, 5–12: Plotinus does not deny that walking is a walking of someone, of feet, but insists that the act is in itself other than, even if expressed *per accidens* by, feet simply occupying changing locations (cf. also VI, 1, 1, 18, 19–21; VI, 3, 21, 14–15). Mechanical toys, in this view, do not "walk," but nor do feet, taken by themselves. The difference (if any) between the cases must have to do with a difference in the actualities that levers or living limbs express *per accidens*. But what is there besides the changing positioning of levers or limbs that allows us to detect the difference? One is reminded in this connection of Chrysippus' claim that the ἡγεμονικόν is walking (*SVF* I, No. 525; discussed by J. Rist, *Stoic Philosophy* [Cambridge 1969], pp. 24, 33–34).

Nor need we say that all actualities (ἐνεργείας) are makings (ποιήσεις) or a making of something. Making occurs *per accidens*. What then? If someone produces footprints (ἴχνη) as he walks, do we deny that he has made something? But they come from his being something else [i.e., his walking]. Or the making and the actuality are *per accidens*, in that he did not aim at such a product. Thus we speak even of inanimate things as making, for example, fire heating and "the drug worked". But enough of these things.[29]

To which I'm tempted to reply, "far from enough!" But what can be made of what Plotinus says here? If change is assimilated to actuality, as it is in VI, 1, then Plotinus' subordination of making to actuality recalls Aristotle's point in the *De generatione et corruptione* (I, 6, 323a20–21) that change is a wider class than making. But in Plotinus this subordination is not one of classes but of realities in which *per accidens*, as "side-effect," things are produced by actualities.[30] The example of the footprint suggests that a substrate of an appropriate sort is required for actualization in a mode related, but not identical, to the actuality whose independence and indifference with respect to this substrate are stressed by Plotinus (22, 5–8). Making is nonpurposive; things are produced as the unplanned precipitates of actuality. This production, however, is not random: actuality produces in function of *what* it is;[31] what is produced is a "footprint" (vestige) of actuality. The relation between an actuality and what is produced *per accidens* from it has to do, I would suggest, with the specific sort of potentiality or capacity a substrate might have as this brings it in relation to a specific actuality.[32]

But surely, we might well ask, must there not be some action, some movement whereby the actuality actualizes the substrate? Plotinus addresses this in VI, 3, chapter 23, with in mind Aristotle's discussion in *Physics* III, 3 of the question whether change is in the agent or the patient. Following an approach suggested by Aristotle, Plotinus places the act that actualizes the patient *in the patient* (*Phys.* 202b7–8), insisting like Aristotle that this is not "cut off" (ἀποτετμημένην) from the agent, but "it [goes] from the agent to the patient, like a breathing on another" (23, 18–20). This last analogy confuses more than clarifies and indeed this is the only time Plotinus uses it. It suggests a corporeal relation between agent and patient which Plotinus has been strenuously trying to avoid. And if nothing "goes" in a corporeal way from agent to patient, what does going consist of here? Little help is given

---

29. VI, 1, 22, 27–34 (my trans.). Cf. Aristotle *Met.* A, 1, 981b1–5.
30. Compare III, 8 [30], chapter 4 where making is described as a παρακολούθημα.
31. On this important principle in Plotinus, cf. my "Gnosticism and the Making of the World in Plotinus," *The Rediscovery of Gnosticism*, ed. B. Layton, 1 (Leiden 1980): 373–377.
32. Cf. my article cited above n. 18, at p. 72.

us at this point.³³ The image at least indicates, albeit poorly, the dependence of the change in the patient on the agent and the presence of this change in the patient. More generally it is clear, I think, that Plotinus deals with the question of how an actuality produces a bodily change with the help of an Aristotelian analysis of the way in which a particular prior actuality brings about the actualization of a specific potentiality. Indeed Plotinus takes advantage of Aristotle's placing of the act that produces change in the patient and insistence that this change is not cut off from the agent, since these ideas appear to lend themselves to Plotinus' isolation of actuality from the bodily changes it produces.

One brief mention of *Ennead* IV, 3 [27] must be made before the implications of Plotinus' ideas in VI, 1 and VI, 3 are considered. In IV, 3, chapter 23, Plotinus discusses the question of the localization of various psychic functions in the body. He is aware of the positions of Plato and Aristotle on this as well as of more recent medical discoveries.³⁴ Briefly, for him, psychic functions are localized in the body in relation to the different aptitudes of different parts of the body to fulfill different functions. Thus the vegetative, growth, and nutritive functions are found in the body as a whole, although nutrition, as involving blood, is more intimately related to the liver. However, it is the *organs* performing these functions that are localized, not the psychic powers that are responsible. Does this mean that there is only one transcendent psychic actuality that actualizes different parts of the body to perform different functions, depending on the difference between these parts? It appears in VI, 3 and elsewhere that Plotinus wishes to retain the distinction between different psychic actualities considered in themselves, although clearly they can only actualize appropriate organs to perform the corresponding functions.³⁵

At this point, I would like to bring together what has been learned so far in order to provide a possible Plotinian answer to our question, "How does soul cause the body to grow?" First, only a certain sort of body can grow, a body such as to admit of the specific sort of actualiza-

---

33. Plotinus' ideas here appear to have been developed in later Neoplatonic theories of imparted power; cf. also Plotinus I, 1 [53], 6; J. Christensen de Groot, "Philoponus on De anima II.5, Physics III.3 and the Propagation of Light," *Phronesis* 28 (1983): 182–194. For discussion of *Physics* III.3 cf. M. Gill, "Aristotle's Theory of Causal Action in *Physics* III 3," *Phronesis* 25 (1980): 129–141.

34. Cf. Blumenthal, p. 74.

35. Cf. VI, 3, 23, 31–33; IV, 7, 14, 1–8; IV, 8 [6], 5, 28–38. In general Plotinus emphasizes the paradigmatic relation between the multiple and united intelligible and the formal differences in the material world; cf. VI, 7 [38], 9; IV, 3, 10. (In Plotinus' theory of immaterial unity and multiplicity, a plurality of psychic powers is not inconsistent with the unity of soul; cf. e.g., IV, 9 [8], 3, 10–18.)

tion that is this sort of bodily change. This change is expressed in the conditions of space, time, and quantity characteristic of body. The actualization of body in this way is in function however of a specific psychic actuality independent of body and its ontological characteristics. This psychic actuality is different from the growing that it produces in a body, and it produces this change not by planning it but incidentally, insofar as a specific sort of body comes into relation with it. The relation is not incidental, however, to the degree that only a certain sort of body capable of a certain sort of actualization is actualized in relation to a specific psychic actuality. The change whereby the body is actualized, i.e., grows, is found in the body that changes, and not in the psychic actuality that remains unaffected and unchanged in itself.[36]

IV

I would like to conclude by suggesting the following points:

1. It is clear, I think, that Plotinus *does* have a way of answering the question of how soul acts on the body. To this extent at least, the question is not for him an insurmountable difficulty entailed by his distinction between soul and body.

2. His answer may be disappointing if we expect some mechanical account of the matter. But such an account he could not consistently give, and indeed his answer is perfectly consistent with his radical distinction between soul and body. He hardly, if at all, compromises the distinction by softening its edges or interposing hybrid intermediaries carrying soul's action to the body.[37]

3. This is not to say that problems are not to be found in Plotinus' answer. What, for example, would that nonspatial, nontemporal actuality be which is expressed *per accidens* in a body growing? Can there be growing without space, time, quantity? What is walking without the walking of feet? In I, 8 [51], 8, 16–18 Plotinus even has "fire itself" acting of itself in a way different from what it produces in matter, i.e., burning. But what is the activity of "fire itself"? Such questions I think could be considered in relation to the wider issue in Platonism concerning the description of a transcendent reality whose characteristics are inferred from their images in this material world. There are also other questions that Plotinus' position raises: is the soul causing growth in a body separate from or part of the soul of the individual body?

---

36. On the question of *non-corporeal* change in the soul, in particular cognitive and moral changes, cf. III, 6 [26], 2–3 with Blumenthal, pp. 48 ff.

37. Blumenthal, p. 139 (with n. 19) rightly argues against the suggestion that Plotinus has recourse to some sort of "pneumatic body" linking soul and body.

How does it relate to the φύσις-soul or to the animation of the world by world-soul?[38]

4. Plotinus' position in relation to Plato and Aristotle calls for a final comment. In general, I believe one can say that Plotinus both sharpens the Platonic dualism of soul and body and provides an account of the relation of the two—all of this, paradoxically, by means of appropriating Aristotelian ideas. In particular Plotinus uses Aristotle's distinction between actuality and change in order to express the difference Plato suggests in the *Laws* between the primary activities or motions of soul and the secondary corporeal changes that they produce. The way in which soul's motions actually "conduct" those of the body, as called for by the *Laws*, is explained in Plotinus by application of the Aristotelian theory of change according to which change is the actualization of a particular substrate by a prior specific actuality. Finally Aristotle's scale of psychic functions allows Plotinus to describe in a precise and detailed way the immanent and dynamic role that Plato gives soul in the body.

But surely, we might object, this is to cut Aristotle's concepts of change and causality loose from their moorings, to rob them of their proper context and therefore of their meaning. Without raising the problem of the adequacy of materialist or functionalist or perhaps dualist interpretations of Aristotle's psychology,[39] I believe we can point to clear instances of causality and change in Aristotle that do not presuppose materiality or local contact (see above Part I). The instance that seems to be of most importance for Plotinus is the relation whereby the pure unchanging immaterial actuality of the unmoved mover in some way brings about the multiplicity of changes in the sublunary region.[40] One might even say that the unmoved mover becomes in Plotinus the paradigm of all immaterial (including psychic) causality in the material world. Hence Nature, the lowest level of soul, emerges in III, 8 [30], chapter 2 very much as a sort of unmoved mover. This presupposes of course the premise that soul at all levels is indepen-

---

38. On these questions, cf. Blumenthal, pp. 27–30; "Soul, World-Soul, Individual Soul," *Le Néoplatonisme* (Paris 1971), pp. 56–63.

39. Cf. above n. 5.

40. On this Adrastus, one of the Aristotelian commentators read by Plotinus and his school, says: ". . . coming to be and destruction . . . growth, diminution, all change and varied locomotion. The cause of these, he [Adrastus] says are the planets. One would not say that the latter, superior, divine, eternal, ungenerated and undestroyed, are for the sake of the inferior, . . . but that [the superior] remain always the same, being the most beautiful, best and most blessed, whereas what is below follows them *per accidens*" (*apud* Theon of Smyrna, *Expositio rerum mathematicarum*, ed. E. Hiller (Leipzig 1878), p. 149, 7–15). This interpretation of Aristotle comes very near Plotinus' theory of changes as occurring *per accidens* in relation to superior unchanging actualities.

dent in its being of body, a premise that Aristotle himself did not generally accept. However, I have proposed to give here for Plotinus, not a defense of the premise, but an account that, assuming the premise, addresses the question of how soul acts on body.[41]

Université de Fribourg, Switzerland

41. For discussion of some elements of this theme in Plotinus' successors, cf. Iamblichus *apud* Simplicius *In cat.* ed. K. Kalbfleisch (Berlin 1907), p. 302, 28 ff. discussed by S. Gersh, *From Iamblichus to Eriugena* (Leiden 1978), pp. 43 ff; J. Barnes, "Immaterial Causes," *Oxford Studies in Ancient Philosophy* 1 (1983): 169–192 (on Proclus *Elements of Theology* 80); J. Christensen de Groot, (on Proclus and Philoponus).

Index of Names

Ackrill, J. L., 236n, 237n, 256n
Adkins, A. W. H., 140n, 142n, 145n, 159n
Adrastus, 261n
Aeschines, 112n
Aeschylus, 104n
Agathon, 39n
Agich, G. V., 10n
Albinus, 113
Alcibiades, 38, 40, 112n, 129, 130
Alcmaeon, 73n
Alexander of Aphrodisias, 112n, 227n, 230n, 242n, 245n
Allen, R. E., 38, 47, 131n, 212n, 244n
Anaxagoras, 133n, 197, 198, 200, 202, 204
Andersen, Hans Christian, 40
Annas J., 202n, 203n, 213n
Antiochus, 112n
Apollo, 74, 118
Apollinaire, G., 65
Arcesilaus, 17n, 112n
Archer-Hind, R. D., 70n
Archilochus, 104n
Ares, 75
Aristophanes, 37–39, 63, 70, 74, 78n, 85, 142
Aristotle, 4n, 7, 8, 10n, 30, 35n, 41, 43, 51, 59, 67n, 69, 79, 96, 112n, 117n, 126n, 133n, 198, 199n, 203, 207n, 208n, 217n, 219–46 *passim*, 248–53, 255–59, 261–62
Aristoxenus, 207n
Athenaeus, 77n
Augustine, 77

Barford, R., 226n
Barnes, J., 222n, 235n, 239n, 262n

Baudelaire, 79n
Beck, L. W., 3n, 5n, 6n, 10n
Berti, E., 222n
Bluck, R. S., 202n
Blumenthal, H., 248, 252n, 256, 259n, 260n, 261n
Bloom, A., 167n, 169n
Boder, W., 26n
Bonitz, H., 67n, 230n, 240n
Boyancé, P., 112n
Boyle, R., 196
Bradley, F. H., 121
Brandt, R. B., 142n, 145n
Bréhier, E., 252n, 254n
Brickhouse, T., 192n
Brumbaugh, R. S., 196n
Brunschwig, J., 131n, 235n
Bubner, R., 24n
Burge, E., 201n
Burnet, J., 197n, 199n, 201n
Burnyeat, M., 28n
Bury, R. G., 38n

Carlini, A., 112n
Cervantes, 53n
Cherniss, H., 86n, 87n, 89n, 90n, 91n, 92n, 94n, 221
Chrysippus, 257n
Cicero, 77n, 112, 130
Clark, P. M., 114n
Clement of Alexandria, 77n
Coleridge, 44n
Cooper, J., 186n, 207n
Cornford, F. M., 56, 57n, 58, 60, 91n, 209, 210n, 214n, 216n, 217n
Coulter, J. A., 59n
Courcelle, P., 112n
Critias, 120, 121, 125, 134
Curtius, E. R., 65n
Cyrus, 114n

INDEX OF NAMES

Damascius, 131 n, 202 n
Dancy R., 245 n
Darwin, Ch., 196
Democritus, 58, 59, 73 n, 112 n
Demos, R., 186 n
Derrida, J., 2, 9, 15 n, 17 n, 18, 20, 23, 30, 32
Descartes, R., 3, 247, 255
Diès, A., 107 n
Dillon, J., 113 n
Diogenes Laërtius, 78 n, 112 n, 113 n
Diogenes of Apollonia, 73 n
Diotima, 38, 186 n
Dodds, E. R., 40 n, 98 n, 141 n, 142 n
Dönt, E., 123 n, 134 n
Dornseiff, F., 78 n
Dorter, K., 201 n, 249 n
Dosiades, 65
Dover, K. J., 37 n, 146 n
Duering, I., 225 n
Dyson, M., 134 n

Ebert, T., 134 n
Empedocles, 57, 58, 63 n, 76
Epictetus, 112 n
Erbse, H., 75 n
Eros, 65
Euripides, 78 n, 104 n, 133 n, 142
Eusebius, 132

Feyerabend, P., 2, 17 n
Fichte, J. G., 4 n, 11
Fine, G., 226 n
Flashar, H., 222 n
Foucault, M., 2
Frede, M., 17 n, 197, 233 n
Friedländer, P., 87 n, 106 n, 112 n, 114 n
Fritz, K. von, 59 n
Furley, D., 207 n

Gadamer, H. G., 2, 9, 23, 25 n, 27
Gaiser, K., 207 n
Gallop, D., 196 n, 199 n, 201 n, 202 n
Garver, N., 17 n
Gersh, S., 262 n
Giannantoni, G., 99 n, 100, 108
Gibbard, A., 142 n, 145 n

Gill, C., 121 n
Gill, M. L., 213 n, 259 n
Goodman, N., 9, 14
Goodrich, W. J., 197 n, 201 n
Griswold, C., 11 n, 16 n, 21 n, 25 n, 55 n, 72 n
Gorden, S., 186 n
Groningen, B. A. van, 60 n
Grott, J. C. de, 259 n, 262 n
Grote, G., 141, 145 n
Grube, G., 169 n

Habermas, J., 2, 10 n
Hackforth, R., 37 n, 98 n, 201 n
Hadot, P., 60 n
Hare, R. M., 176 n, 182 n
Harpocration, 113 n
Harsanyi, J. C., 145 n
Hartman, E., 248 n
Havelock, E., 165 n, 192 n
Hegel, G. W. F., 2, 4 n, 5, 7, 9–12, 15, 16, 18 n, 19, 20, 24–26, 44 n, 64, 79 n, 81 n
Heidel, W. A., 114 n, 115
Heidegger, M., 2, 4 n, 9, 16, 22, 31, 32
Helmbold, W. C., 27 n
Henderickx, A. R., 90 n
Heninger, S. K., 59 n
Heraclitus, 12 n, 29, 119 n, 127–30, 132, 133, 208 n
Herder, J. G., 3
Hermann, K. F., 99 n
Herodotus, 55 n
Hippocrates, 35, 36 n, 75 n
Hirzel, R., 90 n
Homer, 12 n, 29, 74, 75 n, 81 n, 128 n
Hume, D., 6 n
Hunger, H., 66 n
Hyland, D., 11 n

Iamblichus, 113, 256 n, 262 n
Irwin, T., 145 n, 149 n, 151 n, 153 n, 157 n, 158 n, 159 n, 160, 208 n, 223 n, 224 n, 229 n, 233 n
Isnardi, M., 112 n
Isocrates, 104 n

Jaeger, W., 219
Jordan, R. W., 208 n

Index of Names 265

Joyce, M., 163n
Julian Emperor, 112n

Kahn, Ch., 128, 185n, 249n, 253n
Kant, I., 2n, 3–5, 6n, 8–12, 17, 25
Kenyon, F. G., 66n
Keyt, D., 214
Kitto, H., 38
Kojève, A., 20n
Koller, H., 187n
Kosman, L. A., 192n
Kranz, W., 57n
Kraut, R., 87n
Kuhn, T. S., 2
Kung, J., 198n, 207n

Lazerowitz, M., 2n
Lee, E., 181n, 191n
Leibniz, G. W., 44n
Lesky, E., 73n
Leszl, W., 222n
Lloyd, G. E. R., 36n
Locke, J., 3
Long, A. A., 248n
Lucretius, 255n
Lurçat, L., 68n
Lysias, 42, 43

Macrobius, 59n
Marsyas, 1, 40, 165, 187
Martens, E., 134n
Martin, T. H., 70n
Mill, J. S., 142
Miller, M., 16n
Mohr, R., 214n
Morrison, J. S., 37n, 198n
Morrow, G., 209
Mourelatos, A. D. P., 216n
Murray, A. T., 75n

Nagel, T., 161
Nehamas, A., 178n, 179n
Nietzsche, F., 2, 9, 12, 13, 22
North, H. F., 119, 126n, 140n, 142, 145n, 160n
Nussbaum, M. C., 248n

O'Brien, D., 57n
Oedipus, 67
Olerud, A., 59n
Olympiodorus, 113, 131n

Ostenfeld, E., 249n, 250n
Owen, G. E. L., 219–33, 244

Pan, 65
Parfit, D., 148n, 161
Parmenides, 61, 180n, 214n
Passmore, J., 28n
Pease, A. S., 77n
Pépin, J., 112n, 113n
Pericles, 91n, 158
Perry, J., 148n
Perry, R., 215n
Persius, 112n
Philoponus, 255n, 262n
Picard, Ch., 65n
Pindar, 45, 104n
Pinkard, T., 4n
Pippin, R., 2n, 4n, 10n
Plotinus, 78n, 113, 247–62 *passim*
Plutarch, 113n, 127
Polemon, 112n
Polus, 116n
Polybius, 112n
Polybus, 36n
Polyclitus, 61, 62, 64
Popper, K., 32n
Prajapati, 57
Preiswerk, R., 99n
Proclus, 113, 131n, 262n
Protagoras, 7n, 12n, 19, 28n, 29, 30, 36, 41, 48
Pythagoras, Pythagorean, 64, 256n

Raven, J. E., 64n
Rescher, N., 2, 12
Rich, A. M., 248n
Richardson, R., 247n, 255n
Rist, J., 257n
Robinson, H., 248n
Robinson, R., 87, 88n, 89n, 90, 91, 94, 97n, 98n, 100n, 106n, 155n
Rorty, R., 2, 6n, 9, 12n, 13, 17–20, 23, 29n, 32, 33
Rosen, S., 16n, 33n
Ross, W. D., 96n
Rowe, C. J., 226n

Sachs, D., 172n
Santas, G., 134n, 182n, 204n, 214n
Sartre, J. P., 32n
Sayre, K. M., 212n

Schaerer, R., 26n, 90n
Schelling, F., 4n
Schleiermacher, F., 113
Scholasticus, 10
Sextus Empiricus, 17n, 255n
Shipton, K. M. W., 201n
Shorey, P., 87n, 90n, 92n, 93n, 113n
Sidgwick, H., 142
Simias the Rodian, 65
Simplicius, 245n, 262n
Skehan, P. W., 65n
Skemp, J. B., 70n
Solon, 104n
Sophocles, 104n
Sorabji, R., 249n, 251n
Souilhé, J., 112n, 125n
Spivak, G. C., 18n
Sprague, R. K., 124n
Steuben, H. von, 62n
Stewart, J., 38n, 44n, 46n
Stobaeus, 132
Straaten, M. van, 253n
Strycker, E. de, 114n, 223n

Tarán, L., 86n, 98n
Taylor, A. E., 70n, 73n, 74n, 90n
Taylor, C. C. W., 119n, 122n
Thales, 63
Theocritus, 65
Theodorus, 29, 178n
Theognis, 104n
Theon of Smyrna, 261n
Thesleff, H., 114n
Thrasyllus, 112n

Thucydides, 104n
Tobin, R., 62n
Tuckey, T. G., 122n, 134n

Vestinus, 65
Vlastos, G., 87n, 114n, 171n, 181n, 192n, 196n, 200n, 201n, 203n, 209, 210n, 212, 244n
Vretska, K., 99n
Vries, G. de, 43n

Wallon, H., 68n
Westerink, L. G., 59n, 202n
White, N. P., 148n, 150n, 152n, 155n, 156n, 162n, 182n, 184n, 186n, 192n, 204n
Wieland, W., 8n, 23n, 27n
Wiggers, R., 132n
Wilamowitz-Moellendorff, U. von, 65n, 114n
Willis, J., 59n
Witte, B., 134n
Wittgenstein, L., 2, 18, 32, 44
Woodruff, P., 115n
Woods, M., 233n
Wright, L., 198n
Wright, M. R., 57n, 58n

Xenophanes, 57
Xenophon, 63n, 85, 104n, 121

Zeller, E., 86n
Zeno, 114n
Zeus, 37, 40
Zopyrus, 113n

Index of Texts in Plato

Alcibiades I
  105a–b 115
  105b–c 122
  106c–124b 116
  119c–129a 115–118, 129
  124a–b 122
  129b–135e 118, 119, 124, 130, 131

Apology 51n, 56n, 90, 97
  21b–23c 88n, 97n
  26a 89n
  28d–e 90n, 97n
  29b–e 88n
  30e 185n
  39c 97n

Charmides 7, 11, 11n, 111, 115n, 117n, 121, 125, 127, 129, 133, 134, 135
  154e 63n
  155a 90n
  161b 117n
  162d–e 90n
  164c–165b 119, 134
  169e 134
  171e–172a 125
  173a–d 125
  175b 38

Cratylus 113n, 196, 204, 216
  387e, ff 207
  389b–e 205n, 206
  390b–e 206, 207
  403d 50
  439d–440e 208n
  440 210

Critias 86, 96, 96n
  117c 75n

Crito 86n
  49b 104n
  53b 199n

Epistle VII 16, 25n, 51
  335a 42
  341c 51n

Euthydemus 50
  280c–d 50n
  290b–c 90n
  306d 22
  307c 22

Euthyphro 86n, 92, 93n, 112
  5c–d 92n, 95n
  5d, ff 89n, 184n
  6d–e 92n, 95n, 184n
  7b–d 95n
  8b–e 95n
  10e–11b 92n, 108n
  11b–e 87n, 92n
  15b–c 92n

Gorgias 27, 29, 40, 41, 89n, 91n, 99, 104, 104n, 106, 107n, 113n, 115n, 116, 128, 168, 179, 196
  448c 141
  448e 108n
  449a 154
  452a–e 141, 141n
  452e–453a 14
  456a–c 141
  456c–457e 141
  461b 90n
  461e–462a 31n
  462c 154
  466a–e 141, 148
  467c–468c 148, 150

268   INDEX OF TEXTS

471e	90n	194a	22
474c ff	116n	194c ff	93n
480d–e	157	199e	38
482c–e	31n, 104n, 142, 157, 160, 164n	*Laws*	64, 86, 90, 90n, 96, 96n, 97, 98n, 114, 198n, 203, 249, 250, 251, 261
482c–484c	87n		
485a–b	147		
486d	186n		
487b	157, 94n	626b–632d	98n
487e	157, 94n	653b	98n
489b–c	87n	668d–e	64n
490a	154, 160, 161	688b–c	98n
491a–492c	104n	689a–c	98n
491b	154	714a–c	104n
491d	119, 140	731c	98n
491e–492a	141, 146, 150, 154, 161	732a	98n
		734b	98n
492c	140, 154	746c	114n
492d–e	150, 152, 161	860d–e	98n
493c–d	140	863c	98n
494a–e	140, 146, 149	870d	42
495e–497d	150, 151	872c ff	42
497e–499b	152, 153	888e ff	50n
499d–500a	149, 150	889a–890a	195, 195n, 205
500a–501c	149, 150, 158	892c	198n
502c–d	12n	897a	250n
503b–d	91n, 205n	898e–899a	250n
503e–505b	159, 205, 205n, 206	927a	42
505c	156, 157, 158		
506c–509c	129n, 153, 157, 158, 159, 161	*Lovers*	111, 112, 112n, 113n, 115, 124, 125, 127, 129
508a	27	137b–139a	124
509c–511c	157, 158	138a	119
511b–c	147		
511e	40	*Lysis*	
515c–516d	91n, 158	211b ff	90n
521d	185n, 186	218a–b	88n
522c–e	41, 158		
523a	158	*Menexenus*	
523c–525a	40, 130n	238a	59n
Hipparchus	112n	*Meno*	21, 23, 24, 29, 45n, 48, 86n, 91, 95, 97, 97n, 98n, 155n, 168n
Hippias Major			
282d–e	114n		
Ion		71a–b	92n, 94n, 108n
533c	87n	71e–72b	89n, 95n
		72c–d	92n, 95n
Laches	93	74b ff	95n
190e–191e	89n	75b–76a	90n, 95n

Index of Texts   269

76c–e	95n	101a–b	201n
77b–78b	89n, 95n	102b–e	47, 94n, 203, 231n
79a–c	92n	103b	200n, 231n
79e–80d	21, 87n, 88n, 95n, 97n	106e–107b	48, 92n
		110b	42
81a–e	21, 27, 45, 91n	114d	42, 43, 49
82a ff	23, 176n		
84a–c	88n, 97n	*Phaedrus*	7, 11, 15, 16, 19, 21n, 25, 26, 41, 46, 49, 53, 54, 55, 86, 87, 95, 113, 249
85c–86b	39n, 40, 45, 91n, 97n		
86b–e	21, 45, 95n, 108n		
87e–89a	92n		
97d–98a	92n	230d	20
98b	88n	231d	38n
99b–c	88n	237b–c	42
99e–100b	86n, 97n, 108n	243c	31n
		247c–e	8, 95n
Parmenides	38, 86, 96n, 113, 113n, 180n, 181n	249b–c	49, 51, 91n, 95n
		249e–250a	28, 95n
130a–135d	38, 231	250b	95n
135b–c	27n	250e	57n
136d–137b	180n	255d–e	132n
158b–d	179n	257a	20
		258d	43
Phaedo	86, 92, 96, 113n, 130, 147, 164n, 178, 194–204, 208, 209, 211, 212	259e–260a	42, 94n, 95n
		261a–b	43, 72n
		263a–b	95n
		264c	43, 53n
		266b	8
65d	95n	271c	72n
68d–69a	159	275c ff	38, 54
70d	200n	276a	26
71a	200n	278c	12n
72e ff	46, 91n, 155n		
77e	39f	*Philebus*	19n, 86, 96n, 97, 98n, 113n, 114, 196, 204, 249
78c–e	230n		
79e–80b	48, 230n		
81c–d	49	17b	5n
81e–82b	49	18b–d	5n
82b–c	48, 104n	19c	201n
82e–83a	41	22b	98n
84c	49	26e	205
91e	91n	29a–30d	59
95e–96a	200, 201n	38c–e	90n
96c–97b	200	48c–49c	98n, 121
97a–b	197, 197n, 201n	51a–52b	151n
97c–e	197n, 198, 200n, 202	58a–59a	14
98a–b	198, 202	64d–65a	24, 217
98b–99d	198n, 201n, 202		
99a–c	197, 198, 199, 199n, 201, 202, 206	*Politicus*	7, 16, 86, 95, 96, 113n, 114, 172, 196, 205
99d–102a	92n, 96n		
100a–e	8, 46, 197, 203, 203n		

270 INDEX OF TEXTS

268d	42	462b	206
272a	190n	472a	205n
277e ff	5n	476a ff	8, 94n
281a–e	207n, 211, 211n	485b	230n
285e–286a	95n	507a ff	8
287d	207n, 211n	508d	230n
288a	70n	510b–511e	11, 92n
300c	201n	511b–c	221n
308c–311a	207n	525c	230n
		530a–b	205, 205n, 217, 217n

Protagoras 119n, 140, 143, 145n, 146, 149, 167n

		531c	217
		531e	93n
		532e–533b	8
248c	31n	533b–d	92n, 221n
311c	62	534b–c	93n
315b	40	536e	91n
316d–e	12n	537d–539e	98n
320c	41	551d	206
327e–328a	115n	596a–e	8, 12n, 14, 205, 205n, 212n
328c	62		
328d–329b	90n	597a–e	205n, 214n
330c–d	95n	601e–602a	207
334a–335c	90n	607b	14
338b–e	90n	611d	67n
345d ff	89n	619c–d	104n
351b–e	144n		
353e	144n		

Sophist 7, 16, 36, 86, 91, 91n, 96, 96n, 97, 97n, 98n, 113n, 172n, 196

355e–357b	143, 144		
358c–d	89n		
360e–361d	86n, 108n		
		229e–230e	91n, 97n, 98n, 109n, 119
		232c–233c	14
		246b	36
		253a ff	5n
		262b–c	205
		263e	90n
		265c–266c	195n

Republic 8, 14n, 27, 41, 49, 51, 75, 117n, 118, 124n, 125n, 127n, 129, 136, 139, 145, 150n, 152n, 156, 159, 160, 160n, 161n, 163ff, 196, 203, 204

Symposium 35, 36, 36n, 38, 38n, 39, 40, 51, 74, 86, 91, 113n, 167n, 186n, 192

357a	107n	174d ff	185n
358c	104n	175a	49n
367c	104n	175d–e	39, 39n
367d–e	108n	177d	20
368b–c	108n	189c ff	37
414a–e	40	190a	63
430e–431b	119n, 121n	191a	74
433d–e	93n		
437d–439a	155		
442e	93		
443e	159		

Index of Texts 271

192d	37	30c–31b	214, 215
203d	22, 49n	31b ff	214, 215n, 216
205d–e	38	32a	209n
207c–208b	35, 37, 50, 148, 148n	33a–34a	56, 209n, 214, 215, 216
210d	186n		
210e	51n	37b–d	90n, 214
211a–b	182n	37d–e	216
212a	186n	38b–d	209n
212c	38	39b	209n
215a	49n	39d	209n
215c	40, 163	39e–40b	209n, 215
216b	31n	41c	209n
220c ff	185n	41e–42d	91n
221c	186n	44d–45a	58, 67
221d–222a	39n, 49n	46a–d	209, 210, 211
		46c–47c	195n, 209, 209n, 211, 212, 218
Theaetetus	7, 19, 28, 28n, 36, 44, 44n, 86, 90, 96n, 97, 113n, 180n, 208n	48a	209, 210, 211
		48b	210
		51d–52d	90n, 212
149a ff	40n, 193	53b	210
155b	94n	59a	217
155d	51n	62a	217n
160d	12n	64d	217n
161c–d	44	66b–d	217n
161e	29n	67c	217n
165a	178n	68e ff	195n, 209, 209n, 212, 216, 216n
166b	36		
179–183	210	69b–e	69, 210, 211, 212, 216, 207n, 209n
179d	208n		
180d	12n	70a–71b	71, 75, 209n
186a–b	155	72a	121
189e–190a	90n	72b–c	209n
201e ff	5n	73c	215n
		74a–e	209n, 216n
Timaeus	86, 90, 96, 96n, 196, 203, 204, 208, 209, 249	75d–e	79, 209n
		76c–d	209, 209n, 211
		77a–e	209n
19b	55	85c	217n
27a–b	60	86c	217n
27e ff	90n	87c–e	62, 217n
28a–b	205, 206, 214	90a	217n
29a	213n	91a	57
29c–30a	190n, 209	91e–92a	58

www.ingramcontent.com/pod-product-compliance
Lightning Source LLC
Chambersburg PA
CBHW031410290426
44110CB00011B/331